CUISINE AND CULTURE

CUISINE AND CULTURE

A History of Food & People

LINDA CIVITELLO

WILEY

John Wiley & Sons, Inc.

Title page photo by R. Lautman/Monticello. Courtesy of Monticello/Thomas Jefferson Foundation, Inc. Chapter opener photos courtesy Corbis Digital Stock for Chapters 1, 3, 6, 7, and 11.

This book is printed on acid-free paper. ∞

Copyright © 2004 by Linda Civitello. All rights reserved

Published by John Wiley & Sons, Inc., Hoboken, New Jersey
Published simultaneously in Canada

For general information on our other products and services or for technical support, please contact our Customer Care Department within the United States at (800) 762-2974, outside the United States at (317) 572-3993 or fax (317) 572-4002.

Wiley also publishes its books in a variety of electronic formats. Some content that appears in print may not be available in electronic books. For more information about Wiley products, visit our web site at www.wiley.com.

Library of Congress Cataloging-in-Publication Data:

Civitello, Linda.
    Cuisine and culture : a history of food and people / by Linda
Civitello.
        p. cm.
Includes bibliographical references and index.
    ISBN 0-471-20280-0 (Paper)
    1. Food—History. 2. Food—Social aspects. I. Title.
    TX353.C565 2004
    641.3'009—dc21

                                                            2002155889

    Printed in the United States of America

    10 9 8 7 6 5 4 3 2

    Book design by HRoberts Design

Thought: Why does man kill?
      He kills for food.
      And not only food:
      frequently there must be a beverage.

—Woody Allen

Contents

Food Fables and Culinary Puzzles

Holiday History

Antipasto

Antojitos

Amuse-Bouches

Taste is taught. There is no one food that is consumed by everyone on earth except maybe mother's milk. Almost everything we eat, and when, and where, is culturally determined. Some people pay top dollar for escargots in fine restaurants, while others stomp on the same snail when they find it in their garden. One person's haute cuisine is another person's pest. In one South Pacific tribe, couples can enjoy all the sex they want before marriage, but having a meal together is taboo. Among one African tribe, eating shouldn't be done in front of the opposite sex because it's a bodily function like going to the bathroom.*

What we believe about food has also changed over time. Once, people knew for sure that potatoes caused leprosy and sugar cured toothaches. Romans believed that cinnamon grew in swamps guarded by giant killer bats. Americans thought beer was a really good drink for children. A princess was laughed out of town because she dared to use a fork. And Italian food was very, very bad for you. It's all true, and it's all here. Keep reading.

This entire book is an appetizer, a broad overview to put food in historical, political, social, economic, anthropological, and linguistic context. This book could not have been written without everything about food and history that was written before it. Food historians have spent great portions of their lives studying one subject—chocolate, sugar, bread, coffee, corn, salt, codfish, the food of ancient Britain, the Middle East, China, Native Americans, medieval France, the regions of Italy. The list goes on and on. This book cannot go into that kind of depth, but I hope it will whet your appetite to look further into their works.

*MacClancy, *Consuming Culture,* 101.

Food history is a new field. The first full book, British author Reay Tannahill's *Food in History,* was not published until 1973. She put a warning on the copyright page: "I should, perhaps, remind readers that this is a history book, not a cookery book, and urge them not to experiment with the foods described herein. Anyone who chooses to eat unusual and unfamiliar foods may suffer harmful effects." Maguelonne Toussaint-Samat's *A History of Food* appeared in 1987, but her book was not translated into English (by Anthea Bell) until 1992. The anthology *Food: A Culinary History from Antiquity to the Present,* edited by Jean-Louis Flandrin and Massimo Montanari, was published in French in 1996. Seven translators and editor Albert Sonnenfeld were necessary to produce the English version published three years later. The focus of all of these books is European; the editors of the latter two are medieval and Renaissance specialists. In the last five years, there has been an explosion of books about the history of food, much of it by Americans. This book incorporates as much of this new research as possible, but there are still gaps in our knowledge.

This book is the story of humans striving to control their environment, especially their food supply, through thousands of years. Here are legendary kings and queens who set elegant eating habits and the anonymous peasants who grew their food. There are feasts and famines and forks, castles and cannibals and china plates. It tells of a revolution that began partly because of Easter eggs, and a mass migration forced by a potato fungus. It is also about food as aphrodisiac and as medicine, about fortunes made and lost over spices. In these pages you will find famous generals and unknown soldiers, scorched earth and a country so wealthy it fed chocolate candy to its soldiers at the fighting front. There is technology, too, from the mastery of fire to the microwave, from hunting and gathering to take-out food. It is the story of local flavors and global production.

That is a great deal of information, so some events will necessarily be emphasized more than others. Pivotal events in human history include the domestication of plants and animals, the Roman roads and the Silk Road, the spread of world religions and their various dietary regulations, the Crusades, Columbus and the Age of Exploration, the enslavement of Africans to grow sugar and rice, and the addiction of the Chinese to opium to lower the price of tea. This is also the story of the influence American-grown food, technology, and eating styles have had, for better or worse, around the world.

In other words, this book is the short version of the long story of the greatest predator on planet Earth—humans—from the African savanna to the kitchens of California, and what we did with our food along the way.

A Note About Reading History

Reading history takes imagination. We have to forget all of our current comforts and cherished beliefs and leap into the past. Sometimes it isn't pretty back there. People treated each other then in ways that are unthinkable to us now and can still make us angry. As civilizations have come and gone through thousands of years, relationships between men and women and among races, religions, classes, and ethnic groups have changed profoundly. For example, until very recently women were defined by their ability to bear children and confined to tasks they could perform close to home. It was the law. Until 1965, it was illegal in the United States for married couples to use birth control devices (*Griswold v. Connecticut*). Women who did not have children as often as they could were treated with suspicion and disrespect regardless of their status. Queen Marie Antoinette's failure—through no fault of her own—to bring forth an heir for several years after her marriage to King Louis XVI was one of the causes of the French Revolution (Chapter 7). England's King Henry VIII executed or divorced his wives when they didn't have children or had girls. In the American South, slave women who didn't produce children were sold (Chapter 8). Mentally retarded women were sterilized in the United States long before Hitler gave the same order in Nazi Germany because the Supreme Court ruled that "three generations of imbeciles are enough" (*Buck v. Bell*, 1927).

Until very recently in human history, women were "civilly dead"—legally, they didn't exist because they were a man's property, as much as his horse or his house. He couldn't kill or sell them, but there were no laws against other kinds of behavior that we regard as abuse now. According to the famous "rule of thumb," a man could beat his wife with a stick as long as it was no thicker than his thumb. In a divorce, the man always got the children and the woman's life and reputation were ruined. Women had no recourse against this treatment because they couldn't bring lawsuits, serve on juries, or be elected to public office. They couldn't vote in the United States until 1920. A college just for women has been in existence less than 150 years, since Vassar opened in the 1860s (in Chapter 8 you can see what their dining room looked like and handwritten menus of what they ate). A woman couldn't get a credit card in her own name until the 1970s. In restaurants, women's menus had the bill of fare but no prices. The man's menu had prices because he was supposed to pay.

Relationships among races and ethnic groups have also changed. In the United States in 1896, the Supreme Court declared that racism—the concept that blacks are "separate but equal"—was the law. And it was, until 1954 when the Supreme Court reversed its decision in *Brown* v. *Board of Education of Topeka, Kansas.* In the South, it was illegal for "colored" people—anyone who wasn't considered white, like Chinese and Mexicans—to go to school with whites. In 1891, eleven Italians were lynched in New Orleans—one of the largest mass lynchings in American history. In 1942, people of Japanese heritage who were born in the United States and were therefore American citizens were herded into camps and kept there for years. And until 1949, when the all-black Harlem Globetrotters beat the all-white Minneapolis Lakers for the *second time,* most Americans believed that black people were physically incapable of playing basketball.

For most of human history, people of one religion or ethnic group routinely killed those of another. The Romans fed Christians to the lions for entertainment and slaughtered the Jews. In medieval Italy, the word for "human being" was *cristiano*—Christian. Anyone who wasn't a Christian didn't have a soul and therefore wasn't human and was fair game. This belief resulted in the enslavement of millions of Africans, Native Americans, and Asians. The Puritans who came to America to avoid religious persecution hanged Quakers for "polluting" Boston by worshiping differently. In 19th-century America, English-speaking Irish immigrants looking for work found signs that said simply "NINA"—No Irish Need Apply." Why? Because they were Irish and Catholic. Discrimination against Jews kept them out of public hotels, colleges, and jobs. The first movie that dealt directly with this issue was *Gentleman's Agreement,* in 1947.

So, while you are reading, please remember that our lives, relationships, and eating habits would be as much science fiction to people from earlier times as theirs sometimes seem to us. It would be nice to be able to go back into the past and change these injustices, but we can't. These are facts, documented in the notes throughout the book. All we can do is be grateful to the people before us who worked so hard or gave their lives to allow us to enjoy ours, and keep an eye out for what we can do now to make the planet a better place to live. So please, keep these things in mind, enjoy your life, and enjoy the read!

Acknowledgments

This book would not have been possible without the help and support of many, many people. I would like to thank:

My editors, JoAnna Turtletaub for giving me the good news and Julie Kerr for giving me life support in the trenches. The readers, anonymous to me while I was writing, for their persistence and incredible courage in returning to draft after draft until I heard what they were saying and got it right: Jon-Paul Hutchins, Scottsdale Culinary Institute; Mark Berggren, Milwaukee Area Technical College; Stephen Fries, Gateway Community College; Mike Harris, Bethune Cookman College; and Michael Palmer, Western Culinary Institute.

Roger McGrath for his history acumen and his endless patience. Pamala Ferron, Barbara Hartley, and their families; Nancy Uhrhammer, Carol Lynch, Nancy Nelson; Randi Sunshine, Dan Sherkow, and Abigail; Rod Pinks and Susan Quinn for helping to keep me sane and focused. Shela Patel, Beebee Bernstein, Pam Hickey, and Mary Ryan for their support. My ancestors for being Italian, and my aunts Yolanda and Carmela. My brothers Michael and Joe, my sister-in-law Sue, and my niece Dana.

My agent and friend, Sam Gelfman; Tony and Julie LeWinter, just because; Chefs Patricia Greenberg and Gwen Gulliksen of Women Chefs and Restaurateurs for letting me see the interest in this subject among the membership, and Pat for allowing me to sit in her seat at the radio station for a few minutes. Chris Lauderdale, Carol, and Erin for making the food so pretty. Chef Leslie Bilderback. Dr. Randy Schnitman, the best ENT in the business, for restoring my sense of smell. This book is possible because I live in a world-class city between two world-class library systems—the Los Angeles Public Library and its extensive collection of food history books and cookbooks, supported by the Culinary Historians of Southern California (especially Dan Strehl and Nancy Zaslavsky), and the UCLA libraries. The Internet, Amazon.com, and Janet Jarvits, Bookseller, at http://www.cookbkjj.com; and Gary Allen's Web site, http://www.hvinet.com/gallen, provided me with cookbooks, history books, and amazing information.

Claire Criscuolo of Claire's Corner Copia, Cathy Grosfils of the Colonial Williamsburg Foundation, Jessica Tyree at Monticello, Mary Ann Milano Picardi at the Union Oyster House, Susan Greendyke at the Massachusetts Commission for the Arts, for their time, patience, and pictures.

Sony, HP, Canon, Demeter/Ceres, and the Magic Wok Express delivery people. Every under-$7 ethnic restaurant within a 2-mile radius of my apartment.

Whatever it was that kept George Delgado and Carmen Bissell away from work on September 11, 2001.

My high school teachers for teaching me to write; to Vassar College and the history department at UCLA for teaching me to write better and to do research, especially Eric Monkkonen, Mary Yeager, and Jan Reiff. Valerie Matsumoto for bumping into me at the supermarket and lending me her course reader. To Mary Connor, my mentor/teacher, for going down this road first and being my *cicerone*. At Concord, to my students for teaching me what they think I need to know; to my colleagues for their kind answers and help; to Susan Packer-Davis/Hille, Eric, Alex, and Jackson—who will be president. Catherine Evans and the dear departed Jim Kelley, who was a rocket scientist.

$\mathscr{F}$IRST $\mathscr{C}$OURSE

| 7 MIL BC | | 500,000 BC |
| 1.5 MIL BC | | 221 BC |

From Raw to Cooked:
Prehistory, Mesopotamia,
Egypt, China, India

PREHISTORY

Animals don't cook. The ability to use fire is one of the crucial things that separates us from them. Scientists used to think that humans were different from animals because we use tools and have language. Then we discovered that animals use tools and can communicate with each other, and sometimes even with us, like Koko, the gorilla who learned sign language. As Stephen Pyne, the world's leading authority on fire, points out, there may be "elements of combustion" on other planets, but so far "we are uniquely fire creatures on a uniquely fire planet."[1]

Humans Learn to Find Foods: Hunting and Gathering

Scientists believe that humans evolved for millions of years before they learned to use fire somewhere between half a million and a million years ago. The oldest fossils so far, excavated mainly in Africa, put the beginning of humanlike creatures—hominids—at between 6 million and 7 million years ago.[2] From the jaws and teeth of these hominids, scientists deduce that they were primarily plant eaters—herbivores. Our back teeth, the molars, are flat like stones for grinding grain and plants, and that is what we still use them for when we chew.

1

Scientists think that over millions of years, early humans developed two survival advantages: (1) between 4 million and 1 million years ago, human brain size tripled, growing to what it is today, approximately 1,400 cubic centimeters; and (2) they stood upright on two feet—became bipedal—which allowed them to see farther and left their hands free to use weapons for protection and to kill animals for food. Food historians speculate that early humans learned to like the taste of meat from small mammals and animals that could be caught and killed easily, like lizards and tortoises, and from scavenging the leftover carcasses of large animals killed by other large animals.[3] These early humans were hunter-gatherer nomads. They followed the food wherever it wandered or grew. Work related to food was divided by gender. Men left the home to hunt animals by following them to where they went for food, especially salt. Women gathered fruits, nuts, berries, and grasses because their lives revolved around a cycle of pregnancy, birth, and child rearing.[4] Gathering was more reliable than hunting. Becoming carnivores—meat eaters—probably helped humans survive, too. In case of a shortage of plants, there was an alternative food source. Now we were omnivores—we ate everything. We still have the front or canine teeth, sharp like a dog's for tearing meat, to prove it. However, human teeth weren't sharp enough to pierce animal hides. For that, something else was necessary.

Scientists believe that humans invented tools about 1.9 million to 1.6 million years ago. Early humans butchered animal meat, even elephants, with blades made out of stone, which is why it is called the Stone Age (as opposed to the Bronze Age and the Iron Age, which came later). Archeologists call these people *Homo habilis*—"handy man." Then, approximately 1.5 million to 500,000 years ago, another group appeared, called *Homo erectus*—"upright man." These people migrated north to Europe and east to India, China, and Southeast Asia. They had better tools than any of the other groups. And, for the first time, they had fire.

Humans Learn to Use Fire: Cooking

Scientists speculate that lightning started a fire by accident, but humans figured out how to keep it going by appointing somebody keeper of the flame day and night, perhaps the first specialized job. For the first time, humans had a tremendous tool with which to control the environment. It kept night terrors and animals away. It was also sacred, "the only substance which humans can kill and revive at will."[5]

The god who controlled lightning was usually the most powerful god in early religions. Most cultures have creation myths of how humans stole or were given fire by the gods and how they were punished and suffered for this divine knowledge. Fire completely transformed food from raw to cooked, which allowed humans to eat otherwise indigestible foods and made food preservation possible. Control of fire gave humans control of their food supply—a huge survival advantage.

Once humans had fire, how did cooking begin? Perhaps by accident, although anthropologists are still arguing about this. One theory is that an out-of-control fire burned down a hut and accidentally cooked some pigs. People wandered in, tried the cooked meat, and liked it. Another theory is that a forest fire first roasted meat; still others think that cooking was a more deliberate, controlled act by humans.[6] In any case, now there were more options than raw bar and tartare.

We might never know exactly how people mastered fire and started cooking their food; we only know when—between 500,000 and 1 million years ago. Roasting over an open fire was probably the first cooking method. Pit roasting—putting food in a pit with burning embers and covering it—might have come next. Then spit roasting, when hunters came home with the animal already on a spear and decided to cook it by hanging it over the fire and turning it. With sharp stone tools, meat could be cut into smaller pieces to make it cook faster. Food could be boiled in large mollusk or turtle shells where they were available, or even in animal skins,[7] but pots were not invented until around 10,000 B.C., and there were no sturdy clay boiling pots until about 5000 B.C.[8] Cooking in such vessels would probably have produced bacterial contamination, since there was no soap and no effective way to clean them. Finally, scientists believe that *Homo sapiens*—"wise man," the direct ancestor of humans—appeared between 1 million and a hundred thousand years ago.

Humans Learn to Communicate: Dance, Speech, Art

Scientists believe that before language was invented, early humans spoke with actions. They danced, which dance historian Joan Cass defines as "the making of rhythmical steps and movements for their own sake (as against steps and movements done in order to go somewhere, to do work, or to dress oneself)."[9] They danced together in religious ceremonies to ensure fertility of humans and crops, for rain, for a successful hunt. If the dance produced the result they wanted, they

PREHISTORY			
AGE	WHEN (MILLIONS OF YEARS AGO)	LIFE-FORMS	GEOGRAPHY
Archaean	2,500	Earliest living things (single-cell)	
Cambrian	590	Aquatic life-forms	Ural Mountains formed
Paleozoic	450	Major plant groups; life-moves onto land	Appalachian Mountains and Alps formed
Triassic	248	Global warming; ferns; first dinosaurs; mammals	
Jurassic	213	Cone-bearing trees; birds	North Atlantic Ocean and Himalaya Mountains formed
Cretaceous	110	Flowering plants	South Atlantic Ocean formed
	65	Dinosaurs extinct	
Pleistocene	5–13	First hominids (based on fossil skulls, jaws, teeth)	Central America, Caribbean islands formed
Tertiary	2.5–1.5	*Homo habilis* uses tools	
	1.6–0.5	*Homo erectus* uses fire, stone artifacts	
Quaternary	0.01	*Homo sapiens*, ancestors of modern humans	

kept doing it exactly the same way again and again, turning it into a ritual. Music was added—beans or small stones in a pouch shaken or rattled, animal bones with holes drilled in them like a flute, maybe an animal skin stretched over a cooking pot to make a drum.[10] Then, about 100,000 years ago, we developed language. This, too, helped humans to survive. We could warn other members of our tribe of danger, tell them where there was food, plan ahead and cooperate in work, name things and places, and generally organize the world, which is a step toward controlling it.

Early art, too, was often communication connected to fertility and food. Small figures, women with exaggerated breasts and hips, were carved out of rock. Animals were painted on cave walls in France 35 thousand years ago. A mask "changes your actual identity and merges you with the spirit that the mask represents."[11] This is called sympathetic magic. As Sir James Frazer points out in *The Golden Bough: A Study in Magic and Religion,* the principle at work is that "like produces like": if you make a symbol of what you want, it will happen. The woman will have a child, the hunt will be successful, the animal your mask represents will be found. You have control over these things because you have, in a sense, created them.[12] The animals most commonly represented in prehistoric cave paintings are horses, followed by bison, deer and reindeer, oxen, ibex, then elephants and mammoths.[13] So food, art, and religion have been connected since the earliest human times—at least in France.

Corpses, Middens, and Coprolites

How do archeologists know what happened before written history? How accurate is the information? The same scientific tools that solve crimes today, like DNA and microscopic analysis, can solve ancient mysteries. Much of what we know about early humans comes from three sources: corpses—their preserved bodies; middens—their garbage piles; and coprolites—their fossilized feces. Bodies have been found all over the world, preserved by drying in hot climates, by freezing in cold climates, and by bogs in wet climates. Overdeveloped bones in the right forearm tell us that many of these people threw spears.[14] Analyzing their intestinal tracts reveals what these people ate, and also that many of them had the same intestinal parasites that we still have today.[15]

From middens, archaeologists know that in some ways the eating habits of early humans were not that different from ours: They smashed or broke bones to get to the marrow, too. And they did it for the same reason—because they liked it, not because there wasn't enough meat or anything else to eat.[16] Today this is called *osso buco,* Italian for "bone with a hole." The difference is that early humans ate bone marrow with their hands while squatting around a fire, while *osso buco* is eaten with a silver marrow spoon in a fine restaurant. Many of the recipes in French master chef Escoffier's cookbook *Le Guide Culinaire* have marrow as an ingredient, even sweet puddings like his Pouding à l'Américaine (#4438) and Pouding à la Moelle (#4439). Broken jawbones and pierced skulls indicate that early humans savored the taste of animal tongues and brains. The shells of mussels and limpets also survive in middens, telling us that humans ate shellfish as far back as 60,000 to 120,000 years ago.[17]

From coprolites, we know what foods early humans ate because we can see what they excreted. Seeds, fibers, and other indigestible matter ended up in the coprolite. In this way, the human digestive tract was also part of the food chain, helping plants to spread. From these methods, we know that wild crab apples were consumed 750,000 years ago in Kazakhstan, just north of modern Afghanistan.

Dating the items found in corpses, middens, and coprolites is done by several methods. Carbon dating measures the amount of radioactive decay

PREHISTORIC HUMAN ACHIEVEMENTS		
When—B.C.	Where	What
500,000–1 million		Fire/Cooking
Before 100,000		Dance
100,000		Speech
33,000	Chauvet, France	Cave paintings and other art
25,000–20,000	Willendorf, Germany	Stone sculpture—Fertility goddesses
18,000; 15,000	Lascaux, France; Altamira, Spain	Cave paintings and other art
14,000	Middle East	Dogs domesticated from wolves
Before 10,000	Japan	Pottery
8,000	Ice Age Ends—Agricultural Revolution begins in the Middle East	

in the remains of plants or animals. Tree ring analysis—dendrochronology—can reveal what the climate was like and how much rainfall occurred at certain times. Analysis of pollens can also help decipher ancient dates.

THE AGRICULTURAL REVOLUTION

The two most important factors that determine where life is hospitable to plants and animals, including humans, are geography and climate. When the Ice Age ended approximately 10,000 years ago, the last of the glaciers receded and the planet warmed up. This was the first of three major climate changes planet Earth has experienced. The other two were the Medieval Warm Period (950–1300) followed by the Little Ice Age, which ended about 100 years ago. Some scientists think that we are in a new period of global warming caused by pollution from gases produced by car engines and machinery (the "greenhouse effect") and that we have to do something about it fast. Others think it is just part of a natural cycle. Still others think that climate is random and that catastrophic changes could occur suddenly for no reason and are completely out of the control of humans.

Humans Learn to Choose Foods: The Case of the Mutant Almond

Gathering nuts, seeds, and grasses and hunting wild game were unreliable and inefficient, and could support only a limited population. Humans wanted more control over their environment and a guaranteed supply of food, especially food they liked. It is impossible to have some foods if you are a nomad. One of these is wine. It takes two years before vines bear fruit, and there is a very short time frame, just a few days, during which the grapes have to be picked and crushed—until recently, by stomping on them. Then they must be kept at a temperature that will allow them to ferment; finally they need to be stored. It is impossible to chase other food and to make wine, too. So two of the earliest professions were viticulture (growing vines) and viniculture (making wine).

About 10 thousand years ago, humans began to tame wild animals and plants. This was a time-consuming and difficult process, since all plants and animals survive because they have a way to defend themselves. Getting past these defenses can be difficult. Anthropologist Jared Diamond poses some "what ifs"—what if some plants were genetic mutants unable to protect themselves? Wouldn't this make them susceptible to humans gathering food? Diamond uses the almond as an example. It is protected outside by a hard shell and inside by a kernel or seed that contains cyanide. What if some almonds mutated and produced less poison? He speculates that this process must have been repeated many, many times over thousands of years before humans arrived at the edible foods of today.

The first domesticated animals were sheep and goats, then pigs and cows. Barley and then wheat (genus *Triticum*), originally wild grasses, were the first cultivated plants. There are about 30,000 varieties of wheat.[18] Early wheats—emmer, spelt, einkorn—had several layers of protection, including a very hard inedible outer covering called chaff, which had to be roasted to be removed. Then friction had to be applied to the wheat to separate it from the chaff, a process called threshing. This was done by having oxen walk on the wheat or by hitting it. The chaff was lighter than the wheat, so it could be blown or fanned away. Then the wheat had to be ground—by hand, until animals began to be used around 800 B.C.—to make flour. So early flour was stone ground and coarse, and most likely still had bits of chaff or other impurities in it. The problem was that heating the wheat destroyed what makes it rise—gluten. A very important change occurred about 7000 B.C. when wheat with a weaker chaff began to be grown, so the roasting step could be eliminated and the gluten was free to rise.[19] Leavened bread was probably first made in Egypt (see below).

Did domestication occur only once or more than once in different places? Some plants like barley, lentils, and rice seem to have been domesticated in multiple places. There is also evidence that pigs were kept around 7000 B.C. in the city of Jericho in the Near East and thousands of miles away on the island of New Guinea in the South Pacific.[20] Domesti-

THE AGRICULTURAL REVOLUTION		
WHEN—B.C.	WHERE	WHAT
10,000	Southwest Asia	Wheat, barley, sheep, goats domesticated
8000	Mexico	Chiles and squash domesticated
8000	Peru	Lima beans domesticated
7000	Southwest Asia	Bread wheat developed; flax for fabric
7000	Southwest Asia and New Guinea	Pigs domesticated
6000	Northern China (first agriculture in China)	Millet domesticated
6000	Middle East[21]	Apples cultivated
6000–4000	Southwest Asia (modern Armenia)[22]	Grapes cultivated for wine
5000–6000	Southwest Asia	Cattle, chickpeas, lentils domesticated
5000	Yangtze River delta, China; Central India	Rice domesticated
4000	Southwest Asia	Olives domesticated
3000	Southwest Asia	Cities, irrigation, wheel, plow, sail
2686–2181	Egypt	Pyramid building
2500	China	Water buffalo domesticated

cation altered some plants and animals so much that they became dependent on humans for reproduction. Maize (what we call corn), native to the Americas, is an example. The kernels, which are the seeds, no longer fall off by themselves, but have to be removed from the cob.

After domestication came farming. Fire was a force here, too. Slash-and-burn agriculture is the simplest way to clear the land of trees. Once used extensively by primitive tribes, it is still used today in some places, like Borneo. The process begins with slashing the bark on the tree, which stops the sap from flowing and eventually kills the tree. The leaves die and fall off, allowing sunlight to filter onto the forest floor, where the fallen leaves decompose into fertilizer. Then crops are planted. In two or three years, when the soil starts to show signs of being depleted of nutrients, the dead trees are burned, the ash provides fertilizer, and more crops are planted.

THE FERTILE CRESCENT: THE TIGRIS AND EUPHRATES RIVERS

Humans need freshwater to survive, so it is not surprising that the earliest civilizations began around rivers: the Tigris and Euphrates in southwest Asia, the Nile in Egypt, the Yellow (Huang He) in China, and the Indus in India.[23] The Fertile Crescent is an area of land that runs from the Mediterranean on its western end, then curves around in a crescent shape to the Tigris and Euphrates Rivers in modern Iraq, down to the Persian Gulf. It was in this part of the world, the land called Mesopotamia, which means "between the rivers," that scientists believe civilization began approximately five thousand years ago—around 3000 B.C. Even after thousands of years of domestication and farming, of the tens of thousands of edible plant species on earth, only about 600 are raised for food. Many were first grown in the Fertile Crescent.

Some historians think that cities were started for the purpose of worship. One feeble voice raised in prayer might not reach the gods, but thousands would have a better chance of being heard. Early cities were completely surrounded by walls for defense, and inside the walled city was another walled mini-city, the temple. Inside the temple walls was the most important building, the granary, where the city stored its food. This surplus of food made specialized labor possible because not everyone had to farm all the time. The community decided that their resources would be better spent if they had a priest or priestess to honor the gods full-time. This included preparing food offerings for them, honoring them with feasts on their special days, and sometimes inviting gods from other cities to visit. So, from the earliest civilizations, food, religion, and government were all connected. For whatever reason cities arose, they became centers of trade.

Salt: "White Gold"

One of the most valuable trade items from earliest times was salt. It is not a condiment like pepper or mustard or ketchup, but a mineral, NaCl, sodium chloride. Humans need it to live. Our nervous systems can't function without it. Its prevalence shows in the many phrases connected with salt: a valuable person is the "salt of the earth," which is how Christ referred to his apostles; a useless person is "not worth his salt." One of the oldest ways of obtaining salt was by boiling or evaporating seawater. This was done in ancient Egypt; in ancient Gaul (the Romans' name for France); in France in the 18th century, to avoid paying the salt tax; and in India in the 20th century, as a way to gain independence from England and the British salt monopoly. This is a very expensive and labor-intensive way to get salt compared to mining rock salt.

Currently in the United States, between 2 million and 3 million tons of salt are mined each year from deposits that run under the center of the United States, from Detroit and Cleveland south to Louisiana. This salt mountain is as big as Mt. Everest, the tallest mountain on earth. Only 4 percent of the salt that is mined is consumed; the other 96 percent is used to deice roads and by the chemical industry, which breaks it down into sodium and chloride. America also has the Great Salt Desert in Utah, and the Bonneville Salt Flats, where cars are test-raced. Salt will be discussed in more detail throughout this book.

Writing was invented in Mesopotamia, too, to keep track of important information. It was called cuneiform, which means "wedge-shaped," after the shape of the instrument, called a stylus, that was pressed onto blocks of wet clay, which became permanent records after they hardened. Cuneiform went out of use in the 1st century B.C., and over the next several hundred years the tablets were lost or buried or disappeared. In the 1840s, British archeologists discovered 30,000 tablets and pieces of tablets.[24] Now, because of extensive damming of the rivers since 1970, only about 10 percent of the fertile Mesopotamian marshlands still survive. The other 90 percent is now desert.[25] After the first dictionary of cuneiform is published—projected for 2004, after 30 years of work at the University of Pennsylvania—perhaps we will discover more about the food of this area, or even a cookbook.[26]

Fermented Beverages: Mead, Wine, Ale

Mead—fermented honey—was probably the first fermented drink, perhaps another food accident. Maybe honey was left out, rain fell, and yeast settled on the mixture. In both Greece and Rome, before wine making, mead was offered to the gods.[27] Honey was a mysterious substance to ancient people. Greeks knew bees were connected to it, but not exactly how. Romans thought honey fell from heaven and landed on leaves, "the saliva of the stars."[28] Honey is produced from the nectar in flowers gathered by bees to feed young bees. Most of the water in the nectar evaporates, resulting in honey, which contains 35–40 percent fructose, 30–35 percent dextrose, 17–20 percent water, and small amounts of enzymes and other substances.[29]

Humans also started drinking wine very early. Maybe winemaking was done deliberately. Or perhaps wine was another culinary coincidence: grapes left at room temperature fermented naturally. Maybe crushed grapes and their juice left in the bottom of an animal skin fermented. Animal skins are all right for short-term transport of wine, but they aren't an efficient way to store it—pottery is, and by about 6000 B.C. clay jugs were being used. A clay jug with a narrow mouth can be stoppered up to prevent the oxidation that will turn wine to vinegar, while animal pouches can't. It is from the wine residue, tartaric acid, in these clay vessels that we know how long ago humans were drinking wine.

From the beginning, wine was an upper-class drink. Beer was the beverage of the masses, and it, too, might have been the result of an accident. The housewives who were responsible for food preparation malted their grain—they let it sprout because it tasted better and was easier to mill and bake into bread. Somehow the malted grain fermented into an alcoholic beverage and began to be produced on its own. Among the cuneiform tablets discovered in Mesopotamia was the world's first recipe for ale.[30] Sumerians brewed "eight barley beers, eight emmer beers, and three mixed beers."[31] Hops were not added until almost four thousand years later, in the Middle Ages in Europe. Today in some parts of Africa, beer is still brewed in this ancient way without hops. In Sudan, it's called *buza*.[32]

How Humans Eat Together

As thousands of humans came to live together in cities, they needed organization. One leader arose named Hammurabi, who became known as "the lawgiver." The Code of Hammurabi consisted of laws governing every aspect of life, including the management of the irrigation canals; marriage, divorce, and adoption; and construction. The punishment in many cases was literally "an eye for an eye"—say, a broken bone for a broken bone. Punishments were worse for committing crimes against the state than against other citizens. For example, the fine for stealing a sheep, pig, or ox from a temple was triple the fine for stealing from another citizen. The code also governed the wine trade and taverns. Tavern owners, usually women, had to report any talk they heard about plots to overthrow the government. And they were warned about serving watered-down wine—the punishment was death by drowning.[33]

Mesopotamians gave more than laws. By the first millennium B.C., they were also giving elaborate banquets to display the power and wealth of the government. One was a ten-day feast to celebrate the building of the king's palace. Perhaps they served bird bouillon, which is among the earliest recipes.[34]

> 69,574 guests were invited. . . . Dozens of items were served in enormous quantities: 1,000 plump oxen, 14,000 sheep, 1,000 lambs, several hundred deer of various kinds, 20,000 pigeons as well as other birds, 10,000 fish, 1,000 jerboa [a rodent], 10,000 eggs, plus thousands of jugs of beer and skins full of wine.[35]

Oil was also used at banquets, but not in the food—it was perfumed and used in the guests' hair.[36]

Inventions That Aid in Trade: Wheel, Plow, Sail

Three extremely important inventions came out of Mesopotamia: the wheel, the plow, and the sailboat. The wheel and the plow were possible because of the availability of animal labor. Wheeled carts pulled by oxen or horses could transport more goods to market more quickly. They also made waging war with chariots possible. Animals pulling plows to turn the earth over for planting were far more efficient than humans. The sail made it possible to trade with countries that were accessible only by sea or could be reached more quickly by sea, like India. All three inventions made the cities of Mesopotamia powerful trading centers with as many as 30 thousand people each.

The wheel was put to use for one special food. Tannahill talks about the delicate fat from the tail of the fat-tailed sheep. But the four-and-a-half-foot-long tail was heavy and dragged on the ground, so humans made a little wheeled cart so the sheep could carry its tail around. Tail fat from this sheep is still highly prized today.[37]

EGYPT: THE NILE RIVER

The Nile is the longest river in the world. Its headwaters are 4,160 miles upstream from where it empties into the Mediterranean Sea. The Nile was the giver of life for the ancient Egyptians. Water to drink and fish like carp, mullet, and sturgeon came from it. Every spring, like clockwork, it overflowed its banks, bringing rich, fertile soil down from the mountains into the valley to grow food. There were three seasons in Egypt, all connected to the Nile and to planting: flooding was from the middle of June to the middle of October, when the floodwaters receded; sowing and growing lasted until the end of February; and harvesting continued until mid-June or July, when the cycle began all over again. Humans scattered barley and wheat seeds by hand, then sent goats into the fields to walk on them and push them down into the soil so birds couldn't eat them before they had a chance to germinate. By 1300 B.C., apple orchards were planted along the Nile.[38] Like the Mesopotamians, Egyptians irrigated. However, sometimes the water stagnated and became hospitable to mosquitoes and other flies. Other vermin like mice and rats were also a problem because they chewed or burrowed their way into the granaries. Cats were domesticated in Egypt and worshiped because they kept the rodent population down.

Ancient Egyptian culture revolved around this cycle of death and rebirth. Many of the Egyptian gods and goddesses were related to death, but Osiris, who had triumphed over death, was also the god of resurrection and good. Egyptians believed that if they led good and orderly lives, they would be united with Osiris after death. On judgment day, when their hearts were weighed to see if they were heavy with sin, Egyptians made a "negative confession" to prove they had not violated the laws, many of which dealt with food and farming:

> I have not mistreated cattle.
> I have not cut down on the food or income in the temples.
> I have not taken the loaves of the blessed dead.
> I have not taken milk from the mouths of children.
> I have not built a dam against running water.[39]

The pharaoh was equated with the Nile as the giver of life. The people expected the pharaoh, like the river, to reappear after his death. He would need two things to be able to rule properly in the afterlife: an impressive tomb—a pyramid—and his body.

The Embalmers—Cinnamon and Salt

The Egyptians salted human bodies to preserve them so the spirit would be able to find its home again after death. First the brain was removed by drawing it out through the nose. Then the torso was cut open and the bowels and internal organs removed. The cavity was stuffed with pungent-smelling spices like myrrh and cinnamon, then sewed back up. The corpse was submerged in a mineral salt called natron ($Na_2CO_310H_2O$) for 70 days. Then the salt was washed off and the body was wrapped in bandages. Now it was a mummy.

Mummification was done by the high priests, who had their heads shaved to be pure. Before the invention of insecticides in the 20th century, shaving was the only way to guarantee that the servants of the gods would not have lice that could spread to the pharaoh. As a result of embalming, the priests knew a great deal about human anatomy. They used this knowledge to set bones; they also performed the first known brain surgery, around 2500 B.C. They treated wounds with honey and moldy bread. This makes medical sense: the high sugar content of the honey draws moisture out of the cells by osmosis, killing any bacteria,[40] and penicillin comes from a specific type of mold, which was discovered by British scientist Arthur Fleming in 1928.[41]

The Book of the Dead: Food in the Afterlife

The great pyramids were built during a period known as the Old Kingdom, which lasted from 2686 B.C. to 2181 B.C. The pyramids were packed with everything a king would need to live and rule properly in the afterlife, including his wife and servants, who were killed when he died. This custom worked to protect the pharaoh from assassination by those close to him; they knew that if the pharaoh died, they died, too. Sometimes even pets were mummified. Foodstuffs found in pyramids include butter and cheese. Artwork and artifacts in pyramids reveal that the pharaohs ate well: a variety of meats, fish, dairy, fruits, vegetables, ostrich eggs, and pastries.[42] Even beer making is depicted on pyramid walls.

Fermented Food: Bread

If the Nile was the giver of life, then bread *was* life. In ancient Egyptian, the word for bread is the same as the word for life.[43] In the beginning, bread was simple: grain and water patted into a flat circle with the hands, laid on a hot rock next to the fire to cook. Later, more elaborate shapes could be made, but these early flatbreads were more like crackers. Some examples that still exist are Indian *chapati* (cooked on a hot griddle), *poori* (fried); and Jewish *matzoh*, which is baked. As far as food historians know, Egypt produced the first leavened bread, perhaps by accident. One theory is that yeast landed on some dough left out; another is that ale was mixed with the flour instead of water. In any case, the gluten in the flour created pockets that trapped the carbon dioxide produced by the yeast, and the bread puffed up—still an awe-inspiring event. A piece of the fermented dough from the previous batch could be kept to guarantee that the next loaf would rise, and sourdough was born. Or you could just take the head off the beer and add it to the bread. New technologies developed around leavened bread, such as closed ovens and molds shaped like triangles and long loaves. Commercial bakeries in ancient Egypt produced at least 40 different kinds of bread and pastries, according to Tannahill.[44] Such bakeries were necessary to provide some of the food for feasts the pharaohs gave:

> 10,000 biscuits . . . 1,200 Asiatic loaves, 100 baskets of dried meat, 300 cuts of meat . . . 250 handfuls of beef offal, 10 plucked geese, 40 cooked ducks, 70 sheep, 12 kinds of fish, fat quails, summer pigeons, 60 measures of milk, 90 measures of cream, 30 jars of carob seeds . . . 100 heads of lettuce, 50 bunches of ordinary grapes and 1,000 bunches of oasis grapes, 300 strings of figs, 50 jars of honeycomb, 50 jars of cucumbers, and 50 small baskets of leek bulbs.[45]

These foods were eaten with the hands. In early Egypt, upper-class diners reclined on mats or cushions on the floor in front of low tables, but over the years, chairs and standard-height tables came into use. Servants brought the food. The wealthy had a separate room just for cooking, instead of doing it on the roof or in the back of the building. But there was a vast underclass that had completely different eating habits.

Pyramid Builder Food: The Jewish Diet

One of the earliest types of human relationships was slavery. In ancient societies, slavery was based on being in the wrong place at the wrong time: if you lost a war, you became the property of the winners. So the Jews became the slaves of the Egyptians. The Jews were the first people to believe in one god. This type of belief—monotheism—made their religion portable. Their one god was not connected to a particular place, but was everywhere, unlike the many gods in polytheistic religions, which were attached to sacred groves or rivers or mountains. For example, many of the gods of the ancient Egyptians were connected to the Nile, so worshiping them anywhere else would have been impossible.

The Jews have many dietary laws. One of the most important is kosher butchering. The purpose is to inflict as little pain as possible on the animal, one of God's living creatures. The animal is hung upside down, then its throat is cut quickly with an extremely sharp blade. This has benefits for the animal and for humans. It is humane because the animal loses consciousness quickly and doesn't suffer. The advantage to humans is that gravity drains the blood away, so the butcher can easily see any tissue that is white, which means it is toxic to humans. (For a recent case of humans poisoned by improperly butchered meat, see Chapter 12.) Any animal that is not killed in this ritual religious fashion—for instance, if it dies from disease or an accident—is considered *treyf*, impure, and is forbidden. The koshering process continues in the kitchen, where the meat must be soaked, salted, and rinsed to remove all traces of blood.[46] The words *kosher* and *treyf* crossed over into English to refer to things that had nothing to do with food. For example, a person or deal that is kosher is aboveboard, honest, decent. *Treyf* is trash.

Other Jewish dietary laws prohibit eating the flesh of four-legged animals that don't ruminate—that is, chew their cud—or which have cloven hooves. Chief among these is the pig. Also forbidden: rodents, reptiles, and fish that do not swim or have scales, like shellfish. They must not "boil the kid in the milk of its mother," which prohibits eating meat and dairy foods at the same meal or even within several hours of each other. Orthodox Jews must wait six hours after eating meat to have milk.[47] They also keep kosher kitchens so that meat and dairy never touch each other. The kosher kitchen has two preparation tables, two sets of pots and dishes kept in separate cabinets, and two sets of cooking and eating utensils. Traditionally, red dishes are for meat, blue are for dairy. Some modern kosher kitchens have separate sinks and dishwashers.

There is a large third class of foods, neither meat nor dairy, that are safe to eat with anything. These are called *parveh*—neutral—and include plant foods like flour, fruits, vegetables, and sugar; salt; some beverages; and fish. However, there are some restrictions on these foods, too. For example, fruit from a particular tree must not be eaten until the tree has been bearing for at least three years.

While the Jews were enslaved, Moses went to Pharaoh and told him that God had said, "Let my people go, that they may hold a feast to me in the wilderness." But Pharaoh wouldn't let the Jews go. They prayed to their god for freedom; he answered with a series of plagues that were intended to starve and hurt the Egyptians while saving the Hebrews. The plagues turned the Nile to blood so that the water wasn't drinkable and the fish died; covered the land with frogs, which got into the ovens and the kneading bowls; filled the air with gnats and flies; killed the livestock

ℋOLIDAY ℋISTORY
⋙ PASSOVER ⋘

The Jews did as God commanded: they slaughtered a one-year-old lamb, then dipped a bunch of the herb hyssop in the blood and touched the doorposts and the lintel (the beam above the door) as a sign of where they were. Then they roasted the lamb and ate it with unleavened bread and bitter herbs. God saw the blood and passed over the houses of the Jews and did not kill their firstborn sons, but did take the firstborn sons of the Egyptians and the firstborn of their cattle. There was a great cry of grief throughout Egypt, and Pharaoh finally let the Jews go.

God commanded the Jews when to celebrate Passover and how. It begins in the "first month [of the lunar calendar], on the fourteenth day of the month at evening [and continues] until the twenty-first day of the month at evening." God also told the Jews what foods to eat. These ritual foods for the Passover dinner, called a *seder,* include *harosset,* a mixture of chopped apples and nuts that symbolizes the bricks the Israelites were forced to make when they were building the pyramids; horseradish, which represents the bitterness of slavery; and a hard-boiled egg dipped in salt water, which symbolizes the tears the slaves cried. Unleavened bread—*matzoh*—is eaten for seven days because the Jews left Egypt so quickly that there was no time to take leavening.[48]

The Christian holiday of Easter is connected to Passover. (See Chapter 3.)

of the Egyptians but let the Hebrews' animals live; covered humans and beasts with sores; caused it to hail so hard that the plants and the trees died; sent swarms of locusts to eat what was left of the crops and fruit; and covered Egypt with a thick darkness for three days.[49] The final punishment visited on the Egyptians but not the Hebrews is the cause of one the most sacred celebrations in Judaism, Passover.

According to the Old Testament, that is how the Jews finally gained their freedom. The leader in their Exodus from Egypt was Moses, who parted the Red Sea and led them to Canaan (although he was not allowed to enter), the "land of milk and honey," foods that represent a place of plenty.

CHINA: THE YELLOW (HUANG HE) RIVER

China has some of the most dramatic geography on earth, and plant and animal life to match. The Himalayas, the mountain range that forms its border with India, has the highest peak on earth. At almost 30,000 feet, Mt. Everest is nearly twice as high as the tallest peak in the lower 48 states, California's Mt. Whitney. China's lowest point, approximately 900 feet below sea level, is more than three times lower than California's Death Valley. China has climate extremes, too, from tropical rain forest to permanent ice caps. It has no Mediterranean climate, but drenching monsoon rains followed by drought. It also had an enormous population; by A.D. 2, sixty million people.[50]

Historians believe that agriculture arose independently in China and Mesopotamia, because the Chinese cultivated millet, a grain that was unknown in the Middle East, at approximately the same time that wheat was domesticated in the Middle East. The earliest Chinese civilization known, from approximately 6000 B.C., is the village of Ban Po in the floodplain of the Yellow or Huang He River in north-central China. The

---

ℋOLIDAY ℋISTORY
⇒ CHINESE NEW YEAR ⇐

In China, the New Year celebration is called Spring Festival and is deeply connected to China's ancient farming culture. It begins at the new moon closest to the beginning of spring, usually the second new moon after the winter solstice. It always falls between January 21 and February 21.[51] The festival lasts 15 days, although preparations begin much earlier.

New Year's Eve dinner is a feast of traditional foods that are supposed to bring good luck and prosperity in the coming year. Each region of China has its own specialties. Near the sea, the dinner might be prawns, dried oysters (ho xi), raw fish salad (yu sheng), angel-hair seaweed (fai-hai), and "sleep together and have sons"—dumplings boiled in water (jiaozi).[52] A whole animal, like a whole fish or a chicken with head, feet, and tail on, represents abundance. In the south, rice in pudding and wrapped in leaves are favorite foods. In the north, steamed dumplings made of wheat are served. Fresh bean curd is avoided because it is white, the color of death. And don't cut your noodles—long noodles mean long life.

The Festival of Lanterns is the last night of Chinese New Year, when lights drive away demons and promise a good year coming up. Firecrackers explode to drive away Nian, the ferocious beast that eats people. New Year's Day is when hong bao (red packet) takes place. Presents and money wrapped in red paper—the color of good luck—are exchanged, along with greetings to relatives and neighbors.[53]

NEW YEAR'S DAY

February 1, 2003, Year of the Goat
January 22, 2004, Year of the Monkey
February 9, 2005, Year of the Rooster
January 29, 2006, Year of the Dog
February 18, 2007, Year of the Boar

village's defense was not a wall but a moat. The people lived in huts with plaster walls and thatched roofs made of straw. Communal grain—millet—was buried in hundreds of pits scattered in the village. Pigs and dogs were also raised. At around the same time in northern China, salt was harvested when lake waters dried up during the summer. Salt production, either by harvesting or evaporation, predates what is usually used as a source of salt in China—soy sauce. Salt production dates from almost 2000 B.C., soy from around 1300 B.C. Soy sauce began as fish fermented in salt. Then soybeans were added, and finally the fish was omitted, leaving just soybeans and salt. Soybeans are extremely nutritious legumes: they nourish the humans who eat them and the soil in which they are planted. Cinnamon, too, is one of the earliest spices known in China. It is mentioned in the first herbal, in 2700 B.C.[54]

Chinese New Year is perhaps the oldest festival observed anywhere on earth. Around 2600 B.C., the emperor Huang Ti began keeping records based on a lunar month and the twelve signs of the Chinese zodiac. Just as we have Sagittarius, Capricorn, and Scorpio, the Chinese have the Rat, Ox, Tiger, Rabbit, Dragon, Snake, Horse, Sheep, Monkey, Rooster, Dog, and Boar.

The Chinese philosopher known to the West as Confucius (551–479 B.C.) declared that everything on earth would run smoothly if subjects respected rulers, younger brothers respected older brothers, wives respected husbands, and friends respected friends. He also supposedly assembled the *I Ching,* or Book of Changes, and the *Book of Songs,* a combination of court and peasant songs that reveals much about the culture of the time. It mentions 44 vegetables and herbs, including bamboo, Chinese cabbage, celery, peaches, plums, apricots, pine nuts, and hazelnuts. Confucianism was the basis for government in China for many centuries. In the 15th century A.D., the Confucian scholars who ruled China made the decision that China would not trade with the rest of the world, which eventually proved damaging to China.

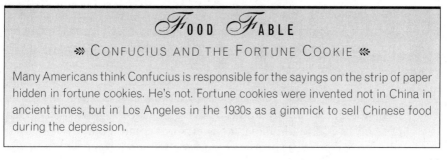

ℱood ℱable

🌾 CONFUCIUS AND THE FORTUNE COOKIE 🌾

Many Americans think Confucius is responsible for the sayings on the strip of paper hidden in fortune cookies. He's not. Fortune cookies were invented not in China in ancient times, but in Los Angeles in the 1930s as a gimmick to sell Chinese food during the depression.

The Wall That Salt Built

In 221 B.C., Shi Huangdi, whose name means "first emperor," decided to build the Great Wall to protect China from attacks by the Mongols to the north. It was an expensive project, paid for with taxes from the state monopoly on salt—the first such monopoly in history.[55] The wall, 25 feet high and thousands of miles long, was built by more than 1 million men. It is one of only a few man-made structures on Earth that can be seen from space. Like the pharaohs before him or the Roman emperors after him, Shi Huangdi began other massive public works projects, including a palace that held 40,000 people. Convinced that he was such a great emperor that he would rule China even after his death, he had 6,000 life-size warriors and horses and 1,400 chariots sculpted out of clay and put in his tomb. Shi Huangdi also standardized written Chinese, which helped to unify China. However, taxed beyond endurance, and with a shortage of crops because farmers were working on the emperor's grandiose projects, the empire collapsed.

INDIA: THE INDUS RIVER

Like the civilizations in Mesopotamia, Egypt, and China, early civilizations in India were centered around a river, the Indus, in the western part of the country. Because of its location at the junction of Asia and the Middle East, India has been the site of a great deal of cultural exchange through many overlapping migrations. The first of these occurred approximately 65,000 years ago. Then, around 6000 B.C., people from the Middle East migrated east into India, bringing domesticated cattle, sheep, goats, and their experience growing wheat. Other people migrated west from China, bringing rice and, later, tea. By 750 B.C., Indo-Europeans had come south into India from the flat, dry grasslands called the steppes. They contributed the horse and their knowledge of iron. Other Indo-European-speaking people migrated into eastern Europe. Today, most of the languages spoken in Europe, India, Iran, and North and South America are based on this common Indo-European parent language. In math, India gave the world the zero and the decimal system.

Some important food firsts came from India: the first plowed field in the world, before 2800 B.C., and the domesticated chicken.[56] The technology for turning sugar cane into granulated sugar existed at least as early as 800 B.C. in India; the word *sugar* comes from the word used in ancient India, *sharkar*. Many words for food come from ancient

Indo-European or other Indian languages, even though the food might have originated somewhere else. The words for a rice dish with spices and meat—*pilaf, pilav,* or *pulao* in Persian and Arabic—come from the much earlier Indian *pallāo* or *pulāo.* The English words for rice (*arisi*), pepper (*pippali*), mango (*mānggā*), orange (*nāgarangā*), curry (*kari*), and chutney all originated in India. *Tamarind* means "fruit of India" in Arabic.[57] Pulses consumed were peas, chickpeas, and lentils. Fruits included coconuts, pomegranates, dates, lemons, some melons, and possibly bananas.[58] In the beginning, India was not a heavily vegetarian country. The sacred cow came later (see below).

Hinduism

India gave the world two major religions, Hinduism and Buddhism. Hinduism arose sometime between 750 B.C. and 550 B.C. after Aryans ("people of noble birth") arrived from the north. It has a body of sacred literature called the Vedas, but unlike the other great religions of the world, no one person was the founder. The Vedas mention barley (but not wheat or rice), sugar, distilled liquor, grinding stones, and the mortar and pestle.[59] They also gave instructions on how to carve beef for the priests who ate it at feasts. The fundamental belief of Hinduism is a rigid caste or class system that determines everything about a person's life, including what and with whom he can eat. There was a racial component to the caste system: those at the top were lighter-skinned Aryans, more likely to be wealthy and educated, while those at the bottom were darker-skinned, poorer non-Aryans. The highest caste is the brahmins, who are often also the priests. Lower down are warriors, then peasants. At the bottom are the untouchables, manual laborers and people in trades the Hindus considered necessary but less desirable or "unclean," like butchers and garbage collectors. The term *untouchable* was meant literally; the slightest physical contact with an untouchable—even his shadow—would contaminate a brahmin physically and spiritually so much that he would have to undergo ritual purification. One of the means of purification involved ghee, clarified butter. By heating butter to remove the milk solids—the part that would cause butter to become rancid—the butter could be preserved for a long time, even in the hot climate of India. Hindus cannot change the caste they were born into during their life on earth. They can, however, move up in the next life. Through a series of reincarnations (rebirths), they can work out bad karma—past wrongs—and eventually achieve divine peace, one of the four goals of Hinduism. The other goals are wealth and power, responsibility, and physical pleasure, which is celebrated in temple carvings of many people having sex in a great variety of ways. The caste system persists today in India in thousands of complex social relationships that determine everything about daily life.

In ancient India, one drink, *soma,* was sacred to the priests, who used it in their offerings to the gods, particularly the goddess of the moon, who gave her name to the drink. This was a controlled substance, far beyond mere alcohol. All-powerful, it produced superhuman feelings and supposedly healed all diseases. It was made by grinding the plant, then "the ground mass was collected on a cowhide, strained through a cloth of sheep's wool, and the sparkling tawny filtered liquid mixed for consumption with milk, curds or flour."[60] There are several candidates for the plant that could have produced these effects, but Indian food historian K. T. Achaya settles on the fly agaric mushroom (*Amanita muscaria*), a hallucinogen.

Buddhism

India's second great religion, Buddhism, arose in the 5th century B.C. Unlike Hinduism, it does have a founder, Siddhartha Gautama, known as the Buddha, who sought to understand the cause of suffering in the world. Fasting by eating only six grains of rice a day didn't help. Wandering didn't help. Finally, he sat under a fig tree and after 49 days of meditation, reached the wisdom of enlightenment. Buddhism rejected the caste system of Hinduism, so it appealed more to the lower classes. It also rejected the many gods of Hinduism but kept the belief in reincarnation as a way to change and achieve perfect peace without pain, which Buddhists call *nirvana.* The Buddha declared that the flesh of many animals, in addition to humans, should not be eaten: elephants, dogs, horses, hyenas, bears, and the big cats—lions, tigers, panthers. But he never said that cattle should not be eaten. That happened around 2,000 years ago, after an ecological disaster in India made it culturally suicidal to raise cattle for food, and long after the Buddha was dead.

The Sacred Cow

A word about the sacred cow. In India, cows are sacred because they produce oxen, castrated male cows. It takes a wealthy culture to support large animals for their meat alone. Sheep and goats give milk

---

𝒞ULINARY 𝒫UZZLE

❖ THE DEATH OF BUDDHA ❖

The Buddha died around 486 B.C. at the age of 80, right after eating a meal that supposedly brought on an attack of dysentery. What did he eat, and did it kill him? As food historian Achaya points out, it depends on the translation of one word, *shukaramaddava*. This could be connected to "boar." It could mean sprouts softened by boars, or mushrooms that grow where boars have softened the ground. Scholars are still debating this one.[61]

---

and hair repeatedly and are killed for food only when they have outlived their other functions. But an ox eats a great deal of food, takes up a great deal of space, and gives no milk. Killing it for food would mean that it has no life as a work animal, which is what cattle are used for in India. They pull plows in the fields and carts on the roads. Their dung is fuel, fertilizer, and free. An Indian farmer who owns an ox can feed his family; if his ox dies, they might starve or be forced to move to the city. He can't borrow oxen from his farmer neighbors, because the cycle of heavy rain followed by a period of no rain means that all the fields have to be plowed at the same time. The zebu cattle native to India survived because they were able to adapt to these rain-drought cycles. They have humps like camels where they store water and fat, and they are resistant to tropical diseases. Cattle are so important to the economy that when India became an independent nation after World War II, it wrote a bill of rights for cattle into its constitution.[62] In India's neighbor, Tibet, its native cow—the yak—serves the same functions today as the cow in India: labor in the fields, transportation, fuel, and fertilizer.[63]

In the ancient worlds of Africa, the Middle East, the Indian subcontinent, and Asia, as humans evolved, so did human interaction. Over millions of years, humans had become bipedal; developed bigger brains; made tools and weapons out of stone, then bronze, then iron; progressed from herbivores to carnivores and omnivores; mastered fire and learned to cook; invented dance, language, art, and religion; domesticated hundreds of species of plants and animals; and created complex systems of irrigation, government, and law. In the first millennium B.C., as merchants from all of these areas traveled the trade routes, so did their food, languages, beliefs, and customs. The knowledge of wine making from the Near East, sheep and goat herding from the Fertile Crescent, olive oil from Egypt, and spices from India, especially black pepper, extended farther west and north than they had before, along the Mediterranean Sea, to another continent—Europe. All of these cuisines and cultures converged on a small, new country that would lay the foundations for Western civilization—Greece.

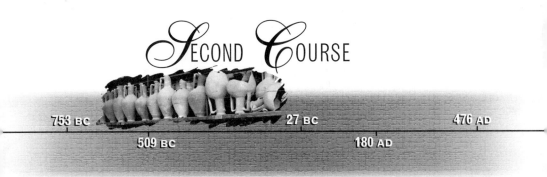

The Goddess of Grain and the God of the Grape: Ancient Greece and Imperial Rome

GREECE

Geography

Greece is a rocky, mountainous country surrounded by sea on three sides. This geography helped to create a political system based on small, local government, affected human relationships, and determined what foods could be produced.[1] Since only 15 to 20 percent of the land was flat enough or fertile enough to farm, the Greeks couldn't grow enough grain to feed themselves. When a country is faced with this situation, it has three choices: (1) trade, (2) colonize, or (3) conquer. Greece did all three. It traded its staple crops, olive oil and wine. It founded colonies to produce grain. But when it tried to conquer other territories, it was defeated and was conquered itself.

The Mediterranean Sea was the center of economic life and food for the Greeks. They were a nation of sailors who lived on the abundant variety the sea provided: fish like mullet, turbot, grouper, and sea bream, and other sea creatures such as eel, octopus, and squid. Especially popular was the bluefin tuna native to the Mediterranean. These large fish—they can weigh almost a ton—could feed many people. And they could be preserved in salt or in olive oil, as they still are today in the Mediterranean. Bonito, the ten-pound version of the bluefin,

25

was wrapped in fig leaves and slow-cooked in the ashes. The measure of an ancient Greek cook was what he could do with fish.[2]

Geography affected government in Greece by keeping it small and local, because travel over steep peaks and down deep valleys was difficult and time-consuming. Each city was like a small country and ruled itself. It is from the Greek word for city-state, *polis,* that we get our word *politics.* The city-state of Athens was a democracy, the form of government in which the citizens rule by voting, and which survives today in the United States. However, Greece was no political paradise: only free males were allowed to be citizens and to vote. Women had no say in the government, and neither did much of the labor force, which was slaves.

Food, too, was democratic in Greece, at least until the 5th century B.C. Everyone ate the same modest meals based on olives and figs, goats and sheep, and barley pounded into a paste, porridge, or unleavened bread. More than any other food, bread represented civilization because it was a completely human product, controlled by humans every step of the way. Vinegar was a favorite ingredient of the Greeks. Black pepper was also used but was considered a medicine. Cows were not kept because of the shortage of pastureland, so a man who owned oxen was considered rich.[3] However, he didn't kill them because he needed them to plow his fields and for transportation. Goats and sheep were kept, but the young ones were reserved for ritual blood sacrifice to the gods, who got the choicest parts, thigh meat and fat. It was a matter of economics, too: goats and sheep produced milk to drink and to make into cheese, and mohair and wool, so they were only killed when they were very old and had outlived all their other purposes.

Greeks ate three times a day: very lightly in the morning and at midday, with a two-course main meal in the late afternoon. The first course was protein—usually fish or cheese—and vegetables. The second course was olives, nuts, and fruit, probably figs or grapes.[4] The philosopher Aristotle noticed the effect of sweet foods: "Why do figs, which are soft and sweet, damage the teeth?"[5]

That was the diet in Athens, in northern Greece. In the southern part of Greece, Sparta was a rigid militaristic society. Infants that were not born healthy and physically perfect were tossed off a cliff. Girls and boys ran and played rigorous sports to toughen them up. When they were seven years old, the boys were sent away for military training. They lived in barracks and slept on hard wooden benches. Spartan food matched the Spartan life. Although cheese, barley, and figs were food fundamentals in Sparta, the staple food was a black broth made from pork stock, vinegar, and salt.[6] It is from their denial of what they considered luxury that we get the word *spartan*.

Geography also influenced human relationships in Greece. Because the land made travel so difficult, the guest-host relationship was sacred. If a stranger, even a poor man, appeared at your door, it was your duty to be a good host, to take him in and shelter him, share your food and wine with him. "We do not sit at table only to eat, but to eat together," said the Greek author Plutarch.[7] Dining was a sign of the human community and differentiated men from beasts. In return, the guest had obligations to his host. These included not abusing his host's hospitality by staying too long, usually not more than three days. A violation of this relationship by either side brought justified human and divine wrath. An example is in Homer's epic poem *The Odyssey*. After the Trojan War, which lasted ten years, Odysseus, king of Ithaca, wandered for another ten years trying to return to his home. In his absence, his house was filled with men who drank his wine, ate his roasted lambs, and pressured his wife to choose one of them as her new husband because they kept assuring her Odysseus was dead. When he finally arrived home disguised as a beggar, the suitors refused to give him food or shelter. Then Odysseus revealed himself and justifiably killed them all.

Olive Oil: Liquid Gold

There was gold in Greece—olive oil. Olives, the fruit of the *Olea europaea* tree, had been cultivated and pressed for their oil in the eastern Mediterranean by Palestinians and Syrians since about 5000 B.C. The dusty gray-green trees are slow-growing but live to be hundreds of years old. Prized for cooking, as medicine, and as fuel, olive oil was one of the basics of trade in the ancient Mediterranean. It was also used as a body lotion, sometimes scented with perfume. For example, in the Olympics, which began in 776 B.C., naked men greased with olive oil competed in the earliest sports: running, the long jump, the discus and javelin throws, wrestling, boxing, and a combination of five events called the pentathlon—all still part of the modern Olympics, which began in 1896. (The winner wasn't totally naked: he was crowned with a wreath of laurel leaves from the god Apollo's sacred tree.) When it was discovered that olive trees, which are very sensitive to cold, grew well in Greece's mild climate, olives became a staple crop. However, the trees' deep roots let the topsoil wash away, finishing off the erosion that had begun centuries earlier when the Greeks started chopping down trees to build houses and ships.

Unripe green olives and even ripe black ones are bitter. Before they can be eaten they must be cured in brine or in oil, or dried in salt. If they are going to be crushed to extract the oil, it must be done very carefully, with just the right amount of pressure to force the oil out of the olive but not smash the pit into it. Ancient people didn't have the levels of labeling that came into existence at the end of the 20th century, but "virgin" means first pressing, "extra virgin" means less than 1 percent acidity, and "cold-pressed" means that heat, which would alter the chemical composition and taste of the oil, was not used.[8]

The olive tree is highly symbolic in Western culture. Jews and Christians know it from the Old Testament story of Noah's ark and the flood. When the dove that Noah sent out to see if the world was still flooded flew back to the ark with an olive branch in its mouth, everyone knew that the floodwaters had receded and that there was peace again. The dove and the olive have symbolized peace ever since. To the Greeks, the olive was the symbol of the goddess Athena, who created it. She was the warrior goddess, helmeted and carrying a shield, who also represented peace and wisdom. Homer's epic poem *The Iliad* describes how she protected Athens and helped the Greeks win the Trojan War.

Demeter, Goddess of Grain: The "Good Goddess"

Another powerful goddess was Demeter, the goddess of all growing things—mother earth. Barley was sprinkled around her temple as an offering to ensure that the earth would be fertile. As time passed, the barley was replaced by wheat, then rice. The custom of scattering rice spread from the temple to the wedding ceremony to guarantee fertility in marriage. This is why we still throw rice at the bride and groom. (Now, however, in an effort to be environmentally sensitive, many people sprinkle birdseed because birds can't digest rice.)

Demeter kept her beautiful daughter Persephone hidden from the roving eyes of the male gods.[9] One day, the thing Demeter feared the most happened: Persephone let out a scream that shook heaven and earth, then vanished. Demeter was devastated. She left Mt. Olympus and wandered the earth disguised as an ordinary human, looking for her daughter. She would not eat or drink the food of the gods, only the little bit of food the reapers ate: barley water with mint, or water, meal, and pennyroyal.[10] Finally, the sun god told her that Hades, the god of the dark kingdom of the dead, had seen Persephone picking flowers and thought she was so beautiful that he opened the earth and captured her. Demeter grieved when she heard this, and so did the earth. Everything stopped growing. Zeus finally stepped in and negotiated a compromise because all the humans were going to starve. Persephone could be with her mother, but only part of the time. She had eaten a pomegranate seed that Hades had given her, which meant that she had to return to the underworld to be with him. That is how Persephone came to be both the goddess of springtime and of the dead. During Persephone's eight months above the ground, joyous Demeter lets things grow and flourish. But when Persephone is in the world of the dead for four months every year, Demeter mourns and nothing grows.

And that is where winter comes from.

Dionysus: God of the Grape

Each winter in Greece, grapevines seemed to die, only to be miraculously reborn in the springtime. Just as the Nile represented resurrection to the Egyptians, Dionysus, the god of the vine, was the sacred symbol of resurrection and immortality to the Greeks. Grapes were plentiful; wine production began by 1500 B.C.[11] The Greeks drank it sweetened with honey, because the amphora—the ceramic vessels they used to store wine—were waterproofed with resin, a sticky secretion from trees that tasted like turpentine. The taste persists today in the Greek alcoholic drink retsina. Like the wine he represented, Dionysus had many sides: he could lift men out of their ordinary state of mind and inspire them, but men also sometimes committed terrible acts under his influence. Women were rarely allowed to have wine. For instance, public banquets were usually restricted to men. On the rare occasions when women were invited, they didn't get the good, strong, aged wine the men got. They were served "sweet wine or barely fermented grape juice."[12] Drinking wine was regarded as sacred because it altered human consciousness and brought men closer to God. At one of the most sacred Greek ceremonies, it was consumed not with dinner as a beverage, but after, at what the Greeks called a symposium.

The Symposium

The symposium was an elaborate ceremony that usually took place in a ruler's dining hall or public building, often a temple. By the 7th century B.C. it was an accustomed practice. The best sources from

---

ℱᴏᴏᴅ ℱᴀʙʟᴇ

⋙ THE ANCIENT GREEK WAY TO DRINK ⋘
AND NOT GET DRUNK

The ancient Greeks were always searching for ways to drink without getting drunk. They finally came up with what they thought was the antidote to the downside of Dionysus. They believed that drinking purple wine from a purple vessel made of semi-precious stone would cause the two purples to cancel each other out and negate whatever was in the wine that caused drunkenness. In Greek, the prefix *a-* means "not," and *methyein* means "drunk" (from *methy,* "wine"), so the Greek word for "not drunk" became the name of the purple stone the vessel was made out of—amethyst.[13]

---

ancient Greece are paintings on vases; the best current source is Massimo Vetta's ten-page essay, "The Culture of the Symposium," in *Food,* edited by Jean-Louis Flandrin and Massimo Montanari (and in English by Albert Sonnenfeld). As Vetta states, the symposium was "a meeting of men that only took place following a meal" to consecrate a special public or private event like a wedding, to thank the gods for a victory in games, or to make a political decision.[14] It began with a blood sacrifice—a religious offering to the gods of an animal, usually a young lamb or goat, that had been ritually killed—followed by eating. Slaves served the guests, who took their sandals off and reclined on couches propped up on one arm. When the eating was over, tables were cleared, hands were washed, and floors cleansed of the scraps thrown on them during dinner. The men were given garlands to put on their heads and chests. Then poetry was recited, flutes played, decisions made. The sense of community was further reinforced because all the men drank from the same cup.[15] Except for a few drops of sacred wine at the beginning of the ceremony, the wine was diluted, often at the ratio of one part wine to two or three parts water. The Greeks regarded diluted wine as a symbol of civilization. It also helped to avoid drunkenness.

Nectar and Ambrosia: Food of the Gods

To the Greeks, the stories about the gods were their religion. Christian writers who came later called them myths. There were twelve major Greek gods, called the Olympians because they lived on Mt. Olympus. They were immortal and ate mysterious food that was forbidden to humans—the sweet drink called nectar, and the heavenly food called ambrosia, which gave its name to the 20th-century fruit salad made with orange sections, sliced bananas, and shredded coconut in an orange juice and confectioners' sugar sauce.

Even though the gods did not eat human food, they were very human in their behavior. They fought among themselves, lied, cheated, got angry, and were not above disguising themselves to get what they wanted, frequently a beautiful young girl. The husband-and-wife team of Zeus and Hera headed up the gods. Both a goddess and a god were connected to fire. Hestia, the goddess of the hearth—the only sister of Zeus, and a virgin—was worshiped in public and in private every day because every city had a sacred fire that was kept burning constantly. In this case, the goddess paralleled what the humans did, since the daughter of the household was responsible for keeping the fire going. Hestia also received offerings at the beginning and end of every meal. One of the rituals of founding a new colony was to take fire from the old city to the new one to guarantee continuity. It survives today in the ceremony of the Olympic torch, which has to be carried by hand from Athens to the site of the Olympic games every four years. The god connected with fire was Hephaestus. Like many Greek gods, he had both a positive and a negative side. On the positive side, he was a blacksmith, which showed the power of fire to create and be useful to mankind. The negative was that he also represented the power of fire to destroy, because he was the only god who was ugly and deformed. However, in another typically Greek contrast, Hephaestus was married to Aphrodite, the most beautiful of the goddesses and the goddess of love. She gave her name to foods that are thought to stimulate the senses, especially sexually—aphrodisiacs. Some foods that are considered aphrodisiacs now are oysters, caviar, Champagne, chocolate, and snails.

Food played a large part in Greek mythology, too. Hunger was used as a punishment for the crime of cannibalism. Tantalus, the only mortal who had ever dined with the gods on nectar and ambrosia, invited the gods to a banquet at which he served a peculiar dish. He had killed his son, boiled him, and now was feeding him to the gods. They figured it out before they started eating (except for one bite of his shoulder) and gave Tantalus a punishment to fit his crime—eternal agonizing hunger and thirst. He was forced to stand in a pool of water, but every time he bent down to take a drink, it disappeared. He reached up to pluck the ripe apples, pomegranates, pears, and figs dangling just over his head, but the wind blew the branches out of his reach. It is from Tantalus that we get our word *tantalize*—to drive somebody crazy with desire.

31

The Golden Age of Greece and the Professional Chef

In the 5th century B.C., Athens and Sparta allied and defeated Persia (modern-day Iran) in a series of wars. The peaceful time that followed was the Golden Age of Greece. Athens grew to between 300,000 and 500,000 people and created the buildings, paintings, and sculptures that are the hallmarks of Greece and Western civilization, like the Parthenon, a hilltop temple with a 40-foot statue of Athena. The Golden Age was the great age of theater in Greece; the comedies of Aristophanes and the tragedies of Aeschylus, Sophocles, and Euripides are still performed today.

The Golden Age was also the beginning of a wealthy class and a split in the culture between rich and poor, which was reflected in Greek cuisine. The poor continued to subsist on barley heated to remove the chaff and ground into cakes called *maza,* wheat pastes or unleavened bread, some sheep or goat cheese, and olive oil.[16] The wealthy had more elaborate meals, with more variety in diet. They consumed legumes like chickpeas, lentils, and vetch, and seeds from flax, sesame, and poppies. They also ate the meat of domesticated animals, including dogs, after observing sacrificial rituals. The forests provided large and small game: boar, deer, hare, and fox. The vegetables commonly eaten were turnips, leeks, watercress, onions, garlic, and purslane.[17] The new profession of beekeeping made honey more available.[18]

The rise in urbanization, wealth, and trade produced a need for more than the free guest-host hospitality of earlier times. City-run inns provided professional hospitality for traveling merchants and businessmen throughout the Greek world, often in waterfront areas.[19] All of these people needed food; cooking became a profession in Greece. Cuisine was not as elaborate as it later became in Rome, but some of the chefs became known. One, Archestratos, evidently wrote much about food, but no whole cookbooks survive, only fragments about foodstuffs and preparation. In addition to being able to afford chefs, the wealthy could afford to buy imported wines. They also drank much more wine than the poor.

Greece's Golden Age ended when it went to war with Sparta. Starting in 431 B.C., Athens and Sparta waged a 27-year war for control of the Greek peninsula. Much of Sparta's strategy was to cut Athens off from its food supply. Knowing this, Athens tried to invade Sicily in 415 B.C. to turn it into a grain-producing colony. Two disastrous years later, the Sicilians emerged victorious after destroying Athens's navy and one-third of its total military force.[20] The war finally ended in 404 B.C., when Sparta blocked Athens's sea route to its grain supply. Without food, Athens was forced to surrender. The Golden Age of Greek civilization was over.

Alexander the Great and the Magic Apples

A new conqueror appeared, from Macedonia, just north of Greece. Alexander was not Greek, but he loved Greek culture. His tutor was the philosopher Aristotle, who had been the student of Plato, who had been the student of Socrates. Alexander's goal was to conquer the known world, and he did. His empire stretched east from Greece through Persia and Iraq to the Indus River on the western border of India, north through what are now Afghanistan and Pakistan, and south into Africa. His conquering created a new culture, Hellenistic, that was a combination of four cultures: Greek, Persian, Indian, and Egyptian. This had an impact on the cuisine of Greece, because new methods of food preparation and new foods were introduced. One writer bemoaned all the changes that were occurring with food:

> Do you see what things have come to? Bread, garlic, cheese, *maza*—those are healthy foods, but not these salted fish, these lamb chops sprinkled with spices, these sweet confections, and these corrupting pot roasts. And by Zeus, if they aren't simmering cabbage in olive oil and eating it with pureed peas![21]

Alexander established cities everywhere he conquered and named at least 15 after himself. The center of learning in the world shifted from Athens to Alexandria, Egypt. It had a library with 700,000 volumes of Greek writing, a zoo, a botanical garden, an observatory, and a great lighthouse more than 400 feet high to keep the ships safe, many of them carrying wheat from the Nile River valley to feed the Mediterranean world.

Alexander was also on a quest for immortality—the legendary water of life or the magic golden apples. He didn't find either one, but he did find other apples that were supposed to let him live to be 400 years old.[22] He didn't live to be 40. He died of a fever, maybe malaria, in 323 B.C., one month short of his 33rd birthday. Still seeking immortality, before his death he arranged to have himself preserved in honey and placed in a glass coffin in Alexandria, Egypt. After his death, as was usual after the death of a powerful leader, there were wars of succession and his empire was split up into smaller areas ruled by several generals. But Alexander's vast empire would soon appear small. Power in the Mediterranean was shifting to a fast-rising country located west of Greece on a peninsula shaped like a boot—Italy.

ROME

The Founding of Rome, 753 B.C.: Suckled by a Wolf

Every country has myths about its founders. In the United States, these myths are about honesty. As a boy, George Washington supposedly chopped down a cherry tree and "couldn't tell a lie" when his father asked him about it. Abraham Lincoln's nickname was "Honest Abe." The myth of the founding of Rome is that Romulus and Remus, twin boys, were born under an olive tree, which symbolized that they were descended from a god—in this case Mars, the god of war—and a Latin princess. Then they were abandoned and found by a she-wolf that saved them by nursing them. Below is a picture of the bronze statue of the wolf, suckling the twins Romulus and Remus, that stands on one of the seven hills of Rome, the Capitoline Hill.[23]

What we know for sure is that Rome was founded in the 8th century B.C. on seven hills 20 miles up the Tiber River for defense—all the better to see invaders' ships coming. There was also a natural harbor there. Salt deposits along the banks and at the mouth of the Tiber provided a valuable item to trade.[24] One of the first roads in Rome was the Via Salaria—the Salt Road.

The Capitoline Wolf.
Photograph © Leo C. Curran

Roman Culture: Gods and Goddesses

Rome absorbed much of its culture from Greece, including the idea that the mind and the body were connected and affected each other—"a healthy mind in a healthy body" (*mens sana in corpore sano*). Greek slaves who were prized for their learning as tutors and their skill as cooks brought their customs and beliefs to Rome with them. Many of the Roman gods are Greek gods with name changes. Dionysus, the Greek god of wine, became Bacchus and gave his name to a wild, drunken feast, the bacchanalia. Jupiter and his wife, Juno, presided over the Roman gods just as Zeus and Hera presided over the Greek gods. Hestia became Vesta; Aphrodite became Venus. She still cheated on her hunchbacked husband, the blacksmith Vulcan, who lived under Mt. Aetna in Sicily and gave his name to our word for erupting mountains—*volcano*. The Roman goddess of the harvest, Ceres, counterpart of the Greeks' Demeter, gave her name to our word for grain—*cereal*.

The Grain Wars: The Punic Wars

From 264 to 146 B.C., Rome and the Phoenicians, whose capital city was Carthage in what is now Tunisia in northern Africa, were locked in a series of wars to the death for control of trade in the western Mediterranean, especially the grain fields of Sicily. To aid them in trade, the Phoenicians had invented a system of writing that is the basis of our alphabet. In the second of these wars, called the Punic Wars, a Carthaginian general named Hannibal made one of the boldest moves in military history. Instead of sailing across the Mediterranean and attacking Italy from the south, which they expected, he marched thousands of soldiers and 60 elephants over the Alps and attacked Italy from the north, taking them by surprise. For more than ten years, Hannibal's soldiers and elephant(s) (historians think that perhaps all the elephants died except one) ate their way up and down the Italian peninsula, through fields of wheat and barley, through orchards of apples, pears, and lemons, and through the vineyards. They devastated the country's farms and economy, especially the rich agricultural areas of northern Italy, so badly that the damage to the fields could not be repaired for many years. Rome eventually won by attacking the city of Carthage, but 50 years later, when it looked like Carthage might make a comeback, Rome finished the Phoenicians off. After a three-year siege, Carthage was burned and razed. The 50,000 Carthaginians who were not killed

35

outright were sold into slavery. Then the ground was spread with salt so that nothing would ever grow there again.[25] Rome now controlled the western Mediterranean Sea. *Mediterranean* means "middle of the land" in Latin because it divides the continents of Europe and Africa, but after Rome gained control of the eastern part of the sea, too, they called it simply *mare nostrum*—"our sea."

Hannibal had long-lasting effects on the Roman economy. Small farmers couldn't afford to replant or repair the damage. They also couldn't afford to compete with the slave labor on the *latifundia,* the large plantation-like estates. So they sold their farms to the wealthy landowners and then either roamed the countryside looking for work as laborers or moved to the cities, where they were poor or homeless. Soon one-third of the population of Rome was slaves and another one-quarter was poor.

The Roman Republic

Rome began as a monarchy but by the 3rd century B.C. it was a republic with a three-part government: 300 senators who made the laws and served for life, two co-consuls who commanded the army and administered the laws, and a court system. Almost 2,000 years later, the Founding Fathers of the United States, fluent in Latin and familiar with the history of Rome, patterned parts of the American government on the Roman Republic and used Rome to justify slavery. The young United States even referred to itself as a republic. We still use Latin words for legal terminology and government positions, like *governor* and *senator.*

The Roman Republic ended when Julius Caesar gained too much power as a general, defied the senate's order to disband his army, and became dictator. In 44 B.C., on March 15, which the Romans called the Ides of March, the senators stabbed him to death in the senate. This plunged the country into 17 years of civil war, during which the Roman general Marc Antony and his ally Cleopatra, the queen of Egypt, committed suicide after they lost a decisive naval battle to Octavian, Julius Caesar's grandnephew and adopted son.

The Roman Empire

In 27 B.C., Octavian emerged victorious as Rome's sole ruler and first emperor with the title of Augustus (meaning "majestic"). The reign of Augustus initiated 213 years of the *Pax Romana* (Roman peace)—for the simple reason that Rome had no enemies left to defeat and no one to stop its expansion. The empire Augustus controlled sprawled across three continents. In Europe, it reached north through Gaul (present-day France) to the island of Britannia (England) and its most important city, Londinium; and west to present-day Spain, Portugal, and the Atlantic Ocean. In Asia, to the east, it extended into Armenia, Syria, Judaea, and Arabia. It also controlled grain-rich North Africa, the breadbasket of the empire; Egypt's rich Nile Valley; and modern-day Libya, Morocco, and Tunisia. Tunisia was the source of most of the olive oil for the Roman Empire. Olive oil was so important to the Roman economy that planting enough olive trees excused a farmer from military service. Through trade with countries outside the empire, Romans now had access to exotic foods and spices, animals, fabrics, and people.

Trade Routes: The Silk Road and Cinnamon Land

Much of Rome's trade with other countries centered around spices. These were acquired over the Silk Road to China and the sea routes from India and Africa. The Silk Road was not a paved road like the other Roman roads, but a series of caravans that traveled through deserts and over mountains to the end of the road—the international marketplace in the capital city of Chang'an in northeastern China, where traders of all races came to buy and sell. What the Romans wanted most, in addition to spices like ginger, turmeric, and galangal, was silk. They prized it and liked to wear it to banquets, where they protected it with large aprons. However, the Romans could only buy silk, not produce it, because silk production was a Chinese monopoly and a closely guarded state secret. Silk was literally worth its weight in gold.

By sea from India and Africa to warehouses in the Spice Quarter in Rome came spices for cooking, for perfume and incense, and for medicine. Cinnamon was the most valuable. It was one of several spices, including white pepper, ginger, and cardamom, that were extremely expensive not only because of the shipping costs, but because a 25 percent tariff—an import tax—was added. The nobles, frequent targets of poisoning, often by their relatives, believed that if you combined almost every spice known to mankind, it would make an antidote that could counteract even the most powerful poison. Black pepper was not on the list of luxury items because the Romans considered it a necessity. Other luxury items subject to the tariff were silk, wool, and cotton; purple cloth (reserved for the upper class); lions, leopards, and panthers; and jewels—diamonds, emeralds, pearls, turquoise.[26] In A.D. 301, the emperor Diocletian set maximum prices for many of these goods to try to stop the runaway inflation that was making them cost increasingly more while Roman money became increasingly worth less.

Arab traders had a monopoly on cinnamon and told the Romans fantastic stories to keep their sources secret. They claimed it grew in remote swamps, high up in trees, where killer bats swarmed. We know now that the Arabs got it from Indonesia, brought by ship to Madagascar and to Somalia on the east coast of Africa, which was called Cinnamon Land. From there it went up the Red Sea, overland to the Nile, and across the Mediterranean.

The culture of Rome—its food, laws, customs, and language— spread on the roads with the governor, the army, and the merchants, and displaced existing cuisines and cultures. In the provinces, Romans replaced local kinds of apple trees with ones they preferred. As early as 200 B.C., the Romans planted apple orchards in Britannia.[27] Roman knowledge of gardening, grafting, and pruning spread, too. Italian wines reached into the provinces and replaced Greek wines, not just because the taste of Italian wines like Opimian and Falernian was preferred, but also because at 1,600 gallons per acre, Italian vineyards produced a volume that Greeks couldn't match.[28] Rome dominated trade so completely that some countries, like the Kush area of northern India in what is now Afghanistan and Pakistan, were forced to develop metal money in order to do business with Rome.

To glorify Rome, the emperors embarked on a massive campaign of public building based on the discovery of a new kind of building material, concrete, that made it possible to create stronger buildings using arches to distribute the weight. It was during this time that many of the greatest buildings of ancient Rome were built: the Forum; the Colosseum, which opened in A.D. 80; the Pantheon, temple of all the Roman gods; and the aqueducts that brought water into Rome. The Forum, four levels high, was the business, political, religious, and market center of Rome, like a giant mall. If all roads led to Rome, all roads in Rome led to the Forum. Spacious, open plazas were surrounded by multicolored marble columns and luxurious public baths and public toilets also made of marble. It contained markets for local and imported produce, restaurants that sold that era's equivalent of fast food, and small boutique-type stores that sold expensive imported spices and other luxury goods under armed guard. It was the location of religious festivals, sacrifices, and offerings of rare scented oils and incense to the warrior god, Mars, and, behind the temples, of dirty deals and prostitution. Government administrators and bureaucrats, the equivalent of the Internal Revenue Service and the Social Security Administration, also had offices at the Forum.[29]

Upper-Class Life and Cuisine: Banquets and the *Convivium*

For the 10 percent of the Rome's population who were the wealthy upper class—called patricians—breakfast and dinner were the main meals, eaten at home. Lunch was lighter, often bought from a street vendor. Breakfast was mostly leftover cheese, olives, and bread. Lunch was called *prandia* and might be followed by a bath at the public baths. Dinner was *cena* if it was only family; if there were guests and it was more elaborate with additional courses like appetizers and desserts, it was a *convivium*.

But what time did Romans dine? The Romans divided the day into two parts, with the middle of the day, noon—*meridiem*—as the dividing line. Midday was important because Rome was a society of laws and lawyers had to be in court before noon. The Romans called the part of the day before noon *ante meridiem,* which we abbreviate A.M.; *post meridiem,* what we call P.M., was after the middle of the day. They read the time on big sundials in their gardens or on one-and-a-half-inch portable, pocket-sized sundials. Neither worked on cloudy days. Water clocks, which measured the flow of water against lines drawn on a basin, served as a backup and were not portable, so people were much more casual about time. Roman dinner would have been in the late afternoon or early evening. Depending on how elaborate the *convivium* was, it could last all night.

Since the dining room was where entertaining took place, it was the best room in the house. It was called the *triclinium,* after the couch on which three people could recline while they ate. The dining room was elaborately decorated with paintings on the walls or a mosaic tile floor that might have pictures of food, like fish and baskets of grain. Romans ignored the religious rituals that the Greeks had observed regarding meat and wine. They didn't make ritual blood sacrifices before eating meat—usually pork, their favorite. They also didn't ritually purify the dining room after eating and before drinking wine because they didn't wait until the end of the meal to drink. They drank wine with their meal, a custom that is still observed in Italy today. At the end of the meal, which was prepared and served by slaves, guests might be offered silver toothpicks.

When the weather was good, wealthy Romans dined outside—*al fresco*. Dining in one of these elaborate sunken or terraced gardens could be just as elegant as dining indoors. They might have ornamental flower gardens as well as food gardens, with separate landscape designers for each. Care was taken to grow special plants for bees—usually rosemary, thyme, and roses.[30] Urns, statues, sundials, shrines, and altars decorated the gardens. Grapevines trained on an arbor or nets that kept birds in provided shade. Water pumped in from the aqueducts splashed in fountains, mosaic-lined pools, and ponds stocked with fish and ducks. The outdoor *triclinium* was built-in, made of marble, cement, or stone, with soft pillows on top. A ledge built into the couch served as a cupholder, so wine was within easy reach. Sometimes the couches were built around a small pool so that the food could float on trays, cooled by the water. Or dinner guests might climb up into a tower and enjoy the view, take a siesta on a sleeping couch in a small outdoor room after the meal, or have dinner in a treehouse.[31]

Some wealthy Romans got out of the city altogether. Like wealthy people today, Romans had vacation houses at the seashore, on a lake, or in the mountains. Their villas (Latin for "farmhouse") were often within 20 miles of Rome so they could visit them easily and oversee their farms. Vacation villas were built for relaxation and to take advantage of the views. Pliny the Younger, a Roman author, had an estate with almost 30 rooms, including quarters for slaves. He called it "my little villa." Eating and entertaining took place in two dining rooms and a banquet room. The main dining room had windows and doors that looked out over the sea on three sides. Glass was very expensive, so windows were usually made of mica or were just holes cut in the walls and closed with shutters. The other dining room and the banquet room were in two separate towers. The second dining room, with eastern and western exposures, faced a vineyard and a garden planted with rosemary bushes and fig and mulberry trees. The banquet room had ocean vistas. Pliny was keenly aware of which windows got breezes and sun from which direction, at what time of day, and in which seasons. There was also an herb garden on the grounds, grain storage, and aboveground wine storage purposely placed near the furnace because the Romans thought smoke helped the wine age. The villa had built-in bookcases, a bathing room with two tubs and a separate room next to it for applying bath oil. In addition, there were three public bathhouses in the small town. State-of-the-art heating in the villa was provided by hot air generated in the furnace room and circulated into the rest of the house through pipes under the floor.[32]

The food had to be outstanding to match such stunning surroundings. Underlying much of Roman cooking was a pungent fermented fish sauce called *garum,* a unique combination of salt, sea, and sun. It originated in Greece and was perhaps the ancestor, in a roundabout way, of Worcestershire sauce. The theory is that Romans exported *garum* to India in ancient times and then the British brought it back from India to England 2,000 years later. *Garum* was readily available commercially; below is a recipe.

To compare: good-quality *garum* cost twice as much as vinegar, the same as lower-grade aged wine, and less than half of what top-quality honey or fresh olive oil cost. Approximately one pint of *garum* cost the same as one pound of pork, lamb, goat, or second-quality fish, and twice as much as a pound of beef. The expensive meats were chicken—one pound cost five times as much as one pint of *garum*—and goose, which cost more than 16 times as much.[33]

RECIPE

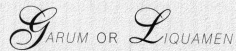

GARUM OR *LIQUAMEN*

"Garum, also called liquamen, is made in this way. The entrails of fish are placed in a vat and salted. Also used are whole small fish, especially smelts, or tiny mullets, or small sprats, or anchovies, or whatever small fish are available. Salt the whole mixture and place it in the sun. After it has aged in the heat, the garum is extracted in the following manner. A long, thickly woven basket is placed in the vat full of the above-mentioned fish. The garum enters the basket, and the so-called liquamen is thus strained through the basket and retrieved. The remaining sediment is allec.

"The Bithynians make garum in the following manner. They use sprats, large or small, which are the best to use if available. If sprats are not available, they use anchovies, or lizard fish or mackerel, or even old allec, or a mixture of all of these. They put this in a trough which is usually used for kneading dough. They add two Italian sextarii [approximately one quart] of salt to each modius [one peck, a quarter of a bushel] of fish and stir well so that the fish and salt are thoroughly mixed. They let the mixture sit for one night and then transfer it to a clay vat which is placed uncovered in the sun for two or three months, stirring it occasionally with sticks. Then they bottle, seal, and store it. Some people also pour two sextarii of old wine into each sextarius of fish."[34]

ℱOOD ℱABLE

⋙ WHO WAS APICIUS? ⋘

Little is known about him; in fact, there are three men named Apicius who might be candidates. One was a high-living man-about-town who loved to eat well and had many dishes named after him, including cheesecakes. He spent a great deal of his wealth on food, endowed a cooking school, and supposedly killed himself when his fortune dropped below a level that could support his expensive habits. Some food historians find this story difficult to digest.[35]

Apicius and the First Cookbook

The first cookbook dates from the 1st century A.D. This compilation of recipes, divided into ten books or chapters, is only a fragment; baking and pastry are missing, which indicates that these were separate specialties. *De re coquinaria* (Cooking Matters) is attributed to a man named Apicius, which just means "epicure," a discriminating eater.

The book was translated from Latin into Italian and German after the invention of the printing press in the 15th century, but an English translation didn't appear until 1936. Only 530 copies of the English version were printed because culinary history was in its infancy and there wasn't much interest in the subject. Translating the manuscript was a lifelong dream and labor of love for Joseph Dommers Vehling, a world-class chef who grew up in a small town on the German-Dutch border and was trained and worked in the grand hotels of Europe before he became an executive chef planning menus for the railroads in the United States. Vehling loved food and cooking as well as the Latin language and Roman culture. A world traveler, he had visited the Roman ruins. In Pompeii, buried suddenly by a volcanic explosion in A.D. 79, he saw ancient bakeries, ovens, and flour mills, with olive oil, figs, lentils, and spices preserved in jugs and jars. On page 43 are pictures of the ovens and the clay vessels—called *amphorae* (pronounced "am-FOR-eye")—still in Pompeii.

Vehling's goal was to set the record straight about the ancient Romans, "for our popular notions about their table are entirely erroneous and are in need of revision."[36] He felt that too many people believed fantastic stories about Roman banquets—which were rare—and satires like Petronius's *Satyricon* because these were the available sources. There is more historical information about banquets because educated, wealthy people wrote about them, whereas information

Pompeii—ovens.
Photo courtesy Nancy Uhrhammer

Pompeii—amphorae.
Photo courtesy Nancy Uhrhammer

about the customs of other classes is sparse. For example, 500 years from now culinary historians will be reading newspaper and magazine articles about what foods were served at the many celebrations of Julia

Child's 90th birthday in the summer of 2002, but probably nothing about the dinner you had last night, which would reveal much more about how Americans really eat.

From the recipes of Apicius it is clear that the Romans liked sauces and meat. Food historian Mireille Corbier states that the ten most common ingredients in Apicius's 468 recipes are black pepper, *garum,* olive oil, honey, lovage, vinegar, wine, cumin, rue, and coriander. Absent is garlic, the seasoning of the poor.[37] For the wealthy, a feast meant meat, and meat meant pork: "nature made the pig for the banquet table."[38] Pigs were fattened and their livers enlarged in much the same way geese were prepared for foie gras until recently—by being force-fed. Pigs were fed dried figs, then guzzled mead. The liquid expanded the figs, which killed the pigs.[39] True omnivores, the Romans ate sow udders, calf brains, flamingo tongues, sheep heads, pork sweetbreads, and capon kidneys. Vehling says that the capon—a castrated male bird—was supposedly "invented" by a Roman surgeon in response to a law that made it illegal to fatten hens. So he castrated a rooster, which caused it to fatten naturally.[40] Romans also raised the dormouse (*Glis glis*) commercially, plumping and tenderizing these small mammals by confining them in earthenware vessels that looked like flower pots with ventilation holes and feeding them a high-fat diet of walnuts, chestnuts, and acorns.[41] Rabbits and hares were also raised commercially. Dogs were eaten, too. Milk came from cows and camels. Cheeses, both domestic and imported, were eaten alone with bread or as an ingredient in other dishes.[42] Olive oil was the main fat; butter—salted—was introduced centuries later, when the Germanic barbarians invaded.

Vinegar added tang in these recipes in combination with honey or *garum,* while raisin wine and honey were the sweeteners for many main dishes. Honey was also used to preserve fruit and meat. Oregano and mint appear frequently but historians are still speculating about silphium. Tannahill says the herb is completely unknown now; others think it might be laserwort,[43] the *fang feng* of Chinese medicine, used to treat sinus infections and fevers.[44] Some historians think silphium was used to extinction because it prevented pregnancy.[45] The use of spices in some of the recipes is eerily modern. A recipe for pears could have come out of California two thousand years later: "Stew the pears, clean out the center, crush them with pepper, cumin, honey, raisin wine, broth and a little oil; mix with eggs, make a pie [custard] of this, sprinkle with pepper and serve."[46]

Apicius also included recipes for drinks, even floral wines. He gives recipes for rose wine, fake rose wine made with citrus leaves but without roses, and violet wine. But most recipes are based on sauces. For example, a fish sauce: "tak[e] one ounce of pepper, one pint of reduced wine, one pint of spiced wine and two ounces of oil." In Roman cooking, a white sauce is made with white wine, white pepper, and egg yolks: "put yolks of hard-boiled eggs in the mortar with white pepper, nuts, honey, white wine and a little broth." Eggs were frequently used as a thickener or binder, along with bread crumbs, honey, and animal blood. The blood could be either from an animal that had been killed, or from a living animal that had been bled. Favorite fruits included grapes, pomegranates, quinces, figs, mulberries, apples, and pears, and the stone fruits (plums, cherries, and peaches). Like a Roman Martha Stewart, Apicius even provided serving tips: "An expensive silver platter would enhance the appearance of this dish materially," he wrote at the end of a recipe composed of sow belly and breast of figpecker (a bird) seasoned with crushed pepper and lovage, sweetened with raisin wine, layered with thin pancakes, and topped with pine nuts.[47]

There are even some medicinal recipes, like one for spiced salts that can be used "against indigestion, to move the bowels, against all illness, against pestilence as well as for the prevention of colds." Apicius didn't need to include many medicinal recipes in his cookbook because a book explaining in detail the medicinal uses of 600 species of plants also appeared in the 1st century A.D. The *Materia Medica,* written by Dioscorides, was one of the major medical textbooks for over a thousand years. The 1st century A.D. also produced Pliny's *Naturalis Historia,* which has several sections on the medicinal uses of plants and animals, even imaginary ones like dragons.

Lower-Class Life and Cuisine: Street Food

The 90 percent of the population that made up the lower classes in Rome—the plebeians—lived in poorly built tenement apartments that frequently collapsed or caught on fire. This was negligence, because the same culture built the Colosseum and the Pantheon, which are still standing. The tenements had no kitchens, so street vendors did a thriving business selling bread and grain pastes. Wheat was the mainstay of the poor. In 122 B.C., reformers lowered the price of grain so that the poor could afford it; in 58 B.C., wheat became free to those who qualified. The wheat was usually prepared two ways: mashed and boiled into porridge, or ground and baked into bread.[48] Leavened and unleavened bread; bread with poppy seeds, with pepper, with salt, with cheese, with honey; and square breads, round breads, flatbreads, and shaped breads could be produced on a massive scale because the Romans had the technology to produce flour on a massive scale. This required more than human labor—a donkey was harnessed to a grinding stone called a quern and walked around it in endless circles to separate the wheat from the chaff.[49] Whether or not wheat was used in a now-popular third way is still not clear. As historian Jo-Ann Shelton points out, "Scholarly opinion is divided on the question of whether the ancient Romans made pasta noodles."[50] For a cold beverage, soldiers and the poor drank *posca,* vinegar diluted with water. *Calda* was wine diluted with hot water. They also had a kind of bread soup with vinegar and mashed cucumber, the forerunner of gazpacho. Indoors at the *taberna* (where we get our word *tavern*), patrons could drink wine and nibble on salted foods, chickpeas, or turnips, the way popcorn and peanuts are served in American bars. The *popina* served simple dinners and alcohol. Both places provided gambling and prostitutes.[51]

In the country, a real villa, the house where the farmer lived and worked, was very different from the vacation villas of the rich. Under one roof were the living quarters for the farmer and his family, an underground prison for chained slaves, a kitchen with high ceilings so the beams didn't catch on fire, baths, a bakery, a dining room, a barn, a stable, a threshing room, separate rooms for olive and wine presses and for wine fermentation. Again, great care was taken with direction: the grain storage should be open to the north, because north wind is the coldest and least humid, so the grain will stay dry and won't rot.[52]

The Persecution of the Christians: Life and Death in the Colosseum

During the *Pax Romana,* Rome didn't wage war against other countries. It did wage war internally, however, against Christians and Jews, who were considered atheists because they refused to worship Roman gods. They also threatened the power of the state because they were willing to die for their god, not for the state. Christianity was only one of the many religions that arose as a response to the excesses of luxury and cruelty among the upper classes in the Roman Empire. Romans persecuted Christians by, among other things, forcing them into to-the-death combat with other humans or animals in the Colosseum, an arena that could hold up to 50,000 people. After some of the human-animal battles, the animals, like bears, were butchered and became upper-class suppers.[53]

A DAY IN THE LIFE OF THE ROMAN EMPIRE		
	PATRICIANS: 10 PERCENT OF THE POPULATION	PLEBEIANS/SLAVES/FARMERS: 90 PERCENT OF THE POPULATION
You are:	A wealthy landowner, in the military, or in the government. You pay for the spectacles at the Colosseum.	Poor or unemployed. You go to free public entertainment at the Colosseum or the Circus Maximus.
You live:	In a many-roomed house with kitchen and dining room, built around a courtyard. You have other homes.	In one room with no kitchen in a poorly built tenement that may catch on fire or collapse.
You wear:	Imported silk.	Coarse homemade fabric tunic.
You eat:	Pork, wine sweetened with honey, food with sauces like *garum,* and expensive imported spices prepared by servants; in your home or at friends' villas.	Grain pastes, bread bought from street vendors or made from free government grain; skin from the fish that made the *garum;* in *tabernas* or *popinas.*

In the Colosseum, completed in A.D. 80, the Circus Maximus (which means "biggest circle"), and other arenas, the Roman Empire could control two of its underclasses at once. Giving the urban poor free entry to these torture spectacles kept them in one place, so they could be managed. It also released anger and was a serious warning about the power of the state. In effect, upper-class Romans were telling lower-class Romans, "Watch out, or you could end up down there, too."

The emperor Constantine ended the persecution of the Christians in A.D. 313 after he supposedly saw a cross in the sky as a good omen just before he won a battle. In A.D. 325, he convened the Council of Nicaea in Anatolia (modern-day Turkey), which made the cross the official symbol of Christianity and set the date for Easter at the first Sunday after the first full moon following the spring equinox.[54] This is why Easter can fall anywhere between March 22 and April 25. Christianity became the official religion of the Roman Empire in A.D. 380, under the emperor Theodosius.

The Persecution of the Jews: Masada and the Diaspora

The *Pax Romana* was not a time of peace for the Jews, either. The Romans killed hundreds of thousands of Jews, most in two separate battles. In A.D. 70, the Romans destroyed the Temple in Jerusalem, leaving only one wall, which is now a holy shrine, the Wailing Wall. In

ℋOLIDAY ℋISTORY
≫ EASTER ≪

Easter is a combination of Jewish, pagan, and Christian rituals. Its name comes from the Jewish holiday of Passover, *Pesach* in Hebrew. In Italian, it is *Pasqua;* in French, *Pâque;* in Spanish, *Pascua.* In English, Easter gets its name from Eostre, the Old English goddess of fertility and dawn. Her festival during the spring equinox celebrated fertility as plants began to grow again and young animals like bunnies, lambs, and chicks were born. The Christian part of Easter is the story of the crucifixion and resurrection of Christ.

Easter is preceded by Lent, a 40-day period of fasting (excluding Sundays) that begins on Ash Wednesday, which signifies mourning. The period before Ash Wednesday is one last celebration of partying and eating the rich foods like cheese, meat, and eggs that are restricted or forbidden during Lent. This is called Mardi Gras (which means "fat Tuesday") or *Carnevale.* Lent made a virtue of fasting during a time of scarcity. At the end of winter there was little fresh food for humans or beasts; even dried or salted food was in short supply. Some monks supposedly survived the winter on triple bock beer, very high in vitamins and carbohydrates.

Lent ends with the Last Supper, crucifixion (on a cross made of olive wood), and resurrection of Christ. On Holy Thursday, Christ gave the ceremony of communion to his followers, the 12 disciples, at the Last Supper: "Take of this bread and eat of it, for it is my body. Take of this wine and drink of it, for it is my blood." Then Christ was betrayed by one of the apostles, Judas, who sold him out to the Romans for 30 pieces of silver. The betrayal is portrayed in Leonardo da Vinci's fresco *The Last Supper* by Judas knocking over the salt cellar, a traditional sign of evil.[55] The next day, Good Friday, is the deepest day of mourning in the Christian religion because it is the day Christ was crucified, died, and was buried. On Easter Sunday, Christians believe that Christ rose again and ascended into heaven.

Eggs were forbidden during Lent but were used heavily in ritual foods when the fast was broken after Mass on Easter Sunday. They were in special egg breads like European Easter breads and Ukrainian *paska.* Sometimes the egg bread is decorated with dyed hard-boiled eggs or shaped into a cross. For Easter dinner, traditional foods depend on geography. In the Mediterranean, it is lamb; in northern Europe, ham; in England, beef.

The custom of giving painted eggs for Easter dates to the later Middle Ages. Baskets to hold the eggs represent birds' nests. The Easter Bunny with his basket of painted eggs came to America with German immigrants in the 19th century and became popular. In Washington, D.C., children used the grounds of the Capitol as a playground and for egg hunts until Congress, unhappy with the torn-up lawn and tired of voting money to keep repairing it, passed a law against it. However, in 1878, children from Washington, D.C., went to President Rutherford B. Hayes and asked if they could have an Easter egg hunt. The president and his wife, Lucy, agreed to let the children use the White House grounds. Easter egg hunts have taken place on the south lawn of the White House ever since. It is the largest public event held at the White House, but it is only for children six years old and under. (See Chapter 10 for Ukrainian Easter eggs and Fabergé eggs, the jeweled eggs made for the Russian royal family.)

A.D. 132, the Jews decided to take the decision about how they would die away from the Romans: they killed themselves at the rock fortress cliffs of Masada rather than let the Romans kill or enslave them. The rest fled their homeland of Judea for safety and scattered in the Diaspora. The Jews were without a homeland for almost 2,000 years, until 1948, when the United Nations created the country of Israel in the old Jewish homeland, so that Jews all over the world could have a safe haven after the Holocaust of World War II. However, in those 2,000 years, Muslims had occupied the land and considered it their home. The conflict between Muslims and Jews continues to this day.

Bread and Circuses: The Decline of Rome After A.D. 180

The *Pax Romana* ended in A.D. 180 when wars with foreign countries resumed. These wars, diseases, loss of loyalty, and economic decline weakened the Roman Empire. The Plague of Antoninus, named after the reigning emperor, was new and terrifying, one of the first zoonoses—diseases that cross over from animals to humans. It began as a disease of cattle but in humans was called smallpox because of the small pus-filled sores that covered the skin. The 15-year epidemic that ended in A.D. 180 killed millions.[56] At one point, 5,000 people a day were dying in the city of Rome alone. Then another plague (some historians think it was measles) struck the empire. The high death tolls left many jobs vacant that were crucial to the running of the empire and killed so many farmers that the empire's food supply was threatened. Rome offered land to people who were not citizens—even to barbarians—if they promised to farm it, then passed laws forcing people to farm and making farming hereditary.

There was also an unfavorable balance of trade. More money was going out of the empire to buy spices, silk, and animals for the contests in the Colosseum, the Circus Maximus, and other arenas than was coming in. By A.D. 250, there were 150 of these spectacles a year, almost one every other day,[57] and the government was giving oil, wine, and pork to 200,000 urban poor in addition to bread.[58] The free food and free admission to the entertainment kept the poor from being hungry and angry and made them grateful to the government instead.

In A.D. 330, the emperor Constantine took a desperate measure to preserve the empire—he split it in half. He made the old city of Byzantium his new capital in the east and named it after himself, Constantinople (Constantine *polis*). The division strengthened the eastern half, which survived; the western half didn't.

The Fall of Rome, A.D. 408–476: "The Funeral of the World" [59]

The 5th century was a time of increasing chaos in the Western Roman Empire, which was completely cut off from the more powerful Eastern Empire. The military was unable to defend the borders against barbarians—Visigoths, Ostrogoths, and Vandals, illiterate Germanic nomadic tribal peoples. The once invincible Roman army couldn't even protect the city of Rome. In 408, invaders held it for ransom: 3,000 pounds of black pepper.[60] In 410, Visigoths ransacked Rome for three days. Wealthy Romans who had estates and villas outside the cities fled to them and buried their silver dinnerware—knives, spoons, cups, dishes, serving pieces—in the fields, where it was still being unearthed in the 20th century. In 452, Attila and his army of Mongol nomads—Huns—appeared outside the city. The emperor of Rome commanded no army and wielded no real power, so Pope Leo I negotiated the peace with Attila. This was the beginning of the ascent of the Christian Church to its position as the most powerful political force in Europe in the Middle Ages.

The barbarian invasion became final in A.D. 476, when the German general Odoacer seized the throne from the last Roman emperor, 14-year-old Romulus Augustulus. The great Roman Empire was broken, its western half destroyed. Rome, the city a million people had called home, was almost a ghost town. Now its entire population—20,000—could fit in the Colosseum two and a half times over. Nature

> ⋙ YOU JUST MIGHT BE ⋘
> A BARBARIAN IF . . .
> (with apologies to Jeff Foxworthy)
>
> > You eat your meat raw
> > You warm your raw meat by putting it between your thighs
> > You warm your raw meat by putting it between your saddle and your horse
> > You have never eaten bread
> > You eat your food without sauce
> > You drink ale because you think wine is for wimps[61]

took over, obliterating the signs of the great civilization. Wind and weather finished off what the barbarians had left of the architectural masterpieces that Rome built. In the once-magnificent Forum, among fallen marble columns and through abandoned buildings where an empire once ruled the earth, down roads where great armies had marched, cows wandered and chewed weeds. Descent began into the decentralized, isolated, rural, illiterate life that would characterize Europe for centuries to come. With the breakdown of the Roman roads came the end of the empire and the beginning of the end of the Latin language. Communication was cut off, trade expired. No more exotic animals or sexy fabrics or spicy foods. For nearly the next thousand years, almost everything in Europe would be homegrown, homemade, and homespun.

| 500 | 732 | 1300 |
| 622 | 1096 | |

Crazy Bread
and Courtly Manners:
The Middle Ages, 500–1300

The Middle Ages is the time between the fall of the Western Roman Empire, at the end of the 5th century, and the start of the modern era, which began with the Renaissance in the 14th and 15th centuries. With the roads no longer safe, Europe became isolated. Literacy and learning declined. Daily life centered around individual farm-based rural societies. Feudalism, a system based on loyalty to a local lord rather than to a distant king or to a country, determined a person's place in society. However, in the eastern half of the Roman Empire, the Byzantine Empire, with its capital in Constantinople, safeguarded Roman culture and laws, mixed with Greek culture. Eastern Christianity developed differently from the Roman version, too, and eventually clashed with it. In the Middle East an entirely new religion—Islam—propelled a great trading empire and created cities where goods and ideas flowed and new cuisines were invented. In the 11th century, Islam was attacked with no warning by European Christians on a series of Crusades, which were unsuccessful from the military and religious standpoints but succeeded in reopening trade routes and in creating hatred that is still with us today.

CHRISTENDOM: THE EARLY MIDDLE AGES IN EUROPE

The early Middle Ages, the period from A.D. 476 to about 1000, was a time of chaos and attempts at political organization. The Christian

53

Church based in Rome and its leader, the Bishop of Rome, called "father" in Italian—*Il Papa*, or the pope—emerged as the most powerful forces in European politics and daily life. The Church controlled every aspect of life in the Middle Ages in Europe, from Spain to eastern Poland, from Italy to England and Ireland. The Church told people what they could eat and when, when to fast and when to abstain. It had guidelines for when married couples should or should not have sex, how often, and in what positions. The Church even controlled time: the bells rang out, signaling when to get up, say morning prayers, go to Mass, say evening prayers, and go to bed.

After the invasions of the Goths in the 5th century, the Church worried that these beer-drinking barbarians would tear up the vineyards, destroy the winepresses, or somehow drive wine—necessary to Christian worship—out of existence. But they didn't. Viticulture continued to flourish, maybe because the barbarians had found a use for wine that made sense to them—as armor. Linen saturated with a mixture of wine and salt dried hard as a board.[1] However, the Church's problem wasn't beer-drinking barbarians but wine-drunk priests and monks who made spectacles of themselves. Attempts to control them weren't very successful, even though public drunkenness was against the law.

Feudalism

Feudalism was a political, social, economic, military, and legal system based on local, personal relationships and loyalties. It was an extension of the class system that had existed in the Roman Empire, transferred to the countryside, where it preserved the unequal percentages of upper and lower classes—10 and 90 percent, respectively. Class divisions in food, clothing, education, and occupation were enforced by law. There was none of the upward mobility that is available to us in modern society through education, changing jobs, or starting over someplace else. People who wanted to be more attractive by decorating their clothes with fur trim or buttons, items reserved for the nobility, attracted the "clothes police," who forced them to dress appropriately for their class. Serfs endured this system because the Church told them it was God's will, their lot in life—and because there was nowhere else to go.

There were few cities, and those were small, with only a few thousand people. Little travel or trade was done because the roads were unsafe and in disrepair, so the manors had to be self-sufficient. The lord of the manor provided land for the serfs to farm; in exchange, the serfs would be the army when the lord needed one. The lord also provided bread. In Old English, the language spoken in England from the middle of the 5th century until the end of the 11th, the word for lord was *hlaford,* meaning "loaf keeper"; the word for lady was *hlaefdige,* "loaf kneader." A servant was a *hlaf-aeta,* "loaf eater."[2] Unlike modern English, Old English divided its words into genders. *Hlaf*—"loaf," the staple of life—was a masculine word. The serfs had to pay a fee to use the lord's mill to grind their grain into flour and to use his oven to bake their bread. Sneaking off to do these things somewhere else resulted in a fine because on the medieval manor the lord was also the law.

The Medieval Mind: The Christian Diet and the Four Humors

The concept of the Great Chain of Being reflected the worldview in the Middle Ages: everything and everybody had a place ordained by God. Off the scale at the top was God; at the bottom were inanimate objects like rocks. Along with this went the theory of the four humors to explain how the human body functioned and how to treat it. This theory was first proposed in ancient Greece by Hippocrates, the father of medicine; it was refined by Galen, a Roman, and turned into rock-solid doctrine by the Church in the Middle Ages. Physicians had nowhere else to get information about the human body because the Church imposed an absolute ban on Christians performing autopsies. There was also no experimentation or firsthand observation of disease or the living human body. Scientists didn't know that the blood circulated through the body until the 18th century. So food was medicine, and the theory of the four humors was the medical bible. It is important to remember when you look at the chart below that what category a food was in had to do not with how it appears, but with the effect it supposedly had on the body. One problem with the chain was that food animals didn't really fit. They

THE GREAT CHAIN OF BEING AND THE FOUR HUMORS[3]					
ELEMENT	HUMOR	EMOTION	COLOR	TEMPERATURE	ANIMAL/PLANT
God					
Angels					
Fire	Yellow bile	Choler (anger)	Yellow	Hot	Dry	Phoenix (mythical); spices
Air	Blood	Sanguine	Red	Hot	Wet	Birds, fowl, meat animals
Water	Mucus	Phlegmatic	Clear/white	Cold	Wet	Whales, fish, crustaceans
Earth	Black bile	Melancholy	Black	Cold	Dry	Trees, leafy plants, roots
Rocks and inanimate objects					

were sandwiched in between air and water, because although they lived *on* the earth, they weren't *in* it like carrots, which were only fit for the lower classes. There were also rankings within each category. Chicken, higher in the air element, was served at banquets attended by the nobility. And, of course, cooking it by a hot, dry fire method like roasting made you that much closer to God. Pork, the least valued of the food animals, was fit for peasants. Veal and mutton were in the middle. Fruit, which grew on shrubs and trees, ranked higher than vegetables, which grew in or on the ground, and the higher up in the tree the fruit was, the more it was fit for nobility.[4]

The theory of humors was that one of these four personality types predominated in each person. If you were sick, your body was out of balance because one of the humors had overwhelmed the others. This could result in anything from pale skin and irritability to cowardice, leprosy, and death. It was crucial to restore balance by eating something that represented the opposite element. For example, brains and tongue were cold and moist, so they had to be counteracted by hot, dry spices like pepper, ginger, and cinnamon.[5] Vinegar (*vin aigre*—literally, "sour wine") was considered cold and dry, so a vinegar-based sauce had to be balanced with hot spices like mustard, garlic, and rue.[6] So did a sauce based on verjus (literally, "green juice"), the unfermented juice of unripe fruit, usually grapes, but also crab apples.

Foods within each humor were further divided into degrees from one to four, the fourth degree being the most intense. In the late Middle Ages, after contact with Muslims because of the Crusades, hot spices included cinnamon, clove, pepper, and others from the Middle East. Cinnamon, cumin, and nutmeg were hot and dry in the second degree, so they were very beneficial to health. Black pepper was a fourth-degree spice, so it was dangerous and had to be used sparingly. At the other end of the scale were mushrooms, fourth-degree cold and wet, to be avoided always.[8] As food historian Jean-Louis Flandrin points out, "In medieval recipes . . . hot ingredients played a

---

𝒻OOD 𝒻ABLE

❯❯"FEED A COLD, STARVE A FEVER" ❮❮

Feed a cold, starve a fever. Have you ever thought that old saying makes no sense because you're supposed to stuff yourself when you're congested? It's a holdover from the Middle Ages in our culture. It does make sense if you look at it from the medieval idea of humors and restoring balance to the system. The theory is that eating will make the stomach work, which will heat it up and counteract a cold. On the other hand, not eating is supposed to make the stomach cool down and counteract a fever.[7] Medieval recipes reflected this—people with fevers had to avoid spices.

crucial role. In fact, they dominated the seasoning."[9] Looked at from the point of view of dietetics, the heavy use of spices in medieval cooking makes more sense. It also explains why so many medieval recipes result in food that is spicy, sweet, and sour. It is not to mask food that had gone bad, especially meat. Bad food smelled as bad to people in the Middle Ages as it does to us, and laws forbade selling meat more than one day old.[10] Among the upper classes, the good host played it safe and served a variety of foods to restore the balance of all personality types. Hungry peasants bent the rules and ate a diet heavy in vegetables.

The Breakdown of the Latin Language

The learned men of the time—the nobles and the clergy—could understand each other when they talked about dietetics and the humoral theory because they wrote and spoke Latin. But the spoken language of the serfs deteriorated into the vernacular—local languages with less complicated grammar. Italian, French, Spanish, Portuguese, and Romanian are called the Romance languages because they are derived from Latin, the language that was spoken in Rome. A Latin saying about food was also preserved in the Romance languages. *De gustibus non est disputandum* means "there's no arguing about tastes." In French, this became *chacun à son goût,* "everyone to his own taste," and in Italian, *tutti i gusti son gusti,* "all tastes are tastes." English is a blend, about 60 percent Latin and 40 percent German. The following chart shows what happened when Latin broke down into the Romance languages, and also the influence of German on English.

THE BREAKDOWN OF LATIN AND THE CREATION OF ENGLISH					
ENGLISH	LATIN	ITALIAN	FRENCH	SPANISH	GERMAN
cook (noun)	coquus (cocus)	cuoco	cuisinier	cocinero	koch
kitchen	culina	cucina	cuisine	cocina	küche
bread	panis	pane	pain	pan	brot
wine	vinum	vino	vin	vino	vein
egg	ovum	uovo	oeuf	huevo	ei
poultry/hen	pullus	pollo	poulet	pollo	henne
milk	lac	latte	lait	leche	milch
cow	va	vacca	vache	vaca	kuh
honey	mel	miel	miele	miel	honig

Note: Even though the word for chicken is spelled the same in Italian and in Spanish, it is pronounced differently. In Italian, it is "PO-low." In Spanish, it is "POI-yo."

While the old Roman Empire in Europe fragmented even further, a vital new religion was gaining strength and unifying territory in the eastern Mediterranean.

THE MUSLIM EMPIRE

Muslims believe that in the beginning of the 7th century, the angel Gabriel came and spoke to Muhammad, a 40-year-old Arab from a powerful family from Mecca, in present-day Saudi Arabia, and revealed the teachings of God, known as Allah. These are written in the holy book, the Qur'an (also sometimes spelled *Koran*). Muslims accepted Jews and Christians because they have holy books, too. Jews have the Torah; Christians have the New Testament. Muslims don't believe in forced conversion; people convert because they believe in Allah. There are five pillars or core beliefs to Islam. Muslims must (1) testify that there is no god but Allah; (2) face Mecca and pray five times a day; (3) give one-tenth of their income to charity; (4) make a pilgrimage to Mecca once in their lifetime; and (5) fast during Ramadan, the holy month.

$\mathscr{H}$OLIDAY $\mathscr{H}$ISTORY
⇒ RAMADAN ⇐

Ramadan is the holiest month in the Muslim calendar. It was during Ramadan that the angel Gabriel appeared to Muhammad and revealed the Qur'an. Ramadan is observed with a monthlong fast that shifts every year because the Muslim calendar has 13 months of 28 days each, based on the cycles of the moon. So, unlike the Christian Lent, which always occurs at the end of winter, when food is scarce, Ramadan can occur during harvest or planting time. The point of Ramadan is to remind Muslims that there is more to life than earthly things, and that fasting is not enough. If a Muslim does not "abandon falsehood in words and deeds, Allah has no need for his abandoning of his food and drink."[11]

Every day during Ramadan, nothing can be eaten from sunup to sundown. Muslims must also abstain from sex and tobacco during this time. Breakfast has to be finished before dawn. After sundown, the daylong fast is broken, traditionally by eating dates and water. Dinner follows. Because the world of Islam is large and spread out through many countries and continents, the foods that break the fast vary from region to region. They often begin with a rich meat soup and end with sweet desserts like baklava or halva.

The Muslims stepped into the vacuum created by the fall of the Roman Empire and controlled much of the same territory across three continents. In Europe, they dominated Spain. Northern Africa, including the Sahara Desert, and the east coast of Africa, along the Indian Ocean, were in their control; in Asia, they extended east into what had been the Persian empire, the modern countries of Iraq and Iran, and India. Their capital city, Baghdad, in present-day Iraq, became the new Rome, a center of trade with a population of almost one million. Muslim ships sailed across the Mediterranean and Arabian seas and the Indian Ocean; camel caravans traveled the Silk Road into China and across the deserts of Africa.

The Muslim religion conquered many regions to create the Muslim empire and a rich blend of cuisines and cultures. They extended as far north as Tours, France, where their advance was halted in 732 by Charles Martel (Charles the Hammer). Making a pilgrimage forced Muslims to travel. Muslim merchants trusted other Muslims: they believed in the same God, spoke the same language, had the same beliefs, used the same money. They even trusted each other across long distances, giving written notes of payment—a *saqq,* which came to be pronounced "check." The Muslims also had something very powerful that they had gotten from the Hindus in India: numbers. What the world knows as Arabic numerals—1, 2, 3, 4—were invented by Hindus. So was the zero. These numbers aided business because they made it possible to add, subtract, multiply, and divide in ways that were impossible with Roman numerals, where I = 1, V = 5, X = 10, and C = 100. It would be very difficult to multiply XVIII by CC. But multiplying 18 by 200 is easy. To India, Muslims brought their religion and foods: melons, pomegranates, grapes and raisins, peaches, almonds, pistachios, cherries, pears, and apricots.[12]

The Muslims also had a vast literature of poetry, stories, and tales like the stories of Aladdin and the magic lamp, Ali Baba and the forty thieves, and *The Thousand and One Nights.* Dreams of flying carpets must have seemed like supersonic travel to people who plodded across the desert on camels for months. Another dream involved turning ordinary substances into gold, or finding a way to turn gold into food. This was the pseudoscience of alchemy. People in the Middle Ages believed that gold could cure dangerous diseases and confer immortality. The alchemy craze spread into Europe. If gold couldn't be turned into real food, then maybe the same effect could be achieved by making real food look like gold. This was done with spices like turmeric and saffron, which was grown in England, Spain, and Italy after a British pilgrim smuggled a bulb out of Asia Minor.[13]

The Muslim Meal

Caliphs and sultans had cooking staffs that might be free or slave labor, under the direction of a master chef whose first priority was to make sure that nobody poisoned the food and killed the ruler. The Mediterranean meal begins with *mazza* (sometimes spelled *mezze* or *meze*), which is often translated as "appetizer." As Mediterranean food authority Clifford Wright explains in his masterwork, *A Mediterranean Feast,* the concept of an appetizer—something to remind your stomach to get excited about eating—is ridiculous to Arabs. You're either hungry or you aren't, and if you are, your stomach doesn't need a warm-up. The only thing *mazza* has in common with appetizers is the small size of the portions. Wright says that since these tidbits can be an entire meal, *mazza* is closer to smorgasbord.[14] (For in-depth Mediterranean food history and unfailingly excellent recipes, see Wright's Web site, www.cliffordawright.com. It is a feast, one of the best on the Web.)

The earliest Muslim recipes date from Baghdad in 1226. They were recorded by al-Baghdadi, who "loved eating above all pleasures," as cookbook author Claudia Roden tells us.[15] Many of al-Baghdadi's recipes are for glorious *tagines*—stews of meat and fruit simmered for hours over a low flame until the meat is falling-apart-melt-in-your-mouth tender. This complies with the Arab dietary law about not eating blood. An example is *mishmishiya,* made with lamb and dried apricots. It gets its name from the Arab word for apricot, *mishmish.* Cumin, coriander, cinnamon, ginger, and black pepper provide the spice; saffron, the color; ground almonds, the thickening.[16] Stews are perfumed with waters distilled from rose petals or orange blossoms. Another recipe is for almond-stuffed meatballs shaped into logs, browned in the fat of the fat-tailed sheep, and simmered in a sauce of almonds, pistachios, and the usual spices—cumin, coriander, cinnamon, and black pepper—and garnished with "sugar candy dates."[17] As in many early cookbooks, al-Baghdadi provides ingredients and instructions but no amounts. Roden remedies this by including al-Baghdadi's recipes alongside her modern versions—with amounts—in *A Cookbook of Middle Eastern Food.*

Milk, usually from sheep or goats, was made into yogurt or preserved in salty cheeses like feta or kasseri. Vegetables and pulses like eggplant and chickpeas were and still are puréed and mixed with garlic, lemon juice, salt, and sesame paste—tahini—to make baba ganoush and hummus. Spinach was eaten often. Starches included bread cooked by slapping it onto the side of an oven called a *tannur* (like the Indian *tandoor*); rice, an import from the East, mixed with dried fruit and nuts to make pilaf; and couscous—steamed semolina—which is the national dish of Morocco, Tunisia, and Algeria, in northern Africa.[18] Grape leaves and eggplant were stuffed with mixtures ranging from the less expensive all-rice to the extremely expensive all-meat. Olive oil can be a garnish or an ingredient. In one famous dish, *imam bayaldi,* olive oil is used in alarming quantities.

ℱOOD ℱABLE

⪼ *IMAM BAYALDI*—"THE HOLY MAN FAINTED" ⪻

The name of the Turkish dish *imam bayaldi* means "the imam (holy man) fainted." According to legend, the imam either swooned in ecstasy when he tasted such a heavenly dish or passed out when he got the bill for the olive oil in it. In any case, Claudia Roden's modern version calls for one-half cup of olive oil for 6 long medium-sized eggplants (not jumbo American ones), with additional olive oil in the stuffing.[19] Clifford Wright's recipe uses ten table-spoons of extra-virgin olive oil for one and a half pounds of eggplant.[20]

The finale to a Muslim meal was a spectacular dessert made with sugar, which the Arabs had learned how to extract from sugarcane through trade with India. Arab conquerors who controlled Sicily from 827 to 1091 introduced sugarcane cultivation there in the 10th century.[21] Much of the preparation of sweets was done in convents, perhaps a refuge for Muslim women used to living in the protection of the harem, who converted to Christianity and joined a convent to maintain their protected status. These are the legendary desserts like baklava (flaky phyllo—also spelled *filo*—pastry layered with butter and ground pistachios and drizzled with sugar syrup scented with orange-flower water) and dates stuffed with sugar and ground almonds and dipped in a rosewater-scented sugar syrup.[22] (Phyllo pastries can also be made savory, like Greece's spinach-and-cheese turnover, *spanakopita.*)

The Muslim Diet

Many Muslim dietary restrictions correspond to the dietary laws of the Jews. For example, Muslims, too, were forbidden to eat pork, blood, and any animal that was dead but not killed specifically for food. Animals that were killed for food had to be killed in a ritualistic way. The butcher had to say, "In the name of God, God is most great," and then cut the animal's throat while it was conscious. This is called *halal* meat, and means to Muslims what meat killed by a kosher butcher means to Jews. Any animal killed in the name of another god is prohibited.[23] In the Middle Ages, Muslims preferred mutton and camel hump.

"Drinking fermented beverages was also prohibited in order to keep Muslims from praying while intoxicated."[24] Muhammad did not like the violence that followed drinking. Wine could be a reward in paradise, where it wouldn't be abused, but it is forbidden on earth. However, a new food-stuff that was becoming popular in the Muslim empire was welcomed by the religion: coffee.

Coffee: Red Berries and Dancing Goats

Food Fable

❯❯ WHERE COFFEE COMES FROM ❮❮

The goats were behaving strangely. Instead of calmly foraging for food, they were running around, leaping up in the air, butting heads. The shepherd boy in 8th-century Ethiopia, on the east coast of Africa, was worried. What could have caused this? When it continued the next day, he watched them closely and saw that they had found something new to eat: the small red berries and glossy green leaves of a strange tree. After they ate the berries, they started dancing and doing what for goats passes for singing—bleating. When the goats showed no other effects from eating this strange new food (like falling over dead, which the boy was afraid of), he tried some, too. He liked the way they made him feel.[25]

The truth: coffee does grow on a tree with glossy green leaves and small red berries. As for the dancing goats, that's anybody's guess. At first people got their coffee just the way the goats and the goatherd did: by chewing the leaves and berries. Then the leaves and berries were steeped in water, like tea. The red coffee berries—called "cherries"—were also ground into a paste and mixed with animal fat. It was not until the 16th century that the berries were roasted, ground into a powder, and mixed with water to produce the beverage we know as coffee. It was accepted by Muslims because it kept them alert through their prayers.[26]

THE BYZANTINE EMPIRE AND RUSSIA

Between Christendom and the Muslim world was the Byzantine Empire. The city of Byzantium was founded in the middle of the 7th century B.C. on the western side of the Bosporus Strait, strategically located at the gateway to the riches of the Black Sea and the lands just to its north. Byzantium had a good natural harbor and an abundance of fish. After the fall of the Western Roman Empire, Byzantium, renamed Constantinople, became the capital and preserved much of the learning, culture, and law of Rome. It also became the center of trade. However, it was more of a Greek than a Latin city. Entertainment in the 60,000-seat Hippodrome (10,000 seats more than the Colosseum in Rome) included horse races but, in this Christian city, no persecution of Christians.

The Byzantine Empire, like the Western Roman Empire, used slave labor. Their slaves came from what is now Eastern Europe: Bulgaria, Russia, Poland, Czechoslovakia, and Ukraine. The people from these places were called Slavs, which is where the word *slave* originated. In the 10th century, an Eastern Orthodox clergyman went on a mission to bring Christianity and literacy to Russia. The Russian or Cyrillic alphabet still bears the name of this traveling holy man, St. Cyril.

How Food Helped Russia Choose Its Religion

In 988, Prince Vladimir of Kiev felt he had to decide on a religion for himself and for his people. He knew his people, their habits, and their likes and dislikes (and his own), so he used food to help him decide. Russians liked pork, so that ruled out Judaism and Islam. Islam had a second strike against it because alcohol was forbidden, which was completely unacceptable to Russians: "We Russians like to drink, and there is no way we can live without it."[27] Christians in Rome fasted too much. False rumors reached Vladimir that Hindus ate humans. So Prince Vladimir chose the Eastern Christianity of Byzantium for his country. It had fast days, too, but peasants could still eat caviar, which was fish, during Lent. In 989, he ordered everyone in the city of Kiev down to the river to be baptized.[28]

Some foods that today are considered traditionally Russian didn't appear in Russia until the end of the Middle Ages or later. The term for sausage, *kolbasy,* appeared in written Russian for the first time in 1292. Vodka (*wódka*) came from Poland after 1500.[29] Sour cream and borscht also didn't appear until contact with the West after 1500. The potato reached Russia around 1700.

CHRISTENDOM: THE LATE MIDDLE AGES IN EUROPE

Wine—the Blood of Christ

The later Middle Ages saw many changes in European culture. It was the beginning of cities and trade routes, of what would soon become modern English and the Romance languages. It was also the beginning of the commercial wine industry. By the 10th century, the sparkling wines of the Champagne region of France had distinguished themselves by vineyard, and were associated with royalty because they were traditionally served at coronations. By the 13th and 14th centuries, there were vineyards in the German Rhineland and in the Tokay region of Hungary.[30] In 1398, a white wine (not the red of today) from a region in Tuscany in northern Italy appeared for the first time—Chianti.[31]

In 1395, Philip the Bold, the duke of Burgundy, ordered that only pinot noir grapes were to be grown in Burgundy. Some vintners had begun cultivating gamay vines, which produced grapes that were hardier and ripened earlier. Philip declared that wine from gamay grapes was foul, bitter, and an offense to the reputation of Burgundy. He ordered the vines torn out. The gamay grape found a home elsewhere and eventually became the basis for Beaujolais wines, but Burgundy is still made from pinot noir grapes.[32]

Other wine-growing regions became known by name to wine connoisseurs. The Church inadvertently helped in this when a political struggle in the 14th century resulted in two popes, one in Rome and one in Avignon in southern France. The wine the French pope drank came from a vineyard that was called Châteauneuf-du-Pape, "the pope's new castle." Later, the Crusades helped further the wine industry because nobles who left to fight often donated vineyards to the Church so that the monks would pray for their success. If they died, their families donated vineyards so that the monks would pray for their souls. By the end of the Middle Ages, one order of monks, the Cistercians, a division of the Benedictines, owned the largest vineyards in Europe. They had been helped in France by King Louis VII, who exempted their wines from taxes on shipping and sales.[33] Wine was also used as currency, and soldiers' rations always included wine. In England, it was cheaper than ale by as much as 12 to 24 times, and it was healthier—wine kills typhoid bacteria in contaminated water.[34]

The wine merchants' guilds had a great deal of political power, because they were often the city government, and taxes on wine paid for many of the expenses of running medieval cities. In London, the Vintners'

Company controlled the wholesale and retail wine trade, and received a charter from the king in 1437. Medieval cities passed laws to control the importation and sale of wine, to standardize weights and measures, and to punish tavern owners who tried to cut corners by adulterating wine or passing cheap or sour wines off as more expensive ones. Punishment included fines, being forced to drink your own rancid wine, and having the barrels of bad wine smashed and dumped in the streets.[35]

Cheese

Many cheeses still important today—Emmenthal, Gruyère, Parmesan—were first produced in the 12th century. These are formed into huge round wheels, each made from as much as 1,000 liters of milk, so the farmers of an entire region contributed. The Latin word for cheese, *caseus,* is the origin of the English word for cheese. The French and Italian words for cheese—*fromage* and *formaggio,* respectively— date back to the Romans, who shaped cheese by putting it into baskets or forms, called *forma.* Some cheeses, like Port-Salut, are named after the monasteries that produced them. "The monks of the Benedictine and Cistercian monasteries, thanks to whom the population did not starve to death entirely during the Dark Ages, were the pioneers of the new cheese-making industry of medieval times."[36]

The Medieval Warm Period and the New Agriculture

Europeans and Russians had a common enemy. Down from Scandinavia swooped the Northmen or Norsemen—the Vikings. Extremely skilled sailors, they built ships with drafts so shallow, they could come within a few feet of shore. They raided towns and monasteries to steal food and left terror everywhere they went. The raids finally stopped because the Vikings were able to grow their own food when the climate changed as Europe entered a time known as the Medieval Warm Period.

The years 950 to 1300 were a period of global warming. Icebergs began to retreat. Northern seas that were formerly frozen became navigable; the growing season was longer, so more food could be produced. The Vikings stopped raiding and started exploring. They settled Iceland, then Greenland, which was colder than Iceland. (The name was a public relations ploy—they thought it would attract settlers.) From Greenland, they went southwest into Newfoundland, in modern Canada. They called it Vinland—Vineland—after the grapes (maybe cranberries?) they found growing wild there.[37] A Viking settlement has been excavated at the mouth of the St. Lawrence River.

Around the year 1000, in addition to the longer growing season, advances were made in agriculture that increased food production. Fields were split into thirds and farmed two-thirds at a time instead of one-half. Crop rotation allowed one-third of the field to lie fallow and regain nutrients while the other two-thirds produced food. New technology in the form of a harness that allowed horses to pull plows more efficiently also aided in increasing crops. However, some of the crops that grew were not necessarily healthier.

"Crazy Bread"

One of the foods that everyone ate during the Middle Ages was bread—when they could get it. Famine occurred twice a year: at the end of winter, when the Church made a virtue out of the shortage of food during Lent; and in the middle of the summer, when the fields were full of crops not yet ready to harvest. Desperate people ate what they could, even if it made them sick. Sometimes they got poisoned by ergot, a fungus that grows on grains, especially rye. Ergot poisoning could cause hallucinations, twitching, and dry gangrene—extremities went numb, turned black, and then fell off, but there was no visible wound. The fungus wasn't destroyed by harvesting, drying, milling, or baking. The loaves that contained the fungus and caused these horrors were called "crazy bread." Over the 500 years from the 11th to the 16th century, there were many episodes of ergot poisoning, which people thought of as epidemics of disease. But in controlled doses, ergot was used as a medicine in the Middle Ages, especially to speed up childbirth.[38]

So, although life in the Middle Ages in Europe improved somewhat because of the Medieval Warm Period, it still left much to be desired. Serfs were still tied to the land, eating bad food, and leading a monotonous existence—all because the Church said it was what God intended them to do with their lives. But soon, a new pope would claim that God had a different plan for them, something much more exciting.

CULTURE CLASH: THE CRUSADES

Russia's conversion to the Eastern Orthodox religion caused friction between the pope in Rome and the patriarch, the leading bishop of the Christians in the East. After years of sparring through letters and threatening each other, both delivered knockout punches in 1054: they excommunicated each other and split into two separate religions. Under the new Eastern Orthodox Church, ministers could marry, people could get divorced, and the government controlled the Church, something Rome would not stand for.

In 1093, Pope Urban II saw an opportunity to regain control over the eastern half of the Church. Alexius, the Byzantine emperor, appealed to Europe for help because he was afraid the Muslims were going to invade Constantinople. The pope decided to kill two birds with one stone: he would send an army of Christians to rescue Constantinople, which would embarrass the patriarch. Then the army would continue on to the Holy Land and reclaim it from the Muslims, revealing the superiority of the Roman Church. As an incentive, the pope guaranteed that all earthly sins would be forgiven for anyone who went on a Crusade—a ticket to heaven. Some of the Christians had questions: Didn't Christ and the Ten Commandments say "Thou shalt not kill"? Yes, the pope explained, but Christ was misquoted. What he meant was "Thou shalt not kill *Christians*." It was the duty of Christians to kill infidels—nonbelievers of other religions.

Between 1096 and 1204, there were four major Crusades to the Holy Land. A Children's Crusade followed in 1212. The Church discouraged those who were not professional fighters from going but was powerless to stop them. Many people assumed that God would provide for them, so they just picked up and left without even taking food. This caused famines along the route when they marched, and tremendous inflation in the cost of food.[39] Along the way they scavenged for food, stole, and even got into riots with other Christians. Other Crusaders went to North Africa, and the Spanish Inquisition began its own crusade against Muslims in Spain.

The Crusades created suspicion and hatred among Muslims, Christians, and Jews in the Muslim world. England's King Richard the Lionhearted ordered the deaths of 3,000 Muslim men, women, and children who surrendered in the city of Acre. Constantinople didn't fall to Muslims then, but did in 1453, when its name was changed to what it is now, Istanbul.

The Crusades caused profound changes in the world and helped to bring about the end of the Middle Ages. After the initial victory in the First Crusade, all the other Crusades were failures—the Christians lost. Jerusalem stayed in Muslim hands after it was recaptured by the Muslim leader Saladin in 1187. The Crusades also weakened the system of feudalism, as the ruling class—lords and knights—spent their fortunes on Crusades, and many were killed. Those who did return found that many of the serfs, left alone on the manors, had taken off to find a better life. They had gone to the new cities that arose along the routes to the Holy Land to provide food and supplies for the Crusaders.

Cities and Guilds: The Butcher, the Baker, and the Wafer Maker

When a serf moved to the cities where there were thousands of people, he needed something he had not needed on the manor: a last name. Everyone had a first name, called a Christian name, which they received when they were baptized, but they had no last names. Many took the name of their profession: Cook, Miller, Smith (for blacksmiths, goldsmiths, silversmiths, tinsmiths), Wright (as in cartwright or wheelwright, the people who made carts or wheels), Cooper (the people who made barrels), or Baker.

One of the ways people could have a better life in the cities was by getting a profession, like the food professions. The way to get into any trade or craft was to join a guild, which was like a union. The purpose of the guilds was twofold: first, to create a monopoly on a certain product, and second, to control the number of people in the profession so that there would not be a glut, which would cause the price people could charge for their goods or services to drop.

There were three stages in guild membership: apprentice, journeyman, and master. Children were sent into apprenticeship as soon as they were able to function by themselves, usually around six or seven years old. They performed menial tasks like sweeping up and running errands. At this stage, they learned by observing. When they got older, they began to learn by doing—hands-on.[40] The apprenticeship lasted until the late teen years, when the journeyman stage began. In this phase, the craftsperson was given increasingly complex projects and responsibility, which could include supervising apprentices. The final stage was becoming a master. To do this, the journeyman had to complete a project entirely on his own, to the satisfaction of the master and the requirements of the guild. Only then could he call himself a master craftsman and set up his own shop. For example, the requirements of a journeyman wafer maker were to produce a minimum of 800 wafers, in three different sizes, per day.[41] Not everyone attained master status; many remained journeymen all their lives, just as today not everyone becomes an executive chef.

One way guilds promoted themselves was by advertising. They donated money for stained-glass windows in the new churches that were being built. Rising sometimes more than one hundred feet, these cathedrals dwarfed every other building in the area and could be seen for miles: Notre Dame and Chartres in France; Canterbury, Westminster, and Durham in England; Dresden in Germany. The cathedrals used new architecture that had narrow stone supports inside leading up to the characteristic pointed Gothic arch. The large spaces between the arches were adorned with something new: glorious stained-glass windows that flooded the cathedral with multicolored, heavenly light. However, the glass could be made only in small pieces, not large sheets, so all the windows were dazzling mosaics. In these windows, in color, we can still see people in the food professions—butchers, bakers, fishmongers, grocers, and tavern keepers—engaging in the daily activities of their professions.[42] Tavern owners also advertised by having criers walk the streets with a bowl of the wine special for the day, beating on it and calling out to entice people to have a taste.[43]

The cathedrals were centers of life for the community. The faithful attended Mass every Sunday (preferably every day); the open space in front of the church was the marketplace; the bells tolled time. One of the bells was at night, to remind people that it was time to attend to the fires in their fireplaces and go to bed. Starting a new fire was time-consuming and difficult, so many people chose to keep the fire going at night. The danger was that the house would burn down, so they covered the fire. "Cover the fire" in French was *couvre-feu,* which became *curfew* in English.

As the cities grew, there was increasing specialization in the professions. They subdivided into narrower and narrower groups. For example, the definition of baker was very strict—the person who kneaded the dough and shaped it into a loaf. The person who tended the fire to make sure the bread cooked at just the right temperature was a different profession. When work was scarce, the two clashed over where one job ended and the other began. Pastry makers made pies, but if the pie had poultry inside, the poulterers wanted control of it. In Paris, bakers controlled pâtés until the pastry guild was formed in 1440, and then pâtissiers had the right to make both sweet and savory tarts. These conflicts sometimes ended in lawsuits.

The Magna Carta and the First Food Laws

1215 was an important year in Christianity and in the history of England. In the world of Christianity in 1215, Pope Innocent III declared that the communion wafer was the literal, not symbolic, body of Christ. In England, King Richard the Lionhearted was on a Crusade and left his brother King John in charge. John was a weak king who spent too much money on wars that he didn't win. This angered the nobles, who forced him to sign a document called the Magna Carta—"great charter"—which guaranteed some of the basic rights of Englishmen, which are still in effect in the United States today: the right to a trial by jury and the right not to be taxed without representation.

Two of the first food laws were also passed around this time. In 1210, King John fixed the price of bread; in 1266, the Assize of Bread regulated the quality. The function of these laws was to prevent bakers from overcharging and from stretching the loaf with things not fit for human consumption, like dirt and stones, and to punish bakers who did.[44]

The King's Court: Table Manners

The rise of the king's court gave rise to manners. People became self-conscious because for the first time there was a right way and a wrong way to behave in social situations, especially at the table. Many words having to do with the new manners came from the king's court (that word originally referred to a court-yard, a farmyard, or any enclosed space): *courtly,* which meant having upper-class manners; *courtesy,* the acts of politeness toward others that were shown by a *courtier,* someone at court; a woman showed her respect when she made a *curtsy;* a young man and woman were on their best behavior when they were *courting* each other; *courteous,* having respectful, pleasant manners fit for the king's court. Just what had people been doing that needed changing? The box to the left shows some of the new rules for upper-class adults at the medieval table.

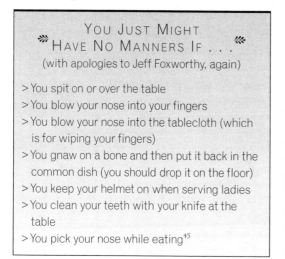

YOU JUST MIGHT
⇛ HAVE NO MANNERS IF . . . ⇚
(with apologies to Jeff Foxworthy, again)

> You spit on or over the table
> You blow your nose into your fingers
> You blow your nose into the tablecloth (which is for wiping your fingers)
> You gnaw on a bone and then put it back in the common dish (you should drop it on the floor)
> You keep your helmet on when serving ladies
> You clean your teeth with your knife at the table
> You pick your nose while eating[45]

Alcoholic Beverages: Bees and Beer

Bees were highly prized for honey; for beeswax, which made sweet-smelling, dripless candles; and for propolis, the bee glue that kept the honeycomb together and which was used as an ointment, like a medieval antibiotic. (The Egyptians had used honey, which completely blocks out air, as an antibiotic, too.) It was not just honey for sweetening and medicine that made bees so valuable; it was also turned into that ancient drink, mead. But bees and honey were difficult to come by, so in medieval England if you saw a bee fly by, you said a quick prayer to get it to stay on your land:

> *Sit down, sit down, bee!*
> *St. Mary commanded thee!*
> *Thou shalt not have leave,*
> *Thou shalt not fly to the wood.*
> *Thou shalt not escape me.*
> *Nor go away from me.*
> *Sit very still,*
> *Wait God's will!*[46]

Calling on St. Mary and God in this prayer is an example of how the Church adopted native pagan rituals and charms. Rather than constantly fighting (and losing against) local customs, the Church allowed the peasants to keep them, but instructed them to substitute "Christ" or "God" for "father heaven" and "Mary" for "mother earth."[47]

By the end of the Middle Ages, hops were used to flavor and preserve beer. Before hops, an herbal mix called gruit was used. This was three herbs: yarrow, wild rosemary, and sweet gale, also called myrica gale. They were considered aphrodisiacs and narcotics.

The Little Ice Age

The Medieval Warm Period in Europe was followed by the Little Ice Age, a period of cooling from about 1300 until about 100 years ago. The temperature change wasn't dramatic, perhaps one to one and a half degrees Centigrade cooler than today. However, the impact on agriculture and shipping ranged from serious to disastrous. The growing season became shorter, food grew scarcer. Wheat did not grow and ripen normally, could not be dried, and rotted. Grapes covered with mildew made sour wine or none. In England, the temperature drop was enough that grapes could no longer be grown at all. It destroyed a commercial wine industry that was so good, France was trying to pass laws to keep British wines out. Fewer ships sailed the seas because of dangerous ice floes, which also kept them from sailing close

RECIPE

𝒲ASSAIL

From the Anglo-Saxon *wes hal*, or "be in good health."

4 large McIntosh apples
¼ cup plus 2 tablespoons dark brown sugar
¼ cup apple juice or cider
3 twelve-ounce bottles of ale
1 cup sherry
1 cinnamon stick
½ teaspoon ground ginger
½ teaspoon freshly grated nutmeg
zest of 1 lemon

1. Preheat oven to 350°F.
2. Slit the skins of the apples horizontally about halfway down. Place in a greased baking dish and sprinkle with ¼ cup of the brown sugar and the apple juice. Bake, basting frequently for about 40 minutes, until apples are soft; remove from oven.
3. Pour the ale and sherry into a saucepan; add the 2 tablespoons brown sugar, cinnamon, ginger, nutmeg, and lemon zest; simmer for 5 minutes. Add the baked apples and their juice, stir thoroughly, and serve hot.[48]

Excerpted from the book *The Apple Cookbook* by Olwen Woodier. Copyright © 2001, used with permission from Storey Publishing, LLC.

to shore. Greenland, Denmark's colony for hundreds of years, longer than the colony of any European country, was isolated by the climate change. Unsupplied and unequipped, the people starved and died and the colony disappeared.[49]

Hungry people left the land and wandered homeless into the cities, begging for food or stealing it. Thousands died and were left to rot, buried in mass graves, or eaten. The ones who were left were too weak to work, suffering from deficiency diseases like anemia, their bodies bloated from lack of protein. Animals suffered from malnutrition, too. Their weakened state made them prone to intestinal parasites, diarrhea, and death. Glaciers crept down into valleys, obliterating farms. In some places the land disappeared—the topsoil literally washed away, down to rock. But farther south, where the sun still smiled, trade flourished and people became phenomenally wealthy—and needed someone to cook for them.

Taillevent's *Le Viandier:* "The Beginning of Cooking as We Know It"[50]

Taillevent (real name Guillaume Tirel, ca. 1312–1395) wrote the first cookbook (with some sections bearing a close resemblance to a book written before he was born). He is an inspiration to anyone in the cooking profession. He began at the bottom of the kitchen ladder as a spit roaster, endlessly turning the meats on the spit in front of an open fire. But he worked his way up quickly and was given a house, a title, travel allowances, and a coat of arms—three little cooking pots. He ended his life as master cook to King Charles VI of France. Cookbooks like his reveal the influence of the Middle East on the cooking of the later Middle Ages in Europe, especially the use of spices: cinnamon, ginger, cumin, coriander, cardamom. In the following recipe for wassail, substitute honey for the dark brown sugar, and it is straight from the Middle Ages. In the United States, people go Christmas caroling from house to house and sing a song that includes the lyrics "Now we go a-wassailing." In England, the songs were sung in the apple orchard, to the trees, or the following year the harvest would be bad.[51]

Sugar: "White Salt"

One food the Arabs had that the Europeans had never seen before and wanted very much was "white salt." Its grains were approximately the same size as those of salt, but it was pure white, unlike salt, which varied from grayish to greenish depending on which minerals were present. And it was sweet. The Arabs had learned how to take the sugarcane stalk, remove the juice, and dry it, leaving only the sweet crystals. This process had existed in India as early as 800 B.C., but it was time-consuming and labor-intensive.[52] Exotic, expensive, and tasty, sugar was highly prized by the upper classes in Europe as a medicine. Apothecaries shaved flakes off cones of sugar and sold them by the gram like other drugs. Medieval physicians considered sugar the perfect medicine for treating toothaches.

The Medieval Meal

The medieval meal began and ended with a prayer and washing of the hands. The best linen was used at the start, when hands were relatively

A DAY IN THE LIFE OF THE MIDDLE AGES		
	NOBLES: 10% OF THE POPULATION	SERFS: 90% OF THE POPULATION
You live:	In the manor house, the largest and tallest structure on the estate after the church.	In a small, one-room, leaky, thatched-roof hut with your family, your animals, their vermin, and your vermin.
You wear:	Fur, velvet; cape, long tunic, buttons.	Homespun flax; short tunic and leg-gings (or the clothes police come).
You eat:	Meat; fine-grained white bread for your delicate health; spices and foods from the Middle East: almonds, dates, sugar; blancmange; wine, beer, mead, cider.	Oat gruel; coarse, dark bread that might poison you with ergot; fruits, vegetables, pulses, cheese; beer, cider.
You do:	Oversee the farming, collect taxes, administer the law. Anything requiring literacy.	Farm. Farm. Farm. Sometimes fight if your earthly and heavenly lord needs you to. You are illiterate.

clean; ordinary napkins were saved for the end, when diners' hands were dirty. The washing bowls were made of silver, or they were gilded—covered with gold. If you were really important, your family crest might be engraved in the bottom of the basin.

Where you sat at the table also indicated how important you were. If you sat at the head of the table or were the guest of honor, you sat in a chair by yourself and you were "above the salt." You got better bread (made of light wheat flour), more of it, and it was served to you. The farther down the social scale you were, the darker the bread. You also got less of it and had to reach across the table to serve yourself. If you found yourself eating one small roll of stale, dark rye bread, sitting on a bench, far away from the salt, you were in social Siberia and no serving person would waste his time on you.[53]

There was no separate dining room, just a room where boards were set up on trestles and draped with cloths for as long as the dinner lasted, then taken down. The permanent piece of furniture in the room was the buffet, where the host displayed his wealth, maybe expensive gold and silver serving pieces and bowls. The kitchen was separate from the main house because of the danger of fire, so the food was probably not warm when it arrived at the table accompanied by an armed guard, even though it was covered. It was delayed again while it was checked for poison in the most elaborate and unsanitary way possible.

At the table, there were serving platters but no plates. Whole-wheat bread, several days old and cut into rectangles, was used as plates called trenchers. Liquids were put into a small bowl that two diners shared. No forks—you ate with your hands, and when you reached into the communal dish for one of the various kinds of meat, you were careful in case somebody else was reaching for something by stabbing it with his knife. (This later came to be known as *service en confusion*.)[54] Wine was served diluted with water (every household has a budget). One of the most expensive and elaborate pieces on the table was the *nef*, the salt cellar in the shape of a ship, perhaps silver or gilt.

Food was fresh in season. Otherwise, meat was preserved by salting or smoking and drying, vegetables were pickled in brine or stored in a root cellar, herbs and fruits were dried. Any-

---

Food Fable
❊ THE POISON TASTER ❊

"Unicorn [a mythical beast] horn, which was thought to bleed in the presence of impurity, was much favored. Agate was in more frequent use, being easier to obtain, as were various objects alleged to be toadstone—that (nonexistent) precious jewel believed to be hidden in the head of the toad. Salt was tested with serpent's tongue, known more prosaically now to be the tooth of a shark."[55]

While everybody was busy looking for exotic poisons, they were missing the bacterial cross-contamination that was right in front of them, especially in the handling of poultry and eggs or in the fingers or spoons dipped repeatedly into pots, and the danger posed by pots made of lead or tinned copper with the tin worn off.

---

body could present a feast in the summer, but to have a feast in the winter indicated great wealth. So did imported foods, at any time of the year.

The Color of Food

Almonds imported from the Middle East were extremely popular in Europe. They spread across Europe in one dish with different names and different forms. In Italy it was called *biancomangiare;* in France, *blancmange;* in Spain, *manjar blanco;* in England, *blanchet manchet.* All meant the same thing: white food. It was based on almond milk and was thought to be the perfect food: it balanced the four humors because it included something from each of them; it was smooth, so it was easy to swallow; it was easy to digest; and it was white and therefore very refined and suitable for the upper classes.

Almond milk—almonds soaked in water and pressed until the water looks like milk—was a useful food during Lent, when any animal products, including eggs and dairy, were forbidden. It could be made the thickness of cream or milk, depending on how much water was added. It could also be drained and pressed to look like cream cheese.

Presentation was extremely important in the Middle Ages, sometimes more important than taste, because the intent was to show off how wealthy you were. At a medieval banquet a feast for the stomach was not a guarantee, but you were certain to get a feast for the eyes. The most elaborate dishes at a medieval feast were peacock and swan, which arrived at the table cooked and dead looking better than they ever had in life. The birds were killed, skinned carefully to keep the feathers intact, then cooked and stuffed back into their skins. Their beaks and feet were gilded. Ideally, a beautiful young upper-class woman would serve the dish, completing the presentation.[56]

Pies were another elegant presentation, and also functional. The crust contained and preserved the filling. Sweet or savory pies could have their lids put back on and be stashed in a cold cellar until the next time they were served. Sometimes live birds were put into a baked pie crust, just like in the nursery rhyme: "Four-and-twenty blackbirds, baked in a pie . . ." When the pie was cut into at the table, the birds flew out for a presentation surprise.

For the upper classes, after the white food, the other courses could be as many colors as the rainbow of fruit and vegetable dyes could make them. Red grapes or cherries tinted garlic sauce pink; blackberries and mulberries made anything deep blue or purple; parsley turned it green. In Europe, as in the Middle East, one color was prized above all others: gold. Humans persisted in their search for two things: eternal life and gold. They thought it might take a while to discover the secret to eternal life, but alchemists were busy trying to find a shortcut that would turn various substances into gold. In the meantime, food could look gold. Spices from the Middle East like saffron and turmeric turned food a beautiful golden color, a practice that continues today in dishes like risotto, even though in the Middle Ages, "one pound of saffron cost as much as a horse" and a pound of nutmeg cost as much as seven oxen.[57] Food could also be covered in gold leaf. Most of the real gold came from Africa, carried in caravans by Muslim traders. Stories traveled on the trade routes, too. Some of the most outrageous came from a Venetian named Marco Polo.

Marco Polo: Fact or Fiction?

Marco Polo (1254–1324) was the son of a merchant from Venice, Italy, a wealthy, prominent city that controlled trade in the Mediterranean. When Polo was 17, his father and uncle took him on a trip to China, which the Europeans called Cathay. The trip was partly business and

𝓕OOD 𝓕ABLE

⫸ MARCO POLO AND PASTA ⫷

For hundreds of years, it was accepted "fact" that Marco Polo discovered noodles in China and brought them back to Europe. Now, in his masterwork, *A Mediterranean Feast,* food historian Clifford Wright states flatly that there is no truth to the story of Polo and pasta. As Wright explains, the origins of pasta are as tangled as spaghetti. He attempts to unravel the strands and comes up with the basic element of pasta: the hard semolina or durum wheat from which it is made.[58] This makes pasta different from bread, which is made from soft wheat. The Chinese did not have durum wheat. Wright places the origins of "true macaroni"— pasta made from durum wheat and dried, which gives it a long shelf life—"at the juncture of medieval Sicilian, Italian, and Arab cultures."[59]

partly political. Polo's father and uncle had been to Cathay before and returned with gifts from the khan to the pope. Now they were bringing gifts and greetings from Pope Gregory X to the great khan. They followed the Silk Road through Armenia, Persia (now Iran), Afghanistan, and eastward. In his writings, Polo described the desert through which they passed as "entirely mountains and sands and valleys. There is nothing at all to eat." He did, however, taste kumiss when they stopped among the Mongols. He compared it to white wine and declared it "very good to drink."[60] Three and a half years and 5600 miles after leaving Venice, the Polos arrived at the khan's summer palace, then went on to the winter palace in Beijing, the capital. They stayed in Cathay for 17 years; the khan appointed Polo to several administrative jobs, including tax collector. After Polo returned to Italy, he was captured when Venice and Genoa went to war in 1298. While in jail, he wrote his memoirs. The book was hugely popular throughout Europe, but some called it *Il Milione*—"the million," meaning a million lies—because it seemed so fantastic. The scale and the grandeur of what he was saying seemed inconceivable.

Polo was impressed with everything he supposedly saw in the khan's kingdom. The canals reminded him of Venice. The summer palace, its walls covered with gold and silver, was "the greatest palace that ever was." Ten thousand pure white horses provided milk for the khan's family. The Chinese bathed several times a week, unlike the Europeans. They also used charcoal for fires instead of wood, and paper for money instead of gold and silver. Polo talked about two-pound peaches and ten-pound pears, giant pearls and pink pearls. Everywhere he went there was salt: in salt beds and salt pans, salt water being boiled to evaporate the water and leave the salt. There was also silk: in clothes, on walls, on furniture, on five thousand elephants passing in review before the khan. There were lions and lynxes and leopards used to hunt bear and deer and wild oxen.

Scholars are still arguing about whether Marco Polo ever went to Cathay. Those who believe he did cite the evidence of silk and other objects in his possession. Those who don't point to the lack of evidence: his name isn't recorded in the annals of the empire, the official records of the Yuan Dynasty. And Polo's book doesn't mention things that were common in China at the time, like tea and foot binding.[61]

True or not, Marco Polo's stories set a fire burning in Europe to find a shortcut to the magic lands of Cathay and Cipango (Japan). The Crusades had gotten people used to traveling and to seeing and hearing about exotic spices and silks and beautiful clothes and carpets, and they wanted them. These things came from Asia. Soon, Europeans would succeed in getting there, and along the way accidentally find something they had not counted on—an entire new world.

Tea, Chocolate, and the
Printing Press:
Asia, the Americas, and the
First Cookbook, 1300–1500

ASIA

The Mongols: Living High on the Horse

In the 13th century, across the vast, dry, flat grasslands of Asia—the steppes—and into eastern Europe, galloped the Mongols, led by Genghis Khan. The Mongols' merciless tactics terrified their enemies. They would surround a city and demand its surrender. If the city didn't surrender, they killed everyone. If the city did surrender, they killed everyone. Soon, the Mongol empire stretched from China in the east to Poland in the west—the largest land-based empire the world has ever seen.

The Mongols were fueled by horsepower. They ate horsemeat; they drank mare's milk, which, unlike cow's milk, is high in vitamin C; they even made an alcoholic drink called kumiss from fermented mare's milk. When there was nothing else to drink or when they were riding and couldn't stop to rest, they drank their horse's blood. They made a slit in the horse's neck and knew just how much blood to suck without hurting the horse.

The Mongols sometimes rode for days, switching horses without ever getting off. They invented stirrups to make themselves bipedal while riding a horse, for the same survival reason early man became bipedal: it left their hands free to use weapons. They could stand up in the stirrups without falling off the horse and still be able to guide it with their knees and feet. They could also twist and shoot to the side or behind them. Standing, they were higher than the horse's head, so they could shoot arrows over it. Their ruthlessness and efficiency earned them the rule of China.

China: The *Tao* of Tea—Tang and Song Dynasties, 618–1279

In 618, a great new dynasty arose in China. The Tang (618–907) reconquered lands that had not been in the possession of China since the end of the Han Dynasty in A.D. 220 and redistributed them to the peasants. Much of the expansion of China occurred during the reign of China's only female emperor, Wu Zhao. She was the power behind the throne for 30 years, ruling through weak emperors before she finally proclaimed herself emperor in 690. During the Tang period, bananas, dates, citrus, and taro palm were grown in the south. So was litchi, of which the emperor's court was especially fond. Foods that traveled to China via Muslim traders on the Silk Road from Persia and Central Asia included sugarcane, spinach, lettuce, almonds, figs, and grapes in various forms—syrup, raisins, wine.[1] However, another beverage had their attention: "The age was marked by an obsessive concern with ale. Rarely in the history of the world has alcoholism been so idealized." The use of hallucinogenic drugs was also widespread. Both seemed to be part of a desire for escapist release in a time of many famines.[2] Costly wars and high taxes to pay for them further weakened the dynasty. One of the items taxed was salt, which provided half of the state's income.[3] Salt smugglers took what they could. Finally, in 907, in a series of events reminiscent of the fall of Rome, rebels from border areas ransacked the capital, Chang'an, and killed the last emperor, a child. After several years of war, the Song Dynasty took power over a China that was smaller but more stable.

During these two dynasties, China's population grew and became increasingly urban and sophisticated. At least ten cities had as many people as Rome and Baghdad at their height: one million. There was also a million-man standing army for which the government bought massive amounts of food. The entire country contained 100 million people, the most in the world, and was the most advanced. It was the only place in the world that knew the secret of how to make silk. Some things in widespread use in China were the fine porcelain that the West still calls china, gunpowder, the printing press, and tea.

ℱᴏᴏᴅ ℱᴀʙʟᴇ
≫ WHERE THE TEA LEAF COMES FROM ≪

The Fable: In the 5th century A.D., Bodhidharma, the monk who brought Buddhism to China, was having trouble meditating—he kept falling asleep. He just couldn't keep his eyelids open, so he tore them off and threw them on the ground. They took root and grew into tea plants. Like all legends, this one has some truth in it: it is possible to see the shape of an eyelid in the oval of a tea leaf, and tea has caffeine, which will keep even sleepy monks awake.

The Fact: Tea is a member of the camellia family, a glossy-leaved bush that also produces large-bloomed flowers. Its scientific name is *Camellia sinensis* or *Camellia assamica*—camellia from China or Assam, a region in northeast India, although it probably originated in Southeast Asia in what is now Vietnam. Mention of tea first appeared in written Chinese around the 3rd century A.D., two centuries before Bodhidharma nodded off, but it was not recognized as a powerful medicine, along with ginseng and certain mushrooms, until the Tang Dynasty.[4] Tea was considered a cure for a wide range of ills, from epilepsy and fever to lung disease and dysentery. While Arabs and Europeans looked to gold to provide the secret of eternal life, the Chinese thought tea was the key.[5]

Tea began as an exotic drink, then got a popularity boost from *The Book of Tea,* written by Lu Yü in the 8th century. Just as Christianity spread on the roads in the Roman Empire, tea spread throughout China on the Silk Road, often with Buddhism. Buddhist rituals were performed in Chang'an, the end of the Silk Road, which was an international trading city.

Yin and Yang

The Chinese also thought that correct balancing of *tao,* the energy force behind the universe, would lead to immortality. Like the Greek gods who had both positive and negative sides, and like the European system of humors on which it is probably based, *tao* has opposing components, *yin* and *yang*. *Yin* is female, passive, cool. *Yang* is male, aggressive, hot. (*Feng shui* is this principle applied to buildings and landscapes.) The Chinese believed that if humans harnessed *yin* and *yang* properly, if they could find the right combination of foods, they could become immortal. To try to attain immortality, five Tang emperors in a row took "immortality drugs"—probably heavy metals—and died.[6]

China's Tang Dynasty was a time of great advances in the arts, such as poetry, but it was during the Song Dynasty, specifically between 960 and 1279, that distinctive regional cuisines emerged in three regions: north; south, around the Yangtze River delta; and Szechwan. Cantonese came later. Northern Chinese cuisine was dominated by the city of Beijing. Millet, meat, and dairy products were a large part of the total food consumed. Wheat was also grown and the flour used for dumplings, fried dough strips, and noodles. It was blander than southern cuisine, which was based on rice, fish, pork, vegetables and fruits. Szechwan cuisine was also based on rice. Tea was popular, too. It was missing two foods that characterize it now, hot peppers and peanuts, because they were from the New World and had not been introduced to China yet. But even then the food was hot, seasoned with a "vegetable that resembles the pea . . . it will cause gasping and gaping."[7]

Historian Michael Freeman's definition of cuisine is "a self-conscious tradition of cooking and eating . . . with a set of attitudes about food and its place in the life of man."[8] So cuisine requires not just a style of cooking, but an *awareness* about how the food is prepared and consumed. It must also involve a wide variety of ingredients, more than are locally available, and cooks and diners willing to experiment, which means they are not constricted by tradition.

All of these prerequisites were met during the Song period, a time of plenty in China. As trade increased, so did the merchant class and so did their desire for new, exciting foods. In 1027, to avoid famine, the emperor ordered green lentils from India and a new strain of rice from Champa (present-day Vietnam) to be grown in southeastern China. The Champa rice matured faster, so two crops could be grown in one season, and it was drought-tolerant, so it could grow where rice had never been grown before. Other kinds were "official" rice, the only kind that could be used to pay taxes; glutinous rice, used to make wine; "red rice, red lotus-seed rice, yellow keng-mi, fragrant rice, and 'old rice,' rice sold off at a discount by the official granaries."[9] However, among the upper classes, polished white rice was the standard, just as refined white bread was the standard in Europe.[10]

There were "seven necessities" that people had to have every day: "firewood, rice, oil, salt, soybean sauce, vinegar, and tea."[11] At various times, the government had monopolies on two of these, salt and tea, and also on wine. The wealthy went far beyond these mere seven necessities. The food explosion was evident in huge cities like Kaifeng and Hangchow, which had separate markets for different foodstuffs in different parts of the city: for grain; two for pork; for meats besides pork, like beef, venison, horse, fowl, rabbit; vegetables, including seventeen kinds of beans; fresh fish; preserved fish; fruit; oranges; and more. In butcher shops, five butchers at a time lined up at tables, cutting, slicing, and pounding cuts of meat to order.[12] The food for the imperial household was bought at its own special markets.

During the Song dynasty upper-class diners moved from sitting on the floor to chairs. Multicourse dinners were brought to lacquered tables set with porcelain dishes and sometimes silver chopsticks and spoons. Meals were prepared by household staffs that could number in the hundreds. The emperor's kitchens had a staff of more than a thousand working under guard. For a change of pace, there were wine houses and teahouses, and restaurants and caterers that cooked food to order that was as good as or better than that available in the wealthiest homes. For the lower classes, there were street vendors, noodle shops, and smaller restaurants like the *tabernas* and *popinas* of ancient Rome that provided prepared food. Some snack shops specialized in one kind of food, like *ping*—cakes that were sweet or savory, stuffed or plain, steamed or fried. All of the chefs who prepared these foods were male, with perhaps only a few female exceptions. If they were literate, these chefs could find recipes printed in Chinese encyclopedias and in *The Illustrated Basic Herbal,* which appeared in 1061 and contained descriptions and drawings of hundreds of foods.

State banquets were the most lavish ceremonies, with over two hundred different dishes and table service of jade, pearl, and silver.[13] A person's importance at a function like this was measured not just by where he sat, but also by how many courses he got. Other festivals celebrated Buddhist holidays. Ancestors were always honored at these events. Much of this new cuisine based on rice and tea, and the culture connected to it, traveled across the sea to China's island neighbor, Japan.

Cipango: Japan and the Tea Ceremony

China and Japan are linked by location. Huge China, wealthy in natural resources and food, lies west of the much smaller Japan, an island country with no natural resources except water and people. Like Greece, most of Japan's land is mountains that contain no mineral wealth. Like California and the Pacific Rim area, it lies on an earthquake fault and has volcanoes. So Japan had to either trade with or conquer other countries to meet the basic needs of its population. Many of Japan's foods—but not its cuisine—and much of its culture, such as art, religion, and pictographic writing, originated in China. The diets of both countries rely on rice. Rice existed in China perhaps 8,500 years ago, but did not reach Japan until between 300 B.C. and A.D. 200. Japanese rice—Japonica—is short-grained and glutinous or sticky.[14]

Japan refers to itself as the "Land of the Rising Sun," which is depicted as a huge red ball on its flag. It is a culture of extremes. On one hand, there is great attention to detail and the creation of beauty; on the other, a violent warrior mentality. In her famous book about Japan, cultural anthropologist Ruth Benedict describes this split as "the Chrysanthemum and the Sword."[15] In Japan, knights in the Middle Ages were called *samurai*. These warriors followed a code called *bushido,* similar to the code of European knights: they were brave and loyal and willing to die for their earthly lord. A samurai would never surrender. If he did, he would have to kill himself to save his honor, so it was more honorable to die in battle. Samurai swords were large and deadly; the same knife-making skills make Japanese kitchen knives some of the best in the world. At the opposite extreme from this warrior culture is a simple activity elevated to art: drinking tea.

In A.D. 804, a Japanese monk brought tea back from China. In 815, he introduced it to the emperor, and that began the tea tradition in Japan. The first treatise on tea, *Kissa Yojoki,* was published in Japan in 1215, the year the Magna Carta was signed in England and the pope declared that communion wafers were the literal body of Christ. The treatise was written by Eisai, the monk who also introduced Zen Buddhism to Japan. However, the rituals associated with tea at this time in Japan had little to do with religion. As a new fashion from China, it caught on among the upper classes. Bored nobles dressed up in their finest satin and brocade and went to teahouses to play games: who could taste a tea and guess its exact place of origin? Then they bet on the outcome and handed out hundreds of prizes, like bags of gold, to the winners. Tea purists objected to this deviation from the Way of Tea. They got the tea games banned. But the games were too popular; finally, the ban went and the games stayed.

The Way of Tea stated that there were four values connected to tea practice: reverence, respect, purity, and tranquility. These were further refined by the greatest master of all, Sen Rikyu, who lived in the 16th century. He added sincerity and genuine consideration of others to the values of tea ritual. Rikyu transformed the tea ceremony from a borrowed cultural practice into something uniquely Japanese. He began by substituting modest Korean-made teacups and dishes for the elaborate imported Chinese ones, and simple bamboo baskets for Chinese vases made of metal or semiprecious stone.[16] He also made the tearoom smaller and more intimate. Then he put a rack by the door where the samurai had to hang their swords. But the sword had served a purpose at the table, as a divider to stake out personal space. A fan was substituted for the sword, which is why it is considered extremely aggressive to open the fan in the teahouse—it is the equivalent of brandishing a sword. The ritual of talking a walk around the gardens in the back of the tearoom before the ceremony serves a similar purpose. It appears to be an appreciation of nature and part of the ritual, but it is also a look-see to make sure no one is lurking in the garden waiting to assassinate the unarmed samurai.[17]

On one level, the tea ceremony is interactive art that heightens and involves all the senses. The first is smell. Incense is burning as you walk into the nine-foot-square teahouse. Then you hear a whisper like a gentle breeze in the trees—the flame under the teakettle. A flower arrangement soothes your eyes. As you sit on the straw tatami mat on the floor, you are aware of the silk of your kimono brushing against your skin. You watch the movements of the tea master as he offers tea to Buddha. Then you drink a bowl of thick, bracing, bitter green tea.

People spend their lives perfecting the tea ceremony. Sometimes it begins with a drink of ice water, plain hot water, chrysanthemum tea, plum wine, or sake—Japanese rice wine. Then food is served. These small meals are called *kaiseki*—the name derives from the words that mean "sitting together." As Jennifer Anderson states, "The food associated with tea gatherings is the flower of the Japanese cuisine."[18] It should be simple and simply prepared. The example Anderson gives is soup, boiled salmon, seaweed, chestnuts, mushrooms, and rice. The eating part of the ceremony begins with two bowls, one of rice, the other of miso soup. Then comes raw fish garnished with horseradish, edible chrysanthemum petals, and chrysanthemum greens. After more sake, the centerpiece is brought out on a separate tray, perhaps "a shrimp ball, a little piece of green *yuzu* citron, a leaf of spinach, and a *shiitake* mushroom in a clear stock of the best quality *dashi*."[19] A grilled course follows, either meat or fish like barracuda. The meal ends with a broth made of brown rice and salt water accompanied by pickles. These foods are served with much politeness and bowing. They are eaten with new chopsticks.

The conversation in the teahouse is about the teahouse, the tea, the flower arrangement. Nothing from the outside intrudes. This forces you to focus on what is in front of you, on the beauty in the simplest everyday things, on how the Zen of the tea ceremony is the harmony of the universe. When you come out, you are altered.[20] The tearoom is a utopia. In the tea ceremony we can see a cultural shift, where old traditions are replaced by something that is completely new, which then becomes the tradition. The tea ceremony is a flawless execution of the combination of art, food, and religion that began in cave paintings 35,000 years ago in Europe.

EUROPE

Bubonic Plague—the Black Death, 1348–1350

The newly reopened trade routes to Asia brought more than silk and spices to Europe. In 1348, rats covered with fleas spread plague quickly by land and by sea, aided by poor nutrition and the absence of personal hygiene and public sanitation. In two years it killed one-third of the population of Europe, about 25 million people. Another 4 million died in Southwest Asia, and 35 million in China. A vicious cycle began. With farmers dead and much of the surviving population weakened, famine followed plague. Then malnourished people were susceptible to disease. Within 100 years, the population of Europe had dropped drastically, as the following chart shows.

EUROPEAN POPULATION BEFORE AND AFTER THE BLACK DEATH (in millions, approximate)[21]		
COUNTRY	POPULATION IN 1340	POPULATION IN 1450
Italy	10	7.5
France and the Low Countries	19	12
Germany and Scandinavia	11.5	7.5
Iberian Peninsula	9	7
Eastern Europe	13	9.5
TOTAL	62.5	43.5

Some people tried to escape the plague by running away from the cities. The *Decameron,* by Giovanni Boccaccio, is a series of stories about young Italians hiding out at a villa in the hills above Tuscany, where they make up stories to pass the time. One is a fantasy about a place called Bengodi, a paradise for people who love food: it is built on a mountain of grated Parmesan cheese, and the vines drip sausages. People who have nothing else to do all day make macaroni and ravioli and cook them in capon broth. There is an endless supply of food because as fast as it gets eaten, more gets made. And through it all runs a stream of white wine.[22]

People who could not escape the cities did what they could to fight the plague. They wandered from town to town, whipping themselves to atone for whatever humans had done to anger God and bring such horror on the world. Others just got drunk and had orgies. Many believed that the plague was caused by foul-smelling vapors coming from swamps, so they made pungent or sweet-smelling pomander balls using herbs like rue and flowers like columbine and marigold, the only things available to them. These, of course, proved useless.[23] (Now, tetracycline kills plague bacteria quickly and easily.)

In an age when nothing about germs was understood, blame had to lie elsewhere. Rumors sprang up that the Jews were poisoning the wells in a plot to kill Christians. The solution: kill Jews. And they did, with a vengeance. As a result of these attacks, a great Jewish migration began from the more heavily populated cities of western Europe to the less populated areas of eastern Europe. The Jews felt they would be safe there, especially in Poland. They were relatively safe for six hundred years, until the middle of the 20th century, when a small town in southern Poland called Oswiecim became known to the world by its German name: Auschwitz.

The severe drop in population caused massive changes in European life. With people in crucial occupations dead, those left alive could command higher wages. Since whatever they produced—bread, barrels, or wagons—was also in short supply, they could charge higher prices. One of the long-lasting effects of the plague was that the populations on the sugar-producing islands like Cyprus and Sicily were severely reduced and slow to increase, so sugar production dropped. It was centuries before sugar production rose to its old levels again, and it would be not in the Mediterranean, but on islands halfway around the world in what came to be called the West Indies—the Caribbean. In some places in Europe, there was chaos. If all the members of a noble landowning family were dead, there was no one left to inherit their land legally. Squatters moved in and fought over it. Serfs fled to the cities as they had after the Crusades. And like the Crusades, the plague, too, weakened the Church, which couldn't explain what was happening or stop it. People in cities began to ignore the Church's prohibition on doing business and just went and did it anyway. They became very wealthy, especially in Italy.

Italy: The Renaissance

Almost one thousand years after the fall of the Roman Empire, Italians rediscovered the cuisines and cultures of the classical Greeks and Romans literally in their own backyards in broken statues, pots, buildings, and in ancient writings. The Renaissance—"rebirth"—of civilization began in Italy in the 14th century. It is important to remember that in the 14th century, "Italy" meant a geographic area, not a unified country. That didn't happen until the 19th century. Until then, the Italian peninsula was occupied by independent city-states, some of which were conquered at various times by Muslims, Spain, or France. The Renaissance was characterized by an increase in trade and in learning, with an emphasis on humanism—the importance of the individual, as opposed to the Church or the state. Famous artists of the Renaissance were Michelangelo, Leonardo, Raphael, and Donatello (long before they were Ninja Turtles). The Renaissance spread north into France and England much later because they were fighting each other in the Hundred Years' War (which lasted 113 years, from 1337 to 1453, until teenage Joan of Arc tipped the balance in France's favor).

Italians rediscovered the cuisine of ancient Rome in 1457, when the Vatican library acquired a manuscript attributed to Apicius. Along with an interest in Roman cooking came a revival of Roman excesses. In the 16th century, Italy was wealthy and powerful, at the height of the European world. And the Medici family was at the height of power in the wealthiest, most powerful city-state in Italy: Florence. They had accumulated wealth by being merchants, the middlemen between Arab traders in the east and Europe in the west. They had so much money they started loaning it out and became the bankers of Europe, with branches in major cities. The Medici family was the new royalty, although they began as what the French called *bourgeoisie* and the Germans called *burghers*: not born nobles, but merchant-class city dwellers. This new class of people had money and wanted to show it off. Fashion and food were two ways. They dressed in layers, all for show: dresses, stockings, shoes, jackets, in great quantities of expensive fabrics like silk, satin, and velvet. Their hair was done into elaborate shapes, increased with fake silk hair and topped with fancy hats in more expensive fabrics and feathers and fur. They used makeup and perfume, and wore jewelry on everything from their hair to their extravagant shoes.

With the growth of cities came an urban population that did not produce its own food. It needed food that was preserved, and for that it needed spices and salt. Flandrin stated it clearly: "At no time in European history did spices play as great a role as in the fourteenth, fifteenth, and sixteenth centuries."[24] The medieval theory of the humors was partly responsible for the spice increase, because now there were more people in classes that could afford them. But which spices were used changed. French upper-class cooking began to consider spices like black pepper unrefined and lower-class. Each class had its own food habits. "Delicate" meats like partridges became increasingly important to the upper classes, who thought they increased intelligence and sensitivity and that spices made them easier to digest. Cooking "correctly" could mean cooking "with correctives"—opposing elements to counteract an unfavorable humor. For example, oysters, extremely cold and wet, could be "fixed" by roasting them with spices.[25] At the same time, bread occupied a larger percentage of the diet and budget of the lower classes, which might spend more than half of their income on it.[26] The breadbasket of Europe was Poland and Ukraine in the east, which meant the grain had to be shipped, which created another wealthy class of shippers. The lower classes sent their children, as early as age 7 or 8, out to be servants in the homes of the new wealthy classes.[27]

Germany: The Printing Press and the First Cookbook

In 1454, a quiet revolution occurred in Europe. A German named Johann Gutenberg invented the printing press. The Chinese had invented movable type centuries earlier but hadn't pursued it because it didn't work very well with their pictographic alphabet of thousands of characters. It worked very well for European languages, which had few letters. The first thing Gutenberg printed, in 1454, was the Bible. A few of these extremely rare and valuable books still exist. There are several in the United States, including one at the Library of Congress in Washington, D.C. Shortly after the Bible was printed, so were books for learned men concerned with their health and, of course, immortality. The first printing press arrived in Italy in 1465.[28] In 1474, *De honesta voluptate et valetudine* (Of Honest Indulgence and Good Health) was printed in Rome. This combination medical manual and life advice book also included recipes, which makes it the first printed cookbook.[29] Written in Latin by an Italian named Bartolomeo Platina, it was translated into Italian in 1487, into French in 1505, and into English in 1967.[30] Apicius and the customs of ancient Rome influenced Platina's book because he was the Vatican librarian—a new position created by the profusion of books created by the printing press—and since 1457, the Vatican had owned the writings of Apicius. As food historian and chef Anne Willan has pointed out, most of Platina's recipes were really written by Martino, an Italian from northern Italy, chef to a cardinal who liked to live very well and threw dinner parties that turned into orgies. Earlier in the 15th century, Martino had written, in Italian, the 250 recipes that appeared in *De honesta voluptate*. Platina acknowledged Martino's contribution.

One of the areas that Platina singled out as excelling in Lenten confections was the province of Catalonia on the Mediterranean Sea at the Spanish-French border. The cuisine and language of this area were connected directly to ancient Rome.[31] The Arab influence is visible, too, in the meat and fruit stews, in the use of spinach and chickpeas, in the melons, and in the orchards of stone fruits—peaches, cherries, apricots.[32] The Arabs also introduced sugar, saffron, and the bitter orange to this region of Spain.

The new interest in wealth and indulging the pleasures of the flesh, including lavish Roman banquets, extended to the clergy. Popes and cardinals employed party planners called chamberlains to arrange spectacles and feasts, and chefs to carry out their every wish. One pope had a lavish public wedding and banquet for his daughter and built a huge bull that was a wine-gushing fountain for his own coronation. Others became wealthy by selling pardons, even to rapists and murderers. No sin was too horrible to keep a sinner out of heaven if he had enough gold. One cardinal who became wealthy selling pardons justified his behavior: "It is not God's wish that a sinner should die, but that he should live—and pay."[33] Ordinary pious people protested; reform movements arose. One was led by Savonarola, a monk in Florence, who urged people to return to the teachings of Christ and lead holy lives. He was burned at the stake for criticizing the Church. It was clear that any movement to change the Church would have to come from somewhere that was not in the pope's backyard.

Germany: Martin Luther and the Protestant Reformation

A monk in Germany finally put down on paper what many people had been thinking. On October 31, 1517, Martin Luther nailed a list of 95 faults he found with the Church to the door of the cathedral in Wittenberg, Germany. He said that the selling of pardons had to stop, and that it would cut down on the immorality if priests were allowed to marry and lead more ordinary lives. After Luther's 95 Theses, as they became known, went to a printer, copies spread like wildfire through northern Europe. At first the Church ignored its wayward son; he was a nuisance, nothing more. But Luther's theses had hit a nerve; people began leaving the Church and worshiping Christ in other ways. The pope excommunicated Luther, which meant that he couldn't receive the sacraments, so he couldn't get into heaven. Then German princes who sided with the pope declared Luther an outlaw: no one was to give him food or shelter. Other princes shrewdly realized that anything that pulled people away from the Church gave them more power. These princes shielded Luther, who spent the next two years in hiding, translating the Bible from Latin into German so more people could read it. When he went back to Wittenberg, he found that many priests had gotten married and were wearing everyday clothes. The Reformation also freed a large part of Europe's population from the Catholic Church's food rules regarding fast days, feast days, and saints' days. European eating habits began to change.

Portugal: The Rise of World Trade and the Search for Spices

Portugal's Prince Henry the Navigator was in love with the idea of exploring. He set up a sailing school where the latest ideas and technology could be exchanged and improved upon. If the Portuguese could find a way to bypass the Arab caravans and Italian fleets, they could lower the price of spices and other precious items and increase their own profits. Just as three important technological developments—the wheel, the plow, and the sail—had helped the Sumerians trade 4,500 years earlier, three new technological developments helped the Europeans. The magnetic compass, invented by the Chinese, always pointed north and helped ships' captains get their bearings on the open sea. The astrolabe, an Arab invention, made navigation using the stars possible. And the new triangular sails allowed ships to sail against the wind, not just with it. The Portuguese ships sailed south down the west coast of Africa, around the Cape of Good Hope, and up the east coast of Africa. They continued across the open sea east of India and arrived in the East Indies in what is now Indonesia—what they called the Spice Islands. They had just found a way to cut out the middlemen.

At the same time, the Chinese were looking for a shorter route to the Middle East and the Mediterranean. From 1405 to 1433, they sent Admiral Zheng He on seven voyages. He explored the South Pacific and reached the Persian Gulf and Africa. The 300-ship fleet must have been an impressive sight, with 9-masted ships 400 feet long, flying red silk sails. They could have kept on going all the way to America, but they stopped. A shift in political power forced the great fleet to retire. The conservative Confucian scholars who were running China did not want the country to pollute itself by engaging in business with foreigners, or any business at all. They declared it illegal to build a ship with more than two masts, which made long-distance voyages impossible. Then they taxed businesses and gave tax breaks to farmers to discourage business and encourage farming. At the same time that the Catholic Church in Europe was loosening its restrictions on engaging in business, China was tightening them. It was a decision that would protect and strengthen China in the short run but prove harmful and make it vulnerable in the long run. For the next 400 years, wealthy, self-sufficient China closed itself off from the world, disdaining to do business with the West. During that time, the West made technological advances that would completely overwhelm China. The next time Europeans came knocking on China's door, they would be carrying new technology made possible by a Chinese invention: guns.

Europeans who had read Marco Polo's stories and believed them wanted to go to China, too, but it was very far and difficult to get to by land. What they needed was a sea route that was a shortcut. It would be worth a fortune to the man who discovered it and to the country that paid for it. Since the Chinese had decided not to become sea traders, Europeans would have to do it themselves. Almost exactly 200 years after Marco Polo published his memoirs, another Italian read his stories, believed them, and was inspired to look for that shortcut. He was known to the Italians in Genoa, where he was born, as Cristoforo Colombo, to the Spanish who financed his expedition as Cristóbal Colón, and to the English as Christopher Columbus. He was an experienced sea captain and had seen the maps of the world. They had three continents—Europe, Asia, and Africa. Jerusalem was at the center of all of them. But some people at the time believed that going west would be the fastest route to the Indies. In Germany, a man named Behaim was building a globe, which portrayed a round world.[34] Columbus trusted his own observations that the horizon never got closer no matter how long he sailed toward it, and that he was not going to fall off the earth. Columbus was petitioning the royalty of Europe to finance his trip to look for spices in the east by sailing west, but he was not having much success. The Medici weren't interested because if he did find a new route, it would cut out their moneymaking position as middlemen. The situation in Spain was tense, as the new king and queen revived the Inquisition as part of their campaign to purify Spain and save its soul.

Spain: The Inquisition and Jewish Cooking

In 1474, the same year that Platina published the first printed cookbook, King Ferdinand and Queen Isabella began their reign. They vowed to unify and purify Spain by making it a completely Spanish, completely Catholic country. To achieve this, they had to cleanse the country of two segments of the population that had been living peacefully in Spain for hundreds of years, the Islamic Moors and the Jews. There were already laws against Jews in place. In 1412, Spain had passed laws that forbade Jews to work at certain trades, including grocer and butcher. They could not employ Christians and could not eat, drink, bathe with, or talk to Christians, and they had to wear only coarse clothes.[35] In 1476, by law Jews had to wear a distinctive symbol. In 1480, the king and queen reconvened the Inquisition. In 1484, Jews were not allowed to sell food. By 1492, the Spanish had driven the last of the Moors out of the country after the battle for the city of Granada, and they had issued an order that all Jews must be baptized Christian or leave the country. The Spanish waged war against the Moors, but they used food to get rid of the Jews. The Inquisition knew that it was possible for people to hide their religious books and lie about their beliefs, but it was impossible for them to hide their food customs.

The Inquisition, under Torquemada, its famous leader whose name has become synonymous with torture, was very thorough and very specific. They went from town to town, called all the people together in the town square—the plaza—and announced what they were looking for: anyone who cooked food on Friday night but didn't eat it until Saturday, because Jews didn't cook on Saturday, their sabbath; anyone who didn't eat pork; anyone who washed blood off meat before they cooked it; anyone who ate foods the Church had forbidden during Lent, like cheese. Disgruntled servants turned in masters and mistresses; neighbors betrayed neighbors. People who were found guilty were marched through the streets to the plaza, then burned at the stake over a slow, agonizing fire. Some Jews "passed" for Christian by pretending to eat like Christians. They made a great show of cooking pork and sharing it with their neighbors; perhaps the neighbors were so overwhelmed by the generosity that they didn't notice that the people who cooked the pork didn't eat any themselves.

Even conversion wasn't a guarantee of safety. Eventually, the Inquisition went after the *conversos,* the Jews who had converted to Christianity but who the Inquisition felt might still be practicing Judaism secretly. In order to survive, the Jews left Spain. Some went west to Portugal, but a great many went much farther away from the Inquisition and from Catholicism altogether: they went north to the only country in Europe that practiced religious toleration, the Netherlands. They took their knowledge of banking and business with them. Ferdinand and Isabella were aware of the economic and intellectual drain on their country but insisted that they had to persevere with their religious cleansing to save the souls of the Christians in Spain.

Waiting to see Queen Isabella was Christopher Columbus, and waiting for Columbus were two new continents, North and South America, and unimaginable mineral, vegetable, and animal wealth. There was nothing in the teachings of the Catholic Church, nothing in the writings of the ancient philosophers, nothing in their scholarly literature or popular folklore or fables to prepare Europeans for the amazing world they were about to encounter.

THE AMERICAN EMPIRES

Before Columbus arrived in 1492, not one person in North or South America had ever had the measles or been scarred by smallpox. No one had ever suffered through those great child-killing diseases, diphtheria and whooping cough, against which nearly everyone in the United States is vaccinated now shortly after birth; nor had they ever had mosquito-borne malaria, or typhus, which is spread by lice. No one had ever gotten the common cold. Those diseases didn't exist in the Western Hemisphere. There were also no weeds like crabgrass and dandelion and kudzu. There were no black rats, no brown rats. American bees buzzed and made honey but they had no stingers.

The people native to North and South America had arrived between 40,000 B.C. and 12,000 B.C. by walking across the Bering Strait between northern Asia and Alaska when the glaciers receded and dried up the Bering Sea, creating a land bridge. These people, relatives of the Mongols, spread from Alaska down to Tierra del Fuego at the tip of South America. They became the Inuit, who ate seal meat; the Kwakiutl, who carved totem poles; the Maliwoo, who lived a laid-back life on the Pacific Ocean at what is now Malibu; the Iroquois, who had a sophisticated system of government, and many other tribes.

Before Columbus arrived, South America, North America, and Central America each had one dominant culture: the inhabitants of Cahokia, located near present-day St. Louis on the Mississippi River; the Inca, in their capital city of Cuzco, in the Andes Mountains of Peru; and the Aztec, whose great capital city, Tenochtitlán, was built on landfill in a lake where Mexico City rises now. Although these three cultures were thousands of miles apart, they had several things in common. All were at the center of complex trade routes. The Cahokians used the Mississippi River and its thousands of miles of tributaries for transportation and trade, including the Ohio and Missouri rivers. The

Inca and Aztec built roads. All three civilizations built enormous pyramids, some larger than the pyramids of Egypt. But none of these three civilizations used the wheel except as a child's toy or in games. Everything on these trade routes was carried on boats or on the backs or heads of people or on pack animals, like the llamas domesticated by the Incas. They didn't have carts because they didn't have strong animals—draft animals—to pull them. There were no oxen, a prehistoric horse had become extinct, and the animals native to the Americas couldn't be domesticated easily or at all: polar, grizzly, brown, and black bears; jaguars, lynxes, and wolves. Although there were few domesticated animals, the Agricultural Revolution had taken place independently in the Americas. The American civilizations had developed new ways of farming and preserving to deal with foods that were beyond the wildest dreams of the people in Europe, Africa, and Asia.

North America: Cahokia, the Mississippian Civilization

In pre-Columbian America, Cahokia, a great city of pyramids, rose from the flatlands on the banks of the Mississippi River, just east of where St. Louis is now. More than one hundred pyramids, aligned with the rising and setting sun and various constellations, spread out over six square miles. Animal images appear on bowls and shells, especially the water spider, which some tribes, like the Cherokee, believed brought fire to humans. Other animals represented are fish, deer, rabbits, raccoons, falcons, snakes, eagles, and frogs.[36] Cahokia reached its peak in the 1100s, when its population was about twenty thousand.[37] Human remains have been found indicating that the Cahokians practiced human sacrifice. Little is known about the civilization at Cahokia, because historians believe that the entire city was wiped out by European diseases that spread from the Spanish in Mexico into the interior of North America. By the time Americans reached the Mississippi River in the 18th century, Cahokia was a ghost town long gone.

South America: Inca—Potatoes and Maize

The Inca ruled over the largest empire in the Americas. Its territory stretched for 2,500 miles along the Pacific coast of South America from the present-day countries of Ecuador, at the equator (which is what the name *Ecuador* means), south through Peru, Bolivia, and western Argentina to approximately where Santiago, the capital of Chile, is now.

Machu Picchu.
Courtesy PhotoDisc, Inc.

This is a territory of geographical extremes. From desert at the Pacific Ocean in the west, the land rises steeply almost 20,000 feet to the snow-covered peaks of the Andes Mountains. The Altiplano (high plain) sits thousands of feet up in the Andes between two parallel mountain ranges. Like the ancient Romans, the Inca built roads and bridges—14,000 miles of them—to connect their empire. Just as in the Roman Empire all roads led to Rome, in the Inca empire all roads led to the capital of Cuzco in what is now Peru, 11,444 feet above sea level. Like the Egyptians, the Inca mummified their dead. They worshiped Inti, the god of the sun, at their most sacred shrine, the Temple of the Sun in Cuzco. They were highly skilled at working with the material they called "the sweat of the sun"—gold. In Cuzco, the walls of buildings were covered in sheets of gold. The Inca also constructed a mysterious city one and a half miles up in the Andes. Called Machu Picchu, it could be reached only by walking over a log bridge with a steep drop below, and is so remote that it wasn't discovered until 1912. Archeologists are still trying to figure out what the Inca used it for.

There was no private ownership of land in the Inca Empire. The government controlled land and the economy and decided which crops would be grown where. Under government direction, farmers built irrigation systems and terraced the hillsides where they grew quinoa, a grain native to the Andes. Inca meats included deer and an animal called a *vizcacha*, which had a body like a rabbit and a tail like a fox. Our jerky comes from the Inca practice of leaving meat out to dry in the desert air and their word for it—*charque*.[38] The difference is that their *charque* was made from llama meat, while ours is more likely to be beef. Dried fish fed the army. Another food staple for a majority of the population then, and now, was *cuy*—guinea pig (*Cavia porcellus*)—which the Inca had domesticated by 2000 B.C. The taste has been described like fishy pork. The *cuy* is a small mammal that reproduces rapidly. It is roasted whole, hair off, skin on, seasoned with chile, gutted, and the cavity filled with hot stones.[39]

The Inca also cultivated more than 3,000 varieties of potato (*Solanum tuberosum*), which they domesticated between 3700 and 3000 B.C.[40] They preserved the potatoes by freeze-drying. Since they were in the Altiplano, a desert at high elevations, the weather was hot and dry during the day and freezing at night. During the day, they squeezed the moisture out of the potatoes with their feet, like crushing grapes for wine, and left them out to dry. Then the dry potatoes froze at night. The freeze-dried potatoes, called *chuño,* could be stored indefinitely in huge warehouses in case there was a shortage.[41] Water was warehoused, too.

Corn, which traveled south from Mexico, was another staple of the Inca diet. To Americans, corn means corn on the cob, with kernels. But the word was in use in Europe long before there was corn on the cob. This has led to some confusion, especially with ancient texts.

𝒞ULINARY 𝒫UZZLE
❊ THE CORN-MAIZE CONFUSION ❊

The word *corn* was first used to describe any grain, even of salt, as in corned beef. It also means the small, hard seed or fruit of a plant, as in peppercorn.[42] So when pre-Columbian Old World writings mention corn, they can mean many things, but maize is not one of them. The word *maize* came from the Spanish, who picked it up from the Arawak Indians of the Caribbean, where *mahiz* means "stuff of life."[43] Maize was domesticated in central Mexico by about 3400 B.C. It quickly became the basic crop and spread north to the cliff dwellers in the American Southwest and to Cahokia, and south to the Inca Empire.[44]

There is further confusion. As food historian Raymond Sokolov points out, "The corn of the Andes [*choclo*] is not our corn. The kernels are much bigger, the taste and texture different."[45] And it was used differently, transformed by a unique technique into a beer called *chicha* (see page 98).

Tomatoes and chile peppers were native to Peru, too. Just as corn migrated south to Peru, tomatoes and chile peppers migrated north to Mexico, where they were domesticated and bred and where Europeans first encountered them.[46]

RECIPE

*C*HICHA—CORN BEER

The method of making *chicha* is this: "women . . . put [the sprouted corn] into their mouths and gradually chew it; then with an effort they almost cough it out upon a leaf or platter and throw it into the jar with [ground corn and water]." Later it is boiled and strained. In her book *The Story of Corn*, Betty Fussell says that *chicha* has "a two-inch head of foam and . . . tastes a bit like English barley water mixed with light pilsner."[47]

Central America: The Aztecs and Cacahuatl

In 1325, a people called the Mexica, or Aztecs, arrived at a valley 7,000 feet above sea level and ringed by mountains—the site of present-day Mexico City. They built their capital city, Tenochtitlán, on an island in the middle of one of the lakes on the valley floor. As they grew more powerful and dominant over Central America, Aztec engineers connected Tenochtitlán to land by roads built above the water.

Like the Inca to the south, the Aztecs worshiped a sun god. But the Aztec god, Huitzilopochtli, demanded human sacrifice every day or he would not appear. Those sacrificed were captured from among neighboring tribes, which, understandably, hated the Aztecs. Those sacrificed were forced to climb many steps up a pyramid to an altar on the flat top. While they were alive, their hearts were cut out, still beating, and offered to the god. The rest of the body was tossed down the pyramid steps, ritually divided, stewed with maize and salt, and eaten. Sophie Coe puts the portions of human flesh at about one-half ounce per person and says that some people declined to eat it. She also points out that the absence of the Aztec staple spice, chile, clearly indicates that this was not an ordinary meal, but a ritual one. Her point is that cannibalism was connected to religion and strictly controlled. It was not a random occurrence when somebody got hungry.[48]

In addition to the sun god, the Aztecs also worshiped the god of fire, who lived among three other gods, represented by three stones on the hearth where all the cooking was done. Much of today's Mexican cooking equipment and the food cooked on it are directly descended from the Aztecs. Tortillas were cooked on a clay griddle called a *comalli* (today, *comal*); corn was ground on a *metate,* a three-legged grinding stone, with the Aztec equivalent of the pestle, a stone that fit in the hand and was therefore called a *mano.* In the Aztec civilization, women were usually the cooks. Mothers taught daughters, and by the time a girl was 13 she was expected to be an accomplished cook. The exception was that men handled the barbecue. Being an Aztec cook could be a dangerous occupation: when the nobility died, numerous male and female cooks were buried with them (the higher the noble person's rank, the

ℱℴℴ𝒹 ℱ𝒶ᴮᴸᴱ
⪼ NATIVE AMERICAN CANNIBALISM ⪻

There is a great deal of misinformation about cannibalism among native peoples in the Americas. It is important to remember the source of this misinformation: the Spanish conquistadors, who needed to justify killing these people. The stories about cannibalism began almost immediately after Columbus's arrival. In fact, the word *cannibal* comes from a variation of the name of the tribe that gave its name to the Caribbean Sea, the Caribe or Canibe. Throughout history, when one group of people decides to kill another, it is easier if the enemy seems not human or is said to engage in practices that are culturally unacceptable. For Christian Europeans, cannibalism was one of those practices.

greater the number of cooks) so that they could cook for them in the afterlife. The nobles were dead but the cooks were buried alive.[49]

As with other cultures, religious festivals played a large part in Aztec life. There were fast days, and on certain feast days several provinces got together, with each required to provide the food on a certain day. But as Sophie Coe points out in *America's First Cuisines,* it is still unclear how many times a day the Aztecs ate. Many sources say two, others say three—at dawn, 9:00 A.M., and 3:00 P.M.[50]

One of the most important foodstuffs, which had more than culinary significance in the Aztec culture, was *cacahuatl,* or chocolate—made from the seeds of the cacao plant, in the genus *Theobroma,* which means "food of the gods." Chocolate was the beverage of Aztec emperors and warriors. They drank it lukewarm, frothed on top the same way it is done today, by rubbing a swizzle stick or *molinillo* between the palms of the hands. In their book *The True History of Chocolate,* Sophie and Michael Coe discuss at length how the Aztecs flavored chocolate. They used finely ground chile powder or sometimes maize, honey (there was no sugar yet), a flower related to the custard apple, another flower related to black pepper, and "black flower"—what they called vanilla because of the color of the pod.[51] Even though the Aztecs had an alcoholic beverage made from agave, they didn't consider it fit for men to drink. Old people could drink it, but chocolate was the drink preferred by nobles and warriors and was restricted to them. It was part of a warrior's food ration, along with tortillas, beans, dried chiles, and toasted maize.[52] Besides, drunkenness was punishable by death. However, chocolate was not consumed indiscriminately. It was served as a ritual beverage after a banquet, by itself, along with tobacco to smoke, in a male bonding ritual that echoes the Greek symposium, where the men drank wine.

The cacao beans were stored in the public granaries, along with maize, but they were much more than food. They were also money in the Aztec empire. They could be used to pay wages and to purchase items. A turkey hen or a rabbit cost 100 cacao beans, an avocado cost 3, a large tomato cost 1.[53] But cacao, like other forms of money, could be counterfeited.

Protein in the Aztec diet came from "deer, peccary, rabbits, jackrabbits, mice, armadillos, snakes, gophers, opposums, and iguanas" that were caught, kept in cages, and fattened up. There were dogs in the Americas, but they were not like modern dogs or the ferocious armored war dogs the Spaniards brought with them. The American dogs were small and soft, like a little rolled roast with feet. They were bred and raised for food, probably fed mostly maize, along with avocados and other vegetables.[54] Also on the Aztec menu were foods from the surrounding lakes: water bugs and their eggs, frogs and tadpoles, lake shrimp, and larvae of the *Comadia redtenbacheri* worm, which today resides at the bottom of the mezcal bottle.[55] These were cooked in a variety of ways: ground up into balls and cooked in maize husks, roasted and salted, and made into tamales. Spaniards who ate them at the time found them palatable; they said the water bug eggs tasted like caviar. One lake food the Spanish could not bring themselves to eat was a plant the Aztec called *tecuilatl*—edible seaweed (*Spirulina geitleri*). It was partially sun-dried, formed into cakes, then completely sun-dried, and used to make tortillas. Supposedly, it tasted like cheese "but less pleasing and with a certain taste of mud."[56]

Most of this culture of corn, squash, beans, and chiles traveled north on the trade routes from the great Aztec civilization into what is now northern Mexico and the southwestern United States.

The Southwest: Three Sisters and Chile Man

In southwestern America, on the edge of the Aztec trade route, efficient native people built communal dwellings, like apartment houses. The largest had perhaps 600 rooms and 1,000 inhabitants. They also farmed efficiently. Instead of having fields that were spread out and time-

CHILE PEPPER HEAT SCALE—SCOVILLE UNITS	
HEAT LEVEL	TYPE OF PEPPER
100–500	Bell, pimento
500–1,000	Anaheim, New Mexican
1,000–1,500	Ancho, pasilla
1,500–2,500	Sandia, cascabel, yellow wax
2,500–5,000	Jalapeño, mirasol
5,000–15,000	Serrrano, early jalapeño, aji amarillo
15,000–30,000	Chile de arbol
30,000–50,000	Aji, piquin, Tabasco
50,000–100,000	Chiltepin, cayenne, Tabasco
100,000–350,000	Habanero, Scotch bonnet

Pepper heat scale chart is reprinted by permission of McIlhenny Company.

consuming to get to and tend, they combined three crops that grew well together—corn, beans, and squash—in a method known as "three sister farming." The corn stalks grew straight up and acted as a trellis for the beans that wound around them. At the bottom of the corn, the big, broad leaves of the squash plants kept moisture in the soil. The people ate the corn, beans, and squash, as well as the beautiful, golden, trumpet-shaped squash blossoms, still widely used in Mexican cooking today. They also ate amaranth, a plant that is very nutritious—but only for a short time. The delicate, new greens are tender and edible like baby spinach, but within a few weeks they are just tough, indigestible weeds.

In the Southwest, as in Mexico, chile peppers figure prominently in the culture as well as the cuisine. Peppers are members of the nightshade family, like their other American relatives the tomato, the potato, and tobacco, and their Asian relative, the eggplant. The heat of peppers, from the large, harmless green bell to the tiny hellfire Scotch bonnet, is measured in Scoville units.

In the 1980s, when the United States became aware of southwestern food, chef Mark Miller of Santa Fe's Coyote Café streamlined the scale and added graphics to it. He put his visual heat scale from 1 to 10, with pictures of chile peppers, on a poster that was very popular. A braid of chiles, called a *ristra,* means good luck to a household, and is given as a housewarming gift. Native people had many different explanations for where chile peppers came from.

Chiles are nutritious, high in vitamins A, C, and riboflavin, but capsaicin, the active ingredient in chile peppers, stimulates pain receptors in the mouth.[57] How odd, then, that the chile pepper is chemically similar to another New World plant, vanilla. Perhaps the heat in the

---

ℱOOD ℱABLE

⋙ WHERE SALT AND CHILE PEPPERS COME FROM ⋘

According to the Papago people of southern Arizona and northern Mexico, the creator of the universe invited all the people he had created to a magnificent dinner. Narama (First Man) "was among the last, and he came naked, covered with salt. . . . [He] took salt from his face and sprinkled it upon the foods. Then he reached down, and his testes turned into chile pods. He began to sprinkle their spice onto all of the foods." This offended the other guests until Narama pointed out that none of the foods on the table—fruits and vegetables, fish and fowl—were complete without salt and chile. The guests tasted the food, and agreed that salt and chile were necessities.[58]

---

chile is a survival adaptation to prevent it from being eaten by the wrong animals, the ones that will not help its seeds spread. For example, small mammals like rabbits destroy the seeds because their bodies digest them. The digestive tracts of birds, on the other hand, remove only the protective outer coating of the seed, which make them the perfect animals to spread seeds.[59]

All of the native peoples in the Americas knew how to farm and preserve their foods efficiently, how to build roads for trade and temples for worship. They knew how to read the heavens and make calendars, how to govern vast empires. Their craftspeople knew how to make objects of great beauty out of gold and silver, and how to cook complex, sophisticated dishes. But what the Inca, the Aztecs, the Caribes, the Papago, and all the other native peoples in the Americas didn't know was that in Europe, Spain's King Ferdinand and Queen Isabella had finally decided to bankroll Columbus's voyage. The monarchs had debated long and hard about spending so much money on a venture so risky. They didn't know then that spending more than one million *maravedis*—the equivalent of $151,780 in 1991 U.S. dollars—would yield a 200 million percent profit and make Spain a great empire.[60]

COLUMBUS SETS SAIL FOR THE AMERICAS: 1492

On August 2, 1492, Columbus and his crew of 90 men attended Mass at the Church of St. George in Palos, Spain. The next day they set sail in three ships, the *Niña*, the *Pinta*, and the ship carrying Columbus, the *Santa Maria*.[61] Six days later, they arrived in the Spanish-owned

Canary Islands off the northwest coast of Africa, the last stop before heading west with the wind that Columbus hoped would carry them to the East Indies—the Spice Islands.

When they set sail from the Canary Islands on Thursday, September 6, 1492, Columbus's men had enough food to last them for one year.[62] They would have packed standard Spanish food that would last, mostly dried or salted: rice and dried chickpeas; beef, pork, anchovies, and sardines preserved in salt. There were surely casks of olive oil and enough wine to provide the one-and-a-half-liter ration that each man expected every day. There was also that misery of the sailor's life, the aptly named hardtack—the unleavened, rock-hard flour, water, and salt biscuit that was more hospitable to parasites like weevils than to humans. The sailors would supplement this with whatever fresh fish they could catch. If any dried fruit was on board, it was for the officers, not the crew. Vegetables, except perhaps garlic and onions, were absent in this diet.[63] There was no cook on board, so crew members took turns at midday preparing the one hot meal a day (at most) on a *fogón,* an open iron box. There was no top and no front, only a bottom filled with sand, a back, and two short, curved sides—just enough to keep the wood fire off the wooden deck.[64] Since the small ships were pitching on the waves nearly all the time, the food would have been a simple, one-pot meal like beans and rice with meat or fish. Below the deck, the hold was packed with food and water, firewood, gunpowder, rope, and other supplies, so the men worked, ate, and slept outside on deck. Rats, roaches, and lice were also standard on ships.

On September 9, when they lost sight of land behind them and there was nothing in front of them but sea and sky, the crew cried. Columbus wrote in the ship's log, "I comforted them with great promises of land and riches."[65] Columbus also led them in prayer several times a day, as Christianity required. After other breaks in morale and false sightings of land in the coming weeks, the crew was near mutiny. Finally, land was sighted for real in what is now the eastern Bahamas on October 12, 1492, thirty-three days after they left the Canaries. Columbus named the island San Salvador—"holy savior."[66]

"We Saw Naked People"[67]

Ashore, Columbus and his men prayed in thanks, claimed the land for Spain, and put up a cross. Natives came to greet them. Sure that he was in the East Indies, Columbus mistakenly called these people *indios*—Indians. The first thing Columbus noticed about these

Indians was that they were naked, good-looking, and friendly, which he assumed would make them easy to convert to Christianity. And they had only wooden weapons, which he knew would make them easy to enslave.

The stage was set for one of the greatest holocausts in human history.

1492   1519   1532   1551   1588

The Columbian Exchange: The 16th Century

The collision of the Eastern and Western Hemispheres—Old and New Worlds—and the foods, plants, animals, and diseases that went back and forth is called the Columbian Exchange. With this contact, humans overrode millions of years of natural development in life-forms on planet Earth. After only a little more than 500 years, it is too soon to tell what the long-term effects of this exchange will be.

Only one food animal went from the Americas to Europe at this time—the turkey. Also, only one major disease traveled from the Americas to Europe—syphilis, which spread through Europe like wildfire and then came back to the Americas in a more virulent form.

Much of the plant and animal life that arrived in the Western Hemisphere from the Old World came as stowaways. Seeds for weeds might get mixed in with grains, dung, or animal feed. Old World dandelions and daisies arrived this way. So did tumbleweed, Kentucky bluegrass, and the black rat, which carries plague and typhus. So did the numerous diseases that went from Europe, Asia, and Africa to the Americas—the common cold, diphtheria, malaria, measles, smallpox, typhus, whooping cough. Ten years after the Spanish arrived in Mexico, the native population had dropped by nearly 10 million.[1] A hundred years later, 90 percent of the native population was dead—a decline from more than 25 million to about 1 million. People native to the Americas had no immunity to any of the diseases Europeans routinely

SOME FOODS FROM EUROPE, AFRICA, AND ASIA TO THE AMERICAS			
ANIMALS	VEGETABLES, HERBS, SPICES	GRAINS, LEGUMES	FRUITS
Cattle*	Anise	Barley	Apple
Goat*	Beet	Chickpea	Banana
Horse*	Broccoli	Lentil	Cherry
Pig*	Cabbage	Oats	Grape
Sheep*	Carrot	Rice	Lemon
Chicken	Celery	Rye	Orange
Donkey	Cilantro	Sugarcane*	Peach
Dog	Cinnamon	Wheat	Pear
Cat	Coffee (1723, by the French)		Plum
Black Rat	Cucumber		Pomegranate
	Eggplant		Quince
	Garlic		Watermelon
	Ginger		
	Lavender		
	Lettuce		
	Mustard		
	Nutmeg		
	Olive		
	Onion		
	Parsley		
	Pepper, black		
	Sage		
	Sesame		
	Soy		
	Turnip		
	Yam		
*Brought to America in 1493 on Columbus's second voyage			

got. In his book *Guns, Germs, and Steel*, Jared Diamond tries to answer the questions that arise from what historians call the "time of contact." Why didn't the people in the New World have any immunities? Why didn't they have diseases of their own to give to the Europeans? Diamond has some theories. One is that New World people didn't have the livestock that Europeans did, which was where a great many of the zoonoses—animal diseases that cross over to afflict humans—originated. For example, the smallpox that ravaged Rome came from cows. Another is that the population of the New World was scattered and not concentrated in cities, where normal human interaction would have exposed people to a variety of diseases and allowed them to develop immunities.

SOME FOODS FROM THE AMERICAS TO EUROPE, AFRICA, AND ASIA			
ANIMALS	VEGETABLES, SPICES	GRAINS, LEGUMES, DRUGS	FRUITS
Turkey	Allspice	Beans, kidney	Avocado
Muscovy duck	Amaranth	Beans, navy	Blueberry
	Beans, green	Beans, lima	Cacao
	Jerusalem artichoke	Corn (maize)	Cherimoya
	Jicama	Manioc (cassava, tapioca)	Cranberry
	Peppers, bell	Peanuts	Papaya
	Peppers, hot	Quinine	Pineapple
	Potatoes, sweet	Quinoa	Tomato
	Potatoes, white	Tobacco	
	Pumpkin	Wild rice (a grain, not a true rice)	
	Sapote		
	Squash		
	Sunflower		
	Vanilla		

OLD WORLD TO NEW

Columbus's "discovery" began a land rush to the Americas. Within two years, Spain and Portugal were ready to fight over boundaries. Instead, the pope mediated, the way the United Nations does now. In 1494, in the Treaty of Tordesillas, the two countries agreed to an imaginary line the pope drew through the New World from north to south. Everything west of the line—Mexico and most of South America—belonged to Spain; everything east—Brazil—was Portugal's.

Columbus's arrival in the Americas and the wealth he found there built Spain into a superpower in the 16th century. The Spanish crown got 20 percent—the "royal fifth"—of everything that came out of its colonies in the New World. But mismanagement, overspending, and wars squandered the fortune. The 16th century began with Spain's rise to power; it ended with Spain starting to decline as the power passed to northern European Protestant countries.

The conquistadors who followed Columbus to the New World in the 16th century conquered the cuisines as well as the cultures of the native people. Spain immediately began to transplant its culture, especially its foodstuffs, to New Spain. Columbus returned to the Americas the following year, 1493, and brought Old World livestock with him: cattle, horses, pigs, goats, sheep. All except the sheep eventually took to the wild and reverted to their pre-domesticated state. The pigs turned into wild boars; the dogs went from protecting flocks to eating them, like wolves; the horses found excellent grazing land and fol-lowed it across the plains—the *llanos*—in Venezuela, Argentina, and Uruguay, and later in North America.

As historian Alfred Crosby points out, "By 1600 all the most important food plants of the Old World were being cultivated in the Americas."[2] However, the vegetable foods were not readily accepted by the native people. The new animals and the products they yielded were another matter and changed native cuisines profoundly. They also changed the landscape, in some cases causing ecological disasters. Livestock reproduced at phenomenal rates. In three years, thirteen pigs produced seven hundred.[3] Cattle grazed on land where natives had grown food plants. A rat-caused famine occurred in Bermuda. With no natural enemies, the rats burrowed into the earth, took up residence in trees, and ate so much that people starved to death. In some cases, however, Indians domesticated livestock themselves.

Mexico: *Mole* and *Carne*

The conquistador Hernán Cortés arrived on the Caribbean shore of Mexico in 1517. He had heard stories about the fabulous wealth of the Aztecs, and he wanted it: "I came to get gold, not to till the soil like a peasant."[4] He had his men burn the ships so they couldn't run away no matter how tough things got. When word reached the Aztecs about these strange beings that had arrived by ship from the east, they thought it was their god Quetzalcóatl returning. The food that Cortés exchanged with the natives he met was passed on to Motecuhzoma (we call him Mon-tezuma), who did not eat it but took the salt pork, dried meat, and bis-cuits to the temple of the god as an offering.[5] When Cortés and his men arrived at Tenochtitlán, they were amazed at its beauty and grandeur; some of them thought it was a dream. The dream continued when the Aztec people and Motecuhzoma welcomed Cortés and his men as gods. By the time the Aztecs realized that Cortés was human and only wanted gold, it was too late. The fierce Aztec warriors were no match for the Spaniards' guns or diseases. A smallpox epidemic throughout the capital ensured Spanish victory. Fevers as high as 107°F turn smallpox's deliri-ous victims into "a dripping, unrecognizable mass of [putrid-smelling] pus." It is spread simply by breathing when the patient is alive and after he is dead by contact with blankets, utensils, or other articles he touched.[6] Soon the entire Aztec empire was under the control of Spain.

After hundreds of years of European influence, modern Mexican cuisine is very different from pre-Columbian native cuisines. One of the most important changes was that the diet of South American natives went from heavily vegetarian and very low in fat to heavily meat-based with a great deal of fat. The "three sisters" of corn, beans, and squash shifted to three different sisters—corn, beans, and rice. Tortillas now came in wheat as well as corn, and were wrapped around stuffings that included *carnitas* (dried shredded pork) and *queso* (cheese). *Chili* (beans in a tomato sauce) became *chili con carne* (chili with meat). Mild chile peppers like Anaheims were stuffed with cheese to make *chiles rellenos.*

Contact with the Spanish changed chocolate, too. Now Mexican chocolate is a combination of chocolate (freshly ground from cacao beans, if possible), *canela* (cinnamon), and granulated sugar. Chocolate *caliente* (hot) is still frothed by hand with a *molinillo* rolled quickly back and forth between the palms of the hands, as if you were trying to start a fire, just as the Aztecs did. But chocolate historians believe that one chocolate dish considered typically Mexican might not be.

Mole poblano is still the signature dish of Puebla. But many more kinds of *mole* come from Oaxaca (pronounced "wa-HA-ca"). There are spicy *moles,* red, yellow, and green *moles,* sweet and sour *moles.* Recently, a restaurant opened in Oaxaca that serves what could be called *nuevo mole,* lighter because it is made with vegetable or canola oil instead of lard. Traditionalists resisted it.[7] American chef Rick Bayless adds red wine to his *mole.*[8]

Other Mexican uses of Old World animals include *pozole* (pork

---

𝓕ood 𝓕able
❧ MOLE MYTHS[9] ❧

As chocolate historians Sophie and Michael Coe point out, there are many myths surrounding the beginnings of *mole* (pronounced "MO-lay"), but it is definitely *not* of Aztec origin. The Aztecs never combined chocolate with food. It was consumed only as a beverage, often ritually after a meal, when they also used tobacco. The Italians, however, experimented wildly with chocolate, beginning in the 1680s. They put it in pasta, in pasta sauce, in polenta, in breading for liver. They fried eggs in cacao butter. Since these recipes predate the earliest recipes for *mole,* the Coes think that perhaps the Italians invented *mole.* Late-17th-century Hispanic stories give different, vague versions of the debut of *mole:* it was created by accident when chocolate fell into a stew—or it was created on purpose. It was made to honor a bishop—no, a Spanish official. The only agreement is that the word *mole* comes from *molli,* the Aztec word meaning "sauce."

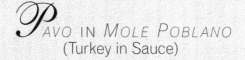

INGREDIENTS

𝒫AVO IN *MOLE POBLANO*
(Turkey in Sauce)

One of the earliest recipes for *pavo* (turkey) in *mole* comes from the state of Puebla, southeast of Mexico City. It was an Old World–New World fusion food. The main ingredients—turkey, tomatoes, and chocolate—were New World. So were the three different kinds of chili peppers—mulato, ancho, and pasilla. But it was seasoned with Old World herbs and spices—black pepper, cinnamon, sesame, cloves, and anise. Sweetness was provided by Old World raisins and sugar, and Old World garlic made it pungent. And even though it contains a New World legume, peanuts, their use as a thickener is a technique that goes back to the ground almond thickeners Europeans learned from the Arabs in the Middle Ages.

and hominy stew), oxtail stew, and tripe stew. There are also many Mexican cheeses made from cow's milk, like *queso fresco, panela,* and *ranchero seco* (a dried cheese, as its name says).[10] Desserts, too, were made from Old World foods. Eggs and sugar make *flan,* Spanish custard. Wheat treats include *churros* made of dough like *pâte à choux,* extruded through a machine or a pastry bag into their distinctive long rope shape, then deep-fried and rolled in cinnamon sugar.

New Mexico: The Pueblo Revolt

In what is now the Four Corners area of the United States, where Utah, Colorado, Arizona, and New Mexico come together, native people lived in villages like apartment buildings—in Spanish, *pueblos.* Around the year 1100, about 1,200 people lived in one of these *pueblos,* the five-story, 800-room Pueblo Bonito in northwestern New Mexico. It was the largest apartment building in the world until 1882, when a bigger one was built in New York City. Descendants of the people spread throughout the American Southwest and built pueblos on mesas (flat-topped mountains), many along the upper Rio Grande. Among them were the Zuni and the Hopi—"the peaceful people." Pueblo men irrigated the fields and farmed; the women ground corn and cooked in the large, flat common area, the *plaza;* the adult males retreated to an underground *kiva* for religious and tribal matters. In 1540, a Spanish soldier reported that the people in a typical pueblo were "usually at work." And efficient workers they were, with very clean buildings for grinding corn and preparing food. Three women would prepare corn at one time, each with a *mano* and a *metate,* like an assembly line: "One of them breaks the corn, the next grinds it, and the third grinds it again. . . . A man sits at the door playing on a flute while they grind. They move the stones to the music and sing together."[11] They also ground ripe pods from mesquite trees into meal, added water, and made sun-dried crackers.

But the Spaniards were looking for gold, and the pueblo people were not Christian. The Spanish soldiers ignored the line of sacred cornmeal the people laid out on the ground as their boundary; took whatever they wanted from them; looked for gold and got angry when they found only beans, squash, tortillas, and turkeys, but took them anyway; told the people if they surrendered they would not be harmed, then butchered thousands of them when they did. The Acoma pueblo was burned to the ground. Everyone in the pueblo— male and female—over the age of 12 was sentenced to 20 years of slavery; all men over 25 also had one foot chopped off. Enslaved, the Indians took care of the cattle, sheep, horses, goats, and pigs, and tended the olive groves and the orchards of peach, pear, fig, date, pomegranate, cherry, quince, lemon, and orange trees.

In 1610, the Spanish founded the city of Santa Fe (the name means "holy faith") in what is now New Mexico and forced the Indians to build it. The pueblo people were willing to accept Christianity, but only along with their own religions, so the Spanish hanged them and then raided the sacred *kivas* and destroyed all the religious items, including the *kachinas,* the masked images of the holy spirits who brought rain and taught hunting and farming to humans. Then came drought and tribes of raiders called *apachu nabahu*—"enemies of the cultivated fields"— which sounded like "Apache" and "Navaho" to the Spanish. The raiders stole all the stored food and ran off with the livestock. The Spanish and the Indians tried to survive on boiled or roasted leather and hides. The Spanish and their god could not help the native people. Starvation was widespread, then disease. Finally, on August 10, 1680, all the pueblos revolted at once. They got rid of anything connected with the Spanish, including the food. They killed the priests, demolished the churches, slaughtered the sheep and cattle and pigs, uprooted the orchards, ripped out the grapevines, and turned the horses loose. The horses headed for the Great Plains, where the Kiowa and Comanche, the Sioux and the Cheyenne learned to ride them. The Spaniards were forced out of New

Mexico entirely, south to El Paso. It was a great victory for the native people. But 15 years later, the Spanish returned to stay permanently.

Peru: Lima Beans and New World Wine

Francisco Pizarro was the conquistador who came to Peru in 1532. The nightmare that had occurred with the Aztecs repeated itself for the Inca—the capture and death of the leader, Atahualpa, and the demands for gold. The Inca, too, died in horrifying numbers from European diseases. The Inca regrouped and attacked Pizarro. In 1535, he founded the city of Lima, now the capital, so he could defend himself against Inca warriors. The city eventually gave its name to one of the members of the bean family native to South America.

Between 1540 and 1550, Spain transplanted foodstuffs to Peru: wine grapes, figs, pomegranates, quinces, wheat, barley, citrus. This explosion of Spanish food was subsidized by the crown, which offered a huge prize—two bars of silver—to the first person in each Peruvian town who produced Spanish foods like wine, olive oil, wheat, or barley on a large scale. There was wealth to be made in cultivating the new foods, but getting them to survive and thrive in the New World wasn't always easy. Of the more than 100 olive tree cuttings that one man imported to Peru, only three survived. These were so valuable that he planted them on a walled farm in a valley and had them guarded by "more than 100 blacks and 30 dogs," which were either bribed or distracted, because one of the plants was stolen and showed up far away in Chile, where it produced numerous trees. Three years later, somebody sneaked back to the farm and replanted the original tree in the exact same spot.[12]

From the early 1520s to the late 1550s, vineyards of European grapes were established in Central and South America, on both sides of the Andes. Wild grapes grew in the Americas, but they were unsuitable for wine. How did viticulture spread so quickly? It was the law. Under the *encomienda* system, Spanish settlers in New Spain (Mexico) were given land and Indians to work it, and were required to plant one thousand vines "of the best quality" for every one hundred Indians they owned. Similar laws were passed in other Spanish-owned colonies. Grapevines did not thrive in Mexico because of the climate, but they did in Peru, especially in the south in the Moquegua Valley. There was a ready-made market for wine in Peru, too, because the vineyards were near the silver mines at Potosí and all their enslaved Indian workers. Peruvian wine makers were so successful after they began producing wine in 1551 that Spanish wine makers protested; in 1595 Spain's King Philip II protected

Spanish vintners by restricting grapevine planting in the colonies. Peru had a thriving wine industry until it was heavily damaged in the late 19th century by an epidemic of phylloxera, a yellow louse almost impossible to see with the naked eye, that eats the roots of vinifera grapevines.[13]

Peruvians took to the coconut quickly. The word *coco* is Spanish for "monkey," because they are both round and have brown fur and eyes. Coconut milk is used frequently, replacing water, chicken or beef broth or stock, or tomato sauce or juice in many recipes.

In 1991, food historian Raymond Sokolov wrote: "Peru's traditional dishes . . . comprise the last great cuisine undiscovered by a world gone mad for new tastes." However, he conceded that "roast or stewed guinea pig has no future in the non-Andean world." And probably neither does roasted llama heart on a stick.[14]

Argentina: Gauchos and Beef

European horses running wild on the *pampas*—the prairies—of Argentina reproduced to the point that it took a day for a herd to pass by. Horses preceded humans into the flat plains of the area around what is now the capital, Buenos Aires, because permanent settlers in 1580 found huge wild herds already there. The Spanish brought their cattle, the ancestors of the Texas longhorns, and those thrived, too. Herds doubled nearly every 15 months.[15] Soon, beef was plentiful and cheap. As historian Alfred Crosby says, "There were probably more cattle in the New World in the 17th century than any other type of vertebrate immigrant."[16] Beef provided food for the enslaved Indians working in the mines. But a more important use was for fat—tallow— to make candles, especially to light the mines. Hides, too, were more important uses of cattle than food. They were tanned and turned into armor and vessels of all kinds, from trunks to drinking cups.

A beef cuisine grew in Argentina, especially using a technique learned from Caribbean natives, the barbecue. What Americans refer to as barbecuing, as in the backyard barbecue, usually means grilling, and is done quickly. True barbecue is pit roasting—originally, digging a pit or providing some kind of enclosure—and takes hours so the meat can attain a smooth texture and smoky taste. Argentine barbecue is basted with brine. Barbecue sauce is the vinegar-based *chimichurri*.[17] Modern Argentine marinades and salsas are often based on reductions of Argentine wines.[18]

Another classic Argentine dish is *empanadas,* roughly translated as "stuffed turnovers." They, too, would not have been possible without Old World foods. The dough is made from wheat and lard; the filling usually contains meat. In Argentina, the meat can be mixed with New World potatoes, or sometimes fruit, like Old World peaches.[19]

Along with the cattle and beef cuisine, the Spanish transplanted their cowboy culture. Americans didn't create the cowboy—Spain did, in the Middle Ages. He was a *vaquero,* from *vaca,* the Spanish word for cow, and he knew how to use a horse to wrangle a herd, how to handle a branding iron, and what to do on a roundup. Americans did invent the long cattle drives to the railheads (see Chapter 8). In Argentina and Uruguay, the *vaquero* was called a *gaucho.* He brought the rest of his Spanish cowboy vocabulary with him: *bronco, lasso, rodeo.*[20]

Brazil: *Feijoada* and *Farofa*

Brazilian food is heavily influenced by Portugal, its colonial master; and Africa, where a large part of its population originated. Approximately 38 percent of the approximately 10 million slaves shipped from Africa to the New World went to Brazil, mostly to work in the sugarcane fields.[21] Brazil's most famous dish is *feijoada,* an elaborate *moros y cristianos* with much meat. It is a fusion of Old and New World foods and shows the influences of slave cooking in the use of pig parts and in the green leafy vegetable accompaniment. It gets its name from the Portuguese word for "bean"—*feijão.* The beans and their liquid provide the sauce. The traditional accompaniments include rice, kale or collard greens, orange slices, and a hot sauce with lime juice.

Bahia, in eastern Brazil, has a very long Atlantic coastline. Shrimp are used frequently—dried shrimp, shrimp in sauce, fresh shrimp garnish. Sometimes dried ground shrimp, with their intense flavor, are used as a sauce base for a fresh shrimp dish. The signature fat is *dendê*—palm oil, an African import. One of the most famous dishes from Bahia, *vatapá*—chicken in shrimp and almond sauce—combines these ingredients and adds many more from the Old World, including coconut milk; rice flour is the thickener. In *vatapá* and another Bahian dish, *xinxim de galinha*—chicken with shrimp and peanut sauce—the *dendê* oil is added at the end, like a butter enrichment. Hearts of palm are eaten fresh in Brazil, but are brined and canned to be sold commercially. In the United States, they are usually used in salads.

Cassava, a root, was a staple starch in pre-Columbian Brazil. It has many other names: *manioc* and *yuca* in Central and South America, *fufu* in Africa, *farinha* in Portugal. But most Americans know it

INGREDIENTS

FEIJOADA

From *The Book of Latin American Cooking* by Elizabeth Lambert Ortiz, p. 215.

4 pig's ears
1 pig's tail
Salt
3 pig's feet, split
a 1-pound piece of *carne sêca*
a 3-pound smoked beef tongue
a ½ -pound piece of lean bacon
4 cups black beans
a 1-pound piece of lean beef chuck or bottom round
1 pound *linguiça* sausage
1 pound fresh pork sausages
2 tablespoons lard or vegetable oil
2 onions, finely chopped
2 cloves garlic, minced
2 tomatoes, peeled, seeded, and chopped
1 fresh hot pepper, seeded and minced, or 1/8 teaspoon Tabasco (optional)
Salt, freshly ground pepper

only as tapioca, which we make into a sweet pudding, often for children and invalids. In Brazil, cassava meal is *farofa,* grains the color of sand and the consistency of coarse talcum powder, toasted in *dendê* and sprinkled over the top of food as a garnish.

A fruit native to northeast Brazil is the cashew (*Anacardim occidentale*), one of the edible members of the poison ivy family (the others are pistachios and mangos). The cashew fruit grows on trees. It is approximately the shape of a Hachiya persimmon, but yellow, with the comma-shaped cashew nut hanging from the bottom. The fruit can be sweetened and preserved or processed and used for juice. Cashew nuts never appear in their shell in a bowl of mixed nuts, like almonds, walnuts, and pecans, because they are doubly protected with a corrosive substance sandwiched between two layers of shell. Human nutcrackers can't get the shell off, but the big beaks of parrots can. So can

115

roasting.[22] The Portuguese were responsible for spreading the cashew from Brazil to their colonies in the East Indies. It also thrives in India.

Plantains (*plátanos*) are also found throughout the Southern Hemisphere and the Caribbean. They are in the banana family, but unlike bananas, they have to be cooked to be eaten. They are usually boiled or fried, or both, and served as a sweet, starchy side dish.

One foodstuff that Europeans invented and that Brazilians took to right away is rum. Brazilians are magicians with alcoholic beverages. Brazilian rum, called *cachaça,* is used to make a cocktail called a *batida*. It is mixed with lime juice and sugar, or coconut milk, or the juice of passion fruit, pineapple, and so on.[23] The history of rum begins with the history of sugar.

The Caribbean: Sugar

For the most part, European settlers were not very interested in New World foods. They were more interested in seeing if Old World foods with already established markets could be produced more cheaply and in greater quantities in the New World. One food in particular fit the bill. It quickly rose to dominate the international market, created huge fortunes on both sides of the Atlantic, caused millions of people to be enslaved, created new professions, and changed the eating habits of *Homo sapiens* completely. It was sugar, from the sugarcane plant, *Saccharum officinarum*.

The introduction of chocolate, coffee, and tea into Europe caused a rise in the demand for sugar, while the availability of sugar increased the demand for chocolate, coffee, and tea. A sugar spiral developed: as sugar became more plentiful, its price dropped; as its price dropped, it became more available to more people. What had been a medicine for the rich in the Middle Ages was a food staple for even the poor by the middle of the 18th century.

Sugar growing, harvesting, and processing was extremely labor-intensive, and the labor was slaves from Africa. Boiling the sugar down to crystallize it was particularly grueling work. Slaves worked in shifts that could last all day and all night; they got Sunday off. They had to stand barefoot on stone floors for the entire shift, which was painful. Tired slaves lost fingers as they fed the cane through the rollers on the grinding machines; "a hatchet was kept in readiness to sever the arm."[24] The majority of the slaves taken from Africa and transported to the Americas—40 percent—went to the Caribbean sugar islands.[25] Life was so harsh that the slaves often died within four years, so a new supply was constantly needed.

SUGAR CHRONOLOGY	
1319	First recorded direct shipment of sugar arrives in England[26]
1493	Columbus introduces sugarcane on his second trip to the Caribbean
1493–1625	Spain dominates the Caribbean and sugar production
1500	Portuguese island of Madeira is world's largest producer of sugar[27]
1544	England begins refining sugar, taking over the industry from the Low Countries, especially Antwerp, Belgium[28]
1585	London is the center of European sugar refining[29]
1588	England defeats the Spanish Armada, allowing England to colonize in the Americas
1619	First Africans arrive in Jamestown, Virginia; attempts to grow sugar fail
1625	Europe gets most of its sugar from Portugal (Brazil); first British settlement in Caribbean at St. Kitts
1650	Lemonade invented in Paris because of drop in sugar price[30]
1650–1850	England, France, Denmark, Netherlands engaged in Caribbean sugar production[31]
1655	British invade Jamaica[32]
1660	British sugar imports exceed all other colonial produce *combined*[33]
1701–1810[34]	252,000 African slaves to Barbados 662,400 African slaves to Jamaica
1733	British Parliament passes Molasses Act to prevent North American colonies from trading with French West Indies
1750	In England, sugar is common even among the poor[35]
1764	British Parliament passes Sugar Act to raise revenue to keep troops in North American colonies after French and Indian War
1791	Successful slave revolt on Haiti (St. Domingue) halts sugar production
1813	First sugar beet refinery, in Passy, France, after Napoleon orders cultivation of the sugar beet to make France self-sufficient
1838	England ends slavery[36]
1848	France ends slavery[37]
1876	Slavery ends in Puerto Rico[38]
1884	Slavery ends in Cuba[39]

Slaves on the plantations had to eat, too. Their food had to be imported because sugar was grown on all available land. The mainstay of the slave diet was salted beef until the British settled North America; then low-grade salted, dried cod was used. In the 18th century, England decided that breadfruit from Tahiti would be a cheap food for its slaves on Jamaica. A relative of mulberry and jackfruit, the melon-sized starchy breadfruit grows on trees and to some tastes like Yorkshire pudding or mashed potatoes. But the crew of the ship carrying the breadfruit, the *Bounty,* mutinied after Captain Bligh withheld their grog ration, accused them of pilfering from his personal coconut stash, and cut their food rations in half. Set adrift in a small boat, Bligh eventually reached land, was given another ship, and got the breadfruit to Jamaica, only to discover that the slaves didn't like it. However, it grew well there and still does. It is valued in some countries as feed for livestock, in Trinidad as human food, and in Hawaii as a substitute for taro in poi.[40]

The Caribbean: Rum

One of the by-products of sugar processing resulted in a new alcoholic beverage. The 16th century was the beginning of what historian David T. Courtwright calls "the psychoactive revolution," the intercontinental traffic in drugs, including sugar and caffeine, that characterizes the modern world. Rum first appeared in the 1640s in the Caribbean. Since sugar production was no longer under the control of Muslims, who forbade alcohol, nothing stood in the way of creating a new type of alcohol from sugar or its by-products. In the hands of the Protestant British, sugar became rum.

There are two different ways of making rum. One, agricultural rum, is made from the fresh-pressed juice of the sugarcane stalk. The other is made from molasses. In both cases, yeast is added to the liquid, which is allowed to ferment, usually for 24 to 48 hours. It is then distilled and aged in oak barrels that formerly held whiskey or bourbon. Most rums are blended after they have aged, but some are blended first, then aged together. It is the aging process in the oak that produces rum's rich brown color. A rum must age for at least three years to be called *vieux* (old).

Rum was first distilled on the island of Barbados, where the Mount Gay label has been in existence for more than three hundred years. The tiny British colony produced more wealth for England than its tobacco-growing colonies of Virginia and Maryland put together. The River Antoine distillery on Grenada, which makes Rivers Rum, still doesn't use electricity. Water powers the wheel that crushes the cane; *bagasse,* the solid crushed cane left after the juice is extracted, is burned to fuel the still. Today, Demerara, a county in Guyana, is the "largest supplier of bulk rum from the Caribbean."[41]

The Caribbean: Slavery—the Notorious Middle Passage

The stench coming from the ship was overwhelming: human excrement, urine, vomit, blood, sweat, and misery. Just as early explorers could smell the blooming flowers of America a hundred miles out to sea, later sailors could smell slave ships a hundred miles away. This was the notorious Middle Passage, the middle part of the triangle trade, the trip from West Africa to the Western Hemisphere. No one wanted to be downwind of a slave ship.

The Caribbean was one of the points on what historians call the "triangle trade": sugar and rum from the Caribbean to Europe (later, New England), goods from Europe to Africa, slaves from Africa to the Caribbean. Portugal had its own triangle trade, which sold "third-grade tobacco soaked in molasses" for slaves in Africa, shipped them to Brazil, then brought the good tobacco to the European markets.[42] On all of these trade routes, the Middle Passage was the same horror.

Why slavery? Why not some other form of labor? Native Americans weren't suitable because they died—in some cases became extinct—from European diseases. Africans from the west coast of Africa were kidnapped by slave traders or African tribal enemies who had guns and nets. One of the first fears of those captured was that they were going to be eaten by the strange creatures that had captured them, "those white men with horrible looks, red faces, and long hair."[43] Sometimes the captives were forced to drink alcohol, which further added to the bizarreness of the experience. Then they were chained two by two and forced to get on the ship. Below is a drawing of how the slaves were packed.

The hold, the part of the ship below the deck, was five or six feet high at the most. The male slaves were laid on the floor, with another layer on a shelf above them. If the hold was six feet deep, there were two rows of shelves. Each adult male slave was allowed a space that was, *at maximum*, six feet long and 16 inches wide. If a man was taller than six feet, he would have to spend the entire voyage with his knees bent; if his shoulders were wider than 16 inches, he would have to spend the voyage lying on his side. Sitting upright was impossible because of the shelf above him. Slaves were sick with vomiting and a violent diarrhea known as the "bloody flux." If they were on the top shelf, it dripped down on those below.

A slave ship.
Courtesy National Archives and Research

Women were not chained so that the sailors could have unlimited access to them. Rape was a standard event for African women on slave ships. But allowing the women to roam freely on the ship backfired. They knew who was drunk on duty and who was passed out; they could find out where the keys to the locked doors and the chains were kept, and sometimes they got them. Women became very important in shipboard slave revolts. The most famous revolt was on the *Amistad* in 1839; director Steven Spielberg made a film about it in 1997. For many years, historians assumed that the revolt on the *Amistad* was a rare event, but after the 1960s, when historians were not just white men but African-Americans, women, and other minorities, their research revealed that mutinies on slave ships were not rare, but common. After all, the slaves had nothing to lose. Unfortunately, the slave revolt on the *Amistad* was rare in its success.

One of the additional ordeals for the captives on the slave ships was the cheap-as-possible food. They despised the horse beans in slimy sauce they got, and threw it around. Sometimes they were fed their native foods, like yams, rice, and palm oil. Some tried to commit suicide by refusing to eat at all. But slaves that weren't eating were valuable cargo in danger of being lost. If whipping or beating didn't get them to eat, forcing their jaws open with a metal device that worked like a car jack usually did. On the other hand, if the voyage took longer than expected and supplies of food or water were running low, slaves were thrown overboard. Ship owners didn't care if part of the cargo was lost this way; it was a business expense and they were insured.[44] The slave trade was very lucrative, producing profits of more than 100 percent.

NEW WORLD TO OLD

Spanish, Portuguese, and British transplants of foods, animals, and people had an immediate impact on their colonies in the New World. Using the Western Hemisphere as a giant plantation for the Eastern Hemisphere made familiar Old World foods more available to people in the Old World. So there was little incentive for Europeans to experiment with New World foods.

"It being new, I was doubtful whether it might not do me hurt."[45] So wrote British writer Samuel Pepys in his diary on March 9, 1669. He was talking about a new beverage made from an Asian fruit that had just reached Europe. He thought it "a very fine drink," but still, he was worried about that glass of orange juice. In the years after Columbus's voyages, every country in the world was bombarded with new food-

POTATO CHRONOLOGY

DATE	PLACE	EVENT
1537	Colombia	Spanish conquistadors eat potatoes for the first time[46]
1550s	Spain	Returning conquistadors introduce potato to the population[47]
1586	England	Chef to Queen Elizabeth I serves potatoes: cook leaves, throws potatoes away[48]
1590	Italy	Pope gives potatoes to botanist Clusius, who paints first pictures of potato[49]
1600	France	Potatoes introduced from Switzerland[50]
1615	India	Potatoes introduced (possibly)[51]
1651	Germany	Government forces people to cultivate potatoes[52]
1660–1688	Ireland	Potato cultivation spreads rapidly; population rises from 500,000 to 1.5 million[53]
1662	England	Britain's Royal Society sponsors cultivation of potatoes[54]
1672–1725	Russia	Czar Peter the Great introduces the potato to the population[55]
1719	North America	New Hampshire—Scotch-Irish settlers bring first potatoes to North America from Europe[56]
1748	Besançon, France	Parliament declares potatoes cause leprosy, forbids growing them[57]
1760–1840	Ireland	Population increases 600 percent, from 1.5 million to 9 million, subsists primarily on potatoes[58]
1756–1763	Poland	Potatoes reach Poland during Seven Years' War[59]
1763	France	Army pharmacist Parmentier promotes potatoes after eating them while a prisoner in Germany during Seven Years' War[60]
1764	Sweden	Government promotes potato growing[61]
1770	Australasia	Captain Cook introduces potato to the population[62]
1780s	France	King Louis XVI grows potatoes in Neuilly. Parmentier sends guards to make potatoes seem valuable; peasants steal the potatoes and plant them, which was Parmentier's goal.
1793	France	*La cuisine républicaine,* first French cookbook written by a woman, Mme. Méridot, is all about potatoes[63]
1835	France	Carême includes recipe for English-style potatoes—mashed—in *The Art of French Cooking*[64]
1830	Belgium	Potato fungus—*Phytophthora infestans*—originates[65]
1837	France	Soufflé potatoes *(pommes de terre soufflées)* created by accident when desperate chef fries potato slices twice[66]
1845	Ireland	Potato fungus wipes out crops.[67] One million Irish die; others leave.
1986	World	The potato is one of the four most important food crops; a staple for 200 million people[68]

stuffs and new cuisines. But cross-cultural change is difficult; convincing people to eat strange foods from other parts of the world is not always easy. People in Europe hadn't been sitting around for centuries wishing they had a tomato or hoping a pumpkin would appear. It took about 300 years for most of the New World foods to be accepted in Europe. Some, such as maize, still aren't fully accepted as human food. Sometimes strange new things can only be described by connecting them to familiar old ones. So Columbus's son described cocoa beans as special "almonds"; the explorer Coronado wrote about strange "cows" with horns, which were buffalo. In Italy, the tomato became "golden apple," *pomodoro,* because some of the original tomatoes, which are heirlooms now, were yellow. The potato became "earth apple"—*pomme de terre* in French, and *erdapfel* in German. The chart on page 121 shows, briefly, how it spread throughout the world.

Two New World items that did find immediate acceptance in the Old World were turkey and tobacco. Europe, used to eating fowl and accustomed to chicken as a special-occasion centerpiece, was ready for a big, new, festive, good-tasting bird. Soon, turkey replaced heron, swan, peacock, and other birds that were nearly inedible but made magnificent presentations. Tobacco grown in the Chesapeake, the area around the bay in what is now Maryland and Virginia, caught on everywhere it went. Within 100 years of Columbus's first voyage, tobacco could be found even in the far reaches of Siberia.[69] Beans were also readily accepted, perhaps because they resembled pulses like chickpeas and lentils. By the middle of the 16th century, they appeared in botanical books, and the kidney bean was known throughout Europe as the "French bean."

Spain: Chocolate and *Paella*

Chocolate probably would have caught on sooner in Europe, but the Spanish nobility considered it a powerful aphrodisiac—the Viagra of the 16th century—and kept the recipe secret by locking it up in a monastery for almost a century. But something so good couldn't be kept under wraps for long; others eventually figured out the recipe and a craze was born. Chocolate was used in different ways in different European countries. Like the Aztecs, the Spanish consumed chocolate as a beverage, but sweetened it with sugar. The French confined it to dessert.

The Spanish immediately developed a liking for the wild chile— the chiltepin or bird pepper (*Capsicum annuum* var. *aviculare*)—which became known throughout Europe as the "Spanish pepper." It was so highly regarded that they kept it whole in salt cellars. Then each diner took out as much as he wanted and crumbled it into his food.

The traditional dish of Spain is *paella valenciana,* and it is a mixture of Old and New World foods. *Paella* refers to the pan in which it is cooked; *valenciana* refers to the region of Spain where it originated. The classic ingredients are Old World rice, several kinds of meat, olive oil, and saffron, and New World green beans, tomato, and paprika.

Don Quixote: The Peasant Quest for Food

That was the how the upper classes ate. The poor were still hungry. Class consciousness, often shown through food, underlies everything in *Don Quixote,* one of Spain's most famous literary works, written in 1602 by Miguel de Cervantes. This satirical novel, which was made into a Broadway musical and movie, *The Man of La Mancha,* is about Don Quixote, a man who still believes in knighthood and sets out on his horse to slay dragons (except that they are windmills) and rescue the fair lady (who is really a woman of low repute). He has a trusty sidekick, Sancho Panza. These two—the noble-hearted cowboy and his pudgy comic relief sidekick, who, like the court jester, is more philosopher than fool—set the standard for cowboy stories and movies for centuries to come. They are also two halves of the human condition. Quixote is spiritual, a dreamer. Panza—his name means "potbelly"—is the realist who lives in the physical world.

Don Quixote made a Spanish food famous. The vegetable and meat stew *olla podrida*—literally, "rotten pot"—appears six times. It is mentioned in the second sentence of the book, to show how poor Quixote is and how expensive food is: "An olla of rather more beef than mutton, a salad on most nights, scraps on Saturdays, lentils on Fridays, and a pigeon or so extra on Sundays, made away with three-quarters of his income."[70] This is a difficult life for a man who knows that "veal . . . is better than beef . . . kid . . . is better than goat."[71]

Most of the time Quixote and Sancho have only bread and water to eat. If they are lucky they might get a bit of cheese, an onion, grapes, acorns, or medlars—fruit originally from Persia that, even ripe, is inedible until it is packed in wet bran or sawdust and ferments internally.[72] A sample of the food at inns explains why upper-class people traveled with their own cooking staffs. One innkeeper tells Sancho, "All I have is a couple of cow-heels like calves' feet, or a couple of calves' feet like cowheels; they are boiled with chick-peas, onions, and bacon."[73] At another, on a Friday, Quixote gets stockfish and "a piece of bread as black and mouldy as his own armour."[74] At a low point, Don Quixote says, "I have a mind to let myself die of hunger, the cruelest death of all deaths." But Sancho loves food and life and says, "I'll stretch out my life by eating."[75]

From the point of view of these starving people, upper-class eating habits and the theory of humors are ridiculous. Quixote says Sancho is such a delicate eater that "he eats grapes, and even pomegranate pips [seeds], with a fork."[76] A starving Sancho sits down to a feast only to have each dish yanked away from him by a Hippocrates-quoting physician:

> I ordered that plate of fruit to be removed as being too moist, and that other dish I ordered to be removed as being too hot and containing many spices that stimulate thirst . . . do not eat of those stewed rabbits there, because it is a furry kind of food; if that veal were not roasted and served with pickles, you might try it; but it is out of the question.

Sancho points out the obvious—"to deny me food is the way to take my life instead of prolonging it"—and asks for some *olla podrida,* "and the rottener they are the better they smell." When the physician says it is not nourishing, fit only for students and peasants, and that a gentlemen should eat "a hundred or so of wafer cakes and a few thin slices of conserve of quinces," Sancho threatens to kill him.[77]

When Sancho finally gets a major meal to feed his *panza,* it is a starving peasant's food fantasy. The wedding of the wealthy Camacho is a utopian exaggeration, the Spanish equivalent of the Italian Bengodi, where the vines drip sausages (see Chapter 4). The first thing Sancho sees is

> a whole ox spitted on a whole elm tree [stuffed with a dozen suckling pigs] . . . and six stewpots . . . [which] swallowed up whole sheep. . . . Countless . . . hares ready skinned and the plucked fowls . . . numberless the wildfowl and game of various sorts suspended from the branches that the air might keep them cool. Sancho counted more than sixty wine skins of over six gallons each. . . . There were . . . piles of the whitest bread . . . a wall made of cheeses . . . two cauldrons full of oil . . . for cooking fritters, which when fried were taken out with two mighty shovels, and plunged into another cauldron of prepared honey that stood close by. Of cooks and cook-maids there were over fifty.

There are trunks full of spices, too. When Sancho begs to dunk a bit of bread into one of the pots, a cook gladly skims three hens and two geese off the top, to hold him until dinnertime.[78]

Sancho is able to eat so well here because Camacho is not a member of the upper class with all of its food rules; he is a farmer who has made good and who appreciates food. It is clear that what the peasants want is meat, and the order of food is clear, too, with chickens and geese still the most expensive and desirable. New World foods are entirely absent.

Mercantilism and the Spanish Armada

Sugar, wine, and other foodstuffs played a large part in an economic system called mercantilism. This was based on a country having a favorable balance of trade—more money coming into the treasury than going out. Economically, it was the end of feudalism and the beginning of capitalism, the accumulation of private wealth. Colonies were an important way to achieve this. They provided the home country with cheap raw materials that the home country then sold to other countries at a higher price or transformed into finished goods like textiles and sold back to the colony. So in the 16th century, hundreds of huge cargo ships, Spanish galleons, sailed across the Atlantic Ocean loaded with sugar, wines, gold, and silver. The heavily laden, slow-moving galleons were tempting targets and an easy way for other countries to accumulate wealth without spending much money. There were some pirates, renegades who belonged to no country, but most of the pirates were in the service of Spain's enemies—other European countries, especially England. Any country that could hijack or smuggle any valuable commodity did. They were all pirates in the Caribbean.

The piracy reached an intolerable level when sugar cost less in England than it did in Spain or even in the Caribbean. King Philip II of Spain complained repeatedly to England's Queen Elizabeth I, who condemned pirates like Francis Drake in public but rewarded them in private. In addition, Catholic Spain hated Protestant England and its Protestant shipbuilding ally, the Netherlands, which Spain had owned until the Dutch revolted. Spain began building a huge armed fleet, an armada, to attack England. The pope promised Spain a huge cash bonus when it invaded England and brought it back to the Catholic Church. In July 1588, the Spanish Armada arrived off the coast of England. But the British won. The decisive factor wasn't men or ships; it was nature. A violent wind came up and scattered the Spanish fleet. The British claimed that "the Protestant wind" showed that their god was more powerful than Spain's. The British victory broke the Spanish stranglehold on sailing in the Atlantic Ocean and allowed the British to do something they had wanted to do for a long time: colonize in North America.

$\mathcal{S}$IXTH $\mathcal{C}$OURSE

Thanksgiving, *Hutsepot,* and *Haute Cuisine:* 17th-Century America, the Netherlands, Russia, France

COLONIAL AMERICA

The Chesapeake: The Starving Time

England's colonies in North America did not get off to a good start. After one, Roanoke, completely disappeared (historians still don't know what happened to it), British settlers came to Chesapeake Bay in 1607. They named the colony Virginia in honor of Elizabeth I, the Virgin Queen; they called the capital Jamestown after King James; and they expected to get rich quick—except that the natives refused to be their slaves. In the winter of 1609–10, when not enough food had been grown, harvested, or preserved, almost all five hundred colonists died during what became known as "the starving time." Captain John Smith later wrote what he had heard about how the colonists were reduced to eating nuts, berries, acorns, horsehide, and worse:

> And one amongst the rest did kill his wife, powdered [salted] her, and had eaten part of her before it was known, for which he was executed, as he well deserved. Now whether she was better roasted, boiled, or carbonadoed [broiled], I know not; but of such a dish as powdered wife I never heard of.[1]

It was not the last time cannibalism would be resorted to in America.

Later Virginians wanted to grow a profitable crop; they tried sugar but the climate was too cold. They settled on tobacco. Soon tobacco was bringing in so much money that people planted it on any available land—they ripped up their gardens, even grew it between graves. But who would hoe and harvest these thousands of acres of tobacco? The Native Americans who didn't die of Old World diseases refused to do it. African slaves were too expensive, although some arrived in 1619. England had the perfect labor force: a surplus of poor, desperate young men in their late teens and early twenties. They signed an indenture—a contract—giving them a free trip to America and free room and board in exchange for four to six years of work. Then they were supposed to get their freedom, tools, corn, and land of their own—something they had zero chance of getting in England. The person who hired the indentured servant and paid for his trip received free labor and fifty acres of land. It was a sweetheart deal all around. Except . . .

Most of these young men didn't live four years after they got to America. They died from dysentery, typhoid, malaria. The ones who did live found that there was only one woman for every six men. And soon the best land was in huge plantations owned by a few wealthy men who also had all the political power. In 1676, when former indentured servants couldn't get land, women, or the vote, they went on a rampage. Bacon's Rebellion ended with Jamestown burned and more than 20 former indentured servants hanged. Planters wanted a labor force they could control, not these Englishmen who used violence to get their rights. In 1698, when England ended the Royal African Company's monopoly on the slave trade, anyone with a ship could get into the slave trade. With competition, the price of slaves dropped. Now it was affordable to own Africans and profitable to sell them.

The Carolinas and Rice

At about the same time, the English established a colony south of Virginia—Carolina, named after King Charles II. Many of the settlers were from Barbados. They intended to grow food for the Caribbean sugar plantations and to export more expensive items, but after failing at wine, olive oil, and silk, they decided on rice as their staple crop. Rice requires skilled labor; Africans had this skill. They were also immune to malaria, and weren't Christian, so according to the Christian world at that time, they could be enslaved for the rest of their lives. The settlers also imported the Barbados slave code, with punishments that escalated from whipping to facial mutilation and sometimes death, which the code said was the slave's fault for forcing his master to discipline him. Charleston, South Carolina, became the primary port through which slaves entered the United States. By 1710, black slaves outnumbered white settlers in the coastal regions of the area that became South Carolina.

In spite of the conditions under which the slaves were brought to America, some of their African cuisine and culture survived. This influenced how cooking developed in the American South, since they were the cooks. Along with their knowledge of rice cultivation, cooking, and storage, they brought yams, okra, watermelon, and their love of fried food. They also brought back foodstuffs that had been taken from the New World to Africa, like the chile pepper and the peanut, and their word for it—*goober*. They brought the banjo and the drum and the music that would become jazz.

New England: "Almost Beyond Believing"[2]

In 1620, Pilgrims—Protestants who wanted to be allowed to worship without being persecuted—landed at Plymouth, Massachusetts. Before they went ashore, the men on the ship entered into an agreement. The Mayflower Compact was the first constitution in America. Only one paragraph long, it sets forth an important principle: that all would be equal and work together as a community.

The Pilgrims, and the Puritans who settled the Massachusetts Bay Colony in Boston ten years later, had their work cut out for them. These were people used to living in towns. They didn't know how to hunt or fish or farm. But they didn't like many of the strange plants and animals in North America anyway—those huge quahog clams, the slimy steamers. And the codfish and lobsters were bigger than they were, sometimes six feet long. They wouldn't eat them at first, even after the Indians showed them how. But with the help of the native tribes, the Pilgrims survived their first year and had a celebration.

Thanksgiving Foods

"The turkey is certainly one of the most delightful presents which the New World has made to the Old."

—Brillat-Savarin[3]

FOOD FABLE

⇒ SQUANTO AND FISH FERTILIZER ⇐

"Contrary to what American myth has long held, it is quite unlikely that alewives or other fish were uses as fertilizer in Indian fields, notwithstanding the legendary role of the Pilgrims' friend Squanto in teaching colonists this practice. Squanto probably learned the technique while being held captive in Europe, and if any Indians used it in New England, they did so in an extremely limited area. Having no easy way to transport large amounts of fish from river to field, and preferring quite sensibly to avoid such back-breaking work, Indians simply abandoned their fields when the soil lost its fertility. . . . Fertilizing fields with fish, as the English eventually did, seemed to Indians a wholly unnecessary labor."[4]

Most of the foods Americans eat at Thanksgiving dinner now are native to the Americas: turkey, cranberry sauce, mashed potatoes, sweet potatoes, corn-bread stuffing, pumpkin pie. In French the word for turkey is *dinde,* short for *poulet d'inde,* which means "chicken from India," because the French, like other Europeans, thought the turkey was from the Indies. Geese, ducks, and other wild fowl were abundant only during certain seasons in the New World, but turkeys don't migrate, so they were available all year. And they had an instinct that helped humans: when one turkey was shot, the others froze in place. It was easy to kill a dozen turkeys in a morning. Nobody ever called anybody a turkey and meant it as a compliment.

Cranberries and blueberries, both members of the heather family and both native to New England, were more than food in sauce and pies. Mashed and mixed with sour milk, they were used as paint. That is why the colors most often associated with colonial American buildings are muted cranberry and milky purple-gray.

Although pumpkin was widely used in the colonies, recipes for pumpkin pie didn't appear in print until the first American cookbook, written by Amelia Simmons in 1796. She called it "pompkin" and gave two different versions. Both had pumpkin, ginger, and eggs, but one used cream and sugar, the other milk and molasses. One used the Old World spices mace and nutmeg, the other New World allspice.[5]

The Codfish

The staple "crop" in the Massachusetts Bay Colony was the codfish, *Gadus morhua.* What sugar was to the Caribbean and tobacco was to the

$\mathscr{H}$OLIDAY $\mathscr{H}$ISTORY

» THANKSGIVING «

The first Thanksgiving was in 1621. Fifty-one Pilgrim men, women, and children hosted ninety men of the Wampanoag tribe and their chief, Massasoit. It was in the fall, to celebrate the good harvest of corn (wheat and barley weren't as successful). The celebration lasted three days. There were "wild fowl" and five deer.

The idea of a national day of thanks was raised in the late 1700s with the first president, George Washington, who proposed November 26 as the date. Nothing came of it until the 1850s, when magazine journalist Sarah Josepha Hale rallied the women of America to pressure the president for a national holiday. In 1863, the third year of the Civil War, President Lincoln declared that the last Thursday in November should be a day of giving thanks. It was the same year that Lincoln issued the Emancipation Proclamation freeing the slaves, and made his speech at the battlefield in Gettysburg, Pennsylvania, in which he said these famous words: "that government of the people, by the people, for the people, shall not perish from the earth."

In 1939, President Franklin D. Roosevelt wanted to extend the Christmas shopping season to give the economy a boost and help it recover from the depression. He moved Thanksgiving one week earlier. Congress objected. The president and Congress did a tug-of-war over the date until 1941, when it was settled: Thanksgiving is the fourth Thursday in November.

In 1970, Wampanoag leader Wampsutta (Anglo name: Frank James) was invited to speak at the Thanksgiving celebration at Plymouth, Massachusetts. When word got out that his speech was about the oppression of Native Americans, the invitation was revoked. He gave his speech anyway, in front of the statue of Massasoit, overlooking the replica of the *Mayflower.* That was the first Native American National Day of Mourning for the culture, the religion, and the lives and lands of their ancestors.

(To find out more about Thanksgiving, log onto www.plimoth.org.)

Chesapeake, cod was to Massachusetts. There were millions off the coast, north to Newfoundland and Labrador. Once it was salted and dried, cod was stiff as a board and could be stacked and shipped like lumber. It was also almost 80 percent protein. In this form it made its way to Europe: *bacalà* in Italy, *bacalao* in Spain, *bacalhau* in Portugal. According to historian Mark Kurlansky, by the middle of the 16th century, "60 percent of all fish eaten in Europe was cod."[6] It was the perfect food for Lent. The best grade was sent to Spain; the worst fed the slaves in the West Indies.[7] It could also be bartered for slaves in Africa. Shipbuilders got rich because of cod, too. The cod was so important to the economy of Massachusetts that a large carved wooden cod hangs in the statehouse in Boston. See page 132 for an example of what it looks like.

The "sacred" cod over the state house door in Boston, Massachusetts.
Courtesy the Commonwealth of Massachusetts Art Commission

Maple Syrup: Tapping the Sap of the Sugar Tree

"Maple Moon" was what Native Americans called the time in the spring when the sap started to flow in the sugar maple tree, *Acer saccharum.* Just as the grapevine was a symbol of resurrection for the ancient Greeks, so the maple was for Native Americans. Flowing sap meant the end of winter and the rebirth of nature. The Iroquois performed a religious ritual, a maple dance, to pray for warm weather and plenty of sap. According to legend, an Iroquois chief pulled his tomahawk out of a tree where he had thrown it the night before and went off to hunt. In the meantime, the weather turned warm and sap oozed into a container left by accident at the base of the tree. On her way to get water for cooking, his wife saw the container of liquid and used that instead; everyone agreed it was much better than water.[8]

Seventeenth-century European writers give Native Americans full credit for knowing how to make maple syrup and sugar, but in the 18th century, Europeans started to claim that they taught the Indians. As historians Helen and Scott Nearing have pointed out, language is on the side of the tribes. All their words for maple syrup translate as "drawn from wood," "sap flows fast," "our own tree," while they called white sugar "French snow"—a clear indication of its origin.[9]

Maple sugar was a primary food in Native American cooking;

among some tribes it was the only condiment. It replaced salt, which they did not like, and it was used to season dried cornmeal porridge, mixed with bear fat as a sauce for roasted venison, sprinkled on boiled fish, and eaten with berries or all by itself, a pound a day.[10] It was reconstituted into a sweet drink that was used in ceremonies, along with tobacco smoked in the peace pipe. Women boiled the sap from maple, walnut, hickory, box elder, butternut, birch, and sycamore trees down to sugar crystals, which was difficult because before Europeans came, they had no metal pots. Their vessels were made of birch bark or gourds which held between one and two gallons and could not be placed directly over fire. Instead, they dropped heated stones into the liquid until it boiled, which involved continuously taking out cool stones and replacing them with hot ones. These small amounts of liquid were then poured into hundred-gallon moose-skin vats. It is not surprising that the Indians began to trade for metal pots and utensils as soon as the Europeans introduced them. Another way to process the syrup was to let it freeze at night, then scrape the ice off the top. This required several nights until just syrup was left. Maple sugar that was to be used for gifts was poured into molds that one European described as shaped like "bear's paws, flowers, stars, small animals, and other figures, just like our gingerbread-bakers at fairs."[11]

The American Culinary Tradition: Pocket Soup and Johnnycake

American cooking developed along two parallel lines. In the South, where slave labor did the kitchen work, cooking could take more time. Labor-intensive cooking, such as barbecue, could be done by slaves. Barbecue needed a great deal of preparation. Either beef or pork had to be properly butchered and marinated. Then the fire had to reach just the right temperature, and the meat had to be added. The fire had to be carefully watched and the temperature maintained. This required a great deal of labor. However, pit cooking developed differently in New England, in the form of the clambake. There, a fire was allowed to burn down in a pit; then clams, lobsters, and corn were buried under wet seaweed and left to steam for several hours. No labor was necessary to prepare the food before or after it was placed in the pit, except to dig it out.

American cooking in the North arose from the middle-class necessity of doing a great deal of work as quickly as possible. They invented shortcuts and new ways to preserve foods. Two examples are pocket soup and johnnycake. Travel was not easy in the colonies. Roads were poor or nonexistent, and there was no guarantee that travelers would be able to find food when they needed it. Sailors, too, appreciated a bit of home. Pocket soup, also known as portable soup, was the solution. This was an early bouillon cube—soup cooked down until it was a condensed gelatinous mass, then cut into small cubes and dried for ten days. Dropped into a cup of water, it reconstituted into soup. Johnnycake or journey cake was a cornmeal cake that would keep without becoming moldy or disintegrating.

Another example of New England fast food was hasty pudding, made famous in the song "Yankee Doodle" (and in the name of a Harvard University club). This was cornmeal—called Indian or "Injun" meal—or rye meal cooked on top of the stove, not baked, so it was ready in half an hour. This is a long time by today's microwave standards, but the baking times for regular cornmeal pudding recipes in *American Cookery* range from one and a half hours to two and a half hours. Sara Josepha Hale's recipes for cornmeal pudding require three to four hours of cooking, even those that are boiled. What makes hasty pudding hasty is that the meal is soaked first and added a bit at a time, and the pudding is boiled and stirred constantly. In this cooking technique, it resembles polenta.

Cobbler, Slump, Grunt, Dumpling, Crumble, and Crisp

Just as regional cooking developed according to the kind of produce and labor available in each area, different areas had different names for the same food. For example, in most of the country, a cobbler is chopped, sweetened fruit with a sweet biscuit dough baked on top. The exception is New England, where it is called a slump, with the further exception of Cape Cod, where it is called a grunt. Other combinations of fruit and dough are a dumpling, pieces of fruit or a whole fruit, like an apple, wrapped in a pastry square and baked. A crumble is a mixture of flour, butter, sugar, and seasonings like cinnamon and nutmeg crumbled over chopped fruit and then baked. A crumble is different from a crisp because a crisp has more butter, which makes the topping . . . crisper. The topping on a crisp sometimes includes oats.

Brown Betty, Sally Lunn, and Anadama

Women, perhaps cooks, have left their names on various foods but not much other information. Brown Betty is a thrifty New England

RECIPE

Buona Forchetta's Anadama Bread

Courtesy of Suzanne Dunaway

1 large or 2 small loaves
2 cups water
1½ teaspoons salt
½ cup stone-ground yellow cornmeal
3 tablespoons melted unsalted butter or olive oil
¼ cup honey or dark molasses
2 tablespoons active dry yeast
½ cup lukewarm water (85° to 95°F)
5 to 6 cups unbleached bread flour

In a large pot, bring the water and salt to a boil over medium-high heat. With a wire whisk, slowly stir the cornmeal into the water, making sure it does not lump. When it has thickened, remove it from the heat and stir in oil or butter and honey or molasses. Transfer to a large mixing bowl and let cool completely.

Dissolve the yeast in the lukewarm water. Stir into the cornmeal mixture. Stir in the flour, a cup or so at a time, mixing well as you go to incorporate it. This will form a firm dough that should not be too dry. When the dough pulls away from the sides of the bowl, stir well a few more times, rub oil on your hands, and transfer the dough to a clean oiled bowl.

Same-day method: Cover the bowl with plastic wrap and let the dough rise in a warm place until doubled in volume, about 1 hour. Proceed with the shaping instructions.

Overnight method: Cover the bowl and refrigerate overnight. The dough will rise in the refrigerator and acquire flavor from the slower yeast action. Remove the dough 3 hours before shaping and let stand, covered, in a warm place. Proceed with shaping instructions.

To shape into loaves: Preheat the oven to 500°F. Oil one seasoned nonstick, oven-proof 9-inch skillet or two 5-inch skillets. Shape the dough into 1 large or 2 small round loaves. Place the loaf or loaves in the oiled pan or pans and let rise for about 40 minutes or until doubled. Brush the tops of the loaves with olive oil, if desired.

To bake loaves: Place the bread in the oven and reduce the oven temperature to 400°F. Bake for about 40 minutes or until nicely browned and loaf sounds hollow when tapped with your finger. Remove the loaf from a pan and cool on a wire rack.

dessert that layers leftover bread with fruit, usually apples, and is baked. It isn't a bread pudding because it lacks eggs to make the custard binder. Sally Lunn is a very light, yeast-risen egg bread. Anadama is supposedly named after Anna, who kept cooking only one thing— a cornmeal and molasses bread—until her husband finally burst out, "Anna, damn her!" Suzanne Dunaway's Buona Forchetta Bakery in southern California makes an updated version of this bread.

"Beer Is a Good Family Drink"[12]

As food historian John Hull Brown points out in *Early American Beverages,* men, women, and children in colonial America drank alcoholic beverages. Beer, familiar from England, was the earliest drink in the colonies. Women were the brewers; they made beer from nearly anything that grew. They made vegetable beers from corn, tomatoes, potatoes, turnips, pumpkins, and Jerusalem artichokes. They made tree beers from the bark of birch, spruce, and sassafras, and from maple sap. Fruit-based beers were brewed from persimmons, lemons, and raisins. There were herb beers using wintergreen, and spice beers made of ginger, allspice, and cinnamon. Even flowers became beer: rose beer. There was molasses beer. They made their ale two barrels at a time, from 8 or 9 bushels of malt, 12 pounds of hops, 5 quarts of yeast, and 72 gallons of water.[13] And, of course, just as in ancient Egypt, once they had beer they had leavening for bread, either from the beer itself or from the "leavins"—the dregs.

They also distilled "spirituous waters" and cordials using spices from the Middle East like coriander, cardamom, and anise seed, and the stones of apricots, peaches, and cherries.[14] Wine was made from ginger, currants, and cherries, but sweet wines, sack, and Madeira were imported. Later, the Scots-Irish brewed whiskey from corn, barley, or oats. Colonial Americans drank hard cider distilled from apples, peachy made from peaches, and perry made from pears. The colonists liked to dress up their alcoholic beverages with cream, sugar, eggs, mace, and nutmeg—like eggnog.

"Kill-Devil" Rum, Stonewall, Bogus, and Flip

Rum, distilled in New England after 1670, was cheap and available. It was called by a variety of names—rhum, rumbullion, rumbooze—and used in a variety of mixtures: stonewall, which was cider and rum; bogus, which was unsweetened beer and rum; blackstrap, made with molasses and rum; and flip, a popular drink that appears at least as far back as 1690 in New England. Here's one way to make it.

RECIPE

*F*LIP

"An earthen pitcher or huge pewter mug . . . would be filled about two-thirds with strong beer to which would be added molasses, sugar, or dried pumpkin for sweetening, and New England rum, about a gill, for flavor. The bitter, burnt taste was gotten by plunging a red-hot loggerhead, an iron poker-shaped stirrer, into the flip making it bubble and foam."[15]

Punch, with its five ingredients of tea, arrack, sugar, lemons, and water, arrived from India via the British East India Company. New Englanders added a sixth ingredient, and rum punch was born. Life was good to New Englanders; they could expect to live ten years longer than if they had stayed in old England. But since they attributed their longer life to drinking alcohol, it became difficult to enforce laws restricting its intake.[16]

Life was longer, but food preparation was still difficult and time-consuming. Before the modern stove with a cooktop and an oven was invented in the mid-19th century, most cooking was done with the quadriceps, because it involved long hours of squatting to stir foods in front of the open hearth. A stool or rocking chair could be pulled up next to the fire, but it still involved long hours next to open flames, as the picture on the following page shows.

On wealthy southern plantations, meats were hung in a separate smokehouse, as the picture on the following page shows.

To see more of a southern plantation, log onto www.cwf.org.

THE GOLDEN AGE OF THE NETHERLANDS

Between England's colonies in New England and the Chesapeake was the Dutch colony of New Netherland. The Dutch knew that they would have to entice people from other countries to settle New Netherland, because the Dutch people, prosperous and free to prac-

Cooking in Colonial Williamsburg.
Courtesy Colonial Williamsburg Foundation

Hog butchering and curing.
Courtesy Colonial Williamsburg Foundation

tice the religion of their choice, had no reason to leave their own country. The Dutch settlers who did go to New Netherland found oak trees that grew seventy feet high and made logs that burned hot and bright for hours. As in the Netherlands, bread was a staple in New Netherland, but it was baked at home. The Netherlands was urbanized, so commercial bakers made bread, but parts of the colony were very sparsely populated, so it was necessary for people to have their own brick ovens built into the wall next to the fireplace. American ingredients like corn and pumpkin found their way into standard Dutch recipes like pancakes. Bread was more than food in the Dutch colony; it was a trade item so much sought after by the Native Americans—especially white breads and sweet cakes—that by 1649 there were laws against making bread to trade with the Indians.[17] New Netherland was just a small part of a vast Dutch empire.

The Dutch replaced the Italians—the Medicis of Florence and the Venetians—as the international bankers, and the world banking center moved to the Netherlands. The Dutch dominated or controlled the world shipping trade in spices, sugar, coffee, slaves, precious gems, and grain. The Dutch fleet of 10,000 ships also delivered oil, wine, and salt from Portugal, Spain, and France to northern Europe, and gold and silver from New World mines to Old World vaults. One of the reasons the Netherlands rose to power was that it was unique—a unified, religiously tolerant republic. During the 16th century, while the European monarchies fought with the Church and within their own countries over religion (and in some places killed a greater percentage of the population than the Black Death had), the Netherlands was open for business. Many of the Jews who had been driven out of Spain by the Inquisition went north to the hospitable Protestant Netherlands and contributed their knowledge of banking and business to an already flourishing economy. The stock exchange, called the *bourse* (French for "purse"), was created in Amsterdam in the middle of the 16th century. In 1609, the Bank of Amsterdam opened. It had an international money exchange, it used the system of writing checks invented by the Arabs in the Middle Ages, and the Dutch government guaranteed the safety of deposits—something not available in the United States until 1933. The Dutch florin was accepted as payment all over the world, much as the American dollar is today.[18]

"God Made the World, but the Dutch Made Holland"[19]

Dutch life was tied to the sea and was a constant battle with it. The Dutch invented windmills to pump water out of the fields and reclaim land from the sea, and dikes, walls to hold back the sea. Much of Dutch food and industry centered around the sea. Twenty-five percent of the Dutch population was connected to the herring industry, from fishing and selling to preserving by smoking, salting, and pickling.[20]

In a time when the economy of other European countries was suffering, the Dutch were extremely prosperous, with a large middle class and a high standard of living. Dutch virtues were cleanliness and thrift. Every morning, Dutch housewives washed not only their own stoops but also the public sidewalks in front of their houses. They lived and ate well. At fish markets, the Dutch bought only live fish. They threw away dead fish, as well as mackerel and red mullet.[21] Even workers could afford meat, cheese, and butter, and the urban poor were provided for in poorhouses that had been recycled from monasteries or convents when the Netherlands converted to Protestant from Catholic. Sailors on warships were fed a 4,800-calorie-per-day diet of mutton, beef, pork, smoked ham, bread, beans, peas, and smoked and pickled fish, much of it herring.[22] They were a country that grew no grain and made no wine, but they controlled trade from the breadbasket of Europe, the countries around the Baltic Sea.

Dutch Cuisine: *The Sensible Cook*

One Dutch cookbook was predominant in the Netherlands (and in New Netherland) in the 17th century. *The Sensible Cook,* published in 1668, contained 189 recipes and two appendices, "The Sensible Confectioner" and "The Dutch Butchering Time." The cookbook and a beekeeping manual were part of the medical section of *The Pleasurable Country Life,* a manual for wealthy bourgeoisie who owned a country house and a garden. The manual was really a compilation of three books: *The Dutch Gardener,* about ornamental gardens; *The Sensible Gardener,* about medicinal gardens; and *The Medicine Shop or the Experienced Housekeeper,* about the care of humans and animals. None of the information in *The Sensible Cook* was available to English speakers until 1989, when it was translated by a Dutch woman, food historian Peter G. Rose. As Rose points out, the gender of the anonymous author of *The Sensible Cook* is unknown, but the book opens with a statement "to all cooks, male and female" and ends with the words "everyone to her own demand."[23] Before mentioning a word about food, the author tells the reader how to build a stove, one of the rare examples before the 19th century of being able to stand up and cook. The recipes are divided into sections: first salads, herbs, and vegetables; then meat, fowl, and fish, followed by baked goods, custards, drinks, and miscellaneous; then a section on tarts, and finally one on pasties. As Rose also points out, the author was an organized person who took the trouble to capitalize the first letters of the main ingredients and to give exact measurements in terms of the *loot* (approximately 14 grams), *pint* (approximately half a liter), and *pond* (approximately 454 grams).[24]

The cookbook also shows the influence of the Middle East and the Middle Ages. Stews and sauces are thickened with bread, toast, ground nuts, eggs, or—a Dutch innovation—cookies. Sauces of sugar and verjus or vinegar continue the sweet-sour medieval cooking tradition. The recipe "To make a proper Sauce" shows its Middle Eastern roots: ground almonds are added to the white bread crumb thickener, while sugar and verjus make it sweet and sour. The only other ingredient is another Middle Eastern spice, ginger. There is little difference in the spices used for meat and for fish. Thirty of the 59 recipes for meat use nutmeg and/or mace; so do ten of the 18 fish recipes. For example, sturgeon is studded with cloves, spit-roasted, basted with butter, then stewed with Rhine wine, vinegar, cinnamon and nutmeg.[25] Bream is also spit-roasted, stuffed with its own roe, chopped egg yolks, parsley, nutmeg, mace, pepper, and butter; sauced with pan drippings, anchovies, and verjus, and garnished with oregano.[26] Many of the recipes contain a butter enrichment at the end; a recipe for hen stewed with greens reminds: "Especially do not forget the butter."[27] Few of the desserts use nutmeg or mace; rosewater is still the flavoring. The Middle Eastern influence was also apparent in cumin-studded Gouda cheese, and in the national dish, *hutsepot* (hot pot), a seasonal meat and vegetable stew.

RECIPE

*H*UTSEPOT, THE DUTCH DISH

"Take some mutton or beef; wash it clean and chop it fine. Add thereto some greenstuff or parsnips or some stuffed prunes and the juice of lemons or oranges or citron or a pint of strong, clear vinegar. Mix these together, set the pot on a slow fire (for at least three and a half hours); add some ginger and melted butter."[28]

The Dutch ate four times a day—breakfast, the main meal at midday, afternoon (at 2:00 or 3:00 P.M.), and evening. They ate bread at all four meals: bread and butter, bread and cheese, bread and meat. It was all washed down, any time of day, with beer. Bread was baked by professional bakers in communal ovens even if the dough was made at home, because few people had ovens in their houses. Bread was the mainstay of the Dutch diet until the potato caught on at the end of the 18th century.[29] Rice was rare; there are only a handful of rice recipes in *The Sensible Cook*. There are also very few foods from the New World. The turkey makes an appearance, as do green beans, called "Turkey beans" because that is where the Dutch got them. But this was a time before the Dutch knew chocolate.

The Dutch displayed their wealth in the furnishings of their homes, their art, their gardens. They had Turkish carpets, Persian silk, Ming china (until Delft began producing homegrown Dutch knockoff blue ceramic tiles and tableware), lace, and linens by the dozens for bed and table. They also adopted an idea from Topkapi Palace, the residence of the sultan of Turkey: gardens for no purpose except beauty, acres of gardens with not one edible plant in them, just flowers, especially tulips and especially red ones. The buying and selling of tulip bulbs was intense in the Netherlands, where fortunes were made and lost on just a handful of bulbs. Dutch art reflected Dutch life: secular, not religious. The still-life paintings celebrated the new, exotic fruits—lemons, oranges, apricots—in settings of abundance and wealth.

All of this abundance presented a dilemma for the Dutch Reformed Church: were the Dutch going to be rich or religious? Were all these spices, sauces, and sugar, these cheeses and meats, all these possessions, the speculating in tulip bulbs, going to cause the Dutch to lose their souls? The response in some cities was sumptuary laws to regulate the sumptuousness—the luxury—of everyday life. For example, in Amsterdam in 1655, no more than fifty guests could be invited to a wedding, the celebration couldn't last longer than two days, and a ceiling was put on how much could be spent on gifts. Some city councils went too far and banned the December 6 festival of food and gift giving in honor of St. Nicholas—Sinter Klaas to the Dutch, Santa Claus to us—along with dolls and gingerbread men. It didn't last—the children rebelled.[30] (We can only wonder what the city fathers would have done about the anatomically correct gingerbread people available today.) While the Church continued to preach thrift, the Dutch made money and spent it—and consumed it. They never stopped eating their pancakes and waffles sprinkled with sugar or swimming in caramel. Before Americans invented baking powder, yeast inflated the waffles. The pancakes were flat as pancakes.

The Spice Islands: Nutmeg versus New York

Much of the wealth of the Dutch empire came from its colonies in the Spice Islands, now Indonesia. In 1602, the Dutch East India Company was founded to trade in Asia. The Dutch East India Company, remote from the Netherlands but having to make decisions for the good of the empire, became so powerful that it functioned like a state: it could coin money, make treaties, and raise its own army. Within a short time, the Dutch broke the monopoly the Portuguese had held on the nutmeg trade for almost a century.

The British were after the spice trade, too. In 1600, they had founded the British East India Company. Like Columbus, they were determined to find their own route to the East Indies. Their quest became more urgent when bubonic plague struck again in the 1660s; physicians believed that nutmeg, the seed of the *Myristica fragrans* tree, was the cure. The maps of the time showed it was possible to get to the Indies by sailing north of Norway and then east. Mistake. The crews starved or froze to death. Determined to do business in the East Indies, the British went to war with the Dutch. They lost, then felt humiliated by the treaty, which gave the Dutch what seemed by far the better deal. The Dutch got to retain control of the lucrative Spice Islands trade, and all they had to give away was their puny colony in North America. The British tried to retain their pride and renamed the colony New York.

THE RUSSIAN BEAR

Peter the Great Modernizes Russia

The Netherlands got a special visitor in the 18th century. Czar Peter the Great realized that if Russia didn't keep pace with Europe, it would be a huge, helpless giant and European countries would come scavenging and pick it apart like vultures. In his program to modernize Russia, Peter visited shipyards in the Netherlands in disguise, which fooled nobody because he was six feet eight inches tall and traveled with an entourage. Peter built a navy and upgraded the army. He hired European officers to train his men. To get a port on the Baltic Sea, he went to war with Russia's neighbor, Sweden. Peter won. He got his port and built a magnificent city that he named St. Petersburg, after the first Christian saint, whose name just happened to be the same as his.

Peter wanted to make Russians behave, look, and eat like Europeans. Europeans read the newspaper, so Peter published Russia's first newspaper, editing it himself. (The newspaper, like the alphabet, was late getting to Russia.) European men were clean-shaven, so Peter taxed men's beards. But it was cold in Russia; men were reluctant to part with their face-warmers and paid the tax instead. Peter had more success introducing European foods to Russia. He sent Russian chefs to European countries to learn the latest cooking methods. One of the things Peter found in Europe was the potato. Russia is now the world's leading producer of potatoes. The Russians used distilling techniques they learned from Poland to make potato-based vodka.

Ukraine: The Breadbasket of Russia

The large, flat plain of Ukraine is like the American Midwest—grain-growing territory, the breadbasket of the region. The peasants there lived harsh lives. Long after the Renaissance, the Reformation, the Scientific Revolution, and many other social and intellectual movements had come and gone, peasants in eastern Europe were still living as they had in the Middle Ages. They were not slaves, but almost. They could not be bought and sold individually, but they were bought and sold with the land. When you bought a farm, you bought the land, the buildings, and the peasants. Laws made it impossible for the serfs to leave the land they worked. They revolted many times, unsuccessfully, until they were finally freed in 1861, the same year America began a civil war to free its slaves. Until then, the lives of Russian serfs were reduced to the basics: work and try to get enough to eat. The scarcity of food was mirrored in the Russian Orthodox Church's fast days—up to 200 a year.[31] The staple food was bread—black bread made from rye in the north, wheat bread in the south. It was eaten at every meal. It was sacred to these people and so was the place it was baked.

The Russian Stove

An old Russian peasant proverb says, "The stove in the home is like an altar in a church."[32] The stove and the fire in it were treated with the utmost respect. For Americans to understand the Russian stove, we have to get rid of all our ideas about what a stove is. In a place where the temperature during the winter routinely drops into double digits below zero, the stove could take up a quarter of the entire hut. It was always built into a corner, made of clay, and functioned as a combination stove, furnace, and fireplace. The stove cooked food, baked bread, and preserved fruits and vegetables by drying. It also kept the temperature just right for fermenting drinks like *beriozovitsa,* made from birch tree sap, and *medovukha,* which was like mead, but with hops added. Later, *kvas*—wheat fermented with water and sugar—became popular.

The stove also warmed the house. Beds were built on top of it and around it, like a sleeping loft. In Russia, people who lounged around on the stove—what we call "couch potatoes"—were "stove potatoes."[33]

Tea and the Samovar

In the mid-18th century, tea became all the rage in Russia, the only country that invented a separate machine to brew it (until the Mrs. Tea machine arrived to keep Mr. Coffee company in the 20th century). The samovar was a large metal urn, usually brass, sometimes steel, copper, or silver, with a spigot to drain the hot water. The first technology to heat water for tea (or anything else) was a charcoal-filled tube in the center of the samovar, but today they are also electric. Samovars ran from the plain, water-boiling variety to very fancy ones that brewed tea on one side and coffee on the other, or had legs that unscrewed for portability. Some were a complete tea service, with creamer, sugar bowl, and cups and saucers.[34] It is immediately recognizable as a Russian appliance.

Peter the Great had visited England, prowled the shipyards in the Netherlands, and met European heads of state. But the ruler and the country he most admired were King Louis XIV and France.

FRANCE

Italy Comes to France: Forks

Beginning in the 16th century in Italy, a new utensil changed the relationship of humans to food, and to each other at the table. The fork created a distance between the diner and his dinner. It also distanced the people eating from each other. No more eating the same food out of the same pot, with the same utensil—their fingers—as they had in the Middle Ages. The fork had been known as a serving tool since ancient Rome, used to spear solid food out of the boiling pot. It arrived at the table as a serving tool to keep the hands of all the diners out of the serving dish. Finally, it became an individual utensil. At first, people had to make a serious effort to use it, because it was two-tined, difficult to maneuver, and not as efficient as fingers. Food kept falling off. The fork also cut out one of the sensations that had always been involved with eating: feel. But it also made it possible to eat some foods, like pasta. Slowly, it spread from the Italian court to France, then England, and finally Germany. It was strictly upper-class, crafted

145

from gold, silver, or crystal. Since primitive people had just been discovered in the Americas, civilized people didn't want to eat like them. One of the means by which the fork began its northward migration was a teenage girl.

Italy Comes to France: Catherine de Medici

ℱood ℱABLE
⋙ CATHERINE DE MEDICI—DID SHE OR DIDN'T SHE? ⋘

In 1533, the same year that Queen Elizabeth I of England was born, a 14-year-old princess left Florence, Italy, to marry a French prince, in a marriage arranged by the pope. Catherine brought her cooks, pastry cooks, confectioners, and distillers, and Italian *alta cucina*—supposedly the end of spicy medieval cooking and the beginning of French *haute cuisine.*

Food historian Barbara Wheaton states that this is incorrect because "French *haute cuisine* did not appear until a century later and then showed little Italian influence; and there is no evidence that Catherine's cooks had any impact on French cooking in the early 16th century."[35] Catherine supposedly introduced frozen ices, artichokes, parsley, and the fork to France.

Wheaton says further that Catherine didn't have much power at court because she didn't have children for 14 years; because her husband was not supposed to become king, but his brother died; and because her husband's mistress set court fashions.[36]

Later, after her husband died and she ruled through her son, Catherine de Medici's court was the height of fashion. In 1581, she was responsible for the first real ballet, the *Ballet comique de la reine*—the Queen's Comic Ballet. She also helped to popularize a new fashion from the New World—tobacco. The active ingredient in tobacco, nicotine, was named after the French diplomat who sent the seeds to Catherine, Jean Nicot.

Catherine survived and even excelled in the backstabbing world of court intrigue. She was involved in the religious wars between the Catholic majority and the Protestant minority, the Huguenots. On St. Bartholomew's Day, August 24, 1572, French Catholics began a three-day coordinated massacre of 20,000 Huguenots throughout France, after which the pope and King Philip II of Spain celebrated. Catherine was not an innocent bystander.

La Varenne and the Beginning of *Haute Cuisine*

There was a dramatic shift in French cuisine in the middle of the 17th century. In 1651, a French chef named La Varenne published a cookbook called *Le Cuisinier françois*—The French Cook. As Anne Willan, who has named her cooking school in France after him, pointed out, *Le Cuisinier françois* "is a seminal work; it marks the end of medieval cooking and the beginning of *haute cuisine.*"[37] Two years after *Le Cuisinier françois* appeared, La Varenne published *Le Pastissier françois*—The French Pastry Cook. (The word *"pastissier"* later changed into the modern *"pâtissier."*)

The beginnings of organization in French cuisine are here with two bouillons, one for meat, one for fish. It is also the beginning of modern sauces—the first roux, the fat and flour thickener. The trademark of most of La Varenne's recipes is subtlety. The hand that sprinkles the spices is light, not heavy like in the Middle Ages. Salt and pepper are the seasonings, with a squeeze of lemon juice and maybe a bouquet garni. Missing are the large doses of cinnamon, mace, clove, ginger. The use of truffles, which have to be dug out of the ground, shows a break with the medieval theory of humors, while the division of the book into meat days and meatless days still shows the influence of the Catholic Church.

More fresh fruits and vegetables appear in these recipes, because they are more readily available and because gardening had advanced considerably, especially among the upper classes. However, there were still not many foods from the New World. La Varenne used the foods that were trendy among the French nobility, like peas, lettuce, and artichokes. People *had* to have peas. Woe to the host who served asparagus instead, although asparagus could be served disguised as peas.

Le Pastissier is the first thorough pastry cookbook, with precise, clear instructions and definitions of weights and measures, perhaps the influence of the Scientific Revolution that was then taking place in Europe. However, Willan thinks that *Le Pastissier* was probably not written by La Varenne or was written by him and an anonymous Italian pastry chef, because Italian pastry chefs were the best in the world at that time. Also, cooking and pastry were two separate professions. In any case, it is sophisticated—there are fifteen varieties of marzipan. It also has the first cakelike biscuit recipes. La Varenne's books were the beginning of a trend. Forty years later, another chef, Massialot, wrote *Le Cuisinier roial et bourgeois*, which continued the style of cuisine La Varenne began.

Vatel: The Chef Who Gave His All

Another giant in food history is Vatel. From all accounts, he was a genius in many areas: planning and managing huge festivals, coming up with imaginative ideas for pageants, and menu planning. He impressed all who attended the gala events his employers hosted. Then, in 1671, disaster. As maître d'hotel to the duc de Condé, Vatel was responsible for planning and executing to perfection a major event for the king, who was coming to visit the duke for several days. The pressure was tremendous. The day a seafood feast and extravaganza was planned, almost no food arrived from the purveyors. Sure that he had destroyed the social and political life of the duke, as well as his own professional life, Vatel fell on his sword. The fishmongers arrived with full carts as he died, but he had left no instructions on how to prepare and present all the food. In 1981, Vatel gave his name to a hotel management school in Paris (it now has seven branches internationally), and in 2000 a movie was made about him starring Gérard Depardieu and Uma Thurman. Thirty-three students from the Instituts Vatel, cutting, chopping, and slicing, made the kitchens look real.

The Frenchman Who Loved His Coffee (Plant)

In 1689, an Italian named Procope opened the first coffeehouse in Paris. Almost everywhere coffee was introduced it met with two responses. The first was overwhelming enthusiasm from the people who drank it. The second was repression by the government. In Mecca, the governor ordered the coffeehouses closed when he heard the patrons were making fun of him. King George II did the same in England for the same reason. The French were going to ban coffee because they were afraid it would replace wine as the national beverage; the Germans feared for their beer. In all these places, people kept drinking coffee and eventually the bans were lifted. An exception was Italy, where coffee was never banned even though Catholic priests appealed to the pope to ban the Muslim beverage. Instead, the pope tried it and gave it his blessing.

From its beginnings in the 9th century, when it was ground into a paste with animal fat, ways of consuming coffee changed. Grinding coffee into a powder made it possible to read the grounds at the bottom of the cup, which gave a boost to fortune-tellers. In 1710, the French, ever neat and efficient, put the ground beans in a cloth bag, poured boiling water over it, and invented the infusion method. The French are also credited with adding milk and creating *café au lait,* which moved coffee from an upper-class evening beverage in a public place to a morning luxury indulged in private. Eventually, *café au lait* filtered down into the general population and became the drink of the working class.

Coffee changed more than just eating habits—it changed social and political habits as well. For the first time, people had a public place and a reason to congregate that did not involve alcohol. It began as a social pastime and became a political one. The rulers who worried about what people in coffeehouses were saying about the government were right to be concerned. In France, the ideas that spread through coffeehouse discussions played a real part in the French Revolution. Coffee is also connected with a food fable about the origin of the croissant.

Food Fable
≫ Where the Croissant Comes From ≪

The Fable: In 1683, the croissant was supposedly invented after the siege of Vienna. Either (1) a baker working late at night noticed the Turks trying to tunnel under the city and saved Vienna or (2) to celebrate their victory over the Turks, the Viennese bakers invented a new pastry in the shape of a crescent—in French, *croissant*—which was either (1) the symbol on the Turkish flag or (2) the shape of the trenches the Turks had dug and were forced to abandon. That would make the Austrians the first people anywhere to have a cup of coffee and a croissant. Not likely, since the croissant is one of the national foods of France and the earliest recipe is from 1905.[38]

The Fact: In 1683, the Turks attacked Vienna and lost. Pulling up stakes in a hurry, they left carpets, clothing, and five hundred huge sacks of strange little round beans. Dark. Hard. Bitter-smelling. Maybe camel food? Torch them. But one soldier had been in the Middle East and woke up and smelled the coffee. The beans were saved—so many beans that he opened the first coffeehouse in Vienna with them.[39]

One Frenchman played a huge role in spreading coffee throughout the world. In 1723, Gabriel Mathieu de Clieu thought coffee would grow well in the Caribbean. He had one plant and nurtured it like a sick baby all the way across the Atlantic Ocean, even giving it his water ration. He was right—the plant loved the Caribbean. A great percentage of the coffee grown in the world today can probably be traced back to that one plant.[40]

COFFEE CHRONOLOGY[41]	
By 1500	Persia, Egypt, Turkey, North Africa have coffee because of Muslim pilgrims
1536	Yemen occupied by Ottoman Turks; coffee exported through city of Mocha
1600s	India begins cultivation from seeds smuggled in by a Muslim
1616	Dutch smuggle a coffee tree from Aden to Holland
1650	England's first coffeehouse opens at Oxford University
1652	London's first coffeehouse
1650s	In Italy, coffee is sold by street vendors
1658	Dutch begin coffee cultivation in Ceylon
1669	Turkish ambassador introduces coffee to Paris; it becomes a huge fad
1670s	Germany—coffeehouses open
1683	Venice, Italy, opens coffeehouse
1683	Viennese defeat Turks, capture coffee, open coffeehouse
1689	Procope, an Italian, opens coffeehouse in Paris
1696	Paris doctor prescribes coffee enemas
1699	Dutch transplant trees to Java, then Sumatra, Celebes, Timor, and Bali
1723	French begin growing coffee on Martinique in the Caribbean
1727	Coffee smuggled into Brazil
1734	Coffee grown in Haiti
1788	Santo Domingo grows half the coffee in the world
WWII	American GI Joes drink so much coffee it becomes known as "a cuppa joe"

Louis XIV: The Sun King

Louis XIV became king of France in 1643. He was an absolute ruler who claimed his power came from God. He said, "I am the state." Louis XIV was the most powerful ruler in French history. He grew up under the threat of assassination by the Fronde, a group of nobles plotting against the king. Louis was suspicious for the rest of his life and took safety precautions, including where he lived and how he ate. He built an enormous palace eleven miles southwest of Paris, in Versailles, and had the nobles live there so his spies could keep an eye on them.

Dinner at Versailles

The palace at Versailles was like a small city. Louis XIV expanded the main building, originally a hunting lodge, to 2,000 rooms that stretched for 500 yards. A 150-yard-long wing at each end of the main building formed a U-shaped courtyard. In the center of the courtyard, Louis XIV placed a huge statue of . . . Louis XIV. The 15,000 acres of gardens, lawns, and woods included 1,400 fountains. One of the centerpieces was the Galerie des Glaces (Hall of Mirrors), a long formal room. A wall of mirrors reflected the gardens outside glass-paned doors (what we call French doors). Ten thousand people lived in Versailles; two thousand worked in the kitchens. Running the palace cost more than half the annual income of France.[42]

Dinner at Versailles was at 10:00 P.M., about the time it gets dark in Paris in the summer. The Sun King took advantage of mealtimes to enforce his power. To guard against poisoning, his food was taken in locked containers from the kitchen to the dining hall, escorted by his private armed guards, the Musketeers. They announced the passage of the king's food through the halls of the palace by calling out, *"Les viandes du roi!"*—"the king's food!"—and everyone had to stop what they were doing and bow. Since he was without equal, Louis dined alone (except sometimes with the queen) in kingly splendor at a huge banquet table high on a platform. Musicians played while he dined; courtiers stood and watched while he ate, hoping for a word of acknowledgment or favor.

The meals Louis XIV ate were legendary. A glutton, he consumed huge amounts of food in no particular order, often against the advice of his physicians. Once, he ate "four full plates of soup, a whole pheasant, a partridge, a big dish of salad, two big slices of ham, some mutton with *jus* and garlic, a plate of pastry, and then fruit and some hard-boiled eggs."[43] And he ate it all with his hands. Although Catherine de Medici had brought the fork from Italy more than a century earlier and it was accepted throughout Europe, Louis didn't like it and refused to use it. He did use something else that Catherine had introduced, the handkerchief.

The *Orangerie*

Oranges became very popular at this time. The first oranges, the ones that the Muslims planted wherever they conquered, were bitter oranges that were called blood oranges, because of their color, or Seville oranges, after the city in Spain. The sweet orange tree—*Citrus sinensis* or Chinese orange—traveled through India to the Middle East. It arrived in Lisbon in 1625 and spread quickly all over Europe, replacing bitter oranges in most places.[44] Orange juice and peel were thought to be the antidote to poisons, colic, and tapeworm. Wealthy people gave theme dinners planned around citrus fruit.

Louis XIV, an orange aficionado, built an *orangerie* at Versailles in the shape of a 1,200-foot crescent and used it as a backdrop for the

MENU

$\mathscr{T}$HE Sixteen-Course Citrus Dinner

"In 1529, the Archbishop of Milan gave a sixteen-course dinner that included:

caviar and oranges fried with sugar and cinnamon
brill and sardines with slices of orange and lemon
one thousand oysters with pepper and oranges
lobster salad with citrons
sturgeon in aspic covered with orange juice
fried sparrows with oranges
individual salads containing citrons into which the coat of arms of
the diner had been carved
orange fritters
a soufflé full of raisins and pine nuts and covered with sugar and
orange juice
five hundred fried oysters with lemon slices
candied peels of citrons and oranges"[45]

masked balls and entertainments he liked so much, especially dancing and the comedies and satirical plays of Molière. It was the job of the royal gardeners to keep the Sun King supplied with oranges and orange blossoms all year round. The trees were usually kept in wheeled pots so they could be moved in from the cold or just repositioned to take advantage of the sun. Painters and weavers provided images of oranges throughout the château in paintings and tapestries.[46]

By the time he died in 1715, Louis XIV had turned France into a superpower, a leader in world politics, fashion, and cuisine. But the palaces and the wars were expensive. He also left France with a debt equivalent to about 20 billion dollars. Since the nobles paid no taxes, the money would have to be squeezed out of the peasants and the middle class. Three-quarters of a century later, the peasants would grow tired of paying half their income in taxes so the nobility could feast on luxuries while they starved. They would make the Sun King's grandson, Louis XVI, pay the ultimate tax: his head.

Election Cake and "Let Them Eat Cake":The American and French Revolutions —the 18th Century

AMERICA: FROM COLONY TO COUNTRY

Migrations: The Pennsylvania "Dutch"

England's colonies in North America continued to grow in the 18th century, partly because England advertised. The mercantile system depended on a large population. The more people in a colony, the more raw materials they could send to the home country and the more manufactured goods they could buy from it. William Penn distributed flyers about how wonderful life was in his new colony of Quakers, people who didn't believe in war or slavery, in Pennsylvania—"Penn's woods." Some of the flyers reached Rhinelanders—Protestant German and Swiss farmers in the Rhine River valley. A winter of unprecedented brutal cold got them thinking about moving to Pennsylvania. New laws that made it easier for foreigners to become British citizens, and therefore to own land in the colonies, got them on ships headed for Pennsylvania. To the ears of the English settlers already there, *Deutsch,* the German word for "German," sounded like *Dutch,* and the Rhinelanders have mistakenly been the Pennsylvania Dutch ever since.

A classic Pennsylvania Dutch dish is *schnitz und knepp,* ham stew with dried apples (*schnitz*) and dumplings (*knepp*). Potatoes also figured prominently in their diet. Mashed potatoes and potato water were in raised breads, cakes, and cinnamon buns (*schnecke*). They made potato fondant candy. On Shrove Tuesday, the day before the beginning of Lent, they made doughnuts (*fastnacht*) with mashed potatoes and potato water. These were solid balls of deep-fried dough; the hole, which allowed the dough to cook faster, was invented later. By 1870, catalogues were selling doughnut cutters with holes.[1]

The Pennsylvania Dutch housewife took pride in her skills at jam making and pickling, her "seven sweets and seven sours." The sweets were fruit butters, conserves, and jams. The sours were pickled vegetables and relishes called chow chow, sweetened with sugar, soured with vinegar, usually seasoned with mustard seed, dry mustard, and celery seed, and colored with turmeric, like chutney. A favorite pickled food still served in bars in Pennsylvania Dutch country are garnet-colored eggs, which go well with beer, along with pretzels (see below).

The Pennsylvania Dutch ate pie at all three meals. They filled their pies and tarts with apples, sour cherries, gooseberries, huckleberries, raspberries, blackberries, grapes, raisins, walnuts, or rhubarb. When they had nothing else to put in a pie, they made vinegar pie—water spiced with vinegar and nutmeg, sweetened with sugar, thickened with egg and flour. Or they baked cakelike shoofly pie—water, molasses, and baking soda with a crumb topping, so sweet you had to shoo the flies away. When the men got together to do serious physical work like building a barn, they also did serious eating. They stacked half a dozen different kinds of pies on top of each other, cut through them all, and chowed down on "stack pie."[2]

INGREDIENTS

𝒫ENNSYLVANIA DUTCH EGGS PICKLED IN BEET JUICE[3]

1 cup beet juice
1 cup vinegar
¾ teaspoon salt
½ teaspoon cloves
¼ teaspoon allspice
¼ teaspoon mace
1 or 2 small cooked beets
Shelled, hard-boiled eggs

The descendants of most of the Rhinelanders moved into main-stream America. But the Amish continue to live a preindustrial life. They do not have electricity. They drive a horse and buggy, not a car. And they still cook good, solid, abundant food. As food historian Nika Hazelton pointed out, "If you want to see what eighteenth-century rural life in Switzerland was like, you'll do far better in a strict Pennsylvania or Indiana Amish settlement than in present-day Switzerland or Germany."[4]

The French and Indian War, 1754–1763

The American colonists' desire to move west began the first global war that started in North America, and led to the American Revolution.* The war that became known as the French and Indian War in America and the Seven Years' War in the rest of the world began in 1754 when the governor of Virginia sent 21-year-old George Washington west of the Appalachian Mountains to stake out Virginia's claim to farmland in the fertile Ohio River Valley. The French, who had fur trading posts there, objected. Washington fired the first shot. When the war ended in 1763, France had lost everything in North America except Haiti. The result of the war: the British forbade settlement west of the Appalachians, which made the Americans very angry (they went anyway). And France wanted revenge.

Taxes, Taverns, and Tea Parties

The struggle between the American colonists and the British Parliament for control of the colonies began the year after the French and Indian War ended. Parliament—where no Americans were represented—taxed sugar in 1764 to pay for the war. The colonists protested. Parliament lowered that tax, then passed the Stamp Act, which taxed paper, from deeds and wills to newspapers and playing cards, in 1765.

---

* There were three world wars before it and five after, including the American Revolution. The wars are: War of the League of Augsburg (1688–1697; in America, King William's War, 1689–1697); War of Spanish Succession (1701–1713; in America, Queen Anne's War, 1702–1713); War of Austrian Succession (1740–1748; in America, King George's War, 1744–1748); the French and Indian War (1754–1763; in Europe, the Seven Years' War, 1756–1763); American Revolution (1775–1783 in America; 1778–1783 was when European countries were involved); Wars of the French Revolution (1793–1802); Napoleonic Wars (1803–1815; in the United States, the War of 1812, 1812–1814); World War I (1914–1918; for the United States, 1917–1918); and World War II (1939–1945; for the United States, 1941–1945; for China (1937–1945). (Bailey, Kennedy, & Cohen, *American Pageant,* 110.)

The furious colonists cried, "No taxation without representation"—you can't make us pay taxes we didn't vote for—and boycotted British wool. Americans stopped eating mutton to let sheep live and provide Americans with wool. The Sons of Liberty, men recruited from taverns by Samuel Adams, a local brewer (yes, that Sam Adams), tarred and feathered the stamp collectors and broke into their houses. The violence forced Parliament to repeal the Stamp Act in 1766, before it went into effect. There were celebrations in taverns throughout the colonies.

Tensions escalated in Boston, a town with fewer than 16,000 people, when the British stationed 4,000 red-coated soldiers—the Bostonians called them "lobsterbacks"—there in 1768 and expected the people to take them into their homes and feed them for nothing. Two years later, after a crowd threw sticks, rocks, and snowballs at them, the soldiers opened fire. They killed four Americans, including a black man, Crispus Attucks. Sam Adams began the Committees of Correspondence, a propaganda letter-writing campaign, to report the Boston Massacre and whip all the colonies up against England. Now he would use the Internet, but in colonial America snail mail traveled on the Boston Post Road through New Haven to New York. Along the way, mail was delivered not to individual houses, but to taverns, where reports of British atrocities inflamed Americans' anger, and strips ripped off dried salted codfish hanging on the wall inflamed their thirst.[5] The Green Dragon Tavern in Boston's North End (now Boston's Little Italy) was where Adams, silversmith Paul Revere (whose name and picture are still on the bottom of the line of cookware named after him), and others got together to plan.

British Prime Minister "Champagne" Charlie Townshend had a new approach: instead of one large tax, many small taxes. The Townshend Acts taxed glass, paint, lead, and tea. The colonists protested. Eventually all the taxes were repealed—except the tea tax. The British East India Company needed the money, so they set the price of the tea *with the tax* lower than what it cost to buy it from American smugglers.[6] The Americans were furious—did the British really think they could sucker them into paying a tax they had no part in passing? The tea had to go.

"Boston Harbor a Teapot Tonight!"

On December 16, 1773, about 150 men in disguise, some dressed like Indians, others with their faces blackened with charcoal, boarded the East India Company ships in Boston Harbor. Hundreds of chests of tea, each weighing 350 pounds, were smashed open with tomahawks and thrown into the harbor. In three hours, it was all over.

The masterminds of the tea party, John Hancock and Sam Adams, made sure they were seen sitting in a tavern far away. Boston wasn't the only place that protested. In Annapolis, Maryland, colonists burned the ships. Other colonies staged public tea burnings.

Parliament retaliated: they shut down the port of Boston until the colonists paid for the tea. Then they came to get the colonists' ammunition and the ringleaders, Hancock and Adams. But Paul Revere made his famous ride, alerting everyone: "The British are coming! The British are coming!" On April 19, 1775, the American Revolution began. The shot that began the revolution was "the shot heard round the world," because it would inspire people in many other countries to fight for their freedom, too. On July 4, 1776, the Declaration of Independence, the document announcing America's freedom from England and using the words "the United States of America" for the first time, was celebrated with fireworks and cheering.

"No Meat, No Soldier"

Under the 18th-century rules of war, fighting was suspended during the winter. In the winter of 1777–1778, British officers were eating and drinking and dancing in New York. British fighting soldiers got rancid, wormy food—rock-hard biscuits that had been captured 15 years earlier in the French and Indian War. They slammed cannonballs down on them to soften them.[7]

Both groups were better off than the 12,000 Americans starving and freezing with General George Washington at Valley Forge, Pennsylvania. They had only animal skulls and hooves that they boiled into thin stews. They had no bread at all for days. Their shoes were worn out or gone, their blankets threadbare. Some of the men were nearly naked. Limbs froze or became gangrenous and had to be amputated. The near-starvation rations weakened the men's immune systems. More than 2,000 died of typhoid, typhus, smallpox, and pneumonia. Finally, the cry went up from the ranks: "No meat, no soldier." Washington wrote to the Continental Congress and made it clear that if his men did not receive food and supplies, the war would be over.[8] He finally got them.

We Couldn't Have Done It Without the French

For almost the first two and a half years of the American Revolution, the French provided the Americans, who had few factories, with ammunition, training, and officers like Lafayette. They did it secretly, to avoid another war with the British. However, after the Americans beat the British at the Battle of Saratoga in upstate New York in 1778, the French went public with their support. This forced the other major countries of the world to take sides—the war went global. One of the reasons King Louis XVI aided America was to keep England from winning and then coming after France's Caribbean sugar property. And to get revenge.

England's other great enemy, Spain, contributed money to the Americans, but it was a French squeeze play that ended the war. Washington's army had the British army, under General Cornwallis, backed up against the sea at Yorktown, Virginia. Cornwallis wasn't worried—the British fleet would sail down from New York to pluck him and his troops to safety. However, the French fleet sailed up from Haiti and sandwiched the British in. Game over. General George Washington said farewell to his men at Fraunces Tavern in New York City after the eight years of war that changed America from a British colony into the United States.

The Whiskey Rebellion and the Bureau of Alcohol, Tobacco, and Firearms (BATF)

In 1787, the year that British sailors on the HMS *Bounty* mutinied against Captain Bligh as he tried to transport breadfruit from Tahiti to the Caribbean, 55 white, middle-class men, mostly businessmen and lawyers, gathered in Philadelphia, Pennsylvania, to draw up a document that would change the world—the United States Constitution. It went into effect on April 30, 1789, when George Washington was sworn in as the first president in the nation's capital, New York City.

Washington had only three cabinet members: Secretary of State Thomas Jefferson, whose job was to deal with other countries; Secretary of War Henry Knox; and Secretary of the Treasury Alexander Hamilton, whose task was to stabilize the economy and ensure that the country had good credit with the rest of the world. One of the first things Hamilton did to raise money was tax luxury items like imported alcoholic beverages, especially wines and distilled liquors. Americans in the 1790s drank about six gallons of alcohol per person each year, twice as much as now. Most was beer; about one-third was distilled liquor.[9] Since efforts to grow vines and make wine had failed in North America in spite of offers of large cash prizes, wine was imported and expensive, so wealthy people would be taxed. This tax proved such a good source of income that Congress extended it to distilled spirits produced within the United States. This caused problems in 1794.

The farmers in western Pennsylvania who grew corn and rye didn't think the "white lightning" alcohol they made out of it was a luxury. It was a necessity, accepted as payment for goods and services. Transporting bulk grain over bad or nonexistent roads was not profitable. Transporting the grain in its liquid, alcoholic form was. They followed their refusal to pay the whiskey tax with boycotts and demonstrations. President Washington knew better than anyone where that could lead. He called up thirteen thousand militiamen to put down the rebellion by a few people. The officers were well fed with "mountains of beef and oceans of whiskey."[10] The organization within the Treasury Department that grew out of the response to this rebellion became the Bureau of Alcohol, Tobacco, and Firearms (BATF), which still oversees alcohol production in the United States today. Jefferson thought that Washington had engaged in overkill. The differences that came to a head over the Whiskey Rebellion were a large factor in the beginning of political parties in the United States.

A New People and a New Cuisine—The First American Cookbook

In 1796, a cookbook called *American Cookery* was published in Hartford, Connecticut. The author was a woman named Amelia Simmons, who described herself as "an American orphan." The book revealed much about Simmons and about the values of the new country. Continuing the country's tradition of self-betterment, Simmons stated in the first sentence that the book was written "for the improvement of the rising generation of *Females* in America" (italics in original). She hoped that the information in her book would make them "useful members of society." She talked about her own situation—"the orphan must depend solely upon *character*" to make her way in the world (emphasis in original).[11] Having a good character was valued in American life until the 1920s, when movies and beauty contests made appearances more important.

On the title page of *American Cookery*, Simmons declared that the recipes were "adapted to this country." Food historian Karen Hess's essay explains the importance of the cookbook: Simmons wrote about the ingredients she knew, many of them New World foods that had been ignored in British cookbooks and appeared in print in Simmons's book for the first time. For example, she published the first recipes for pumpkin and for corn. She used the word *cookie,* the diminutive of the

Dutch word for cake. *Sla* was another borrowing from the Dutch, for salad. Cabbage salad became that American favorite, coleslaw. Simmons also included one very important, typically American first, a leavening shortcut called pearlash, the forerunner of baking powder. This caught on immediately in Europe because it made baking much easier. Before chemical leavening agents, making cakes rise was a time-consuming and expensive process. The cook had to proof yeast and keep it at the right temperature, beat eggs to incorporate air into them, or make pastry with layers of butter that would puff when baked. But baking powder or soda combined with flour and salt produced what Americans called biscuits. American biscuits are not a true biscuit, which is French for "twice cooked" (in Italian, *biscotti*), because American biscuits are cooked only once. They rise twice because of double-acting baking powder. The new leavening gave rise to an entire class of food, quick breads.

Simmons's cookbook was so popular that a second, expanded version was published. It included a recipe for election cake. The biggest holiday in colonial New England, proud of its democracy, was Election Day, in May; it continued to be a holiday in the new republic. Thanksgiving and Christmas were not celebrated until the Civil War, but Election Day was a day off from work for everybody. Even blacks joined the parades, singing and dancing to banjo and drum music. In New England, slaves got to vote for leaders in their slave communities: "The Negro 'government' had its 'judges,' 'sheriffs,' and 'magistrates,' and its courts probably tried trivial cases between Negroes as well as petty cases brought by masters against their slaves."[12] Since the tavern was the polling place, it was also an excuse to have an extra drink or let someone buy you one to persuade you to vote for his candidate. But it was almost not necessary to drink to get drunk—there was plenty of liquor in the election cake. At the end of the 19th century, reformers campaigned to stop holding elections in taverns and getting voters "liquored up" because it undermined democracy and led to violence and riots. By then, the temperance movement had taken firm hold of cooking, too—there was no liquor in the election cake.

The year 1789 saw the birth of the constitutional government that exists to this day in the United States, and the death of the Bourbon dynasty that had ruled France for hundreds of years. Ideas connected with America's fight for liberty, and the money that helped them succeed—taxes paid by the French people—would topple the monarch who had come to America's aid, King Louis XVI of France. This would have profound repercussions for global politics and cuisine.

INGREDIENTS

ℰLECTION ℭAKE COMPARISON

1796—AMELIA SIMMONS[13]	1918—FANNIE FARMER[14]
30 quarts of flour	1¼ cups flour
1 quart yeast	1 cup bread dough
10 pounds of butter	½ cup butter
14 pounds of sugar	1 cup brown sugar
12 pounds of raisins	⅔ cup raisins, seeded and cut in pieces
—	8 finely chopped figs
3 dozen eggs	1 egg
1 pint of wine	—
1 quart of brandy	—
4 ounces cinnamon	1 teaspoon cinnamon
4 ounces fine colander [coriander?] seed	—
3 ounces ground allspice	—
—	¼ teaspoon mace
—	¼ teaspoon nutmeg
—	¼ teaspoon cloves
—	½ cup sour milk
—	½ teaspoon soda
—	1 teaspoon salt
(The finished cake weighed 90 pounds.)	

THE FRENCH REVOLUTION: "LET THEM EAT CAKE"

The American Revolution was one of the causes of the French Revolution. In addition to seeing that an underclass could overthrow a monarchy, the French people were angry because they had been taxed to the maximum to pay for people of another country to win freedoms they did not have. The people in France were divided into three groups, or estates. The first estate was the clergy, which paid about 2 percent of the taxes in France. The second estate was wealthy nobles, who paid no taxes. The third estate paid 98 percent of the taxes and

161

was 98 percent of the population: peasant farmers, urban poor, and the bourgeoisie—the merchant class, an educated middle class that took business risks and brought money into France. The third estate paid 50 percent of their income in taxes but couldn't vote, so they couldn't change the tax laws or anything else—like the Americans' cry of "no taxation without representation."

Haute Cuisine and Fine China

Haute cuisine, or "high cuisine," came out of the large kitchens of France's wealthy nobles. The cooks might be men or women, but the men's salaries were more than triple the women's, and the men were always the managers.[15] Cooking did not include bread, which was bought at the *boulangerie,* or pastry, which was bought at the *pâtisserie.* In a modest household, the cooking might be done by the woman of the house and a maid. In larger establishments, there would be specialized staffs. In charge of everything was the maître d'hotel, who planned all the meals, hired and fired staff, managed the accounts, and kept the keys, because the food, wines, linens, and tableware were locked up. In both kinds of households, the day began by putting the stockpot on the fire—*pot au feu*—and throwing yesterday's leftovers and today's new meat into it.

Much of the silver and gold tableware of 17th century France had been melted down to finance Louis XIV's wars and palaces. In 18th-century France and throughout Europe, tableware was fine china. For centuries, Europeans had been searching for a way to duplicate the delicate, beautiful, and extremely expensive porcelain plates that came from China. Like the silkworm, this was a closely guarded Chinese state secret. Finally, in England in the early 18th century, they came up with a process that duplicated the Chinese plates closely enough. France would not be content to let England have this technology (although they were content to smuggle huge amounts of it). In 1740, at Limoges, the French developed fine china. However, the lower classes in France had neither plates nor food to put on them.

"This Nation Does Not Have a Normal Relation to Food"[16]

It is impossible to separate food from the French Revolution. More than any other revolution in history, food played a crucial part in the French Revolution, literally and symbolically. At the heart of the issue were two foods essential to the French people, bread and salt. And at the heart of the bread issue were the bakers.

The French have been described as a nation of "panivores"— bread eaters—and regard their bread as the best in the world. Bread had both literal and symbolic meaning in French cuisine and culture. It was a source of nutrition, providing most of the daily calories, but it also represented health and well-being, the French identity, and the French religion, Catholicism. French bread was supposed to be wheat and white. In 1775, people rioted because they got dark bread.[17] Scientists and chemists claimed that the bakers baked bad bread because they knew nothing about science; in 1782, a school was established to study bread from milling through distribution, and spread the word to bakers throughout France. Scientist Antoine-Augustin Parmentier was one of the people in charge of the school.

The Bakers and the Bread Police

There was tension between the people and the bakers for almost a century before the French Revolution. Bread was regarded as a public service necessary to keep the people from rioting. Bakers, therefore, were public servants, so the police controlled all aspects of bread production, including making sure that it continued; bakers had to get permission from the police if they wanted to go into another profession.[18] Sometimes the police helped the bakers. For example, when merchants hoarded yeast to create an artificial shortage and jack up the price, the bakers' guild had the police search the merchants' homes and shops and confiscate the yeast.[19]

The master bakers exercised very tight control over the journeymen through a certification system. After 1781, every journeyman baker had to register with the guild and get a *livret*—French for "booklet"—which was like their green card or passport. The journeyman had to show the *livret* to rent a room or to get food in a tavern. When he went to work, he gave the *livret* to the master. When he changed jobs, the journeyman had to inform the guild within 24 hours and pay a fee. He also had to show in the *livret* that the master had given permission. Some masters forced journeymen to work for them by keeping the *livret*. If he left without it, the journeyman was like an illegal alien in his own country. Police raided shops where journeymen were working illegally, the way the Immigration and Naturalization Service (La Migra) raids shops now. The illegal journeymen could be sent to jail or back to their former masters.[20]

The bakers, like the grain and flour merchants, were presumed to be greedy and selfish. People accused them of numerous crimes: adulterating bread with wood chips, soap, or rotten grain, or baking underweight loaves. They made bitter jokes about it: weigh a dead baker and he'll come up short weight.[21] The bakers complained that it wasn't their fault—it was impossible to get absolutely uniform loaves, what bakers call "scaling." The police knew who was responsible because a baker had to carve his initials into every loaf. Making an anonymous loaf was also a crime but, of course, harder to prosecute. The police practiced zero tolerance on short weight; loaves even half an ounce light were seized. Historian Steven Kaplan, who did an extensive analysis of police archives and other public records for his book *The Bakers of Paris and the Bread Question, 1700–1775,* did the math on what short weight cost the people of Paris each day: "perhaps between twenty-five hundred and three thousand four-pound loaves . . . enough to feed several thousand families."[22]

The punishments for bakers included fines, having their ovens destroyed or their shops walled up, having their crimes published in the paper or being forced to wear them on a sandwich board and march through the streets. For serious or repeat offenses there was jail time, loss of master status, or even expulsion from the guild. Sometimes the police just looked the other way and let angry customers—often women—beat the bakers up.[23] At the bread market at Les Halles in Paris on Wednesdays and Saturdays, the average stall displayed "1,530 pounds of bread distributed as follows: 26 twelve-pound loaves, 40 eight-pound loaves, 101 six-pound loaves (mostly round), and 73 four-pound loaves (mostly long)."[24] Competition for customers was fierce. The bakers, male and female—and sometimes bakers' wives—got into fist or knife fights. Women were also the delivery people—*porteuses,* or female porters. On their backs, they carried baskets with as much as a hundred pounds of bread long distances and up four or five flights of stairs.[25]

French bread was made from flour, water, salt, leavening, and massive amounts of human labor. The leavening was a starter that took up to 15 hours to ripen, had to be fed and rested three or four times during kneading, and made a bulky dough that wore the bakers out wrestling with it—they had to knead 200 pounds by hand in 45 minutes. Sometimes they jumped on the dough and kneaded it with their bare feet. As Parmentier knew, this process was brutal on the bakers; the bread got more rest than they did. When some bakers switched to barm (brewer's yeast) because it rose faster and made the dough easier to work with, there was a public outcry. French physicians declared that brewer's yeast "shocked" the flour into rising instead of leading it gently, that it produced bread that was "garbage," and that it would have the same toxic effects on the human body as beer. It also supposedly made the bread less white.

The Salt Tax (*Gabelle*)

Another sore point was salt. French bread needed salt, but because chemistry was in its infancy, the French didn't understand what it did besides improve the flavor. It also controls the yeast, stops bacterial growth, and makes a finer-grained loaf that looks whiter and has a deeper crust. The salt tax (*gabelle*) was levied erratically. The *gabelle* might be high in one village, low in the next. This encouraged smuggling and corruption. Tax collectors were thugs who terrorized the peasants to force them to pay. They broke into houses at dawn, searched people in bed, and took the peasants' property. Sometimes they took the peasants to jail without notifying their families.[26]

Hunger, tension, and street violence mounted. Finally, the king called a meeting of all the classes, the *états generals*. The third estate, which wanted major changes in the government, sat on the left side of the hall; the moderates sat in the middle; and the conservative nobles

---

ℋOLIDAY ℋISTORY

» BASTILLE DAY «

July 14, 1789, is France's Independence Day. It is to the French what the Fourth of July is to Americans and is celebrated the same way—with fireworks and feasting. In the 1970s, Alice Waters began celebrating Bastille Day at Chez Panisse, her restaurant in Berkeley, California, with an all-garlic menu. It works out well because the garlic harvest in northern California is at about the same time. This sample menu is from *The Chez Panisse Menu Cookbook*. Every item, including the sherbets, has garlic in it.[27]

Garlic Soufflé

Baked Fish with Garlic Confit

Roast Squab with Garlic-and-Liver Sauce

Fettuccine with Fresh Chestnuts

Romaine and Rocket Salad with Garlic

Two Wine Fruit Sherbets

of the second estate, who wanted nothing to change, sat on the right. This is where American politics gets its terms "left wing" and "right wing." Since the right wing had all of the political power, nothing changed—then. However, on July 14, 1789, rumors spread through the city that the king had sent armed guards to turn on the people. They stormed the Bastille, the prison in the center of Paris, to get ammunition.

The Women March: "The Baker, the Baker's Wife, and the Baker's Boy"

On October 6, 1789, three months after the storming of the Bastille, French women went to market. There was no bread. Their children would starve. No more! The angry women grabbed stones, sticks, and pitchforks and marched to Versailles. It was 12 miles, and it was raining. They were going to get the queen and "fricassee her liver." The people hated the queen because she spent fortunes on clothes and entertainment, had not produced a royal heir for eight years after she married the king (through no fault of hers), and was Austrian. When she was informed that the people were starving because they had no bread, the queen supposedly laughed and said, "Let them eat cake"—really brioche, bread dough enriched with egg and butter.

When the women arrived at Versailles, the palace guard, whose only job was to protect the royal family, joined the women instead. The women got food: they ransacked the kitchens at Versailles. At gunpoint, King Louis XVI, Queen Marie Antoinette, and their son the dauphin (prince) were taken back to Paris and locked up in the Bastille. On the march back, the victorious women chanted that they had gotten "the baker, the baker's wife, and the baker's boy."

On June 21, 1791, the royal family tried to escape to safety to the queen's brother in Austria. They had almost reached the border when a postmaster recognized the king, even though he was disguised as a servant, because his picture was on all the French money. Rumors spread that the king was disguised as a chef. Historian Rebecca Spang has analyzed political cartoons from the French Revolution and pointed out that they show the royal family with pig faces, or the king eating pigs' feet. They all implied that the king only cared about "pigging out" and sticking the people of France with the bill while they starved.[28] The royal family was brought back to Paris. The king and queen were beheaded by the guillotine; the dauphin died in prison.

The Terror

In 1793, the revolution took a turn toward even more violence and intimidation under the rule of Robespierre. With the nobles executed or out of the country, thousands of ordinary people were accused of being enemies of the state and were sent to the guillotine—a huge blade that chopped heads off—for trivial reasons like serving bad wine. It was during this period that the man who had been the queen's chef for ten years was executed. On July 27, 1794, the Terror ended when moderates seized control and sent Robespierre where he had sent so many others—on a one-way walk up the guillotine steps. The place in Paris where the guillotine stood is now the Place de la Concorde.

THE NAPOLEONIC ERA: 1799–1815

In 1799, a young general named Napoleon Bonaparte seized control of the French government by walking in with the army and declaring he was in charge. The French Revolution and the Napoleonic era that followed brought about cultural changes much more profound than the American Revolution had. The French Revolution created a truly new society with new classes, new values, and new ways of treating people. The first estate, the clergy, was now under the control of the state. The second estate, the nobility, was gone—dead or fled. The third estate, the bourgeoisie, the peasants, and the urban poor, could vote, hold government jobs, and set reasonable taxes for themselves. And their taxes paid for schools for their children, not for some noble's château or banquet. Napoleon wanted to restore France to an empire and recover the land that had been lost in wars with England. He also wanted to rule all of Europe. He was becoming frustrated on both counts.

"Damn Sugar, Damn Coffee, Damn Colonies!"—Napoleon[29]

1802. Napoleon was furious. In the Caribbean, his troops had failed to retake the sugar- and coffee-producing island of St. Domingue (Haiti) from rebellious slaves. Now, 20 thousand of them were dead, killed by Toussaint L'Ouverture, the leader of the slaves, and by yellow fever, a disease spread by mosquitoes. (Yellow fever is the English name for the disease. In Spanish it is much more descriptive: *vomito negro*.)

In Europe, the powerful British navy blocked ships from French ports. Napoleon tried to make France self-sufficient. If he couldn't get sugar from sugarcane in the Caribbean, then he would grow sugar beets at home. The sugar beet proved to be as good a source of sugar as cane. Napoleon's decision contributed to the decline of the Caribbean economy and changed the sugar-eating habits of the world.

Napoleon's wars were becoming expensive. How to finance them? He would have to sell some real estate. Fast. But who would buy?

"The Big Cheese"—President Thomas Jefferson

The 1,235-pound cheese couldn't be ignored. It arrived in Washington, D.C., on New Year's Day, 1802, a gift to President Thomas Jefferson from the citizens of Cheshire, Massachusetts (and 900 cows). This large food also had a political and religious purpose. It was the public relations brainchild of a Baptist minister, one of the leaders of the new religious movement that was sweeping America and came to be called the Second Great Awakening, as people everywhere awoke to their inner religious feelings. The cheese had a motto printed on it: "Rebellion to tyrants is obedience to God."[30] People everywhere made a pilgrimage to see the big cheese in the White House. And that is how the president of the United States became "the big cheese."

In 1803, the Big Cheese was worried. President Jefferson had just bought 828,000 square miles of land and his conscience was bothering him. Nowhere did the Constitution say that the president, by himself, could pick up a pen and double the size of the country, not even at three cents an acre. He had authorized the American ambassador to buy New Orleans so that the American farmers who were swarming west over the Appalachians into the Ohio River valley would have a seaport to get their produce to Europe. To trade with other Americans, any foodstuffs from the Ohio River valley could be floated downriver to where three rivers— the Ohio, the Allegheny, and the Monongahela—met at Pittsburgh. But to trade with Europe, they had to continue down to the mouth of the Mississippi, to New Orleans. The Americans owned Pittsburgh; the French owned New Orleans, which angry Americans were talking about attacking and taking by force. This would throw the new, small United States into a war with a European superpower headed by Napoleon, a military genius. President Jefferson hoped that Napoleon would sell New Orleans to the United States instead. He was stunned when Napoleon gave the go-ahead to sell everything France owned on the North American mainland. It was one of the greatest real estate deals in history.

But what, exactly, had America bought? A shortcut to the riches and markets of China and India, they hoped. Maybe this, finally, was the Northwest

Passage, the water route through North America to the Pacific Ocean that Columbus, Hudson, Champlain, and the other explorers had not been able to find. Maybe by going north, up the Mississippi River to its headwaters, they would discover a route to Asia. Two years later, Lewis and Clark returned from their exploration with disappointing news—no Northwest Passage.

New Orleans—Creole Cuisine

New Orleans, however, was not a disappointment. Its Creole cuisine—the French- and Spanish-influenced cuisine of the ruling class, prepared by African cooks—is unique in America. Beginning in 1791, New Orleans residents could buy fresh turtles, crabs, vegetables, or slaves at La Halle, the French marketplace. After 1812, travelers, gamblers, and other characters sailed up and down the Mississippi on luxurious steamboats with ballrooms, bars, and casinos.[31] Famous New Orleans foods include gumbo—an African word and concept. This is a roux-based sausage-and-seafood stew thickened with okra (an African word for an African vegetable) and seasoned with filé (powdered sassafras leaves obtained from Native Americans). The name *jambalaya* comes from *jambon,* French for "ham," and *ya,* an African word for "rice"; *étouffée* means "smothered," but is more like a stuffing for seafood. Louisiana bills itself as the "Sportsman's Paradise" because of the abundance of deer, quail, duck, and other wild fowl. Prepared

---

ℋOLIDAY ℋISTORY
◈ MARDI GRAS AND *CARNEVALE* ◈

In Christianity, January 6, twelve days after Christmas, is when the three kings who had been searching for the newborn Christ child found him. In Louisiana, it marks the end of the festive Christmas season and the beginning of the festive Mardi Gras season. *Mardi Gras* is French for "fat Tuesday," the last day of feasting before Lent and its 40 days of fasting begins. The first official Mardi Gras celebration in New Orleans was in 1827, although other celebrations had been occurring in French America since 1718.[32] A fancy dress ball kicks off the series of parades with kings and queens, special Mardi Gras jewelry, and a special king cake in the official colors of Mardi Gras—purple, gold, green. Other Mardi Gras celebrations occur around the world. Perhaps the largest is in Brazil, where it is called *Carnevale,* and samba clubs practice special dances all year for the festivities.

INGREDIENTS

*K*ING *C*AKE—
THE CAKE WITH A BABY INSIDE[33]

2 cups sugar
½ cup butter
2 cups flour
½ cup water
5 egg yolks
6 egg whites
½ teaspoon baking soda
1 teaspoon cream of tartar
juice of 1½ oranges

meats are everything from sophisticated sausages like boudin to barbecue and real fried pork rinds with streaks of pork (nothing like the prepackaged Styrofoam-like version). The Gulf of Mexico provides shrimp, oysters, and crawfish. As elsewhere in the South, corn appears as grits and hominy. Louisiana is also famous for its rice and sugar. Pralines are a pecan, butter, and brown sugar patty. At sidewalk cafés, people snack on beignets—fried pastry puffs dusted with confectioner's sugar—and chicory coffee. It is also the home of bananas Foster, oysters Rockefeller, Tabasco sauce, and a very special holiday, Mardi Gras.

The king cake has a tiny plastic baby doll baked inside. Traditionally, the person who gets the piece of cake with the baby in it is king or queen for a day and then has to provide the next party. The custom dates back to the ancient French custom of baking a lucky bean (*fève*) into the bread. The baby refers to the Christ child.

Jefferson, the Francophile President

Jefferson was a Francophile—he loved France and all things French. While he was the American ambassador to France, he ate and loved Continental food. He took a slave with him to be trained by French chefs. After he returned to America, Jefferson granted the slave his freedom, but only after he trained a replacement. Jefferson also brought crates of pasta and the word *macaroni* back with him. (The word *spaghetti* didn't appear in America until the 1849 edition of *Modern Cookery for Private Families* by Eliza Acton.)

Jefferson's plantation, Monticello, had 5,000 acres of orchards and fruit and vegetable gardens, plus numerous outbuildings. Below is a blueprint of the house. Notice that although there are a tea room (7) and a dining room (8), there is no kitchen in the house. The kitchen was a separate building. Rooms of the "original" Monticello, before it was expanded, are shown with solid lines. To take a virtual tour, log onto www.monticello.org.

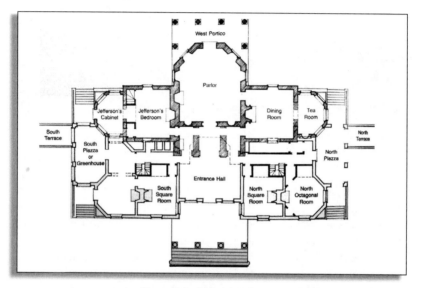

Blueprint of Monticello, home of Thomas Jefferson.
Courtesy of Monticello/Thomas Jefferson Foundation, Inc.

1. North Octagonal Room
2. North Square Room
3. Entrance Hall
4. South Square Room
5. Library, or Book Room
6. South Piazza, or Greenhouse
7. Tea Room
8. Dining Room
9. Parlor
10. Jefferson's Bedroom
11. Cabinet

The kitchen at Monticello. Photo by R. Lautman/Monticello.
Courtesy of Monticello/Thomas Jefferson Foundation, Inc.

The kitchen was one of several outbuildings on a typical southern plantation. It included a large fireplace, storage shelves, and equipment. It was separate to keep the heat out of the main house, and also to avoid accidentally burning the main house down.

Thomas Jefferson, the third president of the United States, and John Adams, the second president, died on the same day, within a few hours of each other. The day was July 4, 1826—exactly 50 years after the Declaration of Independence.

"An Army Marches on Its Stomach": The Invention of Canned Food

In 1803, armed with the $15 million he got from the United States for the Louisiana Purchase, Napoleon proceeded with his plan to conquer Europe. He needed to make sure his troops had good food. He offered a prize of 12,000 francs (U.S. $250,000 today) to the first person who could find a way to do this.

In 1810, Nicolas Appert published his book *L'Art de conserver pendant plusieurs années toutes les substances animales et végétales* (The Art of Conserving for Several Years All Animal and Vegetable Substances). Appert, born in 1750, grew up in the wine cellars and inns of Champagne, helping his father, an innkeeper. By the time he was 22, he was an accomplished chef; by 31, he had his own confectionery shop in Paris. He was also passionate about preserving foods. He wanted to find a new method, because the old ones—salting, drying, and smoking—altered the taste and texture of food, and not for the better.[34] For ten years, he experimented with ways to preserve food. He finally settled on packing the food in glass bottles—Champagne bottles at first, because he could get so many—and boiling them in a *bain-marie* or water bath. The food tasted good, much better than what other methods produced. Then Appert got lucky. The food critic La Reynière liked what Appert was doing and wrote about him in his food column. However, food packed in glass was impractical in the navy. The country that ended up getting the patent on Appert's invention and mass-producing it was England, because it was more industrialized than France and had a highly developed tin industry. The cans, made by hand and flat on top, had to be opened with a hammer and chisel until the middle of the 19th century, when Americans mass-produced them, recessed one end of the can, and invented the can opener.

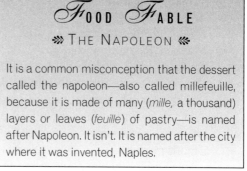

Food Fable

❊ THE NAPOLEON ❊

It is a common misconception that the dessert called the napoleon—also called millefeuille, because it is made of many (*mille,* a thousand) layers or leaves (*feuille*) of pastry—is named after Napoleon. It isn't. It is named after the city where it was invented, Naples.

Scorched Earth in Russia

Losing his colonies in the Americas increased Napoleon's obsession with conquering Europe. That included Russia. To stop Napoleon, the Russian people destroyed their own food. They burned their grain and slaughtered their livestock, and Napoleon did not get their country. He marched into Russia with 500 thousand men. He limped out with 50 thousand. The Russian people and the Russian winter were formidable foes, and Napoleon lost. It was an expensive lesson, but not one that another European dictator, 130 years later, would learn from. Hitler, too, would be beaten by the fierce determination of the Russian people and the ferocious Russian winter. After Napoleon's final defeat by the British at Waterloo in Belgium in 1815, he was exiled to the tiny, remote island of St. Helena in the Atlantic Ocean, originally founded as a refueling port for the British fleet on its way to the Spice Islands, and he died there.

"And the Restaurants, How Many New Marvels!"[35]

The changes in the world of cuisine were also profound. The French Revolution changed what, where, and how people ate. The bourgeoisie had more money, since 50 percent of their income wasn't going for taxes anymore, and they wanted to eat well. Out of the ashes of the French Revolution emerged the modern restaurant, a purely French invention that began in Paris.

The revolution also ended the medieval guild system. The food industry shifted from arguing over which guild controlled which food to which establishment could sell what kind of food to the public. In 1830, a café owner was sued for impersonating a restaurateur because his menu contained 120 items, too many for a café, and he also served lunch.[36]

These new eating habits needed new words to describe them. The words connected with the restaurant are French. A man named Boulanger had opened the first restaurant in 1754, in Paris, well before the revolution. He served a soup that was supposed to restore the health, called a *restaurant*. Other French words are *restaurateur*, for the owner of a restaurant, and *menu*, from the French word for "small," because the menu is a small description of the larger dishes. Grimod de la Reynière was the world's first restaurant critic; his *Almanach des gourmands* was the world's first restaurant guide, before the brothers Michelin and the husband-and-wife team of Tim and Nina Zagat. In 1801, the word *gastronomy* appeared for the first time, as the title of a poem. It referred to the Greek *Gastronomia*, written by Archestratos in the 4th century B.C. This was followed by *gastronome*, a person familiar with good eating.[37]

Brillat-Savarin: "You Are What You Eat"

Perhaps the first gastronome was Jean Anthelme Brillat-Savarin, whose most famous quote was "Tell me what you eat, and I will tell you what you are." His book of meditations on food, *The Physiology of Taste*, was published in 1825. He also said, "Gastronomy is the intelligent knowledge of whatever concerns man's nourishment."[38] As an upper-class man, he spent two years of the French Revolution hiding out in America, part of the time in Hartford, Connecticut (if he ate election cake, he didn't mention it). He also lived in New York City. He had nothing but praise for the American table. The food was absolutely fresh—freshly grown, freshly milked, freshly killed—and there was plenty of it. He knew, because while he was there, he went on a turkey shoot. A true food lover, Brillat-Savarin said that the riches of the Americas were not gold but potatoes, vanilla, and cocoa. He loved the treasures of France, too: "The truffle is the diamond of the art of cookery."[39]

Brillat-Savarin listed the reasons he loved restaurants: you can choose when to eat, how much to spend, and what kind of meal to have; you can have the best of what France has to offer, and luxuries imported from all over the world. He was an observer of the wide variety of people who eat in restaurants, too—the ones who eat alone, the country families, married couples, lovers, the "regulars," the foreigners. He pointed out a pitfall: eating in restaurants is so seductive that it is easy to get into debt doing it. After all, "a restaurant is Paradise indeed to any gourmand."[40]

The Chef's Uniform

The word *chef,* short for *chef de cuisine,* also came into use at this time. Earlier, chefs were called cooks or master cooks. With professionalization came the language of the kitchen, names for positions in the profession, and a way to distinguish this profession—a uniform.

The chef's uniform has two practical functions: (1) to protect the chef from the food, and (2) to protect the food from the chef. In the first case, the long sleeves, long pants, and double-breasted jacket are a barrier against burns, spills, and splatters. The black-and-white houndstooth check pattern on the pants is camouflage—try to find the stain. Sturdy shoes guard against falling equipment and knives. Nonskid soles provide traction on floors slippery from spilled food and grease. In the second case, the long sleeves, double-breasted jacket, and neckerchief protect the food from a sweating chef. The *toque blanche,* the tall white chef's hat, keeps the chef's hair out of his eyes and out of the food and also, like the stars on a general's hat or the distinctive hat of an admiral, makes it easy to see who is in charge in a crowded kitchen. Before Carême, the chef's hat was floppy; Carême put cardboard in his to make it stand tall. The toque is supposed to have one hundred pleats, to represent the minimum number of ways a good chef can prepare eggs. In *The Culinary Guide,* master chef Escoffier lists 202 ways to prepare eggs, *excluding* omelettes, which are another 82 recipes and a note that "using the basic recipe for Omelette Norvégienne it is possible to produce an almost infinite number of variations of this type of omelette (Omelette Surprise)."[41]

The uniform couldn't protect cooks against one serious kitchen hazard: carbon monoxide poisoning. Carbon monoxide binds strongly to the hemoglobin in blood, thus preventing it from carrying oxygen to the body's tissues, including the brain. Carbon monoxide gas is odorless, colorless, and therefore impossible to detect. It is produced by using charcoal fires indoors with inadequate ventilation. Carbon monoxide poisoning was so common among cooks in France that it was called *folie des cuisiniers*—cooks' craziness—because of its symptoms of bizarre behavior, disorientation, and loss of muscle coordination. It also turned the face a bright cherry red, which could make a person suffering from carbon monoxide poisoning look drunk.[42]

Carême: The Architect of French Cuisine

"Antonin Carême is probably the greatest cook of all time."
—*food historian Anne Willan*[43]

Carême came to food as a profession not out of love, but out of dire necessity. In 1793, the year Louis XVI and his head parted company on the chopping block under the guillotine, Carême's impoverished parents turned the illiterate ten-year-old boy out into the street and wished him good luck. The boy was no fool—he found work in a kitchen. He rose quickly and became a *pâtissier*. He taught himself to read and in 1815, by the time he was 32, had published two books, *Le Pâtissier royal* and *Le Pâtissier pittoresque*. Twelve years later, he had learned everything he could about the other branches of cooking and was one of the best chefs in France. He decided to try working for royalty in England but became frustrated when he realized after two years that even the best French cooking couldn't make a dent in hundreds of years of bland British food.

> The essentials of English cooking are the roasts of beef, mutton, and lamb; the various meats cooked in salt water, in the manner of fish and vegetables . . . fruit preserves, puddings of all kinds, chicken and turkey with cauliflower, salt beef, country ham, and several similar ragoûts—that is the sum of English cooking.[44]

Carême went to Russia—too cold. Vienna was better, but France was just right, and that is where he spent the rest of his life. Carême was a genius at organization. He brought order and consistency to French food. One of his greatest contributions to the world of cuisine was that he organized the sauces on which French cuisine is based. His system was modular: five leading or mother sauces were the basic building blocks. By adding wine, herbs, cheese, vegetables, and so on to these five basic sauces, hundreds more could be created. These were called small or daughter sauces. Now there was a clear progression in French cooking: first, master the five leading sauces—béchamel, velouté, espagnole, hollandaise, and tomato. Two sauces—espagnole and hollandaise—are named after the countries where they originated, Spain and Holland; béchamel is named after the chef who invented it; tomato is named after its main ingredient. Only one sauce, velouté, has a name that describes the sauce. In French, *velouté* means "velvety," and when it is made right, that is the truth.

Carême also stressed presentation. The part of him that was an architect created elaborate tall constructions, often spun sugar, called *pièces montées,* to decorate his tables. He also created art in the new branch of cuisine that arose after the French Revolution, the cold buffet with *chaud-froid* (hot-cold) dishes—foods that are cooked first, then coated in aspic and served cold. In 1833, this genius wrote his last book, which defined French cooking throughout the 19th century. He died the same year.

America's Second War for Independence; South America Revolts

England took advantage of France's preoccupation with its business in Europe to try to retake the United States. In 1815, the same year Napoleon was defeated at Waterloo and Carême published his book, in New Orleans the United States won the last battle of the War of 1812. (The treaty that ended the war was signed in December 1814, but news hadn't reached the United States yet.) No land changed hands, but the United States retained its independence and was beginning to gain respect as a power to be dealt with.

Napoleon's reign as emperor caused revolutions all over Central and Latin America. When Napoleon invaded Spain and Portugal in 1808, he placed his brother Joseph on the throne. The Spanish people refused to accept this Frenchman as their king. Instead, they waged a guerrilla war for years. Spain's colonies felt even less loyalty to a French king. By 1841, all of the New World colonies that had belonged to Spain since the late 15th and early 16th centuries had formed into the countries that still exist today. Brazil won its independence from Portugal, too. Then these independent new colonies began to split up. In 1830, Colombia splintered into modern-day Colombia, Venezuela, and

Ecuador. Eleven years later, in 1841, Guatemala, Honduras, El Salvador, Nicaragua, and Costa Rica broke away from Mexico, weakening it. This was of great interest to Mexico's neighbor to the north, the United States, which was expanding rapidly and wanted more land.

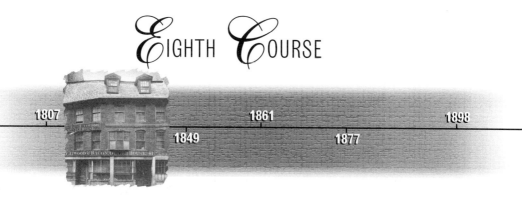

From Coyotes to Coca-Cola: The 19th Century in America

"GO WEST, YOUNG MAN!"

America was in a fever to head west. "Manifest Destiny" was the idea that the restless American people were destined to rule North America "from sea to shining sea." And they were inventing the technology to get there. In 1807, Robert Fulton's steamboat sailed up the Hudson River, against the current. In 1825, the Erie Canal cut the time it took grain to go from Buffalo to New York City from three weeks to less than one, lowered the price from $100 to $5 per ton, and turned New York into the Empire State. At the end of the 1820s, the first railroads were built in the United States. In 1844, the wires talked—the first telegraph message was sent. Most of this new technology was in the northern United States. West of the Mississippi there were no steamboats, no railroad, no telegraph. But there was good farmland in California and Oregon.

Going west in a covered wagon was not cheap. Each adult needed 400 pounds of provisions. The majority of those who went were prosperous white farmers from families who had been in the United States for generations. Because of the expense, few free blacks could afford the trip. Some immigrants went, usually as servants. Inexperienced pioneers overloaded their wagons and ended up jettisoning about half their goods. They brought milk cows because there was no dairy

179

industry in California yet and milk was very valuable.[1] Breadstuff was the staple on the overland trail—wheat flour baked into yeast-risen bread in a Dutch oven when they had the time and the fuel; biscuits, crackers, cornmeal. They also brought coffee, sugar, salt, bacon, and dried fruit. These midwestern farmers counted on shooting or trapping game along the way. Sometimes they could, and sometimes they couldn't. They also had no concept that the short stretch on the map called "Forty-Mile Desert," west of the Humboldt Sink in what is now Nevada, would take them not two days of walking but at least five; that many of their oxen would die or go crazy from thirst; that the curved wood in their covered wagon frames and wheels would dry out, straighten, and splinter; and that this 40-mile crossing would leave them exhausted, weak, and low on food. Desperate people ate "bush trout"—rattlesnakes. People dying of thirst drank their mules' urine or paid $15.00 for a glass of water when they could get it.

How to Cook a Coyote

After the desert, they faced the hardest part of the trip—the more than 14,000-foot-high peaks of the Sierra Nevada ("snowy peaks" in Spanish) Mountains. The famous Donner Party from Illinois, stranded for months in the snow above 6,000 feet in the Sierras during the winter of 1846–1847, butchered their dead. They took great care to label the body parts so no one would accidentally eat a relative. Some of the 47 people who survived did so by eating some of the 40 who died.[2]

In another case of being stranded in the snow, desperate 18-year-old Moses Schallenberger, who had fallen behind and been left by his wagon train, decided to try to trap something, anything:

> I found in one of [the traps] a starved coyote. I soon had his hide off and his flesh roasted in a Dutch oven. I ate this meat, but it was horrible. I next tried boiling him, but it didn't improve the flavor. I cooked him in every possible manner my imagination, spurred by hunger, could suggest, but couldn't get him into a condition where he could be eaten without revolting my stomach. But for three days this was all I had to eat.[3]

Moses was also able to trap foxes, which he found delicious, though their meat was "entirely devoid of fat," which he craved. He also caught many more coyotes, "but I never got hungry enough to eat one of them again."[4]

The Gold Rush: Feeding the Forty-Niners

After a war with Mexico from 1846 to 1848, the United States reached to the Pacific Ocean. In 1848, at Sutter's Mill near Sacramento in northern California, gold was discovered. The stories were fantastic—men dammed a river and found $75,000 worth of gold nuggets just lying in the dry riverbed; a man and his two sons picked up gold worth more than $9,000 each in a short time.[5] And this was at a time when the average unskilled laborer earned $1.00 for a 12-hour day. Historian John Holliday described the gold rush in the title of his book *The World Rushed In*. And it was an almost totally male world. In the first five months of 1850, of the 17,661 people who passed through Ft. Laramie, Wyoming, on their way west, 17,443 were men.[6] They gravitated to taverns, saloons, and bars.

No matter where the miners came from or what language they spoke, they all had to eat, and all the food had to be shipped in. Merchants who sold food got rich by mining the miners—they gouged. Some food costs less today than it did more than 150 years ago.

FOOD PRICE COMPARISON 1850–2002 (PER POUND)[7] ($1.00 IN 1850 = $20.00 IN 2002)		
Item	1850—California Gold Fields	2002—Los Angeles Supermarket
Coffee	$ .50	4.17
Sugar	.75	.89
Beans	1.00	.75
Potatoes	1.00	.99
Tea	2.50	(in bags) 5.38
Vinegar	5.00	.90

Cooking equipment suffered the same markup: tin pans and coffeepots cost $8 each, frying pans, $6. Water in a boardinghouse cost $20 per week; rent was $500 per month. With saleratus—sodium bicarbonate—selling for $6 per pound, the men opted for flour and water left out to ferment, leavened with wild yeast that settled from the air. A portion of each batch of this bread could be kept aside and fed to start the next batch. From these bread starters, the men became known as "sourdoughs." (For those who claim that San Francisco sourdough bread doesn't taste like any other, they're right. The yeast in the air there—and only there—is *Lactobacillus sanfrancisco*.)[8] Even when food and equipment were available, nobody wanted to work unloading it or getting it out of the warehouses. Literally tons of food rotted, and there was nobody to clean it up. The men hated to waste time doing anything except looking for gold. Even roasting and grinding their coffee beans took too long. Folger's stepped in with the first preroasted coffee.[9] When the men complained that their pants kept ripping from all the hard work, a Jewish merchant from Bavaria named Levi Strauss teamed up with a Lithuanian tailor and took out a patent for denim pants held together with metal rivets—Levi's blue jeans.[10]

Yes, there was gold "in them thar hills," but there was malnutrition, too. No one who wrote home mentioned dairy or eggs except to note their absence. Butter from New York arrived brown after a year-long sea voyage around "the Horn," the tip of South America. Cooks had to sift flour to get rid of weevils and pulled long black worms out by the handful. Gunpowder substituted for salt. A meal usually consisted of "coffee, bacon, beans, and hard bread," eaten standing up or sitting on a log.[11] Men who worked outside all day in the rain or waded in streams freezing with snowmelt got sick and did not get well on this food. In the 1850s scurvy killed about 10,000 miners until they started eating winter purslane, which they called "miners' lettuce."[12]

The Native Americans of California, who were described as "timid and friendly," lived on acorns and wild game they shot with bows and arrows. The massive population invasion had the same disastrous effect on them that the arrival of the Spanish had had on the natives of Central America 250 years earlier: they died. By 1860, the native population of California had dropped to about 30,000.[13]

The gold rush in California in 1849 was just the first of several mineral rushes. Later silver was discovered in Nevada, gold in the Black Hills of South Dakota in the 1870s, and gold again in the Alaskan Klondike/Canadian Yukon in 1898. But the sane Canadians sent the Royal Canadian Mounted Police or "Mounties" in first. They turned back anyone who didn't have a six-month supply of food.

The people in the California territory wanted to become a state. But slave or free? Either way, California's entry into the union would destroy the balance in the Senate of 15 free and 15 slave states. In 1850, California joined as a free state because the sourdoughs didn't want slave labor competing with them in the gold fields. The South's solution: buy Cuba from Spain and turn it into a slave state. But Spain wasn't interested. In the Compromise of 1850, the slave markets, but not slavery, ended in Washington, D.C., and the South got a tough new Fugitive Slave Law. Southerners claimed the slaves were happy and well treated. Was that the reality?

THE CIVIL WAR AND RECONSTRUCTION—1850–1877

Slavery and Soul Food: Not "Livin' High on the Hog"

The slave-owning planter class, the ones who lived in mansions and had overseers, like in the movie *Gone with the Wind*, was a very small percentage of the white population in the South. In 1850, only about 25 percent of white families owned slaves, and of those, only 1,933 families owned more than 100 slaves.[14] Seventy-five percent of whites in the South owned no slaves; many were subsistence farmers who led difficult, hardworking lives:

> By any standards their lives were drab. Their houses more nearly resembled shacks than the mansions of tradition. . . . The produce of their small plantations included meat, grain, and vegetables for subsistence and tobacco, rice or other staples that could be sold for cash. [15]

Still, this was luxury compared to how the slaves lived. Booker T. Washington, who was born into slavery and was the first principal of the Tuskegee Institute in Alabama (opened July 4, 1881; now Tuskegee University), wrote his autobiography, *Up from Slavery,* and described the slave cabin where he grew up. It was one room, 14 by 16 feet, where Washington lived with his mother, brother, and sister. It had a dirt floor, a hole in the center to store sweet potatoes, another hole in the corner to let the cats out, holes in the log walls to let light in, and a door falling off its hinges. His father was a white man, but Washington never knew who he was. The cabin was not just their home; Washington's mother was the plantation cook, so it was also the plantation kitchen. There was no stove; all the cooking was done on an open fire on the floor. Washington remembers his mother waking the children up in the middle of the night once for a feast, a chicken she had stolen.

Slave cooks in the wealthy plantation households were almost all female. They usually learned by doing, often a daughter at her mother's side, using recipes and methods passed on from earlier generations of female cooks. The white plantation mistress gave instructions but she did not cook, so the black female slave cook reigned supreme in the southern kitchen. She had a skilled, high-status job with a great deal of prestige. She worked in the house, not in the fields, and she was proud of it.[16] Slave owners were afraid of their cooks because the cooks had the power to poison them and sometimes did.

Fine southern cooking and legendary southern hospitality were made possible by the labor of women slaves. Food historian Karen Hess states that in the first half of the 19th century, all southern cookbooks by white women were recipes that they got from black cooks.[17] The first cookbook by an African-American, *What Mrs. Fisher Knows About Old Southern Cooking*, was published in 1881 in San Francisco, but it was not until the 1990s that food historian Dan Strehl discovered that the author, Abby Fisher, was a mulatto, born a slave in South Carolina to a slave mother and a French father. She was illiterate, so the book was dictated. There are 160 numbered recipes in 72 pages. The majority, 58, are for breads, cakes, pies, puddings, and sherbets. Forty-one are for Mrs. Fisher's prize winning pickles, sauces, and preserves. Her pastry is rolled out "to the thickness of an egg-shell for the top of the fruit, and that for the bottom of fruit must be thin as paper."[18] "Compound Tomato Sauce" is more like a ketchup, left to stand for 24 hours with onions, allspice, cloves, black pepper, and cayenne pepper, then cooked with vinegar.[19] South Carolina was rice country, so rice appears in one of the earliest recipes for jambalaya. Chicken, crab, oysters, and fish are mixed with crackers and turned into croquettes, baked into pies, broiled, fricasseed, stewed with rice in gumbo, or made into chowder. Potatoes are "Irish potatoes." Corn appears in fritters, boiled, in "Circuit Hash" (succotash), in hoe cake, in pudding, and in corn bread with rice. Eggplant, introduced to Africa by the Arabs, is stuffed, as are tomatoes. Tomatoes *and* milk are used in clam chowder.

The labor force was not the only difference between kitchens in the North and the South. In the North, the kitchen hearth was the heart of the house. In the South, the plantation kitchen was separate from the house, just another outbuilding along with the dairy, the stable, and the outhouse. On large plantations, supplies were bought and animals slaughtered and processed in bulk—barrels of flour and whiskey, dozens of chickens. In one day, 17 hogs totaling 2,077 pounds were killed and turned into sausage and tallow.[20]

In the South, what part of the hog you ate was a clear indication of your rank in society. The plantation owner and his family ate the meat from "high on the hog"—ribs, roasts, hams. The slaves got the food from the outer limits—ears, snout, tail, feet or "trotters"; or from the inner wasteland—the small intestines, called chitterlings or "chitlins." Chitlins were sometimes used by the whites, but as casings for sausage, not alone as food. Slave cooks prepared the meat from high on the hog but weren't allowed to eat it. They were also not allowed to eat beef, lamb, mutton, chickens, turkey, and geese, which were reserved for the plantation house.[21]

Slaves had no control of any part of their food supply. If the master allowed, they could supplement their diet with vegetables they grew on their own time on a patch of land near the slave cabin or with fish they caught. If the master didn't allow them to, they couldn't. Slave women, in particular, were at the mercy of the masters for food. Slave women who were good "breeders" and produced many children sometimes got extra food for their families. Often, those who didn't have children were sold.[22]

The Underground Railroad and the Taste of Freedom

Some northern white women began to think they had something in common with slaves, and to agitate for freedom for both. In the first half of the 19th century, a man could beat his wife legally as long as he used a stick no thicker than his thumb—the "rule of thumb." In 1848, approximately 100 white women and men gathered at Seneca Falls in upstate New York. They drafted a document that was for women what the Declaration of Independence was for the nation. Their document, the Declaration of Sentiments, stated that "all men and women are created equal," that they were being taxed without representation, and that they should have the right to vote. Just as the Declaration of Independence had a list of grievances against King George III, the women had a list of grievances against men: men prevented women from going to college or into professional careers; passed divorce laws so that women could never get the children; made all property that a woman owned, whether inherited or earned, the property of her husband; and turned public opinion against women by having different moral standards for men and women.[23] The people who signed the declaration were ridiculed mercilessly in the press. Nevertheless, a powerful movement had been set in motion, and women became more involved in efforts to abolish slavery.

Lydia Maria Child was one of these. She began as a novelist, then wrote *The American Frugal Housewife*. Published in 1829, it was the only cookbook she wrote and it was immediately a best-seller. However, her books about rights for slaves and her position as editor of the *National Anti-Slavery Standard* put her on the fringes of American politics; *The American Frugal Housewife* was not reprinted after 1850.

Catherine Beecher's *Treatise on Domestic Economy* was published in 1841 and became the new household standard. Beecher opposed the women's movement, but she was a practical person and her book explains clearly how to manage a household with few or no servants. She was deeply concerned with all aspects of the health and well-being of everyone in the household, down to what the milk cow was eating.[24] Her *Treatise* provided anatomy lessons and life advice. Her sister, however, was very involved in the abolition movement, and in 1852, Harriet Beecher Stowe wrote *Uncle Tom's Cabin,* which electrified northerners about the horrors of slavery and attempts by the slaves to escape, especially a young mother with her baby.

One of the ways slaves escaped was via the Underground Railroad. This wasn't a literal railroad. Rather, it was a series of "stations" or "safe houses" where the runaway slaves could hide and get food until they got to freedom, sometimes Canada. Many of the organizers of the Underground Railroad were blacks who were either born free in the North or escaped to freedom, especially black ministers. Quakers, who founded the first anti-slavery society in America in 1775, were also very active in the Underground Railroad. A famous "conductor" was Harriet Tubman, an illiterate black slave who suffered brain damage at the age of 13 when her white master, in a fit of rage, smashed her in the head with a lead weight and nearly killed her. She escaped, then made 19 trips back into slave territory and smuggled more than 300 slaves out to freedom. The North called her the "Moses" of her people; the South put a $12,000 bounty on her head.

What some runaway slaves remembered most about their first day away from slavery was the literal taste of freedom: the food, and how it was served. Sometimes they couldn't eat even though they were starving, because they were so overwhelmed. They couldn't believe they were sitting at a table with white people who treated them not just as equals, but as betters: these white people waited on *them,* encouraging them to eat all the food they wanted. And what food it was!—food they had cooked and smelled and looked at and longed for all their lives but had never been allowed to eat, food they could get only by stealing and would have been punished for taking. But once they started eating, they couldn't stop, as one runaway slave recounted:

> I ate straight on for an entire hour, quite steady. I demolished all the ham and eggs and sausages they placed before me, with their due accompaniment of bread, and then a round of cold salt beef was brought up, from which I was helped abundantly.[25]

Finally free and livin' high on the hog!

Scorched Earth in the American South: "War Is Hell"

In April 1861, one month after Abraham Lincoln became president, the Confederacy fired on the United States at Fort Sumter in South Carolina, and the Civil War began. In the beginning, under the command of Robert E. Lee and other brilliant generals, the South won. Gradually, however, the North's greater population and industrial power—including two-thirds of the railroad track and all the gun factories in the country—began to overpower the South's cotton-based economy.

Like Napoleon, the north's General Ulysses S. Grant knew that a commander can move his troops only as far as he can supply them. He also knew that his army was in the United States, where there was plenty of food, and gave orders to take it from the enemy. General William Tecumseh Sherman did this in his six-month march through the South on a front 60 miles wide. Sherman burned Atlanta to the ground, then led troops to Savannah on his famous "March to the Sea." Then he headed north through South Carolina, North Carolina, and Virginia, doing more than $100 million in property damage (estimated in 1865 values), a great deal of it to railroads.[26] As he started his march, news reached him and his troops about the Confederate prison in Andersonville, Georgia, where Union soldiers were being held.

> Inside the camp death stalked on every hand. . . . one-third of the original enclosure was swampy—a mud of liquid filth, voidings from the thousands, seething with maggots in full activity. Through this mass of pollution passed the only water. . . . We could not get away from the stink—we ate it, drank it and slept in it.[27]

"War is Hell," said Sherman. Southerners in northern prison camps and in Sherman's path in the South agreed and went one step farther: Sherman was Satan. But the slaves he freed along the way thought he was God.

In the midst of all of this war and carnage, Americans turned to God. "In God we trust" was added to American money for the first time. In 1863, Lincoln declared Thanksgiving a national holiday. Christmas was also becoming a popular holiday.

The Civil War ended on April 9, 1865, when General Lee surrendered to General Grant at the courthouse in Appomattox, Virginia. Less than a week later, President Lincoln was assassinated. The country immediately plunged into deep mourning. And the slaves finally got news they had been praying for all their lives: they were free.

Reconstruction

The new president, Andrew "Tennessee" Johnson, had serious problems. How would the Union be reconstructed? On what terms would the rebellious states be allowed back into the Union? The economy of

ℋoliday ℋistory

⇨ Christmas ⇦

Christmas Day, December 25, as it is celebrated in the United States today is a mixture of German, English, and American traditions. It also has remnants of pagan rituals. The Romans had an end-of-the-year festival called the Saturnalia, for which the color red had special significance, especially red hats. The original Santa Claus was Saint Nicholas, a true saint who lived in what is now Turkey in the 4th century.

In the mid-1800s, England's Queen Victoria and her husband, Prince Albert, were photographed in the royal palace celebrating Christmas in the German tradition of Victoria's childhood—with a Christmas tree. The pictures were printed in American magazines and the Christmas tree caught on instantly, along with other German Christmas traditions like singing "O Tannenbaum" (German for "Christmas tree"), bringing fresh greenery into the house in the middle of winter, candy canes, and gingerbread. Plum pudding became a British Christmas tradition. There are no plums in it; *plummy* means "something wonderful" or "choicest"; also, *plums* sometimes meant raisins. Christmas became commercialized in the middle of the 19th century, when the new department stores used their display windows to tempt people into buying gifts. In the middle of the 20th century, Irving Berlin wrote the song "White Christmas," sung by Bing Crosby. It became hugely popular during and after World War II.

In some countries, the Christmas celebration continues until Twelfth Night, the twelfth day after Christmas. January 6 is also known as the Epiphany, when the three wise men reached the Christ child. In England, the song "The Twelve Days of Christmas" with its famous lyrics, "and a partridge in a pear tree," commemorates the observance. In New Orleans, it is the beginning of the celebration that ends with Mardi Gras. In Italy on Twelfth Night, La Befana, the good witch, flies in and brings gifts to children. If they are bad, they get only *carbone*—a lump of coal.

the South, much wealthier than the North before the Civil War, was destroyed. And 4 million slaves were now free. What would they do? How and where would they live? The United States Constitution was amended quickly to grant rights to the freed people. In 1865, the 13th Amendment granted freedom to all slaves; in 1868, the 14th Amendment guaranteed former slaves the rights of citizens; and in 1870, the 15th Amendment gave black men—but not black or white women—the right to vote. The first thing many of the freedmen did was try to find their family members who had been sold. This was difficult and in some cases impossible for people who didn't know where or when they were born because it was illegal for them to read. And, like serfs on feudal estates in the Middle Ages, they didn't have last names. They were only

---

$\mathcal{H}$OLIDAY $\mathcal{H}$ISTORY

≫ JUNETEENTH ≪

Juneteenth—June 19—is a very special day for African-Americans. It was on June 19, 1865 that the news first reached slaves in Galveston, Texas, that they were free. There was much jubilation then and much speculation now about why they did not find out sooner. The Civil War had been over since April, and Lincoln had issued the Emancipation Proclamation two and a half years earlier, on January 1, 1863. But then, some masters told their slaves that since Lincoln had freed them and he was dead, they were slaves again.[28]

Frederick Douglass, a famous black leader who escaped from slavery, made a speech in which he told white people that the Fourth of July was *their* holiday for *their* country. Juneteenth finally gave the freed slaves something to celebrate, which they did with barbecue and music. Ntozake Shange's book *If I Can Cook/You Know God Can* is part cookbook, part memoir, part history of Africans in the Western Hemisphere, and all soul. It is as if Shange is in the kitchen with you at the prep table, telling stories about the ingredients as you do your *mise.* The recipe for the traditional good-luck New Year's dish, Hoppin' John (Black-eyed Peas and Rice), ends with: "Yes, mostly West Indians add the coconut, but that probably only upset Charlestonians. Don't take that to heart. Cook your peas and rice to your own likin'."[29] Shange has recipes for every day and for special occasions, like Pig's Tails by Instinct, French-fried Chitlins, Cousin Eddie's Shark with Breadfruit, and Collard Greens to Bring You Money.

For more on the history of Juneteenth, check out www.juneteenth.com.

"Mammy" or "Sam." Many took the names of presidents, especially Lincoln and Washington. They went to school for the first time. Parents wanted their children to be able to read so that they could have a better life. The older people wanted to read the Bible before they died. And finally, they could get married legally. They also insisted on being addressed respectfully, as "Mr." or "Mrs." This angered whites.

The Black Codes and the Ku Klux Klan

Many white southerners didn't want to lose the social, economic, and political superiority they had enjoyed over black people and their labor. If black people could make a living and feed themselves and their families, they wouldn't have to go to work for whites. In November 1865, just seven months after the end of the war, Mississippi was the first southern state to pass "Black Codes." These laws made it illegal for black people to hunt or fish; to own a hunting dog, a gun, or land; to preach or assemble without a license. The codes also made "intent to steal" a crime. The punishment: black men and women went to jail and were leased out to white plantation owners as convict labor, sometimes chained together on gangs.[30] Whites who went to prison served their sentence in prison.

Confederate army veterans went out at night to terrorize and kill the freed people. They based their name on the Greek word for circle, *kuklos*—the Ku Klux Klan or KKK. When the angry Republican Congress sent the United States Army to occupy the South as if it were a foreign country, klansmen started wearing sheets to hide their identity. In 1877, the Republican North and the Democratic South made a compromise after the most corrupt election in American history, the presidential election of 1876. Northern Republicans kept the presidency, while southern Democrats got the troops removed. Northerners were well aware that when the troops left, black people would lose their rights and their lives at the hands of the KKK. It remained that way until the civil rights movement in the 1960s.

THE WEST: THE RAILROAD AND THE INDIAN WARS—1860s–1886

Stagecoach Food

Mark Twain, who later wrote the American classic novels *Tom Sawyer* and *Huckleberry Finn,* went from Missouri to the Nevada Territory by stagecoach in July 1861, and wrote the book *Roughing It* about his adventures. He described eating at the stage stops. The cups and plates were tin, the main course was condemned army bacon, and the breakfast beverage was called slumgullion: "It really pretended to be tea, but there was too much dishrag, and sand, and old bacon rind in it to deceive the intelligent traveler. He had no sugar and no milk—not even a spoon to stir the ingredients with." The manners matched: "Pass the bread, you son of a skunk!"[31] Only once was there real food between the United States and Salt Lake City, a breakfast of "hot biscuits, fresh antelope steaks, and coffee."[32]

One thing most Europeans agreed on was that American frontier eating was fast. People didn't taste their food, they inhaled it. They sat down at the table and were done in five minutes. In boarding houses, service was *à la française*—all the food put on the table at once—but speeded up by an American invention called the Lazy Susan. This was

---

ℋOLIDAY ℋISTORY
❧ CINCO DE MAYO (MAY 5ᵀᴴ) ❧

Cinco de Mayo commemorates the day in 1862 when a small group of Mexican patriots defeated a much larger and better-equipped French force at Puebla and prevented them from taking the capital, Mexico City. (It is *not* when Mexico won its independence from Spain, which is September 16, 1810.) France invaded when Mexico couldn't repay a loan. With aid from the United States, the French were gone by 1867. But the festival lives on in Puebla and even more in parts of the United States with large Mexican populations. Mariachi music, *folklórico* dancing, parades, and street fairs include traditional foods like margaritas (classic, strawberry, melon, and more), guacamole and chips, green corn tamales at the beginning of the season, and cook-offs of *menudo* (a stew of tripe, hominy, and chile).

For more information, see www.mexonline.com/cinco.htm.

---

a large platter on ball bearings in the middle of the table, which rotated so that every diner could reach every food.[33] (Does this qualify as *service à la Susan?*)

While America was fighting its Civil War, France took advantage of the situation to send troops into the Western Hemisphere and try to take Mexico.

"I've Been Workin' on the Railroad"

After the Civil War ended in 1865, the United States turned to the West again. The first major task was to complete the transcontinental railroad, even though the United States already had almost half of all the railroad tracks in the world. Finding workers wasn't easy; any able-bodied male in California wanted to look for gold, not work for $3 a day. Finally, Leland Stanford had an idea: Chinese. The Chinese were already in California; they had come looking for gold but discrimination by whites had forced them out. Mark Twain visited San Francisco's Chinatown in the 1860s and wrote that the Chinese "are quiet, peaceable, tractable, free from drunkenness, and they are as industrious as the day is long. A disorderly Chinaman is rare, and a lazy one does not exist."[34] Some whites said that the Chinese—on average, under 4 feet 10 inches tall—were too small to build a railroad. Stanford shot back, "They built the Great Wall of China, didn't they?"[35]

And like the workers on the Great Wall of China and the pyramids in ancient Egypt, the men who built the railroad had to eat, too. Whites were often sick with intestinal illnesses. Chinese weren't. Diet made the difference. Whites ate what the Central Pacific gave them— boiled beef and potatoes—and drank water from polluted streams. The Chinese got food from Chinese merchants in San Francisco, paid for and cooked it themselves, and drank tea made from germ-free boiled water. They ate

> oysters, cuttlefish, . . . abalone meat, [Asian] fruits, and scores of vegetables, including bamboo sprouts, seaweed, and mushrooms . . . rice, salted cabbage, vermicelli, bacon, and sweet crackers. Very occasionally they had fresh meat, pork being a prime favorite, along with chicken.[36]

Because they didn't get sick, the Chinese were accused of being "devilish." They also bathed daily and didn't drink alcohol. Their only vice was that they smoked opium on Sundays—a habit acquired from the British (see Chapter 9).

In October 1869, the last spike of the Transcontinental Railroad— the Golden Spike—was driven in Ogden, Utah, and the east and west coasts of the United States were connected by rail. Food on the trains was considerably better than it had been at the stage stops where Mark Twain ate. The Chicago-based Pullman Company manufactured "palace" cars, luxurious "hotels on wheels" with leather seats, brass lamps, and curtains. The dining cars were equally elegant. White linen and solid silver were on the table; Champagne, antelope steaks, mountain trout, and fresh fruit were on the plates. The contrast between the wildness of the country outside and the civilization on the train with a chef and a French-influenced menu impressed diners.[37] Also impressive was the excellent service. All the waiters and porters on the Pullman cars were black; until the middle of the 20th century, these were some of the best jobs black men could get in the United States. Pullman porters also created one of the first labor unions for blacks.

When the transcontinental railroad was finished, the Chinese were 25 percent of the labor force in California. There was not another project that needed as many laborers, so desperate Chinese would work for less than whites. Angry white workers retaliated with mass lynchings of Chinese in Wyoming, San Francisco, and Los Angeles. In 1882, Congress passed the Chinese Exclusion Act to keep the Chinese, the poor, the mentally retarded, and prostitutes out of the United States. With the Chinese gone, whites turned their attention to the Native Americans.

Scorched Earth in the West: Buffalo Culture and the Plains Indians

The United States Army used the same scorched-earth policy on Native Americans that it had used in the Civil War: it wasn't necessary to kill the people, just destroy their food supply. The buffalo was more than just the main source of food for the Plains Indians; it was their entire culture. Buffalo hides made their homes (teepees), clothes, blankets, robes, and shoes (moccasins). Buffalo horns were used for ceremonial costumes, the bones became sewing needles, the ligaments and sinews were used like rope and wire. Buffalo bladders and stomachs became containers. Millions of buffalo were killed by the army and by "sportsmen" who rode the new railroads out onto the plains and used long-range repeating rifles to pick off buffalo as if they were in a shooting gallery (with free bullets provided by the army). Sometimes the entire carcass was left to rot except for the tongue, which was prized as food in the eastern United States. Sitting Bull, the chief of the Lakota, said, "A cold wind blew across the prairie when the last buffalo fell—a death wind for my people."[38] But it opened up the land for white people.

The Family Farm Economy

The midwestern farm economy was a household economy. Everyone participated; the work of women and children was essential. Labor was divided by gender. Because of frequent pregnancies, women stayed closer to the house, but if it became necessary, for example, at harvest time, they worked in the fields, too. Women planted, hoed, weeded, and harvested the garden, milked cows and churned butter, fed chickens and collected eggs. The men spent the days plowing, building or mending fences, and tending to the barn and the large farm animals.

The Locust Plagues

In spite of the incessant hard work by everyone in the family, nature was still a huge variable. In the Bible, locusts were one of the ten great plagues the God of the Hebrews sent to force the Egyptians

	WOMEN AND CHILDREN	MEN AND BOYS
You do:	All food preparation: three big meals a day	Chop down trees to clear land
	Feed and milk cows	Chop wood for fuel
	Feed chickens, gather eggs, clean hen-house	Build and mend fences
	At hog butchering time, make sausage and prepare hams	Plow and spread manure in fields
	Tend domestic garden near house	Sow
	Preserve fruits and vegetables	Harvest
	Make cheese	Maintain and repair farm equipment
	Churn butter	Care for oxen, mules, horses
	Clean house	Herd and feed hogs and sheep
	Spin wool and flax into yarn	Clean and maintain barnyard
	Weave cloth from yarn; dye or bleach it	Slaughter and butcher large farm animals
	Cut, sew, mend clothes for entire family	Hunt
	Make soap	Make cider
	Wash clothes, hang up outside to dry	Make maple sugar
	Knit socks, mittens, and caps	
	Pluck down from geese and ducks, stuff pillows with it	
	Make cider	
	Make maple sugar	
	Assist in cornfield in emergency	
	Bear and nurse children	
	Take care of children	
	Make everything look nice	

A DAY IN THE LIFE OF A MIDWESTERN FARM FAMILY[39]

to let the Hebrews go. *Locust* is another word for grasshopper or cricket and means "burned-over place," which is what the land looks like after these insects have been there. A locust can eat as much as 38 pounds of food in its lifetime, which is only a few months.[40] From 1873 to 1878, grasshoppers descended on midwestern farms like a biblical plague. Year after year, they ate everything in sight. First, the large adult grasshoppers swarmed down on the fields with a deafening noise like a million scissors and ate the ripening wheat, oats, barley, and corn. Then they laid eggs. Farmers in Minnesota were sure the tiny eggs wouldn't be able to survive the brutally cold winter or the rainy spring. They survived both and hatched just in time to eat the sprouting wheat, oats, barley, and corn. They repeated this pattern for half a decade. The farmers burned the fields, but the grasshoppers flew away and came back. The farmers covered the crops with sheets and blankets, but the grasshoppers ate them. The farmers invented "hopper dozers," pieces of metal they smeared with molasses and dragged through the fields. Not enough grasshoppers stuck to the molasses to make a difference. Children running home crunched grasshoppers under their bare feet. Finally, unable to control the grasshoppers or make a living, people moved away. In the middle of one of the greatest westward migrations in history, some states *lost* population.[41]

"Don't Fence Me In": Cattle Drives, Cow Towns, and Barbed Wire

There was no railroad in the South, so the cattle in Texas had to be herded north to the railheads, to the legendary tough cow towns—Wichita, Dodge, and Abilene in Kansas; Omaha in Nebraska. These were the towns of lawmen like Wyatt Earp. The trails had names like Chisolm and Goodnight-Loving. Each cattle drive had a cook who managed the chuck wagon and dished out grub. After the foreman, the cook was the most important man in the outfit. Other cowboys packed his bedroll and harnessed his team. And they'd better stay out of his way. Cooks were notoriously temperamental. After all, they were cooking for as many as 100 men, outside, in a different place every day, from the back of a wagon. The pots, Dutch ovens, and frying pans were heavy cast iron. The fare was coffee, beans, coffee, beef, coffee, biscuits, and coffee. Coffee came in 100-pound sacks; a coffee grinder was on the side of every chuck wagon. With the coffee was the equally essential granulated brown sugar, so dried out that chunks had to be chipped off and put through a meat grinder. There was nothing raw and green like vegetables, although canned peaches were a favorite, and canned tomatoes provided enough vitamin C to keep scurvy away.[42] Chiles were the main spice. Sometimes they killed one of the cows and made stew.

The legendary blizzards of 1886 were one of the reasons the cattle drives ended. When the snow cleared, thousands of cattle were found frozen, stacked up where they had been trapped against the barbed wire fences. Cattlemen called it "the big die-up."[43]

The Indian wars ended in 1886, too. Every Indian who had been at war with the United States was either dead or on a reservation. The last Indian to surrender was Geronimo, leader of the Chiricahua Apache, in Skeleton Canyon in southeastern Arizona, not far from Tombstone. In 1887, Congress passed the Dawes Severalty Act to break up tribal lands and force Indians to dress, speak, worship, and live like white Americans.

Also in 1886, a bombing in Chicago's Haymarket Square killed 7 policemen. The Knights of Labor, the major union at that time, was blamed. Membership dropped so drastically that it went out of existence. A new union, the American Federation of Labor (AFL), which still exists today, began later in 1886. Some of the first to join were restaurant workers.

EARLY HOTEL AND RESTAURANT EMPLOYEES UNIONS IN THE AFL[44]		
DATE UNION FORMED	LOCATION	ORGANIZATION
1887	New York	Waiters Union
	New York	Bartenders
1888	Brooklyn	Bartenders
	Boston	Bartenders
	St. Louis	German Waiters Union
1890	St. Louis	American Waiters and Bartenders
	St. Paul, Minnesota	Waiters Union
	Chicago	Waiters League (founded 1866 under the Knights of Labor)
	Brooklyn	Waiters Union
1891	Indianapolis	Waiters
	Minneapolis	Waiters
	Denver	Cooks
	St. Louis	Cooks
	Logansport, Indiana	Bartenders Mutual Aid

THE GILDED AGE

In the cities in the last quarter of the 19th century in America, everything seemed covered in gold. It was the Gilded Age, after the title of a novel written in 1873 by Mark Twain and Charles Dudley Warner. The Industrial Revolution and America's abundant natural resources were making Americans tremendously wealthy, and they were showing it off. The word *millionaire* didn't exist before the 1840s; by 1901, America had its first billion-dollar corporation, United States Steel. The wealthy built mansions that rivaled European palaces and often included pieces of real ones that had been dismantled, shipped across the Atlantic, and reassembled. Ceilings and walls were covered with gold leaf, gold paint, gold draperies. Dishes were trimmed in gold, flatware was gold. After silver was discovered in America's Comstock Lode in 1859, tables were also set with silver: rings for elaborately folded damask napkins, forks for asparagus, oysters, pie, and pastry; mustard spoons, grape shears, fruit knives, sugar tongs, salt spoons, sardine servers, orange peelers, coffee and tea services; ice cream spoons, knives, and forks. There were pitchers for molasses and maple syrup, and containers for cans of condensed milk. Crystal finger bowls on lace doilies appeared at the end of the meal. Ceramic dinner service for home use came in enormous quantities; in one case, a set of 514 pieces, including twelve dozen 10-inch dinner plates, six dozen "muffin" plates between 4 and 7 inches in diameter, and 18 serving platters.[45]

Shopping and Eating

Galloping consumerism characterized the Gilded Age. Factories produced massive amounts of goods and advertised to get people to buy them. Two new technologies helped Americans to become good shoppers: structural steel and plate glass. The new structural steel was much stronger than the old wrought iron, so less of it was needed to support a building. Like the Gothic cathedrals of the Middle Ages, there was now more space between beams. Into this space went plate glass windows—one huge piece, six feet high or more. Behind these windows, goods were displayed; the department store was born. At the end of the 19th century, when Otis invented the elevator, the skyscraper was born. Going shopping was one of the only excuses a respectable middle-class woman had for leaving the house.

If the shopper couldn't get to the department store, the department store came to the shopper. Catalogues hundreds of pages long from Sears Roebuck and Co., headquartered in Chicago, tempted readers with pictures of stoves, dishes, pots and pans, farm tools, seeds, tractors, hot-water heaters, rugs, shoes, ready-made clothes, and furniture. All of it could be ordered by mail and delivered by train—even the house to put it in.

Houses were beginning to have indoor plumbing and electricity, and more than one room for eating. The dining room was formal, while there might be a separate, less formal breakfast room for just the family. Middle- and upper-class meals were breakfast, dinner, and supper. There were other meals for women: the "ladies' luncheon" and high tea. Two things made this increase in the standard of living possible: tin cans and refrigerated railroad cars. Tin cans—Appert's invention, mass produced on American assembly lines by 1876—made previously exotic, out-of-season, or extremely perishable foods affordable and convenient. Canning began in America in the 1820s with lobsters, oysters, and salmon. By 1882, tomatoes, corn, beans, and peas were the most popular canned foods of the at least 51 kinds available.[46] Refrigerated railroad cars made meat, especially beef and pork coming out of the world's largest meat market, the Union Stockyards in Chicago, available throughout the country.

Eating Disorders: Anorexia and Bulimia

In Victorian England and America, an appetite for food was equated with an appetite for sex, which was taboo. The foods that were thought to arouse unhealthy appetites in girls and women were coffee, tea, chocolate, mustard, vinegar and pickles, spices, nuts, raisins, warm bread, pastry, candy, and alcohol. Meat was the worst—it would surely lead to insanity or nymphomania or both.[47] A woman seen eating meat and potatoes put herself on a level with a barnyard animal. Many women took to eating in secret—reversing the trend for women to eat in public that was begun by Catherine de Medici almost four hundred years earlier. Men's sexual impulses needed to be controlled, too. Piano legs were covered so that men's wicked thoughts would not be stimulated by the sight of a leg—any leg. A glimpse of a lady's leg was nearly impossible because her ankle-length skirt and petticoats would have to ride above her knee-length high-button shoes—and even then she was wearing stockings you couldn't see through. These sexual avoidances carried over into the language of food. Polite people offered their guests "white meat" or "dark meat" because one simply did not utter the words *breast* or *leg*.

In this world of rigid control of women and sexuality, manners and food, a strange malady began to appear, mostly in middle- and upper-class teenage girls. In a time of an abundance of food and wealth in their own families, these girls wasted away and sometimes died because they would not eat. The disease was first described in 1868 by an English physician who named it *anorexia nervosa*.[48] It experienced an upsurge in the 1960s.

There are two forms of the disease. Anorexia involves starving. Bulimia is binge eating, then purging the food from the body by extreme exercise, laxatives, enemas, and vomiting—at first forced by putting the fingers down the throat, later at will. Sufferers of both are more than 15 percent below minimal normal body weight, have missed three consecutive menstrual periods, and are abnormally preoccupied with appearance. The numbers on the scale tell these young women that they are seriously underweight, but when they look in the mirror all they see is fat. These diseases are ten times more common in women than in men, especially now in professions like modeling and ballet, although male wrestlers, for example, who have to stay within strict weight categories, also abuse food. Malnutrition unbalances metabolism and depletes vitamins and minerals. Loss of body fat causes the person to feel cold all the time, so the body grows fuzz all over—like fur—to try to warm itself. Calluses develop on the back of the hands from sticking fingers down the throat; the acid in vomit erodes teeth and the esophagus; blood pressure drops because the heart slows down. About 11 percent die.[49]

Good Help Is Hard to Find

In contrast to these wealthy young women who starved them-selves, working-class young women who smoked, drank, and kept "bad company" with people their parents didn't like were sent to prison, sometimes for years. These young women felt that because they were earning their own money, no one could tell them what to do. Their offense was that they were behaving like men. In New York, they were sent to the women's reformatory north of New York City at Bedford Hills. From there, they were paroled as kitchen help to mid-dle-class women who were having trouble finding servants. It was an ideal situation for the housewives: if their "girl" didn't do what they wanted, they had the entire prison system and the police force to dis-cipline her.[50]

Middle-class women were unhappy with their servants. The "ser-vant problem," as it was called, was really this: young women who had a choice went to work in factories. They didn't want to work six and a half days a week in somebody else's house, have their mail opened, and their social lives monitored. In America, there was not a class of people raised to be servants as there was in Europe. Immigration, dis-rupted by the Civil War, resumed with a flood of immigrants at the end of the 19th century. But these people weren't coming to America to be servants for the rest of their lives.

Vassar—The First College for Women

Life was changing drastically for middle-class women. In the 1860s, an English immigrant in Poughkeepsie, 72 miles north of New York in the Hudson River Valley, decided that he wanted to use the

Vassar College menu, 1860s
Special Collections, Vassar College Libraries

money he had made brewing beer to make his name known all over the world. He opened a college that he declared would be for women what Harvard and Yale were for men. He did this in the face of the best (male) medical advice at the time: that if women used their brains excessively, they would damage their reproductive systems. The brewer named the college after himself—Vassar. Menus from shortly after the college's founding reveal typical American institutional food. It is extremely heavy on meat and starches. It also clearly fits into the 19th century trend to have a substantial breakfast with protein, the main meal at midday, and a light supper—in one case, only prunes.

For almost a century, these meals were cooked in individual dormitory kitchens and served in wood-paneled dining rooms on tables covered with white cloths, under chandeliers. The young women had to dress up for dinner, which until the late 1960s meant wearing skirts.

However, in the last decades of the 20th century, it became too expensive to have a dining room in every dormitory, so one central dining hall was created; by then, the college had also become coeducational. Women attending Vassar and the other colleges that opened to them in the late 19th and early 20th centuries had a profound impact on America and the world in the coming generations.

One of the things college girls did was popularize chocolate. The first written reference to fudge making comes from Vassar in 1887.[51] The craze spread to other women's colleges, especially Smith and Wellesley. The Vassar recipe is a simple, basic one of cream, sugar, butter, and chocolate. The Smith recipe added brown sugar; Wellesley added marshmallow creme. Ninety percent of the recipes for fudge in the United States today are based on these three recipes.[52]

The main dining room, Vassar College, 1889.
Special Collections, Vassar College Libraries

As chocolate became more popular, it became associated with one very romantic holiday that began to be celebrated in the 19th century, Valentine's Day. (See Holiday History on page 203).

American Restaurants

In the 19th century, Americans also began to eat at restaurants. The Union Oyster House in Boston, Massachusetts, claims to be the oldest continuously operating restaurant in the United States. It is located in the North End, near the wharves and where Paul Revere lived (his house is still standing, too). Nearby is the historic Quincy Market area and what is now the Boston Market. The building that houses the restaurant was built before 1742 and used for other purposes before it became the Atwood & Bacon restaurant in 1826, as the photo on page 202 shows.

The fare was simple: mostly oysters, clams, eggs, pie, beverages, as the menu on page 204 shows.

Oysters were a craze in the 19th century. Oyster houses and bars sprang up all over the United States. For people in the middle of the country, with no ocean, there were "prairie oysters"—raw eggs replaced raw oysters, which had a similar consistency. The same condiments were used, such as Tabasco, Worcestershire sauce, vinegar, and ketchup. Farther west, in the Rocky Mountains, prairie oysters were neither oysters nor eggs, but calf's testicles. Oysters (the seafood) sold for 15 or 20 cents a dozen in the 19th century; in the 21st, they were almost ten dollars a half dozen.

Boston boasts another "continuously"—the Parker House, in the center of town, is the oldest continuously operating hotel in the United States. It was there that Parker House rolls were invented, as well as Boston cream pie, which is really a layer cake with a custard filling and chocolate frosting.

Exterior, Atwood & Bacon restaurant.
Courtesy the Union Oyster House

ℋOLIDAY ℋISTORY
❧ VALENTINE'S DAY, FEBRUARY 14TH ❧

Valentine's Day is the second most popular day for dining out (after Mother's Day) and for sending greeting cards (after Christmas). It has its own cuisine and rituals based on a combination of Greek, Roman, and Christian cultures. In the Roman Empire, February 14 was a fertility festival, but around 498, Pope Gelasius declared it St. Valentine's Day. Like Apicius, there are multiple candidates for St. Valentine. All were Christian martyrs. Supposedly, Valentine performed secret marriages for young lovers. Or he helped Christians escape from prison. Or he was in prison and sent a love letter and signed it "From your Valentine."[53]

Cupid, the winged chubby little cherub who shoots his arrows into the hearts of unsuspecting humans was originally the ancient Greek god of love, a physically perfect and gorgeous athlete. (In Rome he was called Eros and gave us our word "erotic.") His mother—Aphrodite in Greece, Venus in Rome—was jealous of all the attention a beautiful young woman named Psyche (Soul) was getting, so she sent Cupid to make Psyche fall in love with someone ugly. But when Cupid saw Psyche, he fell in love with her himself. He made her promise never to look at him or they would be separated forever. Psyche loved him blindly, and promised. But when her sisters came to visit, they kept pushing her to find out what he looked like. Maybe he was a monster, and she should kill him. One night, Psyche got a lamp and a knife and snuck a look at Cupid while he was asleep. Her happiness made her hand tremble. Some hot oil from the lamp fell on Cupid's shoulder, burning him. He woke up and left, angry, saying, "Love cannot live where there is no trust." Broken-hearted and remorseful, Psyche searched for him everywhere and in desperation went to Aphrodite and begged to see him (he was at his mother's, recuperating). Instead, Aphrodite made Psyche perform impossible tasks like separating wheat, poppy, and millet seeds mixed into one huge pile. Psyche was fortunate and got help for every task, even going to the Underworld. Finally, Cupid recovered from the wound Psyche had inflicted on him and he yearned for her. After all, she had gone through hell—literally—because she loved him. Cupid didn't want his mother to make any more trouble, so he went to Zeus, the king of the gods. Zeus called all the gods together and declared that Cupid and Psyche were officially married. Then he gave Psyche some ambrosia to eat, which made her one of them.[54]

So Cupid and Psyche—Love and the Soul—can't live without each other and remain united forever (in spite of the mother-in-law from hell).

During the Middle Ages, St. Valentine and Cupid mingled and Valentine became the patron saint of lovers. Cards were exchanged. The oldest valentine in existence was written in 1415. In the 1840s, an American woman, Esther A. Howland, is credited with the first mass-produced valentines. Now, in addition to cards, lovers send flowers, especially roses, and especially red roses to symbolize passion.

Valentine's Day cuisine is associated with aphrodisiacs: Champagne, caviar, oysters, foie gras, passion fruit, and truffles (fungus, chocolate, and ice cream). Restaurant decor goes pink and red: menus, linens, flowers, aprons. So does the food; raspberries appear in vinaigrette, coulis, gelée, soufflé. Food is also heart-shaped: pâté, ravioli, cakes, tarts, muffins, pancakes, cookies, candies. But all of these offerings to the Greek god and the patron saint of love are not guarantees—Cupid is still very mischievous.

In New York, Swiss immigrant brothers opened Delmonico's Restaurant at No. 2 South William Street in 1831. They served Continental cuisine. The restaurant became more than just *the* place to eat for Wall Street financiers. It also served at various times as a telegraph office and a bank. In 1832, President Jackson vetoed the recharter of the Bank of the United States, and by 1836, it was closed. Without one central bank in control, after 1837, any institution with enough credibility to back up its name could issue its own money. Delmonico's and the Parker House did. Examples of the currency they issued appear on the opposite page.

Delmonico's is credited with creating many new foods, among them Baked Alaska, to celebrate America's purchase of Alaska in 1867. This is an elaborately molded frozen biscuit with ice cream on top, covered with meringue and heated briefly until the meringue colors.

World's Fairs and Amusement Parks—the "All Electric Home"

On September 4, 1882, at 3:00 P.M., an event that changed the world occurred: a switch was thrown, and New York City lit up with Thomas Edison's new invention—electricity.[55] It transformed night into day. Broadway became the "Great

ATWOOD & BACON,

ESTABLISHED 1826.

OYSTERS.		SCALLOPS. (in Season.)	
VIRGINIA:		Fried,	35
Stewed,	15	Stewed,	30
" large,	20		
Roast,	15		
" Fancy	20	Crackers and Milk,	15
NARRAGANSETT:		Bread and Milk,	15
Raw, plate,	doz. 15	Dry Toast,	10
Half-Shell,	half-doz. 10	Buttered Toast,	10
Stewed,	25	Milk Toast,	15
" bench-opened,	30	Boiled Eggs, (3)	20
Roast,	25		
" bench-opened,	30	Fried Eggs, 3)	20
Fried, crumbs or batter,	25	Dropped Eggs, (3)	20
" bench-opened,	35	Eggs on Toast,	20
Roast in shell,	35	Bread and Butter,	5
CAPES:		Extra Crackers,	5
Half-shell,	doz. 20		
"	half-doz. 10		
Stewed,	35	Apple Pie,	5
Roast,	35	Mince "	5
Fried,	40	Lemon "	5
Roast in shell,	40	Squash "	5
CLAMS.		Custard"	5
IPSWICH:			
Stewed,	15	Tea,	5
Steamed,	25	Coffee,	5
Fried, crumbs or batter	25	Milk,	5
Chowder,	15	Ginger Ale, (Pureoxia)	5
LITTLE NECKS:		Sarsaparilla,	5
Dozen,	20		
Half-Dozen,	10		
Stewed,	40		
Fried,	45		
Quahaugs, Stewed,	25		
" Fried,	35		

PLEASE PAY THE WAITER.

Atwood & Bacon restaurant menu, 1826.
Courtesy the Union Oyster House

Delmonico money.
Courtesy of the Federal Reserve Bank of San Francisco, American Currency Exhibit

Parker House money.
Courtesy of the Federal Reserve Bank of San Francisco, American Currency Exhibit

White Way," and New York became famous for its night life. Electricity and machines were used for play, too, in New York's playground, Coney Island. After 1884, people out to enjoy themselves could get on the gravity-powered ride that became the roller coaster. They could eat a Coney Island red hot before it was called a hot dog. At Nathan's Famous, they could feast on huge clams on the half shell. They could stroll while eating cotton candy, a spun-sugar confection invented by German immigrants.

Eleven years after New York was illuminated, electricity lit up a building in Chicago. The 1893 World's Fair in Chicago was called the

Columbian Exposition, in honor of the four hundredth anniversary of Columbus's discovery of the New World. (They were a year late because it took longer than expected to arrange it.) Its intention was to do for America what the Crystal Palace Exhibition in London had done for England in 1851—show off the wealth and power of the country. Pavilions and exhibits at the Columbian Exposition had to adhere to strict architectural guidelines to create a giant "White City"—so white that black Americans, even famous ex-slaves like Frederick Douglass, were not allowed in as either workers or spectators. One exhibit was about electricity and the "All Electric Home" of the future, a paradise of "electric stoves, hot plates, washing and ironing machines, dishwashers, carpet sweepers, electric doorbells, phonographs, fire alarms, and innumerable lighting devices"[56]—all of which eventually came into widespread use, but more than 50 years later.

THE 19TH-CENTURY HEALTH FOOD MOVEMENT

In 1857, German physicist Rudolf J. E. Clausius discovered a unit of heat that he called a "calorie." It was the amount of energy required to raise the temperature of one gram of water one degree Celsius. With the discovery of the calorie, could health food and dieting be far behind?

Vegetarianism

One idea behind health food in the 19th century was that if men stopped eating like animals—that is, eating meat—they would stop behaving like animals. This objectionable animal behavior included selfishness, sex, and war. There were two phases to 19th-century vegetarianism. The first began in the 1830s. The second was in the Gilded Age.

In the 1830s, Dr. Sylvester Graham objected to the refined white flour that was the sign of upper-class food. He claimed that refining was a sign of man's fall from his wholesome natural state to an artificial, civilized one. He advocated healthy flour made from coarsely ground whole wheat, the rough kind fed to the peasants in the Middle Ages. And he claimed that no commercial baker could make real bread. That could be done by only one person: "It is the wife, the mother only—she who loves her husband and her children as woman ought to love."[57] The flour was named after him first, then the crackers made from it. Today, it is almost impossible to find just graham crackers. They are marketed as "low-fat grahams" to differentiate them from Honey Grahams, Cinnamon Grahams, Teddy Grahams, Cheddy Grahams, and the other grahams that mock their inventor's intentions. Often, graham flour is the third or fourth ingredient, after fat and sweeteners. Serving suggestions on the box: dip graham crackers into frosting or Cool Whip.

One person who carried health and self-sufficiency to an extreme was philosopher Henry David Thoreau. He believed in vegetarianism, which most Americans did not:

> One farmer says to me, "You cannot live on vegetable food solely, for it furnishes nothing to make bones with"; . . . walking all the while he talks behind his oxen, which, with vegetable-made bones, jerk him and his lumbering plough along.[58]

From July 4, 1845, to September 6, 1847, Thoreau engaged in an experiment to prove that man didn't need meat or civilization. He lived simply in the woods at Walden Pond in Massachusetts, and recorded his observations about the meaning of life, what he ate, how he prepared it, and how much it cost.

He lived simply on food he purchased, picked, or planted. He bought rice, molasses, rye and cornmeal, flour, a bit of salt pork or lard, and sugar. He supplemented these with seasonal wild fruits and nuts like grapes, wild apples, chestnuts, and groundnuts (*Apios tuberosa*). He also cultivated enough beans, potatoes, and peas that he was able to sell his surplus for a profit. Thoreau's total food cost per week: 27 cents.[59] He proved that it could be done, but being alone almost all the time is not for everyone.

Kellogg vs. Post: The Race for Breakfast

There was a battle going on in Battle Creek, Michigan, between the Kellogg brothers. John Harvey wanted to keep the cereal they made sugar-free. W. K. wanted to add sugar. They were both blindsided by C. W. Post, who didn't have a brother to argue with. Post wanted to add sugar to the cereal he made, so he did. W. K. finally added malt sweetener to Corn Flakes. John Harvey, a physician, went his own way and established the Battle Creek Sanitarium—known as the San—which became the center of the late-19th-century health food movement and the forerunner of modern spas. By 1888 its staff of doctors, nurses, physical therapists, and dietitians was handling 600 to 700 patients at a time. Vegetarian, it catered to upper-class patrons like Eleanor Roosevelt (later First Lady) and Henry Ford. John Harvey Kellogg emphasized the importance of chewing food. Another 19th-century health food doctor, J. H. Salisbury, was obsessed with chewing, too. He invented a patty of prechopped meat formed into the shape of an oval for those who couldn't or wouldn't chew properly. It was named after him: Salisbury steak. Kellogg wrote a song about chewing. (Although the original song is gone, it was re-created for the 1994 movie about the San, *The Road to Wellville*.) He was terrified of constipation because he believed it caused "autointoxication"—self-poisoning. Absolutely convinced that masturbation was one of the greatest sins, he advised parents to raid their children's bedrooms at night to catch them in the act. He also advocated what is now called "female circumcision"—cutting the female genitals to prevent sexual enjoyment. He said this should be done without anesthetic.

Kellogg wrote many treatises on diet and food. Aided and abetted by his wife, Ella, he came up with the idea that pasta should be boiled for an hour. He ignored humans' flesh-tearing teeth and claimed that all animals were originally nut eaters. Many of his recipes included imitation meat made of nut butters. Those opposed to vegetarianism argued that eating meat must have been the right thing because the human race survived, and along the way invented cooking to make meat digestible. But Kellogg's goal was "to rescue civilization from the 'race-destroying effects of universal constipation and world-wide autointoxication.'"[60]

"Atlanta Holy Water"—Coca-Cola

Just as apothecaries in the Middle Ages sold sugar and drugs, pharmacists in the Gilded Age sold sugar-water beverages in their drugstores. The drugstore soda fountain, a long counter like a bar where patrons are served non-alcoholic beverages, is an American invention. So is the soda jerk, so called because he jerks down on the handle of a machine that mixes soda—artificially carbonated water, invented in 1767—and flavorings into hundreds of combinations. By the 1880s, several of these beverages were patented. Their inventors became millionaires by selling for a nickel what cost less than half a cent per portion.[61] Most were root and herb concoctions; all claimed to benefit health.

Atlanta physician and pharmacist John Stith Pemberton's goal was to invent a potion to free himself from his morphine addiction. In 1885, he invented Pemberton's French Wine Coca, patterned after other fortified wines, like Vin Mariani. Pemberton's drink contained two new wonder drugs, coca from Peru's coca leaf and caffeine from the African kola nut. Both were stimulants and also supposedly aphrodisiacs. He claimed it was good for what ailed Americans: exhaustion,

EARLY SOFT DRINKS[62]			
YEAR	BEVERAGE	WHERE	HEALTH CLAIM
1876	Hires Root Beer	Philadelphia, PA	Purifies the blood
1885	Moxie Nerve Food	Lowell, MA	Cures nervousness and paralysis
1885	Dr Pepper	Texas	Aids digestion

constipation, melancholy, impotence, headaches, hysteria, and addiction to opium and morphine, both legal then. (These claims were wrong, of course.) When Atlanta banned the sale of anything with alcohol in it, Pemberton took the wine out of his Wine Coca and added seven secret ingredients, known only as "7X."

The first ad for Coca-Cola appeared on May 29, 1886. The year after that, Pemberton took out a patent on Coca-Cola; the year after that he died. The Coca-Cola Company became a corporation in 1892. The formula for Coca-Cola was super-secret for more than a century, until 1993, when journalist Mark Pendergrast, researching the history of Coca-Cola, went through their archives. By mistake, they gave him a file that contained Pemberton's original formula for Coke. Here it is:

Almost all of the ingredients in Coca-Cola, including all seven of the super-secret flavorings and the sugar, are Middle Eastern and

RECIPE

𝒯HE ORIGINAL FORMULA FOR COCA-COLA[63]

Citrate Caffein	1 oz.	Flavoring	
Ext. Vanilla	1 oz.	Oil Orange	80
Flavoring	2½ oz.	Oil Lemon	120
F.E. Coco [Fluid Extract of Coca]	4 oz.	Oil Nutmeg	40
Citric Acid	3 oz.	Oil Cinnamon	40
Lime Juice	1 qt.	Oil Coriander	20
Sugar	30 lbs.	Oil Neroli [from orange blossoms]	40
Water	2½ gal.		

Caramel sufficient

Alcohol 1 Qt.
let stand 24 hours.

Mix Caffeine Acid and Lime Juice in 1 Qt Boiling water add vanilla and flavoring when cool.

Indian in origin. Using orange blossoms is distinctively Middle Eastern. It could almost be out of al-Baghdadi's medieval cookery book. The only New World ingredient is vanilla.

Coca-Cola was marketed as a medicine until 1898, when Congress taxed medicines. Then Coca-Cola decided it was a beverage. Until 1899, it could only be enjoyed at soda fountains, because the one ounce of Coca-Cola syrup mixed with carbonated water went flat quickly. Then two lawyers from Chattanooga, Tennessee, had what Coca-Cola's board of directors thought was such a waste-of-time idea that they signed a contract giving the lawyers—for nothing—the right to sell Coke *in bottles*. (As stupid business deals go, this one is right up there with IBM's declaration that computer software would never be worth anything, so Bill Gates could keep all the rights to his programs.)

In April 1898, the United States went to war and Coca-Cola played a part. The name of a new drink made with rum, Coca-Cola, and lime juice represented what Americans intended to do. It was the Cuba libre—free Cuba. Four months later, Spain had been driven out of its last colonies and the war was over. In the Caribbean, the United States acquired Puerto Rico and Guantánamo Naval Base in Cuba. In the Pacific, it gained Guam and the Philippines. It was on its way to becoming a world power.

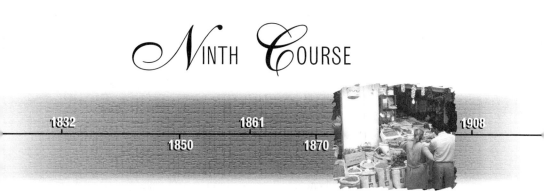

Sanitation, Nutrition, Migration:
The 19th Century in Europe, Asia, and Africa

While Americans in California gold fields were trying to figure out how to grind coffee and keep their pants from falling apart, scientists in Europe were making huge strides in discovering the causes of disease. The last half of the 19th century was also a time of increased awareness of health and of the belief that science could make human life better. In France and Germany, a war was on to see which country could find the most microbes. France had Pasteur; in Germany, Koch led the way.

DISEASES AND GERMS

In the 18th and 19th centuries, the Industrial Revolution drove millions of people from the country into cities looking for work. Crowded slums, poor nutrition, and lack of sanitation caused hundreds of thousands of deaths. Life at sea was no better.

Scurvy, the "Plague of the Sea"[1]

In 1657, in the sparkling seas off of Acapulco, Mexico, a ship was drifting, bobbing with the waves, shifting with the wind. It was a ghost ship, the entire crew dead from scurvy.

211

Scurvy is a deficiency of vitamin C—ascorbic acid—which works with iron to make red blood. It also makes collagen, which holds tissue together. Unlike some animals, humans can't make or store vitamin C, so we have to eat or drink it every day. In the absence of vitamin C, the symptoms of scurvy can appear in little more than a month. They start with tiredness and muscular weakness; then new wounds fester and ulcerate instead of heal; old wounds pull apart; small pinpoint purple spots on the skin indicate internal hemorrhaging; the gums get sore and bleed; the teeth fall out; the eyes and nose drip blood; then death comes.

The Latin word for scurvy is *scorbutus,* so the foods that fight scurvy are known as anti-scorbutics. The most common anti-scorbutics are citrus—orange, lemon, lime, grapefruit; cruciferous vegetables—kale, broccoli, cauliflower, cabbage, Brussels sprouts; and the nightshade family—bell pepper, potato, tomato. There is the exact same amount of vitamin C in half a cup of broccoli and half a cup of orange juice—62 milligrams. Half a cup of kale has almost 50 percent more than either—93 milligrams.[2] Merely by looking at this list of fruits and vegetables, it is not apparent to us now that they have anything in common; we know this only because vitamins were discovered in the 1920s. In the 18th and 19th centuries, all kinds of theories were put forward: the crew got scurvy because they hadn't been on land in a while; a piece of whale meat tied around a weak arm or leg would cure it; the acidity in certain foods counteracted scurvy. (Asians ate fresh ginger that they grew on their ships and didn't get scurvy.)[3]

The problem was that with a shortage of trees for fuel, the world was turning to whale blubber. Whaling ships from England or New England gone for three or four years to the whaling grounds in the Pacific could never carry enough food and water; they had to rely on what they could pick up along the way. In the Galapagos Islands, west of Ecuador, they got giant 200-pound tortoises, which they somehow hoisted onto the ship, where they spent the time walking around—very slowly—until they were needed for stew. Sometimes sailors were able to buy sheep or other food animals. But the biggest problem, and what the men needed most, were fresh fruits and vegetables, because the greatest killer, "the plague of the sea," was scurvy.[4]

The United States: Cholera and the Water Supply

In 1832, America experienced a new phenomenon: cholera. This disease caused death by depleting the body of fluids rapidly. Even though there had been cholera epidemics in other parts of the world,

Americans weren't concerned. They called it "the Asiatic cholera," and believed that because it originated in China, a "heathen" land, good Christians would be immune to it. Americans also didn't consider themselves at risk to get this disease because America was the New World; it lacked the slums, vices, and corruption of the Old World. To their surprise, Americans were hit very hard, both physically and psychologically, when cholera arrived in 1832. Cholera in the 19th century, like bubonic plague in the 14th, followed the trade routes. The difference was that in the 19th century, the trade routes extended all over the world. Wealthy Americans fled to their homes in the country. Of those who remained in the city, who lived and who died was puzzling: seemingly upstanding members of the community died while lower-class people lived. The reason: fine, upstanding citizens drank water from wells they didn't understand were contaminated, while street people drank germ-free wine, rum, or gin. Americans were terrified; a group of ministers appealed to president Andrew Jackson for a national day of prayer. He told the ministers to go ahead, but cited the separation of church and state to decline the participation of the presidency.[5]

Cholera struck the United States again in 1848–1849, from east to west. It swept through the poor Irish neighborhoods in eastern cities like New York, killing the Irish just after they arrived, already weakened from the potato famine and weeks on the coffin ships. In the west, travelers on the trails added cholera to the list of dangers they faced. Sometimes they had to leave people with cholera behind; with the certainty of approaching winter, they didn't have time to stop.

England: Dr. Snow and the Water Supply

1850. A mysterious cholera epidemic struck London. People on one side of town got cholera; on the other they didn't. This time, a physician, Dr. John Snow, figured out the cause. He traced it to one well with water contaminated by people dumping the contents of their sick babies' diapers down it. From this and other scientific experiments came germ theory and an understanding of how diseases spread. The British established a department of public health. It became the model for New York City's public health department, the first in the United States, in 1866. It was a response to the third and last major cholera epidemic in the United States. In a little more than 30 years, the American attitude toward disease had changed completely. Disease had gone from being divinely caused to being preventable by science, from a religious problem to a secular one: clean up the water supply.

France: Yeast and Phylloxera

Something was destroying the wines of France; it was a national disaster. In the middle of the 19th century, the wine in France went sour. It smelled bad and tasted worse. It was not even good vinegar. Vintners were mystified: there was nothing wrong with the grapes as they grew on the vines, and they had been harvested, stored, and processed as they had for centuries. But there was no wine in France. This was a tremendous blow to the national economy and to the national pride. Perhaps the scientists could help. Louis Pasteur discovered what made wine ferment. Although the process of fermentation had been known for 5,000 years, nothing was known about what caused it. The ancient Egyptians knew that fermentation turned grain into beer and made bread rise, but they didn't know why. What Pasteur discovered under his microscope was why: yeast. He also discovered that if you heated the wine to a certain point, the organisms that caused the wine to sour were killed, while the ones that made it ferment lived. This process of heating foods to destroy organisms that cause spoilage still bears the name of its discoverer: pasteurization.

As science expanded, plants and animals were exchanged worldwide. One of the plants sent to Europe was vinifera vines from North America. Europe was struck by an epidemic of phylloxera, a tiny yellow aphid that sucks the sap out of the roots of vinifera grapes, while the aboveground parts of the plant show no signs of illness. Then the whole plant dies. Phylloxera spreads easily on wind, water, and soil stuck to shoes and equipment. Between the 1860s and 1900, it killed off about one-third of the vinifera grapes in Europe. The cure: import phylloxera-resistant American rootstock and graft French grapes onto it. By 1900, less than one-third of the vinifera grapes growing in France were on original French rootstock; the rest were growing on American vines.[6]

THE BRITISH EMPIRE

The Industrial Revolution

The Industrial Revolution—the use of machines to do work—began in England in the middle of the 18th century. People streamed from the country into the cities where they lived in crowded conditions and worked 15 or more hours per day, even children as young as six. The first industry to be mechanized was textiles—spinning and weaving cloth.

This made clothes more affordable for more people. The people who owned the factories, supplied the raw materials, and sold the finished product became a prosperous new middle class with new eating habits.

Isabella Beeton: *The Book of Household Management*

A book that describes this new middle-class life is Isabella Beeton's 1,112-page *Book of Household Management*, published in London in 1861. It contains:

> Information for the Mistress, Housekeeper, Cook, Kitchen-Maid, Butler, Footman, Coachman, Valet, Upper and Under House-Maids, Lady's Maid, Maid-of-All-Work, Laundry-Maid, Nurse and Nurse-Maid, Monthly, Wet, and Sick Nurses, Etc. Etc.; Also, Sanitary, Medical, & Legal Memoranda.[7]

Clearly, the new British middle-class housewife was a household manager, in charge of a many-roomed house, nutrition, and sanitation for her family and a large staff, including child rearing, invalids, what invalidates a will, and how to keep hair from falling out.

These new middle-class people were meat-eaters. Out of 845 pages of recipes, 255 are for meat, most cooked by boiling. She cites laboratory studies supporting the health benefits of boiling, because "the juice of flesh is water, holding in solution many substances . . . which are of the highest value as articles of food."[8] A 53-page chapter about vegetables—mostly boiled—even has a recipe for boiled salad: boil 2 heads of celery and 1 pint of French beans separately until tender; cut celery into 2-inch pieces. Garnishes are chopped lettuce, blanched endive, or boiled cauliflower.[9] Suggested sauces are made of (1) milk, oil, vinegar, mustard, sugar, salt, and cayenne; (2) eggs, cream, vinegar, mustard, salt, white pepper, and cayenne pepper; or (3) egg, oil, cream, vinegar, mustard, sugar, and salt.[10] There are also four chapters that reflect the British love of dessert and teatime—one chapter on puddings and pastry; one on creams, jellies, soufflés, omelets, and sweet dishes; another on preserves, confectionery, ices and dessert dishes; and one on bread, biscuits, and cakes.

The book is a masterpiece of organization. Each recipe provides information on ingredients, method, time, average cost, how many portions it makes, and when the ingredients are in season. Most measurements are by weight; exceptions are "a heaping tablespoonful" or "2 dessert-spoonfuls." Each recipe is numbered, so cooks can find them and cross-reference them easily.

It is ironic that the woman who was an authority on sanitation died from a sanitation disease. Isabella Beeton was 24 years old when she died after giving birth to her third child, a victim of the professionalization of medicine. In earlier times, a female midwife stayed with a woman during her "lying-in," and did only that. When men took over the medical profession, they came to women giving birth after setting broken legs, treating infections, doing autopsies. Maybe they washed their hands. Women began to die of an infection called childbed (puerperal) fever, and so did Isabella Beeton.

Russian Table Service—*Service à la Russe*

Around 1860, Russian table service—*service à la russe*—replaced French table service—*service à la française*—which had been in style in Europe since the Middle Ages. In *service à la française,* all the food was placed on the table at once. Several dishes containing the same food were placed in different areas of the table, but this was no guarantee that every diner would get every food. Some food would get cold while other food was eaten. The advantage to *service à la russe* was that food was served in courses, one after the other, by attentive waiters who took away empty dishes and replaced them with new full ones. This way, food that was meant to be served hot would be hot when it arrived at the table. The host got to show off his wealth in the array of the food, numerous sets of dishes and glasses, and many servants. A new utensil came into use—the crumber, to brush crumbs off the table between courses. In Ireland, however, there was neither table nor crumbs for the peasants.

Jonathan Swift's "Modest Proposal" for Ending Famine in Ireland

In 1729, Jonathan Swift, the British author who is most famous for writing *Gulliver's Travels,* wrote a short piece called *A Modest Proposal,* subtitled *For Preventing the Children of Poor People in Ireland from Being a Burden to Their Parents or Country, and for Making Them Beneficial to the Public.* It was bitter, dark satire about the extreme poverty among the Irish:

> [A] young healthy child well nursed is at a year old a most delicious, nourishing and wholesome food, whether stewed, roasted, baked, or boiled, and I make no doubt that it will equally serve in a fricassee, or a ragout. . . . A child will make two dishes at an entertainment for friends, and when the family

dines alone, the fore or hind quarter will make a reasonable dish, and seasoned with a little pepper or salt will be very good boiled on the fourth day, especially in winter.[11]

The starving Irish missed the humor, because they felt the British would have done it if they could have gotten away with it. There was no shortage of food in Ireland—there was inequality in food distribution. The Irish, like the serfs in the Middle Ages and the slaves in the American South, raised the food but were not allowed to eat it. There had been famines in Ireland before, but nothing of the magnitude of the 1846 famine.

ℋOLIDAY ℋISTORY

≫ ST. PATRICK'S DAY, MARCH 17TH ≪

St. Patrick's Day is the most widely celebrated festival in the world.[12] It honors the patron saint who arrived in Ireland—called the "Emerald Isle" because of its lush green landscape—in A.D. 432, converted the people to Christianity, and banished all the snakes (although evidence indicates there never were snakes in Ireland). The 75 St. Patrick's Day festivals in the United States involve much wearing of the green; dancing to Irish drums, strings, and bagpipe music; and eating traditional corned beef and cabbage and drinking green-colored beer. The first St. Patrick's Day celebration dates back to 1762. It was in New York City because the Irish in Ireland, under British rule, couldn't celebrate being Irish. Chicago was the first city to dye its river green (www.chicagostpatsparade.com).

The Potato Famine in Ireland

The potato, which grows in poor soil where nothing else as nutritious will, allowed the population of Ireland to increase more than it would have on any other food. The potatoes were usually eaten boiled in their skins. The pot was placed on the floor, and everyone squatted around it. Condiments were salt, mustard, and sometimes buttermilk. Mashed potatoes were invented here: take the potatoes, mash them with some of the potato water, add the condiments. An adult male ate 13 or 14 potatoes per day, and very little else. Occasionally there were eggs or oats.[13]

Then a disease turned the leaves and stems of the potato plants black and rotted the roots. The potatoes died, and so did the Irish. As a solution, corn (maize) was imported from America. But Irish mills, made for processing soft grains like oats and wheat, could not make a dent in corn. The corn rotted; the people starved. They picked nettles that grew on graves. Like the Mongol horsemen 500 years earlier, they slit the necks of their farm animals and drank the blood. Sometimes the animals died, too. Approximately 1 million Irish died during the famine; another million left.

They would go to a new place, a place where there was food, where they could keep their religion, and where the land was rich and the streets were paved with gold. They would start over in America. And they would bring their strong Irish identity with them.

COLONIAL CUISINE

The new European factories needed raw materials, and the displaced farmers and their families who came to the cities by the millions to work in them needed food. The European powers turned to other continents to provide the raw materials and food they needed, and markets to sell the goods they manufactured. In the 19th century, the major explorations were to Africa, India, and Asia.

Africa Enslaved: Working for Peanuts, Cocoa, Rubber, Diamonds, and Gold

Africa is an enormous continent. It has the longest river in the world, the Nile; by far the largest desert, the Sahara; and the fourth tallest mountain, Kilimanjaro, which at 19,340 feet is almost a mile higher than the highest peak in the continental United States, California's Mt. Whitney. Its other climate zones range from Mediterranean in the north to rainforest at the equator. It also has vast savannas—grassy plains—where lions, zebras, giraffes, and other animals roam.

In the 19th century, Europe invaded the continent of Africa. Between 1878 and 1913, every country on the continent with the exceptions of Liberia on the west coast and Ethiopia on the east fell to a European power, and in 1935, Italy took Ethiopia. Three things enabled Europeans to colonize Africa: quinine, a New World herb that warded off malaria; the steamship, which made sailing upstream into the interior of Africa possible; and machine guns, which allowed a handful of men to control millions. France had the greatest amount of territory, almost 36 percent of the continent, which it controlled with the French Foreign Legion. Most of it was in the northwest, the modern countries of Algeria, Morocco, Mauritania, Mali, Niger, and Chad. England followed with more than 32 percent, mostly in the east and south, including modern Egypt, the Sudan, Uganda, Kenya, part of Tanzania, Zambia, Zimbabwe, Botswana, and South Africa. Germany and Belgium had almost 8 percent each. Portugal, Italy, and Spain split what was left. This is why there are croissants and baguettes in Ivory Coast in west Africa, spaghetti in Ethiopia and Eritrea on the east, and curry and chutney in British east and west Africa.

The British attitude toward people of other cultures was profoundly racist. Cecil Rhodes stated it clearly: "I contend that we [Britons] are the first race in the world, and the more of the world we inhabit, the better it is for the human race."[14] These colonial powers caused complete disruption of the life and the land, the cuisine and the culture. They forced the native people to grow non-native staple crops like peanuts and cacao, which displaced native African food. By the end of the 19th century, Africa was the world's leading producer of cacao. This caused the economy to shift from a self-sufficient barter system to cash, because the native people now had to buy food with money, so they had to work for wages. Some went to work on rubber plantations in the Belgian Congo, under the extremely harsh rule of King Leopold. Workers who didn't do their work well enough or quickly enough had their hands or feet cut off. The Congo was also rich in copper and tin. But South Africa was a gold mine—literally.

African Cuisine

Much of modern African cuisine is the colonial cuisine that Europeans forced upon Africans in the 19th century. Africa was blessed with relatively few native food plants and animals, but many from around the world grew well there. African cuisine came in waves. First, the plants and animals that were indigenous, like okra and yams—an 18- to 20-pound bland starchy vegetable (not like the small sweet tubers that Americans call yams, which are really a variety of sweet potato); then, in antiquity, Near Eastern, Greek, and Roman peoples came to trade in Alexandria and introduced wheat, barley, sheep and goats. From the 7th through the 15th century, the Arabs dominated and brought spices like cumin, coriander, cinnamon, ginger, and black pepper to the northern and eastern coasts of Africa. The slave traders brought New World peanuts to grow to feed slaves during the Middle Passage. Chili peppers migrated south from the Iberian peninsula. But Europeans were restricted to the coasts until the 19th century, when they began to penetrate the interior. First came missionaries. The most famous was David Livingstone, who finally questioned what he was doing there when the

Africans had their own religions. Farmers followed missionaries, and the military came to protect them and businesses.

Because of Africa's geographical and cultural diversity, it has developed distinct regional cuisines. Common to the cuisines of north Africa—the region called the Maghreb—is the chile pepper, used in *harissa,* Tunisia's main condiment of dried chile peppers, olive oil, garlic, cumin, cinnamon, coriander, and caraway.[15] Throughout Africa, chile peppers are the main spice; there are words for them in many languages in Africa—*piment* in French; in Swahili, *pili-pili, peri-peri,* and *piri-piri,* which is also the name of the chile-spiced stew that is the national dish of Mozambique. In Africa, chiles are spice, medicine, aphrodisiac, and the food that was supposed to make people immortal.

A stew of meat and fruit or meat and vegetables, in Arabic, the *tagine* or *tajin* of al-Baghdadi (plural, *touajen*) is prepared in the cooking vessel of the same name, with a cone-shaped top to allow steam to escape. Or the *tagine* can be cooked in the bottom of a pot with a steamer insert. The steam from the *tagine* wafts up to cook the couscous in the top section. Couscous, the staple food in northern Africa, probably originated with the native Berbers. It is tiny balls (one-eighth to less than one-sixteenth of an inch) of semolina wheat (the kind used for pasta), barley, millet, or maize flour mixed with salted water.[16] It can also be steamed by itself in a *couscousière* (a French word), or cooked in the stew.

Spiced meat is cubed into *kebabs* or ground into *kefta.* Both are cooked on a skewer over a charcoal fire. *Kefta* can also be fried or shaped flat like a hamburger. Spiciness is provided by a Moroccan spice mix, *ras el hanout,* and olives and lemons cured in salt. Spices are sold in bulk at the *souk* or marketplace.

The Moroccan masterpiece is bastilla (one of various spellings), layers of contrasting tastes and textures wrapped in flaky dough. The Moroccan pastry, even thinner than phyllo (or filo), is called *warqa* (meaning "leaf"). The layers inside are chicken (originally pigeon or squab) stewed in spices until it falls off the bone. Some of the reduced stewing liquid, along with lemon juice, is mixed with eggs and scrambled until silky. Crunchy chopped almonds are sautéed in butter, dusted with cinnamon and sugar, and sprinkled on top before it is all enveloped in buttered *warqa* and baked. You break off a piece and eat it with your hands—only the right hand, because Arabs reserve the left hand for personal hygiene. It is customary to use only the thumb and the first two fingers, to show restraint, instead of greedily using all five.[17] As rich as it is, bastilla is not the main course—just the first or second. The desserts in northern Africa are also Arab-influenced and very sweet with sugar syrup or honey. In the book *Best of Regional*

Souk in Tunisia.
Photo courtesy Nancy Uhrhammer

African Cooking, Hachten includes one that is a serious aphrodisiac—it contains both Spanish fly and hashish. Everything is washed down with spearmint tea.

West Africa has tropical beaches and tropical fruit: pineapple, mango, papaya, coconut. An abundance of fish is preserved by drying, smoking, or salting. Although West Africa is a large grower of cacao, it is not processed there. The beans are shipped to Europe or the United States for processing, then shipped back to Africa as candy, so it is expensive and usually found only in cities and eaten by foreigners.[18] West African meals are one course, and one-pot stews, often thickened with peanuts. Foods are cooked in palm oil. The staple starch is *fufu* (also *foofoo* and numerous other spellings)—cassava, maize, yams, plantains, or rice boiled, steamed, baked, or fried, then pounded and mashed.[19] Chicken is the most valued meat, but snails are eaten more often. One popular Nigerian street food sounds perfect for Super Bowl Sunday: beef marinated in beer, rolled in ground peanuts and chile, then grilled over charcoal.[20]

In the absence of Muslim influence, there are also palm wine, roast pork, and homemade beer, brewed from "corn, sorghum, or millet; in the rain-forests, mashed bananas are the base." In southern Africa, beer is brewed from the fruit of the maroela tree, which falls to the

221

ground and ferments. What the humans don't harvest, the elephants eat. It makes them drunk and dangerous.[21]

Snack foods include locusts, steamed or sautéed and then seasoned with chile. Termites are a delicacy. African termites build enormous mounds above ground; aardvarks (sometimes mistakenly called anteaters) use their sharp claws to tear down the claylike walls, and long snouts and sticky tongues to penetrate the narrow tunnels inside the mounds. When the termites swarm, looking for a new place to build, humans catch them and eat them. They are very high in protein and because they are white, they are sometimes called "rice ants." Their flavor has been compared to peanut butter, sugared marrow, and almond paste.[22] Sometimes humans eat the aardvarks, too. Other meats are eland (a large antelope), venison, ostrich, gazelle, hippopotamus, giraffe, crocodile, seven-pound frogs, rats, and bats.

Many of the ports of Africa were originally settled by European countries as stations where their ships could stop for repairs and supplies, including food. South Africa, almost halfway on the sea voyage between Indonesia and the Netherlands, served this purpose for the Dutch East India Company, which first established a colony there in 1652. They immediately planted fruits and vegetables that would keep the ships' crews healthy and free from scurvy and other vitamin-deficiency diseases: "sweet potatoes, pineapples, watermelons, pumpkins, cucumbers, radishes, and citrus trees such as lemons and oranges."[23] By the 18th century, they brought slaves from Malaysia and their spicy cuisine, including one dish called *kerrie-kerrie,* later shortened to *curry.* Another Malaysian spice mixture composed of onions, ginger, dried shrimp or prawns, and chile powder is called a *sambal.*[24]

In eastern Africa, in Ethiopia and Eritrea, *injera,* like a thick, elastic sourdough crêpe, is "the daily bread, tablecloth, and silverware."[25] The bottom of an enormous round tray the diameter of a small table is lined with *injera;* the stew is on top of the bread, soaks into it, and is used to scoop up the food with the hand. The east also has strong Indian influences because the British brought experienced workers from India to work on the railroad in Africa, including one young man named Mohandas K. Gandhi, who later led the successful fight for India's freedom.

India: "The Jewel in the Crown"

India was called the jewel in the crown because it was England's most valuable colony. Its fertile land produced foodstuffs like tea and coffee. In the 1860s, cotton for England's textile factories also became extremely important when American cotton was cut off by the Civil War. India's population of 300 million provided a huge market for England's manufactured goods.

The British in India were the ruling class, so they lived and ate very well. Breakfasts were substantial: boiled or fried fish or prawns, a curry or casserole, cold mutton, bread and butter or rice, plantains or oranges. Kedgeree (Isabella Beeton spells it *kegeree*) was a popular British breakfast of "any cold fish, 1 teacupful of boiled rice, 1 oz. of butter, 1 teaspoonful of mustard, 2 soft-boiled eggs, salt and cayenne to taste," all mixed together and served hot.[26] The household of a British official had its own deer, cows, calves, sheep, kids, ducks, geese, and rabbits, so an important dinner could include 15 or 16 meat courses. One woman described an average daily main meal in 1780: "We dine at 2 O'clock in the very heat of the day. . . . A soup, a roast fowl, curry and rice, a mutton pie, forequarter of lamb, a rice pudding, tarts, very good cheese, fresh churned butter, excellent Madeira."[27] Nap time followed, then socializing and visiting. Supper was a light evening meal.

A century later, the meals were reversed—the midday meal was light, while the heavy main meal was a social event at 7 or 8 P.M. After 1807, the word *tiffin* appears. This is a light midday meal, from the British word that is the equivalent of *snack*. The arrival of wives shifted food away from native Indian to Anglo-Indian or purely British food like roast meats, puddings, and sandwiches. Curry was popular with Anglo-Indians, but not in its original meaning as a spiced relish from south India. Instead, it became a catchall word that could mean broth, a wet stew, or a dry dish. Drinking increased. The beverage of choice was claret. A man could drink three bottles after dinner; a woman, one a day. They also drank Champagne, brandy, and beer. Servants prepared and served the food.[28]

In 1857, beef and pork caused the Hindu and Muslim sepoys—Indian soldiers in the British East India Company army—to mutiny. A rumor, untrue, spread that the rifle cartridges were smeared with beef and pork fat. The sepoys were incensed because they had to break the cartridges open with their teeth. It took a year for the British to regain control of India. In 1869, the same year that the United States completed the transcontinental railroad, Lucknow—the last province that was resistant to the British—fell.

India also produced a crop that proved crucial in expanding the British Empire. It was grown cheaply in India, then transported to China on British ships and sold to the Chinese. The plant's name in

Latin is *Papavera somnifera*—"poppy put-you-to-sleep"; the product processed from its sticky juice is opium.

China: Tea and Opium

In the 19th century, the British treasury had an unfavorable balance of trade with China. The British wanted tea; the Chinese wanted nothing except payment in silver. The British had to find something to sell to China. They decided on opium—a depressant drug, a "downer." It was highly addictive, so there would be return customers. The Chinese emperor objected in writing to Queen Victoria. She responded the way Elizabeth I responded to the king of Spain in the 1580s when he complained about pirates hijacking British ships in the Caribbean—she ignored him. There was a war, but the Chinese navy was no match for British steamships and guns. By 1842, the Opium War was over and China was forced to give the island of Hong Kong to the British. Before the Opium War, the emperor had allowed foreign ships to anchor only in the city of Canton (now Guangzhou) in southern China. Afterward, five major ports were open. In effect, foreign money, businesses, governments, and guns were calling the shots in China. This destabilized the government, caused civil wars in China for almost a century, led to the end of thousands of years of empire (and the emperor) in 1911, and made China vulnerable to invasion by Japan in 1937.

China: Cantonese Cuisine

Historian E. N. Anderson, in *The Food of China,* states: "Cantonese food, at its best, is probably unequalled in China and possibly in the world."[29] The freshest ingredients, drawn from all regions of China, split-second timing, a wide variety of techniques, hundreds of superb dishes, and the ability to quickly absorb new foods and techniques—like baking—from other cuisines make for an ever-expanding, innovative cuisine. Unfortunately, what most Americans know as Cantonese cuisine isn't. The sweet-and-sour pork, chop suey, chow mein, greasy egg rolls, and fried rice that became popular in the United States in the 1950s and 1960s are not at all representative of Cantonese cuisine. It was "dumbed down" and sweetened up for American taste buds. The Cantonese have even fewer desserts than other areas of China, so they do not use sugar with a heavy hand in their main dishes. Cantonese cuisine uses—sparingly—chile sauce, hot mustard, vinegars, sesame oil, and soy and oyster sauces. Fish and seafood, from oysters to sea cucumbers, squid, jellyfish, and croaker, are Cantonese specialties. They are often steamed, stir-fried, or deep-fried. They are not slathered in cornstarch, canned pineapple juice, and questionable flavor enhancers like MSG (monosodium glutamate). The Cantonese regard this kind of cooking and the people who eat

ℱood ℱABLE

≫ THE ORIGIN OF CHOP SUEY ≪

It is a myth that chop suey is of American origin. As the story goes, someone went to a restaurant in San Francisco's Chinatown just before closing time, so the chef threw together all the leftover odds and ends. Chop suey is leftovers, but from Canton, where *tsap seui* means "miscellaneous scraps."[30]

it the same way the Romans regarded people who had never had bread and put meat under their saddle to warm it up—as barbarians.

The delicacy of Cantonese cuisine comes out in *tim sam* (*dim sum*), which means "small eating." These are bite-sized dumplings, pieces of dough wrapped around a spiced meat or seafood filling, then steamed. Sometimes they are wrapped in lotus or bamboo leaves and steamed, the way Mexican cuisine uses corn husks to wrap tamales. Cantonese cuisine is also the cuisine of the islands of Macau and Hong Kong. By treaty, England gave Hong Kong back to the Chinese on July 1, 1997. Many people left Hong Kong and brought their cuisine with them; there are now many fine Cantonese restaurants in the United States.

China and India: "Coolies," the New Slaves

In the 19th century, Chinese and Indians became a new source of slave labor throughout the world. They were known as coolies, a word with obscure origins. In Chinese, the word *coolie* means "bitter labor," while in Hindi it means "bonded labor." The African slave ships were the model for the coolie ships, and as on the African ships, the coolies died and mutinied. Chinese lured other Chinese into servitude with offers of jobs as cooks for the French in Canton, or with the Chinese army. Chinese and Indian workers were shipped as far away as the Caribbean, where they worked 21 hours a day making sugar. Some Chinese went to New York City, where they intermarried with the Irish. And, of course, they brought their cuisine and their culture with them. Others ended up in California, in the gold fields or working on the railroad.

EUROPE

Ludwig, the Mad King of Bavaria, and the Fairy-Tale Kitchen

Ludwig became the king of beautiful Bavaria, in the Alps in southern Germany, when he was 19 years old. Most Americans know Bavaria because of the cars made by Bavarian Motor Works (BMW) and because in German, the word for "Bavaria" is *Bayern*—as in aspirin. Ludwig loved palaces and swans, the Bavarian coat of arms. To provide work for his subjects in a slow economy, he began building castles. They were 19th-century Gothic, patterned after the medieval castles he grew up in. The paintings, frescoes, tapestries, and sculptures celebrated heroes from German mythology like Siegfried slaying the dragon. The ceilings were decorated with scenes from the operas of famous German composers like Wagner. Mechanical swans swam in man-made streams. The castles were spectacular but they were bankrupting the kingdom. In 1886, when Ludwig announced he was going to build a fourth castle, he drowned under mysterious circumstances. Some say that nobles lured him onto a boat, went to the middle of the lake, and pushed him overboard.

At one castle, Neuschwanstein—New Swan Castle—built between 1869 and 1886, Ludwig spared no expense in creating an ultra-modern kitchen. Huge round polished granite columns supported an arched and vaulted ceiling. The kitchen also boasted a granite fish tank, hot and cold running water, a grill, an enormous cooktop that vented under the wood floor, and a wall oven. Rising heat was put to work in two ways. As it passed from the stove to the chimney, it was directed through a plate warmer. Then, hot air in the chimney turned the blades of a turbine connected to a gear that automatically turned the spit roasters. Before elevators, dumbwaiters hauled firewood for the stoves and sent the cooked food up three floors to the elaborate dining room.[31] Most Americans have never seen Neuschwanstein, but they would recognize it instantly—it is the model for Sleeping Beauty's Castle at Disneyland, but infinitely more beautiful. (To see the castle, log onto www.germanworld.com/neu.htm.) For two weeks every year, starting the last week of September, nearby Munich hosts the world's largest beer festival, the Oktoberfest.

The Franco-Prussian War of 1870: Escoffier Cooks for the Army

When France declared war on Germany in 1870, French military officers raced everywhere trying to be first to corner the best cooks. It just wouldn't be civilized to go to war without a chef. One of the rising chefs in Paris was Auguste Escoffier, a 22-year-old from the French Riviera. He was gifted and he was motivated, and he became the chef to the General Staff. At the beginning of the war, Escoffier was preparing *blanquette de veau,* roast sirloin, and rabbit in pork fat, cognac, and white wine close to the battlefield. He knew that as the war went on food would become scarce, so he planned ahead. Preparation is everything. He became his own farmer, purveyor, and forager. He set up a secret little farmyard so he could have fresh eggs, milk, chickens, geese, rabbits, pigs, sheep, and turkeys. Supplemented with the officers' own stashes of wine and brandy, it paid off. During a siege, the General Staff continued to eat well long after the other cavalry officers had eaten their last good meal—and their last horse. Eventually, however, Escoffier too was reduced to using the cavalry officers' horses in *pot-au-feu de cheval* and *cheval aux lentilles.* He and another chef were taken prisoner of war and escaped, but they were captured again when they tried to get jobs in a German *pâtisserie.*[32]

Alsace: Franco-German Cuisine

One disputed area was the province of Alsace, east of Champagne, on France's border with Germany along the Rhine River. Not surprisingly, the cuisine shows a hearty Franco-German fusion. The food from this area that is probably most familiar to Americans is quiche, the savory custard tart with bits of bacon or ham (traditionally, no cheese) that became popular in the United States in the last decades of the 20th century.[33] Quiche goes well with the white wines the region produces, like Riesling. But Alsatians consume twice as much beer as people in other parts of France; like the inhabitants of nearby Belgium, they use it in cooking, too, especially in soup. Alsatians love *choucroûte garni*—sauerkraut with pork and sausages. Strasbourg is famous for its Gothic cathedral and *pâté de foie gras* baked in a pastry crust; Münster is famous for its soft cheese. The bread, unlike the white bread so prized elsewhere in France, can be dark like German bread, made with rye or whole wheat. Typically German seasonings found in Alsatian cuisine are juniper, caraway, and horseradish.[34]

Along with French *tartes* and *petit fours,* pastry shops in Alsace make German Black Forest cake (*Schwarzwalder Torte*), layers of chocolate genoise, whipped cream, and morello cherries drenched in kirsch—cherry brandy—and named after the nearby forest. No Alsatian bride set up housekeeping without the distinctive deep, swirled mold for *kugelhopf,* a sweet bread studded with nuts and raisins that used to be for special occasions but now is a breakfast standard. The mold gets its name from *kugel*, meaning "ball," and *hopf*, "hops," because formerly beer made the batter rise. Terra-cotta molds were preferred over copper because they absorb butter, making the crust on each bread better than the last. In addition to the molds for wafers—*gaufres*—Alsatians have numerous molds for shaped spiced cakes or gingerbreads: a star for Christmas, a fish or eel (once abundant in the Rhine River) for New Year, a fleur-de-lys for Epiphany, a lamb for Easter, a baby for a baptism, and the famous French rooster for patriotic events.[35]

ITALY: UNIFIED COUNTRY, REGIONAL CUISINE

"Una tavola senza vino é com'una giornata senza sole" ("A table without wine is like a day without sunshine")

—*Italian saying*

In the beginning of the 19th century, Italy was eight separate states. One was ruled by Italians, one by the pope; the others belonged to foreign countries. Since the fall of the Roman Empire in A.D. 476, Italy's city-states had been conquered and reconquered, ruled by French, German, Spanish, Arabs, Byzantine Greeks, and Normans who enriched themselves at the expense of the people, then left. In 1871, Italy ceased being a series of loosely connected city-states and became one country. It was unified politically, but still fragmented culturally. Each former city-state had its own cuisine, culture, and dialect. These differences in Italian were not like the differences in American English, with merely slightly different accents. They used different words. To overcome this, Italy made education mandatory in 1879.

Northern Italian Cuisine

Two years later, the most influential cookbook in Italy was published, *La Scienza in Cucina e l'arte di mangiar bene*—The Science of Cooking and the Art of Eating Well. It was subtitled *Manuale practico per le famiglie*—Practical Manual for Families. It reflected the styles and eating habits of the new middle-class city dwellers, especially in the north. This type of Italian cuisine didn't become popular in the United States until the end of the 20th century, because only 20 percent of the Italian immigrants who came to America at the end of the 19th and beginning of the 20th century were from the north.

Emilia-Romagna has been called the "richest gastronomic region in Italy."[36] This area is rich in dairy farms that produce Parmesan cheese and butter, the main ingredients in alfredo sauce, the Italian cream sauce. Grains in the north also include rice and corn for *risotto* and *polenta*, often to accompany *osso buco*, stewed veal shank. From the seaport city of Genoa comes *pesto genovese*, a sauce made of basil, olive oil, pine nuts, and Parmesan cheese. *Prosciutto di Parma* is a northern Italian ham. Dried sausages like *salame* are also from the north. *Mortadella*, an uncured sausage, is known in the United States by the mangled pronunciation of the name of the city where it is made, Bologna, which Americans call "baloney."

The meal begins with *antipasti*, appetizers, but there is no one main course, as meat often is in an American meal. As cookbook author Marcella Hazan explains: "There are, at a minimum, two principal courses, which are never, never brought to the table at the same time."[37] But this was very different from how the vast majority of the population of southern Italy ate.

Southern Italian Cuisine: The *Mezzogiorno*

The southern half of the Italian boot, the part below Rome, is known as the *Mezzogiorno*—literally, "midday" or "noon"—because it is where the sun shines brightly. In 1806, feudalism ended in Italy, but not the extreme class divisions between the minority of upper-class wealthy and the majority who were barely surviving as farmers. Most people in southern Italy lived in a one-room, two-level hut. On the dirt floor on the bottom level lived the animals—a few chickens, maybe a pig for sausage. Up a ladder in a loft was where the family slept. The food was not very different from what Don Quixote and Sancho Panza had in Spain 200 years earlier, or medieval peasants one thousand years earlier: lentils, bread, onions, maybe some cheese and fruit. Meat was on the peasant table only twice a year, at the major Catholic holidays—a chicken or capon for Christmas, roast kid at Easter. Pasta, too, was a luxury. Like the peasants in Ireland or the slaves who did all the work in the American South, southern Italian peasants raised the animals, sowed the seeds, and harvested the crops, but they didn't get to eat them. The food went to the upper classes.

In the cities, it was different. Upper-class cuisine made full use of the bounty for which the Mezzogiorno had been famous and fought over since it was settled by the Greeks in the 4th century B.C.—wine, figs, raisins, spinach, citrus fruit, sheep and goat, cheese, olive oil, grain. The sea was rich with *frutti di mare* or seafood (literally, "fruit of the sea"): *calamari* and *polpi,* squid and octopus. By the 18th century, Naples had become the pasta capital of the world, with almost three hundred pasta businesses. Some of it was sold by street vendors and eaten, in those long strands, by hand.[38] Sauce made with plum tomatoes, especially from the area of San Marzano, has also come to be identified with southern Italian cooking, although the tomato does not appear in Italian cookbooks until almost 1700, and then the recipe is for "Spanish-style" tomato sauce.[39] Pasta was layered with tomato sauce and ricotta cheese and topped with mozzarella to make lasagne, or stuffed with ground meat or ricotta cheese and herbs to make square ravioli or round agnolotti and then covered with sauce. Parmesan cheese is traditionally grated over the top. Meat sauces and meatballs—*polpette*—were reserved for special occasions. Pasta was eaten with peas—*pasta e piselli;* or with beans—*pasta e fagioli,* which became *pasta fazool* in Neapolitan dialect.

Pizza, a round, flat bread with various toppings, is another typically Neapolitan food. The word *pizza* is related to *pita,* and has been used since the 10th century. Neapolitan pizza has a crisp, thin crust, while Sicilian pizza has a thicker, more breadlike crust. Simple pizza is dough topped with tomatoes, olive oil, garlic, and oregano. A more elaborate version is *pizza margherita,* created for Italy's Queen Margherita. It is *tricolore*—three-colored—to represent the Italian flag. The tomato sauce is red, the mozzarella is white, and the fresh basil leaves are green. A flat wooden paddle called a peel is used to slide the pizza into a very hot—750°F—brick oven.

Baking in Italy was very connected to religion. Each one of the numerous festivals required its own special breads or desserts. Some holidays were celebrated throughout Italy, like Madonna Assunta, the Assumption of the Virgin Mary into heaven, August 13 to 15, and St. Lucy's Day, the Feast of Lights, on December 13. Breads in the shape of *ossa di morti*—bones of the dead—were baked in honor of the Day of the Dead, November 2. For Easter, a special, rich, yeast-risen egg bread was baked, as well as pies filled with ricotta and rice, barley, or kernels of wheat. Another Easter pie is savory, baked in a crust spiced with black pepper and filled with cubed prosciutto, other meats, cheeses, and an egg binder. But many feast days were for local patron saints. For example, San Maura, the patron saint of people with arthritis and rheumatism, January 15, is celebrated with small breads in the shape of canes.[40]

The pastry and confectionery arts were highly developed in southern Italy because the Arabs cultivated sugar in Sicily since the Middle Ages. Italian sponge cake might originally have been called *pan di spugna* (sponge bread), or it might be Spanish in origin—*pan di Spagna* (Spanish bread). It is deliberately a bit dry and lightly sweetened, so it can be sliced into layers and moistened with liqueurs like rose-scented *rosolio* or *strega,* made from herbs and elderberries, and topped with fresh fruit or jam. A more elaborate version calls for the cake to be sliced, drenched in rum, spread with vanilla and chocolate *crema pasticciera* (pastry cream) or ricotta cream, and topped with whipped cream. This is similar to an English trifle and is called *zuppa inglese*—English soup—because of the rum; it needs to be eaten with a spoon. *Zeppole,* fried and filled with pastry cream, are made for St. Joseph's Day on March 19. The technique for making *zabaglione* (now *zabaione*) *marsala* is the same as the beginning of a *semifreddo:* whisk egg yolks and sugar for several minutes to aerate and thicken. Various areas of Italy (and other parts of Europe) make a simple pastry of dough, twisted or knotted, fried, and sprinkled with confectioners' sugar. *Struffoli* are small fried dough balls coated in warm honey and topped with colored sprinkles. Ricotta was also given special treatment in desserts in southern Italy and Sicily.

Sicilian Cuisine

Ricotta means "recooked," just as *biscotti* means "twice cooked." Originally made from goat or sheep milk, ricotta was a by-product from making a sharp, hard, aged Italian cheese, provolone (nothing like the tasteless round rubber log that is sold as domestic provolone in the United States). Now, ricotta is made on its own. Dried, it becomes *ricotta salata,* tangy and crumbly.

It is used in Sicily's most famous dessert. Cannoli is a study in contrast: a crunchy unsweetened fried pastry tube filled with smooth, sweetened ricotta. Now the dough is wrapped around hollow metal cannoli forms (*cannolini* are the small version), but in the 19th century, pastry chefs used *canna*—cane stalks or reeds. *Cassata* is another Sicilian dessert made with ricotta, a combination of sponge cake and ricotta wrapped in green-tinted almond paste (in earlier times, pistachio paste). *Cassata* can be traced back to the Arab *qas'ah,* the mold that shaped it.[41] *Cassata gelata* is its frozen cousin, which adds layers of three different flavors of *gelato.* Traditional Sicilian *gelato* is different from French and American ice creams. French ice cream is thickened and enriched with eggs. American ice cream—Philadelphia ice cream—has more cream than French ice cream, but no eggs. *Gelato* was originally made with goat's milk, which has more fat than cow's milk but less than cream; it was originally thickened with wheat starch, then in the 19th century cornstarch. There are also refreshing ices—*granita*—made with water, sugar, and lemon juice, mulberries, cinnamon, or jasmine flowers.[42]

Sugar is also used in Sicilian main dishes, which can be often *agrodolce*—sour and sweet. *Caponata* is an eggplant relish made with vinegar and sugar. Sometimes foods are sweetened with orange or tangerine juice, raisins, or currants. Caper berries are common, too. The north African and Arab influence shows in *cuscus* (couscous), the use of rice, spinach, and the many dishes with chickpeas. From the sea come swordfish, sardines for stuffing, and tuna and anchovies for pasta sauce. Again, these were upper-class foods. The American ex-slave Booker T. Washington visited Sicily and was shocked at the lives of the peasants:

> The Negro is not the man farthest down. The condition of the coloured farmer in the most backward parts of the Southern States in America, even where he has the least education and the least encouragement, is incomparably better than the condition and opportunities of the agricultural population in Sicily.[43]

In the early 1890s, successive years of drought damaged the grain, grape, and citrus crops in Sicily, and phylloxera wiped out vines throughout the *Mezzogiorno*. But hunger was not the only thing that drove 40 percent of Sicily's population away. Lack of industrialization and sanitation also played a part. A government that demanded seven years of service in the armed forces and that turned troops loose on its citizens with orders to arrest anyone with "the face of an assassin," 20 thousand deaths from malaria every year, and American industrialization that undercut the price of sulfur, Sicily's chief export, all churned up the idea of leaving. Finally, three years of cholera epidemics in the mid-1880s that killed 55,000 people, and volcanic eruptions and a tidal wave that killed 100,000 more in 1908, seemed like signs from God to the 1.5 million people who decided, weeping and cursing, that leaving Sicily was the only way they could survive.[44]

They would go to a new place, where the land was rich and the streets were paved with gold. They would start over in America.

*T*ENTH *C*OURSE

The Purity Crusade, *Cuisine Classique,* Communal Food, and Prohibition: The Early 20th Century in the United States, Europe, and Russia

THE NEW IMMIGRANTS AND THE MELTING POT

They came to America by the millions. Between 1870 and 1920, 26 million people migrated to the United States—Italians, Jews, Poles, Hungarians, Greeks, Lithuanians, Czechs, Rumanians, Russians, and others.[1] They arrived at Ellis Island in New York Harbor with few possessions and almost no money—the average male had 17 dollars.[2] Immigrant labor helped to make the United States an industrial giant and a world power. From a late start in the Industrial Revolution, American factories were now outproducing England, Germany, and Belgium, the most industrialized countries in the world—*combined.*

Italian-American Cuisine

"Not yet Americanized. Still eating Italian food." The late-19th-century female social worker who wrote this might have been referring to macaroni, which horrified meat-and-potatoes-eating Americans. If the pasta wasn't bad enough, that sauce of olive oil and garlic and tomatoes would surely kill you. And pizza—that same tomato sauce,

233

Holiday History

❯❯ San Gennaro in New York's Little Italy, ❮❮
September 12–22

The *festa* of San Gennaro, the patron saint of Naples who was decapitated on September 19, A.D. 305, for believing in Christ, is the largest Italian-American celebration in the United States. The street fair began in New York's Little Italy in 1926. It takes place from September 12 to 22 every year (except 2001, when it was canceled because of September 11). More than a million people turn out to watch the religious processions as the statue of San Gennaro is paraded down Mulberry Street, and to buy Italian food—especially sausage and pepper submarine sandwiches—from more than 300 street vendors. In 2002, a cannoli-eating contest began.

---

but on bread. Only one thing could make it worse—fry the bread dough, then ladle tomato sauce on top and sprinkle it with cheese. The name said it all: *pizza fritta,* fried pie. And when their babies teethed or had colic, these people rubbed wine on their gums or even gave them a sip. Italians would never become real Americans or understand American food.

Usually, the Italian men came to America first. They learned to cook or found rooming houses run by other Italians where they got meals. About 50 percent of the Italians saved money and went home for good. Others sent money back, or sent for their wives and families later. As the people became more prosperous in America, these women who could make a meal out of very little in the old country found they had a great deal to work with in the new one. Meat began to appear more often. On Sundays and holidays there might be a special tomato sauce with meatballs, sausage, pork spareribs, and *braciole*—flank steak sprinkled with salt, pepper, Parmesan cheese, chopped garlic, parsley, and fresh basil in season, rolled and tied with string, browned in olive oil and garlic, then simmered in the sauce. Mothers taught daughters to cook without recipes, just by feel. They avoided cooking classes. The second generation, the children of the immigrants, who went to American schools and learned to read and write English, began to figure out the measurements and write recipes down. The Christmas and Easter traditions of making mountains of pastry, sweetened egg bread, and ricotta pies to offer to the relatives and friends who dropped by continued. So did the festivals that reinforced the immigrants' sense of community in their new country, like the Feast of San Gennaro.

However, Italian immigrants, with one foot in Italy and one in America, celebrated holidays with the cuisines of both countries. For example, on Thanksgiving, Italians ate soup, lasagne, meatballs and sausage, and Italian bread. *Then* they ate the full American Thanksgiving dinner with turkey, cranberry sauce, stuffing (made with Italian bread, Italian sausage, and giblets), mashed potatoes, and sweet potatoes. There would also usually be an Italian vegetable like broccoli with olive oil, lemon juice, and garlic; then a salad of fresh greens followed by fresh seasonal fruit like pomegranates, pears, and tangerines; pumpkin and apple pie; and finally, a bowl filled with walnuts and almonds to munch on. For Italians, Thanksgiving was a traditional Italian holiday meal with a traditional American holiday meal sandwiched in the middle.

Jewish-American Cuisine

Many foods that Americans think of now as typically American, or typically New York, originated with the 2.5 million Jews who migrated from eastern Europe. Jews settled on New York's Lower East Side, the alphabet avenues—A, B, C, D—east of First Avenue. Like the Irish and the Italians, the Jews took advantage of the abundance of food in America to develop their own cuisine and cook every day the food that previously had been reserved for holidays or for the upper classes in Europe. Noodles and dumplings like kreplach and knishes could be filled with meat in addition to the traditional potatoes. Chicken soup, bagels, bialys, lox and cream cheese, sour cream, cheesecake, borscht, and gefilte fish could be eaten often. German Jewish delicatessen food, heavy on meat—kosher sausage, salami, pastrami—became the new tradition for all Jewish immigrants. Delicatessens called "appetizing" stores sprang up only in the New York Jewish community.[3]

Jewish women, responsible for food preparation, demanded high-quality food and boycotted and demonstrated when they didn't get it. American food companies advertised in the Yiddish press; some, like Heinz, even started producing kosher foods. These people who had known starvation in the old country pushed food on their children. Rabbis and the Yiddish press reminded Jews to observe the dietary laws, because temptations to eat outside the culture were everywhere. Some Jews were curious, especially those who worked closely with Italians. Jewish children were exposed to the foods of Americans and of other immigrants at school. Words like *macaroni* show up in some of the first American cookbooks published by Jews.[4]

$\mathscr{H}$OLIDAY $\mathscr{H}$ISTORY
≫ Polish Fest ≪

America's largest Polish festival is the Milwaukee, Wisconsin, Polish Fest. For three days in June, thousands of people feast on Polish, German, and other European specialties. *Feinschmeckers* (gourmets) will be glad that *wurstmachers* (sausage makers) have been busy turning out more than 70 varieties of sausage—bratwurst, beerwurst, knackwurst, yachtwurst, wieners, liver sausage, braunschweiger, salami, bologna, German-style mortadella with pistachios, and summer sausage—along with pastrami, ham, smoked pork butt and shoulder, and bacon. Beer is the beverage of choice, to quench the thirst from nonstop polka dancing. See www.polishfest.org for more details.

Cookbooks written by Jewish women or by settlement houses—places the immigrants could go to learn how to settle into the United States—helped the Jewish community learn how to use the resources available to them. The first one was published in 1901 by Lizzie Black Kander. *The Settlement Cookbook: The Way to a Man's Heart* had Jewish and non-Jewish recipes. Unlike Italian women, Jewish women eager to improve their skills signed up for free cooking classes provided by local governments and charities. Another group with a strong culinary tradition settled farther west, and still celebrates its cuisine and its culture today.

PROGRESSIVES AND THE PURITY CRUSADE

The Progressive era, approximately 1901–1920, was a time of intense, profound change in America. In 1903 in Detroit, Henry Ford mass-produced cars with gasoline combustion engines; in Kitty Hawk, North Carolina, the Wright brothers flew the first airplane; and in Hollywood, *The Great Train Robbery,* at 20 minutes long the first movie that told a full story, was released. At the St. Louis World's Fair to celebrate the 100th anniversary of the Louisiana Purchase, an ice cream vendor supposedly ran out of dishes, took waffles from the vendor in the booth next to him, and wrapped them into cones. In Europe, it was also the year that Escoffier published *Le Guide Culinaire,* his masterwork of recipes and cooking techniques.

The Progressive reformers, middle-class men and women, wanted to clean up democracy, the food supply, and human behavior. This is reflected in four Constitutional amendments. In 1913, the 16th Amendment created an income tax; the 17th Amendment took election of senators away from the state legislatures and put it in the hands of citizens directly. The 18th Amendment made alcohol illegal. In 1919, the 19th Amendment gave the vote to the last group of Americans that still had no voice—women.

The Meatpacking Industry and *The Jungle*

One of the first targets of Progressive reformers was the meatpacking industry. In 1905, a stomach-turning story about the meat processing industry appeared in a series of magazine articles. Upton Sinclair's book *The Jungle* was the caboose on the train of events that led to the passage of the Meat Inspection Act in 1905 and the Pure Food and Drug Act in 1906. Women's groups had been lobbying for years for laws to clean up the food supply. During the Spanish-American War in 1898, young men in the prime of life had died from eating bad food, canned meat they called "embalmed beef." The process that began with Napoleon and Appert to guarantee safe food for the army was used to pawn off rotten food that the corporate giants couldn't sell anywhere else. Americans were outraged. They were further outraged when Sinclair described meatpacking plants where animal blood flowed in rivers, food and humans were covered with flies, workers fell into vats and were processed as lard; rat feces, rat poison, and dead rats ended up in sausage along with rusty, filthy water from garbage cans; and chemicals made rotten meat odorless and healthy-looking. Sinclair wrote the book to show the terrible working conditions of the immigrants—his main characters are a Lithuanian family in Chicago—but readers panicked over what was being done to their meat. Sinclair said, "I aimed at the public's heart, but I hit its stomach." In an unprecedented display of power, the federal government stepped in and regulated the country's meat and food processing plants.

The Basement Bakers: the *Lochner* Case

Along with meat, the bread supply was of great concern to Progressives. In 1894, the *New York Press* printed an editorial about the horrendous working conditions of bakers. American food professions still operated like medieval guilds; journeymen bakers worked more than 100 hours a week, usually in very unhealthy conditions in primitive tenement basements. They worked at night, breathed in flour dust, and had a lower life expectancy than other workers: "most of them dying between the ages of forty and fifty."[5] In 1897, the state legislature unanimously passed the New York Bakeshop Law, which limited the number of hours a baker could work to 10 per day or 60 per week. It required "all buildings or rooms occupied as biscuit, bread, pie, or cake bakeries" to have ceilings at least 8 feet high; floors of cement, tile, or wood (meaning not dirt); walls of plaster or wood (meaning not dirt); "air shafts, windows, or ventilating pipes"; drainage and plumbing; and a bathroom separate from the food prep and storage areas. It also stated, "No person shall sleep in a room occupied as a bake room," and barred all domestic animals except cats from bakeries, indicating there was a rodent problem.[6] In 1905, the year *The Jungle* was published in magazine form, the United States Supreme Court overturned the section of the New York Bakeshop Law that limited working hours. *Lochner* v. *New York* stated that the government has no right to interfere with business. For the next 32 years, until it was overturned in *West Coast Hotel Co.* v. *Parrish* in 1937, the *Lochner* decision blocked attempts by working people to improve their working conditions.[7] But what the bakers couldn't get by law, they got by bargaining. In 1912, union bakers in New York City negotiated their workday down to 10 hours.

The men in the food trades wouldn't have been successful in their bid for better working conditions if it hadn't been for the 148 girls, most of them teenagers, who had burned or jumped to their deaths the year before when a fire swept through the Triangle Shirtwaist Company clothing factory where they worked. The girls had been locked in to keep union organizers out. New York State launched a four-year investigation that aimed to improve working conditions in all industries.

Efficiency Experts and Domestic Science: Ellen Richards

In the beginning of the 20th century, efficiency became almost a new religion. Scientists, engineers, and efficiency experts like Frederick Taylor, and Frank and Lillian Gilbreth, were the saviors of time. They believed everything could be measured, and the measurements used to improve society. They used standardized tests, like the IQ (intelligence quotient) test, to measure human potential. Recently, scientists taught sign language to Koko, a gorilla. Then they gave Koko a standard IQ test. Normal human IQ is between 85 and 115. Koko scored 95 points, and would have scored higher but the test was culturally biased against gorillas. It was a food question that tripped Koko up: "Of the following five things, which two are good to eat? 1. a flower;

Holiday History
≫ Mother's Day ≪

Mother's Day, the second Sunday in May, is the most popular day to eat out in America.[8] In 1914, Congress passed a resolution making it a national holiday, and President Woodrow Wilson issued a proclamation. The Mother's Cookies Company began the same year and continues today. Many songs celebrating mothers soon followed.

Mother's Day came about because Anna Jarvis, a West Virginia woman, vowed to fulfill her mother's wish to have one special day set aside to honor every mother "for the matchless service she renders to humanity in every field of life." Anna's mother, also named Anna Jarvis, spent her life in service to others. Before the Civil War, she initiated Mothers Day Work Clubs to try to remedy the horrifying infant mortality rate caused not just by disease but also by poor nutrition and sanitation—seven of her eleven children died in childhood. During the Civil War, the Mothers clubs shifted to nursing injured soldiers, regardless of which side they were fighting for.

After Anna Jarvis died in the second week in May 1905, her daughter began a letter-writing campaign to state and federal legislators and other prominent people to make Mother's Day a national holiday. She intended Mother's Day as an emotional and spiritual tribute, and handed out white carnations, her mother's favorite flower (now the traditional Mother's Day flower). She was horrified when the holiday became commercialized. The church where Anna Jarvis worshiped, Andrews Methodist Episcopal Church in Grafton, West Virginia, built in 1873, is now the International Mother's Day Shrine.[9]

Brunch

Brunch, a traditional way to celebrate Mother's Day, is purely an American invention. The word "brunch," a combination of "breakfast" and "lunch," is not even in the *Oxford English Dictionary,* although it is in American dictionaries.[10] It originated during the Gilded Age in 19th-century America, when women began having "Breakfast Parties."

Brunch is an opportunity for chefs to go past the customary breakfast and lunch foods to quiche, seafood Newburg, frittatas, and even more elaborate creations. In Kennebunkport, Maine, chef Christian Gordon at Federal Jack's has revamped a Delmonico's invention from the 1920s, eggs Benedict—an English muffin topped with ham, poached eggs, and hollandaise sauce—into a croissant topped with poached eggs, lobster, and hollandaise.[11] Mother's Day brunch in the elegant Raffles Hotel in Singapore has featured a salmon station, a carving station, and a "Live Station" with pan-fried foie gras with rhubarb grenadine compote and Old Port Wine jus.[12]

Brunch is also an excuse to start drinking early in the day. A traditional brunch drink is the mimosa, made with Champagne and orange juice. The Mimosa Royale adds Chambord. At the Kapalua Bay Hotel in Hawaii, mimosas also come in Tropical—

Champagne, Peach Schnapps, and orange juice; Strawberry—Champagne and strawberry juice; and Plumeria Terrace—apricot brandy and orange juice.[13] Other traditional brunch drinks are the Bloody Mary—vodka and tomato juice; and its nonalcoholic cousin, the Virgin Mary.

Eventually, fathers demanded equal time, and Father's Day began to be celebrated unofficially. In 1966, President Lyndon B. Johnson made it official when he declared Father's Day, the third Sunday in June, a national day.

2. a block; 3. an apple; 4. a shoe; 5. ice cream." Koko picked flower and apple, but the correct answers were apple and ice cream. However, a case could be made for Koko's choices, especially now when edible flowers are not unusual in salads and soups.[14]

Ellen Richards, a graduate of Vassar, was the first woman to get a Ph.D. from MIT, the Massachusetts Institute of Technology. In 1870, she had to enroll as a special student because no woman had been there before. She used her knowledge about chemistry to improve the lives of the women who managed households, and to teach them to identify adulterated foods. She published many books about sanitation and nutrition, in addition to cooking. Her first book was *The Chemistry of Cooking and Cleaning.* She spearheaded a movement to teach women the cutting scientific edge of food preparation and housekeeping, because with good household help hard to find, many more women had to do these things themselves with the help of the new electric appliances. Women formed many organizations to spread this information, like the Cooking Teachers' League and the National Household Economic Association. Ellen Richards was president of the American Home Economics Association until 1910. By then, the new profession of domestic science was firmly established.[15] Ellen Richards was just one of the many women who crusaded for change. One woman was responsible for creating a new holiday to honor mothers in the United States.

The recipe on the following page is an Italian specialty that can be served as a brunch treat or as a side dish with dinner.

Guess Who's Not Coming to Dinner?

President Theodore Roosevelt didn't understand the public's reaction. He had simply invited a great American leader to dinner. Except that the leader was black—Booker T. Washington, the former slave and founder of the Tuskegee Institute in his native Alabama. Senator Benjamin

RECIPE

ℂLAIRE CRISCUOLO'S
SQUASH BLOSSOM PANCAKES

Serves 6 (makes about 32 pancakes)

2 cups unbleached all-purpose flour
2 teaspoons baking powder
3 eggs
1 cup water
8 to 10 squash blossoms, rinsed and coarsely chopped
¼ cup finely chopped flat-leaf parsley
Salt and pepper to taste
½ cup olive oil

1. Measure the flour and baking powder into a large bowl. Stir to combine. In a separate bowl, whisk together the eggs and water. Add the egg mixture to the flour mixture all at once, using a rubber spatula to scrape out the bowl. Stir to combine.

2. Add the squash blossoms, parsley, salt, and pepper to the batter. Stir well to combine.

3. Line a cookie sheet with a double layer of paper towels and set it by the stove. Heat 3 tablespoons of the oil in a large nonstick skillet over medium heat. Drop heaping teaspoons of the batter into the hot oil, fitting as many as you can without crowding. Cook for 2 to 3 minutes, or until the undersides are medium golden brown. Turn and cook the other sides for about 2 minutes, or until medium golden brown. Transfer to the towel-lined cookie sheet.

4. Continue frying the remaining batter, heating additional oil as needed. Serve hot, at room temperature, or chilled.

From *Claire's Italian Feast* by Claire Criscuolo, chef-owner of Claire's Corner Copia, New Haven, CT (www.clairescornercopia.com).

Tillman of South Carolina said, "The action of President Roosevelt in entertaining that n——r will necessitate our killing a thousand n——rs in the South before they will learn their place again."[16] When Ida B. Wells, a black southern journalist, wrote articles against lynching, she got out of the South one step ahead of the lynch mob herself. W. E. B.

Du Bois (pronounced "doo-BOYCE") became the first African-American to earn a Ph.D. from Harvard and was one of the founders of the NAACP (National Association for the Advancement of Colored People) in 1910. Then Woodrow Wilson, the son of a minister, former president of Princeton University, and the Progressive governor of New Jersey, was elected president in 1912. His high moral ground appealed to many voters, but Wilson was from Virginia. He segregated the White House, installing separate drinking fountains, bathrooms, and cafeterias. The rest of the government followed suit. For the next 20 years, until President Franklin Delano Roosevelt and his wife, Eleanor, moved there in 1933 and desegregated it, the only blacks in the White House were the kitchen help.

DINING *DE LUXE* IN THE *BELLE EPOQUE*

Escoffier and Ritz: *Cuisine Classique* and the Grand Hotels

In Europe, the man who brought cuisine to its highest levels didn't want to be a cook. Like Carême before him, Auguste Escoffier, "the king of chefs and the chef of kings," wanted to be an artist, a sculptor. He was born on October 28, 1846, in the south of France. At the age of 13, he became an apprentice cook in a restaurant owned by his uncle in Nice, the Restaurant Français. His brilliance was noticed and when his apprenticeship was over, he was presented with the dream of every cook in the provinces: a job in Paris. He went. After the Franco-Prussian War in 1870, Escoffier returned to Paris.

At a time when grand hotels were being built all over the world to cater to wealthy travelers, the meeting of Escoffier and César Ritz changed the food and hotel industries forever. The Savoy Hotel in London was built with American hotels as a model and to rival them in attracting wealthy patrons. Americans invented the electric light and the telephone and expected these things when they traveled. Always looking for a shortcut, Americans also invented the shower, known then as the "shower-bath," and really liked indoor plumbing. Ritz understood this; his hotel reflected it.

Escoffier invented new dishes, many named after famous people, usually women. For example, *pêches Melba* (Peach Melba) was named after the famous Australian opera singer Nellie Melba. Originally, the dish was too complicated and might not have caught on, but Escoffier replaced an elaborate ice swan and spun-sugar sculpture with a raspberry sauce, and it became a hit. Other dishes were named after princesses and the actress Sarah Bernhardt, who became a personal friend of Escoffier; she sent him a heartfelt note of sympathy when his son was killed in World War I.

Escoffier Organizes the Cooking: *Le Guide Culinaire*

"I wanted to create a useful tool rather than just a recipe book."

–Escoffier

In 1903, Escoffier's massive book, *Le Guide Culinaire—The Culinary Guide*—was published. It does not just tell *how* to cook foods, but *why,* and in detail. With 5,000 recipes, it has stocks, roux, and sauces, the bases of French cuisine, first. Then garnishes, soups, hors d'oeuvres, eggs (202 recipes), fish, meat, poultry, and game. One separate chapter is about roasting; Escoffier had held the difficult position of *rôtisseur,* or roasting chef. This was a real juggling act. The chef had to constantly turn a giant spit over an open fire with different kinds and cuts of meat and poultry on it and make sure that they all cooked to exactly the right degree of tenderness at exactly the right time. He recommends which cuts of meat are best for formal presentation, like beef ribs (which need a trained carver); and which ones are suitable only for the family table, like pork shoulder. He advises tearing the ears of a hare to determine its age (the younger, the easier to tear); and warns about English puddings and meat pies because once they are assembled, nothing can be done to correct the seasoning or any mistakes. He instructs that poultry and game should be barded—partly covered with thin slices of salt pork or pork fat—to retain moistness while roasting. He puts the nail in the coffin of some older ways of presentation: "The Medieval way of decorating roast game birds with their feathers has fallen into disuse."[17]

Escoffier is also very concerned with safety. His section on deep-frying recommends using beef kidney fat but not mutton fat, because it froths up and might overflow. (He also doesn't like the taste, unlike Middle Eastern cooks, who prize it.) It is also crucial to have equipment that is easy to use and not defective. Although he does not come out and say so, it is clear that Escoffier has witnessed some terrible kitchen accidents and is very protective of his kitchen staff. Also increasing kitchen efficiency and standardization were the professional cooking schools that had begun in France in 1895 with the Cordon Bleu (blue ribbon).

Escoffier Organizes the Kitchen: The Kitchen Brigade

Escoffier made the second great step to standardizing French cuisine. Just as Carême organized the sauces, Escoffier organized the kitchen. The man who was born in the 19th century and trained in a medieval system of apprenticeship brought 20th-century methods of organization to the kitchen. The kitchen brigade was a military-style chain of command from the top to the bottom. The chef is in charge of food production. He or she plans menus, decides what food and supplies need to be ordered, determines costs of menu items, and plans work schedules. In some large establishments, the chef's duties are more administrative and creative, so the sous chef (*sous* means "under" in French) supervises the kitchen and the staff. Each area of food production has a station chef or *chef de partie*. A *chef de partie* sometimes has an assistant, called a *commis*. The *tournant*—swing cook—fills in as needed. The *aboyeur* (literally, "barker") calls out the orders. Depending on the size of the establishment, the kitchen brigade can be expanded or condensed. This is the classical kitchen brigade.

THE KITCHEN BRIGADE[18]				
CHEF				
SOUS CHEF (UNDERCHEF)			PÂTISSIER (PASTRY)	
Chefs de Partie (Station Chefs)			Confiseur	Boulanger
Saucier	Poissonier	Rôtisseur	(candy)	(baker)
(sauces)	(fish)	(roasting)	Glacier	Decorateur
Grillardin	Friturier	Entremetier	(cold desserts)	(specialties)
(grilling)	(frying)	(hot appetizers)		
Potager	Legumier	Garde-Manger		
(soup)	(vegetables)	(pantry, cold food)		
		Boucher		
		(butcher)		

The organizational model of the kitchen brigade has been used for a brigade for the front of the house, supervised by the maître d'hôtel or the host who greets the customers. The wine steward controls the house wine stock, list, and table service. The headwaiter supervises the wait staff.[19]

"Where Ritz Goes, We Go!"—The Prince of Wales[20]

The Prince of Wales, the future King Edward VII of England, was an admirer of Escoffier and Ritz and made the Savoy *the* place to be. The Prince also turned out, accidentally, to be Ritz's undoing. Edward's coronation celebration was going to be the most important event ever held at the Savoy. The driven, perfectionist Ritz planned for months so that every detail would be flawless. Two days before the coronation, Edward developed appendicitis and the coronation was postponed. The effect on Ritz was nearly fatal. He didn't fall on his sword like Vatel, but he went into shock and had a complete emotional breakdown. He never worked in a hotel again. The man who brought electricity and private indoor plumbing to hotels, who elevated a chef to management for the first time, who always made sure that everything ran smoothly, who could fix anything, couldn't be fixed. He died 16 years later, alone in a sanitarium in Lausanne, Switzerland, not far from where he was born and where he had made his brilliant beginning.

Cooking became more professional and the standards rose at the same time that cars were becoming popular. The two came together in 1900 in France in the first guide for travelers, the Guide Michelin. It was the brainchild of brothers André and Edouard, owners of the Michelin Tire Company, who wanted people to drive (and use their tires). Their symbol is the Michelin man, made of tires stacked up on each other. His name is Bibendum, after the Roman saying, *Nunc est bibendum:* "Now let's drink."

"The Paris of the West" and the Escoffier of the West

San Francisco, California, wanted to become "the Paris of the West," and they had a chef who fancied himself the Escoffier of America—chef Victor Hirtzler of the Hotel St. Francis. He was born in Strasbourg, was apprenticed at 13, trained at the Grand Hotel in Paris, and served as food taster to Czar Nicholas II of Russia. On April 18, 1906, at 5:13 A.M., the St. Francis and the Fairmont hotels rode out the great San Francisco earthquake, 8.3 on the Richter scale, with some cracking and buckling. The kitchens were open, serving thousands of hotel guests and displaced San Franciscans and visitors, including opera singer Enrico Caruso and actor John Barrymore. But they couldn't withstand the fires that erupted all over the city when the gas lines ruptured and the water ran out. The two-year-old St. Francis Hotel was completely destroyed.

Two years later, the new St. Francis opened on the same spot with Hirtzler still the chef. In 1910, he published his own book of recipes, *L'Art culinaire*. In 1919, it was expanded and set in a day-by-day format: breakfast, lunch, and dinner 365 days of the year. Hirtzler was clearly competing with Escoffier. Like *Le Guide culinaire, L'Art culinaire* contained 202 recipes for eggs. It too had recipes for calf's brains, sweetbreads, foie gras, truffles, tongue, lobster, lamb kidneys, rooster combs, and oxtails. But Hirtzler also specified American foods: California oysters, California raisins, California artichokes, avocados (called "alligator pears"), Alaska black cod, reindeer. Most of Hirtzler's dishes reflect his classical French training, like puff pastry, sauce périgord, hollandaise, and béarnaise. But Hirtzler was also feeding Americans, so hamburger, steak and beef stew are on the menu, along with gingerbread; cobbler; Southern corn pone; cactus fruit; cream of celery, Kalamazoo; hare soup, Uncle Sam; Maryland beaten biscuits, Philadelphia pepper pot; Kentucky sauce; Petaluma cream cheese; Boston baked beans; Boston brown bread pudding; and Boston and Manhattan clam chowders. Escoffier lists only one recipe using chocolate; Hirtzler, in the hometown of Ghirardelli, has many, including chocolate cream pie. Hirtzler also did something that Escoffier never did—he named dishes after himself. There is Celery Victor, Chicken Salad Victor, Crab Cocktail Victor, Victor Dressing, and Coupe Victor. Chef Victor Hirtzler lives on today in the Victor Restaurant at the top of the St. Francis Hotel.

However, a classically trained chef from Europe would have to make accommodations to cooking in the United States. Even if dishes had the same name, *charcuterie* was very different in France and America, as the illustrations on pages 248 and 249.

"I've Been Dining on the Railroad": The Harvey Girls Civilize the West

Anywhere that considered itself civilized served French food, even remote regions of the American West. Disgusted with the poor food at railroad stops, British-born Fred Harvey established a string of first-quality restaurants that stretched from Chicago south and west to San Francisco, along the Atchison, Topeka, and Santa Fe Railroad. In the 30 minutes patrons had while their train was stopped, the Harvey houses served food that was perhaps French, or at least French-sounding. For example, Cream of Chicken Reine Margot, Consomme Careme, Jumbo Bull Frog Almandienne, and Medaillon of Salmon Poche, Sauce Mousseline (their spellings). American foods included mashed potatoes, raspberry sundae, Manhattan clam chowder, roast home-made veal loaf, broiled live baby lobster (whole), and Saratoga chips (aka potato chips).[21] These dishes were served in Wichita, Kansas; Guthrie, Oklahoma; Amarillo, Texas; Trinidad, Colorado; Clovis, Deming, and Raton, New Mexico; and Needles, Mojave, and Merced, California.

At first, waiters served the food, but they got into fights—with their fists, with knives, with guns. They destroyed kitchen equipment and missed work. Harvey's solution: fire the men and hire women. The Harvey Girls—the first professional waitresses—were single white women "of good character" from 18 to 30 years old who responded to ads in newspapers in the East and Midwest. Some came because there were many more men than women in the West, but the six-, nine-, or twelve-month contract each woman signed said she could not get married during that time without losing her job, her pay, and her railroad pass.[22] Even so, from 1883 to the late 1950s, about 100,000 women chose to become Harvey Girls.[23]

A large staff was necessary to get food on the tables so quickly in the à la carte lunchroom and a dining room, and the waitresses were the majority: "in order of importance, a manager, a chef, a head waitress, between fifteen and thirty Harvey Girls, a baker, a butcher, several assistant cooks and pantry girls, a housemaid, and busboys."[24] Harvey chefs were mostly European. The front of the house—the Harvey Girl waitresses—were all white. (The first Hispanic Harvey Girl wasn't hired until the 1930s, and then the railroadmen threatened to quit.[25]) Their professional waitress uniform was long and black—dress to the floor, sleeves to the wrist, high collar. Over this was an immaculate white apron. They worked ten hours a day, six or seven days a week. But the kitchen workers reflected the population of the southwest—black, Hispanic, and Indian.

The railroad subsidized the restaurants, which they allowed to operate at a loss, because "Fred Harvey meals all the way" was a guarantee of good food that sold train tickets. Harvey was a perfectionist who showed up in his restaurant kitchens unannounced and "looked the place over as if he suspected a murder had been committed and the search was for clues."[26] He fired people if he didn't like their attitude or if they tried to cut corners by squeezing orange juice ahead of time instead of when it was ordered. The Harvey Girls were immortalized in the 1946 MGM movie musical *The Harvey Girls,* starring Judy Garland. One of the musical numbers explains the importance of the uniform and how to set a table properly.

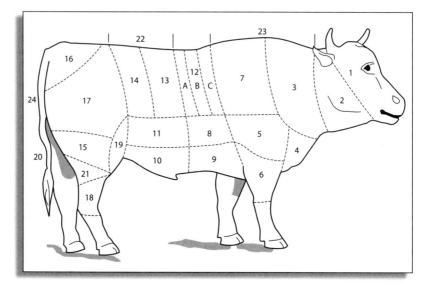

Beef, American Cuts (Boeuf Coupe à l'Americaine).
From The Epicurean *by Charles Ranhofer. Chicago: The Hotel Monthly Press, 1920. Copyright © 1920 by Rose Ranhofer.*

1. Head

2. Beef jowl

3. Neck

4. Brisket

5. Cross ribs

6. Shin

7. Chuck ribs

8. Plates

9. Navel

10. Inside flank

11. Thick flank

12. Six Prime ribs, A first cut, B second cut, C third

13. Short loin

14. Hip

15. Round

16. Aitchbone rump

17. Round bottom

18. Leg of beef

19. Butt

20. Oxtail

21. Horseshoe legs

22. Hip and loin

23. Whole chuck

24. Round top

Beef, French Cuts (Boeuf Coupe à la Française) [original spellings].
From The Epicurean *by Charles Ranhofer. Chicago: The Hotel Monthly*
Press, 1920. Copyright © 1920 by Rose Ranhofer.

1. Culotte

2. Tranches petit os

3. Milieu du gîte à la noix

4. Derrière du gîte à la noix

5. Tendre de tranches intérieure

6. Tranche grasse intérieure

7. Pièce ronde partie intérieure

8. Aloyau ave filet

9. Bavette d'Aloyau

10. Côtes couvertes, à la noix

11. Plat de Côtes

12. Surlonge partie intérieure

13. Derrière de paleron

14. Talon de Collier

15. Bande de Macreuse

16. Milieu de Macreuse dans le paleron

17. Boite a molele [moelle?]

18. Collier

19. Plat de joue

20. Flanchet

21. Milieu de poitrine

22. Cros bout

23. Queue de gîte

24. Gîte de devant

25. Cros du gîte de devant

26. Gîte de derrière

27. Cros du gîte de derrière

Mobile Dining *de Luxe*—the *Titanic*

The same stringent standards applied on ships. Crossing the Atlantic Ocean by luxury liner was done by a small elite; only 205,000 passengers crossed in 1902.[27] An acronym to describe the way the wealthy made the crossing became a synonym for luxury: *posh*. It stood for "port out, starboard home," which ensured that the cabin would always be facing the south and the sun.

The 883-foot-long *Titanic*, 46,328 supposedly unsinkable tons with eleven decks, struck an iceberg in the North Atlantic on April 14, 1912 at 11:40 P.M. and sank less than three hours later, at 2:20 A.M. on April 15, 1912. Its lounge was patterned after the Palace of Versailles; it had a marble drinking fountain, Turkish baths, and a gymnasium, and was the first ocean liner to have a swimming pool and squash courts. Among its passengers were ten millionaires, people with names like Astor, Guggenheim, Widener, and Rothschild. For the dinners that were served to the 322 first-class passengers in their own dining room, the Goldsmiths and Silversmiths Company of Regent Street in London had provided 10,000 pieces of plate.[28]

It was a British ship, so dinner was announced by buglers playing "The Roast Beef of Old England."[29] The last meal served was on Sunday night, April 14, 1912, and it was supposedly the most lavish served on the ship: oysters, salmon, filet mignon, roast duckling, foie gras, squab, asparagus, chocolate and vanilla éclairs, and French ice cream for the finale.[30] It took a staff of about 60 chefs and 40 assistants (mostly French) and 50 waiters (mostly Italian) to get the 2,000 breakfasts and dinners prepared and served.[31]

That last night, Sunday dinner had been served and the kitchens were closing down. The shipbuilder popped in to thank the baker for a special bread. Almost everyone on the ship retired for the night, looking forward to being in New York in 48 hours. But the ship sideswiped an iceberg, which slit a 300-foot gash in its side. For the first time, radio operators used the new code—SOS for "save our ship"—at sea. The ship *Carpathia* picked up the last of the 711 survivors by 8:00 A.M. This was fortunate, because no one had bothered to put food or water or compasses on the lifeboats of the unsinkable ship. A total of 1,490 people drowned on the *Titanic*. The highest proportion of passengers saved was from first class; the lowest, from third class. The staff couldn't even think about getting on a lifeboat until all the passengers were on. As far as historians can determine, all of the kitchen staff died except one. A 17-year-old cook was saved by accident.

He was helping a woman carry a child and was swept overboard when the ship went under. He was picked up by a lifeboat.[32] Almost twice as many kitchen staff died on the *Titanic* as at Windows on the World on September 11, 2001. The press busied themselves with obituaries of the rich and famous on the *Titanic,* but only one person tracked down the names of as many of the kitchen staff as possible and printed obituaries of them—Escoffier.

Escoffier at Sea: Bigger than the *Titanic*

Germany had been competing with England ever since the Industrial Revolution began in the 1750s in England. As the British expanded into Africa and Asia, so did the Germans. Now the kaiser was increasing the German navy in a direct threat to British supremacy on the seas. Nationalism was rising in Germany, but in the kitchen the kaiser wanted only French food and French cooks. On May 25, 1912, the Hamburg-American liner *Imperator,* 52,000 tons, 900 feet long, was launched. It was Germany's answer to the *Titanic* and had learned its lesson from the *Titanic's* sinking a month earlier: the *Imperator* was bigger, and it carried extra lifeboats. The *Imperator* had a swimming pool, marble bathtubs, and other fittings that made her top-heavy, so that she rolled badly.[33] It was Escoffier's first trip across the Atlantic, on his way to open the kitchen at the Hotel Pierre in New York City. Tensions were high in Europe; the smell of war was in the air. After an imperial banquet for more than 100 people, Escoffier talked to the kaiser, hoping to influence him to keep the peace in Europe. Escoffier had been through one war with Germany and did not want another one.

WORLD WAR I AND THE RUSSIAN REVOLUTION

Two years after Escoffier and the kaiser spoke, World War I began. In 1914, in the city of Sarajevo in what is now the country of Yugoslavia, Archduke Ferdinand of Austria was assassinated. Germany, the Austro-Hungarian Empire, and Italy went to war against France, England, and Russia. Later, Italy would change sides, Russia would leave the war, and the United States would join France and England. The ability of technology to inflict wounds was much more advanced than medicine's ability to heal them at that time. The new technologies were airplanes, chemical gases, motorized tanks, and machine guns. The defense against these was primitive: dig a trench in the mud.

One million men died in major battles like Verdun and the Somme. And as always in wartime, getting supplies to the front and feeding the fighting men was a difficult problem.

Armenian Cuisine

The fighting in World War I extended east to Turkey, which had a large population of Armenians. Armenian cuisine is a mixture of Turkish, Greek, Syrian, Persian, and Arabic influences. Like the cultures to the east of it, Armenian cuisine has flat bread, rice pilaf, and barley; like the cultures to the west, it has noodles. Like the cuisine of its neighbor to the west, Bulgaria, yogurt is a staple food, used in everything from hot and cold soups to dips, cheeses, stews, pastries, beverages, salads, and cakes. Chickpeas and lentils are widely used. Eggplant appears fried, stuffed, baked, mashed, in hot and cold casseroles, in salad, and with and without meat, usually lamb, like the layered Greek casserole moussaka, and the Persian *imam bayaldi*, which the Armenians call *iman bayeldi*. Okra finds many uses here, along with zucchini, cauliflower, spinach, cabbage, and dolma—stuffed vegetables, especially grape leaves. An Armenian specialty is bulghur—cracked wheat—used in tabouleh and pilaf. Desserts are made of *kadayif* (the Persian *kataif,* a shredded wheat dough) and phyllo, and are drenched in sugar syrup, like *paklava* (Greek *baklava*). They use the fruits and nuts of the eastern Mediterranean—raisins, dates, apricots, walnuts, almonds. Sesame is used in oil and paste form (*taheen, tahini* in Lebanon and Syria, to the south).

During World War I, the Turks massacred almost two million Christian Armenians at Musa Dagh. Many of the surviving Armenians migrated to the United States, to the Central Valley of California and the city of Fresno, where they grew grapes and went into the dried fruit business, especially raisins. Some famous Armenian-Americans are the writer William Saroyan and actress-singer Cher (Cherilyn Sarkisian).

The United States: From Hot Dog to "Liberty Dog"

The United States joined World War I in 1917, after Germany resumed unrestricted submarine warfare and sank American merchant ships in the Atlantic. The war was not popular; the draft was difficult to enforce. Many isolationists felt that the United States had no business in a European war. Approximately a quarter of a million men simply didn't show up, and before Social Security numbers (with the

Social Security Act of 1935) there was no way to track them. World War I was also a problem for many American immigrant groups. The Irish hated the British, America's ally; the Jews objected to another ally, the Russia from which they had fled. America also had a large population of German-speaking immigrants and citizens of German descent, but Germany was the enemy. Americans turned against everything German—in principle. They wouldn't eat hot dogs and sauerkraut, which were German, but they would eat "Liberty dogs" and "Liberty cabbage," which were 100 percent American. Italy and Italian immigrants, too, were the enemy—for a while, until Italy switched sides midway through the war. Then Italian food became acceptable, even desirable: "Spaghetti, food of the ally."[34]

Men and women volunteered for the war effort. Many, like the writer Ernest Hemingway, went to Europe and drove ambulances. On the home front, Americans grew victory gardens to feed themselves and to add to the national food supply. At Vassar College, students volunteered to work on the Vassar farm during the summer. They planted, hoed, weeded, milked cows, and drove tractors, as the following picture shows. Notice the modest bloomers.

World War I ended in 1918, at the eleventh hour on the eleventh day of the eleventh month: 11:00 A.M., November 11. The day and time were chosen purposely so that no one would ever forget the horror of

Plowing at Vassar Farm.
Courtesy of Special Collections, Vassar College Libraries.
Photo by Brown Brothers.

the "war to end all wars." There certainly would never be another war. Who would be insane enough to go through anything like that again?

The Punitive Treaty of Versailles and the Seeds of World War II

In 1919, the leaders of the world got together at the Palace of Versailles to draw up a peace treaty. France and England wanted to punish and publicly humiliate Germany. The United States objected; they felt that harsh conditions would only enrage the German people and make them want revenge. But England and France overruled the United States, and the punitive Treaty of Versailles passed. Germany had to publicly admit that it started the war; it had to repay England and France for the war; it could only have a very small army; its colonies in Asia were given to Japan; its colonies in Africa were divided between England and France; its western border, the province of Alsace-Lorraine, was returned to France; its eastern border, a strip of land known as the Danzig Corridor, became part of the newly created country of Poland.

These conditions made economic recovery nearly impossible for the Germans. Money became worthless. One American dollar was worth more than 800 million marks. Food prices skyrocketed—a loaf of bread cost a supermarket cart full of money. Germans fed instead on despair and dreams of revenge.

Working as a dishwasher in the kitchen at Ritz's Savoy Hotel in London was a young man from French Indochina who wanted freedom for his country. He tried to see President Wilson to show him the document he had drafted for his country patterned after the American Declaration of Independence, but Wilson wouldn't see him. More than 40 years later, the United States was forced to deal with Ho Chi Minh on his own terms in his own country, Vietnam.

The Russian Revolution

In 1917, the year the United States entered the war, Russia left. It had already lost more than seven million men and was facing a revolution. Food played a huge part in the Russian Revolution in 1917. Peasant farmers made up the majority of the army, so crops didn't get planted or harvested. There were food shortages in the country and food riots in the city. Finally, even the czar's close advisors begged, pleaded, then demanded that he give up the throne. Later, the czar, czarina, their four daughters, and one son were executed, shot to death by communist revolutionaries.

Russian Cuisine

In the 200 years since Peter the Great had decided to westernize his country, Russia had become a power in European politics and cuisine. The potato had become a staple. So was the dark rye bread called pumpernickel. In the cold Russian climate, root vegetables like turnips and beets were staples, too, in *borscht*—beet soup with a sour cream enrichment. Dill and caraway were the common herb and spice. From Russia's Siberian side, bordering China and Mongolia, Russia gets *pel'meni*—dumplings like ravioli or wontons made of flour-and-egg noodle dough filled with fish, mushrooms, or meat (originally horsemeat). Preserving foods was not a problem in Siberia, where even the ground was frozen a great deal of the year. A wide variety of foods in Russia were also preserved by pickling—cucumbers, mushrooms, apples, lemons, and cabbage (as sauerkraut).

The European influence, especially French, is apparent in *pierogi,* turnovers made from a flaky sour cream pastry filled with ground meat, rice, eggs, mushrooms, or cheese. *Pirozhki* are the smaller version. These versatile pies can be either street food or served at a banquet. A more elaborate upper-class filled pastry is *kulebiaka,* fish *en croûte*—poached salmon, sturgeon, or whitefish between layers of a fish, rice, and mushroom filling, baked in a yeast dough or pastry crust. Another luxurious Russian dish, Chicken Kiev, is named after the capital of Ukraine.

The upper-class food trio was small buckwheat crêpes called *blini,* the caviar that was placed on them with a small silver spoon, and the vodka that washed it all down. *Blini* were also traditional during Butterweek, the Russian equivalent of Mardi Gras, when they were buttered and topped with sour cream. Caviar is the roe, or eggs, of the sturgeon fish, found in the Caspian Sea. It comes in several grades—

INGREDIENTS

*C*HICKEN *K*IEV

Chicken Kiev has only six main ingredients: chicken breast filets pounded and stuffed with unsalted butter, then rolled, dipped in flour, beaten egg, and bread crumbs, and deep-fried in oil. When the diner cuts into the chicken, the butter bursts out. In some restaurants, the server makes the first cut because it can be messy.

osetra, sevruga, and beluga, the largest. Vodka was "infused with any-where from 3 to 40 flavors—sage, heather honey, angelica root, ginger root, anise, juniper berries, Crimean apple and pear leaves, mint, young shoots of mountain ash, nutmeg and nutmeg blooms, vanilla, cinnamon, cardamom, cloves."[35]

The Fabergé Russian Royal Easter Eggs

The Russian royal family had an Easter tradition based on the peasant tradition of painting eggs. Some of the more elaborately deco-rated eggs come from the Russian Orthodox Church in eastern Europe, especially Ukraine. *Krashanky* are hard-boiled eggs dyed one solid color, meant to be eaten. *Pysanky,* purely decorative, are made from raw eggs dyed many times in elaborate multicolored patterns. Each color has a symbolic meaning: yellow means a successful harvest, green represents the rebirth of spring, and black is the dark before the dawn, when the souls of the dead travel, especially between the first and third crows of the rooster. The dyes were made from plants: red from beets, orange from onion skins, blue from red cabbage leaves, brown from nutshells. Now, everything from tiny quail eggs to enor-mous ostrich eggs are decorated.

Every year the Russian royal family exchanged Easter eggs, but they weren't folk art. They were made by Fabergé, the royal jeweler, out of gold, silver, platinum, and crystal studded with diamonds, rubies, pearls, emeralds, and sapphires. Each egg had a surprise inside, often mechanical. For example, a platinum egg 10¼ inches high opened up to reveal miniature gold railroad cars that hooked together and ran when wound up with a key. A tiny golden replica of the royal yacht floats in a crystal sea; the whole thing is 6 inches high. A miniature version of the coach in which the czar and czarina rode to their coro-nation in 1896 comes out of a golden and jeweled egg 3¹¹⁄₁₆ inches high. The last egg was relatively modest, a red cross on a white back-ground, because the royal family felt it might be in poor taste to flaunt their wealth in the face of famine and war. It was too late.

One egg was a miniature orange tree, 11¾ inches high, with a gold trunk, studded with "oranges" and "orange blossoms" made of precious stones. A secret "orange" made a little bird pop up out of the tree and sing. The Fabergé Orange Tree Egg was made for the Russian royal family in 1911.

In 2000, when an exhibit of Fabergé eggs was on display at the Riverfront Arts Center in Wilmington, Delaware, executive pastry chef

Fabergé Imperial Orange Tree Egg.
Courtesy the FORBES Magazine Collection, New York.

Michele B. Mitchell (a 1988 graduate of the Johnson & Wales Pastry Arts Program) at the Hotel du Pont in Wilmington, Delaware, and her staff recreated the Orange Tree Egg out of sugar work, chocolate, fondant, gold leaf, and silver dust. It was three and a half feet tall and took about one hundred hours to create. They also made forty-five miniature Orange Trees as room favors. The top half of the small tree dome came off to reveal truffles inside, as a turn-down service for the VIPs at the gala opening of the exhibit, which was held at the hotel. The chocolate sculpture is on page 258.

Chocolate Fabergé Egg Sculpture.
Chocolate Fabergé Egg Sculpture created by Michele Mitchell, Executive
Pastry Chef of the Hotel du Pont, Wilmington, DE.

The Cities: People Eat Communally

Lenin, the leader of the new communist Bolshevik government, pulled Russia—the Union of Soviet Socialist Republics, or USSR—out of World War I. After a further four years of civil war, from 1917 to 1921, there was no more private ownership of property; it all belonged to the state, communally. Gone, too, were the titles. No more princes or princesses, dukes or duchesses. Everyone was equal in the new class-less society, where people addressed each other as "comrade." This meant drastic changes in all levels of society and in the food people ate, where and when they ate it, and how they grew it.

In the cities, the government took over the restaurants, hotels, and mansions that had been used by the upper classes and turned them into communal dining places where all workers had to eat.[36] Then they organized food preparation and distribution throughout the entire country as if it were one enormous kitchen. Communal dining was also intended to free women from their traditional kitchen duties so they could work in factories or on farms. Shortages of skilled kitchen staff resulted in small portions of food that tasted terrible prepared in unsanitary conditions and led to epidemics and strikes. Meals were "tiny plates of barley gruel" or "soup with herring head or rotten sour cabbage." Moldy grains, bread the consistency of clay, and "coffee" made from acorns rounded out the meal.[37] People still wanted the food they were used to, and some of them had the money to pay for it. As Mauricio Borrero points out, secret restaurants sprang up, like speakeasies in the United States where Americans went to get alcohol after it became illegal in the 1920s. But in Russia, they were risking arrest to get a meal. With the right connections and the right password, you might be lucky enough to find yourself in a place with tablecloths and napkins, eating roast meat and vegetables and something made with flour and sugar.[38] The country desperately needed to produce more food; the daily bread ration had dropped from one pound per person in 1917 to two ounces in 1919.

The Country: People Farm Communally

After Lenin died in 1924, St. Petersburg, the city founded by Peter the Great in 1703, was renamed in Lenin's honor: Leningrad. Stalin took over the USSR, with a five-year plan for agriculture and industry. His goal was to make the country an industrial giant equal to the United States. To do this, he needed equipment and engineers. To buy the heavy industrial equipment the USSR needed, they sold the only thing they had: grain. They sold millions of tons of grain; millions of people starved. International Harvester operated a factory in the USSR. Large farms were split up and people were forced to farm together. Without the incentive of keeping food for themselves or selling it at a price they wanted, food production dropped. Many of the successes that Stalin claimed in food and industrial production were only numbers on paper that bore no resemblance to reality.

THE ROARING TWENTIES IN THE UNITED STATES

The threat of communism caused violence in the United States immediately after World War I. When the police went on strike in Boston, the entire country panicked and blamed communism. In a little room in Washington, D.C., a man sat filling stacks of index cards with the names of suspected communists. The little room grew into the Federal Bureau of Investigation—the FBI—and the man, J. Edgar Hoover, spent every day until he died in 1972 hunting for communists.

The year 1920 was another watershed in American history. For the first time, more Americans lived in cities of 2,500 people or more than in the country. It was the year of the first transcontinental airplane flight—no passengers, just mail—and of the first international black congress, at which African-Americans issued their own declaration of rights, just as white women had done at Seneca Falls, New York, in 1848, 72 years earlier. In 1920, Americans heard the first radio broadcast. Six years later, they heard the first radio advertising jingle; it was for a new breakfast cereal, Wheaties. Two Constitutional amendments went into effect in 1920. The 18th Amendment outlawed alcohol. The 19th Amendment granted women the right to vote.

A major change occurred in the global economy as a result of World War I. The United States emerged from the war a creditor nation—for the first time, other countries owed the United States money. The war was expensive; European countries had borrowed money from the United States to pay for it. As a result, the center of world banking shifted to New York City, where it remains today.

American soldiers returning to the United States found that much had changed at home, too: their jobs were gone and for some, their neighborhoods had changed because of African-Americans who had migrated north to work in factories during the war. Angry whites rampaged through black neighborhoods in Chicago and East St. Louis; they burned the entire African-American section of town to the ground in Tulsa, Oklahoma.

"The Manufacture, Sale, or Transportation of Intoxicating Liquors … Is Hereby Prohibited"

On January 17, 1920, the 18th Amendment to the Constitution shut down the 7th largest industry in the United States. This didn't occur overnight. The temperance movement began in the early 19th century as religious opposition to rum drinking. That is why coffee replaced rum as the standard beverage of the United States Army in 1832. The temperance movement gained momentum in the middle of the 19th century when beer-drinking German and whiskey-drinking Irish immigrants began arriving in large numbers. At the end of the 19th century came wine-drinking Italians and Hungarians, vodka-drinking Poles and Russians, beer-drinking Czechs and Lithuanians. American women countered with the Women's Christian Temperance Union and took to picketing in front of bars and sometimes smashing them with hatchets. Progressive reformers thought that alcohol caused a wide variety of social ills. Workers who spent the weekend binge-drinking missed work on Monday, or showed up hungover and had accidents. Factory workers who got paid in cash on Friday went to the bars across the street and drank and gambled their pay away, so their families had no money for food. Young sons who went into bars looking for their fathers became juvenile delinquents. Daughters turned to prostitution to put food on the table. And a drunk voter could be bought. Progressives thought that prohibiting alcohol would cure all these problems.

The alcohol industry didn't mount a serious campaign against the prohibition movement because beer and wine producers couldn't believe it would affect them. Beer and wine were like water; you drank them with food. At the worst, only hard liquor—distilled spirits— would be prohibited. But *all* alcohol over half of one percent was prohibited. There was a loophole: suddenly, many people were getting prescriptions for alcohol "for medicinal purposes." Hard-core alcoholics sneaked into churches and synagogues to steal the sacramental wine, or drank the alcohol that fueled small appliances like curling irons. Wine production plummeted from 55 million gallons in 1919 to 4 million gallons in 1925. However, grape production dropped right after the 18th Amendment was passed, then rose again. Clever vintners marketed grape juice and "bricks" of dried grapes with labels warning consumers not to add water and yeast or the grapes would ferment and turn into wine. Some estimates are that wine consumption doubled by the end of the decade.[39]

Crime: The Beer Wars and Al Capone

Prohibition caused crime to increase, not decrease. It turned law-abiding Americans into casual lawbreakers. When drinking was legal, bars had to close. When it became illegal, bars could stay open all the time. People went to the new underground drinking places, called speakeasies, where they knocked on the door and whispered the password. In the countryside in cold parts of the country, anyone with a water tank filled it with cider, let it freeze, and skimmed the ice off every morning until it reduced down to applejack—homemade apple brandy. Prohibition also caused a huge rise in violent crime, as the gangs that smuggled liquor into the country in trucks from Canada or by ship along the coasts fought each other using World War I surplus Thompson submachine guns—tommy guns. And since they were taking a risk, it was much more profitable to sell distilled spirits with a higher alcohol content than bulky beer.

Crime was especially violent in Chicago, where gangsters killed each other for control of breweries, which continued to operate by bribing officials. Innocent bystanders got caught in the crossfire of drive-by shootings. On Valentine's Day, February 14, 1929, Al Capone's gang machine-gunned seven rival gang members in a garage on Clark Street. This was too much. The government sent in federal agents, who became known as "the Untouchables," to get Capone. They realized that it would be impossible to convict him on criminal charges because he would just kill anyone who testified against him, so they convicted him of not paying $215,000 in income taxes. He was sent to the federal prison in Atlanta, Georgia, until 1934, when he was shipped to the first super-prison on an island in San Francisco Bay—Alcatraz.

The architects of Alcatraz thought of everything, including the food. They decided that, since poor food contributed to so many prison riots, the food in Alcatraz would be far superior to that in any other prison in the United States. This advice was forgotten later at Attica, a maximum-security prison in upstate New York, where one of the causes of the prison riot on September 9, 1971, the worst up until that time, was food. On a food budget of 63 cents per man per day, the prison administration bought pork, an inexpensive meat. However, a large percentage of the prison population was African-American Muslims, who couldn't eat it One of the demands of the rioters, ahead of education, health care, a grievance committee, and recreation, was "Give us a healthy diet, stop feeding us so much pork, and give us some fresh fruit daily."[40]

The Good Humor Man Meets the Mob

Americans went crazy for candy in the 1920s, which saw the birth of Milky Way, Butterfinger, Oh Henry!, and Mounds bars. These followed the Hershey bar, which had been created by Milton Snavely Hershey, the son of German immigrants in Pennsylvania. In Youngstown, Ohio, Harry Burt invented a hard candy on a stick, which he called the Jolly Boy Sucker. What he really wanted to do was put a chocolate coating on an ice cream bar. The problem: the ice cream melted or the coating clotted. He finally got it to work, but holding it was messy. The solution: put it on a stick like his other candy. He called his confection Good Humor because he said it put him in a good humor to eat it. Harry Burt got a patent, then he got an old truck, painted it white, put on a white uniform, took the bells off a sleigh, and rang them as he drove slowly down the street, attracting children. As he became successful, gangsters wanted a percentage of the profits. When he refused, they blew up the trucks. The Good Humor man and his white truck were a standard fixture in the 1950s and 1960s as Americans moved to the suburbs, and the ice cream was one of the last foods still delivered to homes. Now, Good Humor is just one product of the company that makes Breyer's ice cream and Klondike bars. Good Humor trucks still exist, but they don't travel down city streets anymore. Some refurbished ones are available for rent from private companies.[41]

The Immigration Door Slams Shut; The Harlem Renaissance

In 1924, the Immigration Act cut immigration for two groups—southern Europeans and eastern Europeans, mostly Italians and Jews—to a minimum. By this time, many Americans regarded Italians as a "criminal class" and Jews as anarchists who wanted to overthrow the American government. Italy's fascist dictator, Mussolini, also stopped the population hemorrhage that had reduced the population of Italy by one-third by refusing to allow any more people to leave. Exceptions: Mexicans were not restricted from coming into the United States because farmers needed cheap labor. But once in, they were severely restricted as to where they could go and what they could do. Mexicans who attempted to leave the fields and move to the cities were stopped—by the police, if necessary. Mexicans were considered "colored" and were subjected to the same Jim Crow laws as African-Americans in the South: forced to ride in the back of the bus, to use separate public facilities, waiting rooms, and water fountains, and to go around to the back door of restaurants to get food. In 1927, Asians were added to the list. The United States Supreme Court ruled, in the case *Lum v. Rice,* that a Chinese girl could not enroll in a Mississippi school because the students were white and she was "colored."

There was another unintended loophole in the immigration laws. People with British passports were always allowed into the United States. Britain owned many islands in the Caribbean, so all the inhabitants were British citizens with British passports. And they were black. Many people from the Caribbean used this opportunity to migrate to New York City, where they became one-quarter of the population in Harlem and the heart of a cultural flowering of poetry, novels, art, and music called the Harlem Renaissance.

At Harlem nightclubs like the Cotton Club, performers and staff were all black, but only white customers were allowed in. Jazz and blues, uniquely American music with roots in Africa, came up from New Orleans to St. Louis, Kansas City, and Chicago after World War I when the United States government forced New Orleans to close down the red light district, Storyville, because too many sailors were getting into trouble (or ending up dead) there. Jazz greats like Louis Armstrong said good-bye to their families and got on the trains headed north.

A black leader emerged from this movement: Marcus Garvey, a Jamaican. He said that his people were not "colored," they were Negro, and make sure you spell that with a capital N. He preached pride and urged blacks to go to black stores, black banks, and black businesses. The United States government deported him back to Jamaica.

The Ideal American Woman

In the 1920s, Americans became obsessed with appearances. People stopped asking what good deeds a person had done and said instead, "What does he or she look like?" Americans discovered beauty contests, diets, salad, and sliced bread. Women cut their hair short like men, raised their hemlines to the knees, and declared that they were liberated. The year 1921 saw the birth of two mythical American women. One sprang from the glitz of Atlantic City, New Jersey; the other was conceived in a board room in the grain-growing heartland in Minneapolis, Minnesota. One was all about appearance; the other was pure function. One had physical reality but no substance; the other was all substance but a physical fiction. Miss America and Betty Crocker were flip sides of the same coin, two opposite images of the ideal American woman. They have both changed over time to reflect how women's appearances and roles have changed, as the official Betty Crocker portraits show.

The evolution of Betty Crocker—Betty Crocker's official portraits.
Courtesy General Mills Archives

Betty Crocker began as a serious-looking, unsmiling housewife. By the 1950s, she still looked like somebody's grandmother or aunt, but she was smiling. The women's movement that crystallized around the publication of Betty Friedan's book *The Feminine Mystique* in 1963 showed in the Betty Crocker pictures of 1968 and 1972, which looked like professional women who worked outside the home. The 1986 Betty Crocker looked a little more shrewd and tough than the others, as if she had a master's in business administration and wouldn't cook food as much as order others to do it. The Betty Crocker of 1996 was softer, more casual and approachable, and had the biggest smile yet. There was also a search for handwriting that would look like Betty Crocker's, because she answered thousands of letters about cooking from American women. Betty Crocker became a merchandising empire. She had her own radio show and cookbook.

The emphasis on appearances extended to food. The invention of color printing made advertising in magazines, newspapers, and posters easy and affordable. Consumers wanted food that looked just like the perfect pictures. This explains why the Red Delicious apple, which is tasteless but looks like every picture of an apple, including the ones in children's alphabet books (*A* is for *apple*), is by far the best-selling apple in America.

Movie Star Cuisine

Hollywood movie stars represented the ultimate in appearances. In the 1920s, Hollywood movie stars lived in multiroom palaces that looked like French châteaus, Italian villas, Spanish haciendas, or European palaces. Their estates had swimming pools, tennis courts, marble floors, gatehouses, vast lawns. Wild parties took place. They ate at the It Café on Vine Street in Hollywood, owned by sexy Clara Bow, who had "It"; or at the Brown Derby on Wilshire Boulevard, shaped like a derby hat, where Bob Cobb invented the chopped salad of lettuces, chicken, bacon, and avocado named after him. In Tijuana, chef Caesar Cardini supposedly invented the Caesar salad, which became popular in California. Sometimes actors overdosed on drugs or were murdered under mysterious circumstances.

One movie star never got into trouble. He made $100,000 per year and was insured for five times that amount. His Beverly Hills estate was complete with all the trappings that Americans found irresistible in the 1920s: an electric refrigerator in the hygienic white kitchen, electric lights, fans, heating, a radio. His dinner service was silver. His yard was screened in to keep flies away. He traveled with "the best of everything, beds, drawing rooms on trains, private baths," and with his usual entourage: personal valet, bodyguard, trainer, and special chef.[42] He received more than 10,000 fan letters a week, sometimes a million a year. He made public appearances and visited children in hospitals and orphanages. He was studio head Jack Warner's favorite star because his movies made so much money they saved Warner Bros. from bankruptcy, and because he never gave the studio any trouble. He didn't care if his movies got bad reviews; his ego didn't become hugely inflated if they did well; he didn't drink, smoke, do drugs, or have affairs, and he never talked back.

He was a dog.

Rin Tin Tin was a pedigreed German shepherd bred to be a war dog for the German army in World War I. His owner, American soldier Lee Duncan, found "Rinty" in a trench in France when he was just days old and brought him home to California. Rin Tin Tin was a merchandising empire. He was spokesdog for Ken-L Ration dog food; dog biscuits were passed out in theater lobbies where his movies played. There were Rin Tin Tin statuettes, buttons, pins, photographs, and fan clubs. He mailed not autographs but "pawtographs" to his fans by the thousands. And he had his own radio program, *Rin Tin Tin Thrillers*— just like Betty Crocker.

The Discovery of Vitamins and Penicillin

In the 1920s, scientists began to discover exactly what was in food. They called these properties *vitamins,* a combination of *vita-,* meaning "life," and *-amine,* as in amino acid, and named them with letters of the alphabet. Vitamin A, in liver and carrots, affects eyesight. Deficiency causes night blindness; excess results in nausea, joint pain, and death. B vitamins, in brown rice, pork, and liver, make the nervous system function. Vitamin C counteracts scurvy. Vitamin D, the "sunshine vitamin," is in milk and helps to build bones. Without it, bone-deforming rickets occurs. Vitamin K causes blood to clot. There are other vitamins, and scientists are still discovering the properties of foods.

In 1929, Alexander Fleming, a British physician, noticed that something was destroying his bacteria-growing experiment. Some mold from bread had gotten into it and killed the bacteria. He had discovered *Penicillium notatum,* the first antibiotic. The word *antibiotic* comes from the Greek: *anti-,* "against," *bios,* "life." Soon after, other antibiotics like the sulfas, the mycins, and tetracycline were discovered. Penicillin came into widespread household use in the United States after World War II, when it was mass-produced for use in the war. Fleming was knighted and was one of the winners of the Nobel prize in 1945 for his discovery.

The Rise of the Supermarket and the Fall of the Stock Market

As 1929 began, life was looking good. The Industrial Revolution had arrived in the American home. Electricity and new appliances replaced household servants: electric stoves and refrigerators, vacuum cleaners, washing machines, toasters, sewing machines, teakettles. People could save time by purchasing their bread already sliced and their vegetables frozen in a process invented by Clarence Birdseye after he saw Eskimos quick-freezing food. (Then Marjorie Merriweather Post, of the Post food family, bought Birdseye's operation and changed the name to General Foods.) Americans ate canned food and fed their infants the convenient new baby foods made by Gerber. They bought all these foods in the new one-stop supermarkets. The Alpha Beta supermarket had everything in alphabetical order; customers could walk up and take what and how much they wanted instead of waiting for a clerk to help them, like in the old general stores. Another food giant, the A&P—the Great Atlantic and Pacific Tea Company—was selling one-tenth of all retail food in the United States and doing one billion dollars a year in business.[43] The USDA was inspecting meat, and Coca-Cola was free of coca. The Public Health Service monitored 29 diseases, including food-borne illnesses, in every state, the District of Columbia, Hawaii, and Puerto Rico. There was one car for every five people in the United States, compared with one for 43 in England, and one for 7,000 in Russia.[44] There were many fun things to do, like driving around in the car with friends, going to movies and dances and parties. Anyone who really wanted a drink could get one. America was in a party mood. Party party party.

In October 1929, the stock market crashed. It was the greatest financial flop in American history up to that time. Stock prices dropped; millions of people lost their jobs. People who had been worth millions were suddenly wiped out. They committed suicide by jumping out of their office windows. During the presidential campaign in 1928, Herbert Hoover promised Americans that if he was elected, he would put "a chicken in every pot." After the stock market crash, many Americans not only didn't have a chicken, they didn't have a pot.

The party was over.

Soup Kitchens, C-Rations, and TV Dinners: The Depression, World War II, and the Cold War

THE GREAT DEPRESSION AND THE NEW DEAL

Soup Kitchens and Bread Lines

With millions of people out of work, public funds and private charities were quickly overwhelmed. Gangster Al Capone saw the depression as a public relations opportunity to present himself as the patron saint of Chicago; he set up its first soup kitchen and fed 3,000 people a day. It didn't keep him from being sent to prison. Some organizations handed out free bread, but accepting charity at that time was regarded as shameful, and people standing in line to receive free food often tried to hide their faces. The Los Angeles County sheriff's department did better than soup and bread lines—it hosted an annual barbecue. It was pit-cooked for 14 to 15 hours, the West Coast equivalent of the New England clambake, but with beef. First, they cut the number of people who needed food by shipping thousands of Mexicans back to Mexico.

Unemployment across the United States reached deep into the middle class. Many people lost their homes. They lived in empty lots or down by the railroad yards, in shacks made of old pieces of tin or cardboard boxes. They heated themselves by making fires in barrels; they ate garbage and food scraps they scrounged or begged. These new

269

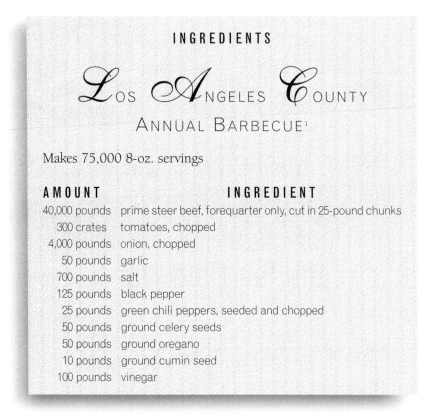

INGREDIENTS

Los Angeles County
ANNUAL BARBECUE[1]

Makes 75,000 8-oz. servings

AMOUNT	INGREDIENT
40,000 pounds	prime steer beef, forequarter only, cut in 25-pound chunks
300 crates	tomatoes, chopped
4,000 pounds	onion, chopped
50 pounds	garlic
700 pounds	salt
125 pounds	black pepper
25 pounds	green chili peppers, seeded and chopped
50 pounds	ground celery seeds
50 pounds	ground oregano
10 pounds	ground cumin seed
100 pounds	vinegar

"towns," called "Hoovervilles" in bitter honor of President Herbert Hoover, sprang up all over the United States. Hoover, a Republican, told Americans who saw their lives getting worse and worse, "Prosperity is just around the corner." He lost resoundingly in his bid for reelection in 1932 to Democrat Franklin Delano Roosevelt (FDR). Polio had almost killed FDR; it left him in a wheelchair (although he was always photographed without it). It also left him knowing what human beings can accomplish if they have enough willpower

> "I see one-third of a nation ill-housed, ill-clad, and ill-nourished."
> *—President Franklin Delano Roosevelt*[2]

Roosevelt, inaugurated on March 4, 1933, told the American people the truth—the depression, entering its fourth year, was getting worse, not better. This, along with an unprecedented, steep rise in violent crime, had Americans hungry, angry, scared, and losing confidence in their government. The economy was worse in the United States than in any other industrialized nation. Many Americans wondered if capitalism and democracy were going to survive or needed to be replaced with something else. In Russia, Stalin's communist five-year plan was succeeding, according to Stalin; in Germany, Hitler's National Socialist party, the Nazis, were turning the economy around. FDR reassured the American people: "We have nothing to fear but fear itself."

Roosevelt had a three-pronged approach, the three R's: relief, recovery, and reform. He would provide financial relief to people in the form of jobs and money; begin programs to help economic recovery; and reform the laws controlling banks and the stock market so that this would never happen again. In the first hundred days after his inauguration, Congress was happy to pass any programs the president proposed. He immediately declared a bank holiday and closed every bank in the country until federal auditors could decide which ones were healthy. Deposits in the banks that reopened were insured up to $5,000 by a new agency, the FDIC—Federal Deposit Insurance Corporation. There were so many agencies that they were referred to only by their initials. These "alphabet agencies" had names like CCC and AAA.

CCC: Civilian Conservation Corps—Paying People for Real Work

On March 31, 1933, FDR signed the bill creating the Civilian Conservation Corps. The CCC's goal was to prevent the many angry, unemployed young men living in Hoovervilles and hanging around street corners from forming gangs and revolting against the United States. Just as almost two thousand years earlier, the Romans gave free bread and entertainment to the urban poor to avoid civil disorder, the Roosevelt administration got 19- to 22-year-old men off the city streets and into the countryside. Soon, there were men in 1,450 CCC camps throughout all 48 states building roads, clearing trails, and planting trees. They were supposed to receive the standard army ration—12 ounces of flour, 10 ounces of fresh beef, 10 ounces of potatoes, and 5 ounces of sugar per man per day—but army physicians increased it by 5 percent when they discovered that all the men were undernourished. The menu included a variety of foods, but the constants at all three meals were the basis of the typical American diet: meat, potatoes, bread, butter, coffee. Dairy products were also abundant in fresh milk, butter, creamed vegetables, and puddings. (Under "fresh vegetables" the army lists canned corn, green beans, and peas.)

The men had to send their pay home so their families could buy food and pay mortgages. Now these men and their families felt good about their country. So did the farmers who sold their food to the government.

MENU: CIVILIAN CONSERVATION CORPS[3]		
BREAKFAST	*DINNER (LUNCHEON)*	*SUPPER*
Oatmeal	Roast Pork and Gravy	Braised Ribs of Beef
Fresh Milk	Baked Potatoes	Mashed Potatoes and Gravy
Fried Eggs and Bacon	Creamed Peas	Creamed String Beans Fresh
Hashed Brown Potatoes	Cabbage Slaw	Fresh Fruit Salad
Bread and Butter	Rice Pudding	Apple Pie
Coffee	Bread and Butter	Bread and Butter
	Coffee	Hot Cocoa and Coffee

AAA: Agricultural Adjustment Act—Paying People Not to Work

The problem with American farms was the same as with American industry—overproduction. Food cost very little. Shipping it, however, was expensive. It cost farmers in the Midwest more to ship their food to the cities than they could charge for it. They would lose money. So they destroyed the food. Newsreels showed farmers dumping gallons of milk, rivers of milk, into the gutter while hungry babies in cities cried and got rickets. Something had to be done. Roosevelt's solution was the AAA—Agricultural Adjustment Act. This revolutionary law paid farmers *not* to farm. They had to plow their fields under. The AAA was eventually declared unconstitutional and replaced with other farm subsidies.

The New Deal changed the relationship between the American people and their government profoundly. The government giving charity was contrary to the American myth of rugged individualism, the idea that people would take care of themselves without help from anyone, especially the government. On the other hand, European countries, where social welfare programs had existed for decades, considered America backward and barbaric because it didn't have these programs.

The New Deal also changed the relationship between the government and black Americans. FDR immediately ended segregation in the White House, and his programs gave professional jobs to black people. The First Lady, Eleanor Roosevelt, had many black friends and worked actively to help them achieve equality. She was also the president's "legs," going places he couldn't. There were jokes about Eleanor sightings, just as there are jokes now about Elvis sightings—Eleanor was spotted down a coal mine, on a bridge, on a farm, in a school. But the Eleanor sightings were real; she *was* everywhere, making the federal government a living presence for ordinary Americans. She was more of a force in the life of America than any other first lady.

Alcohol in the New Deal

One of the first things FDR did after his inauguration was ask Congress to make beer and wine legal again. On March 22, 1933, they passed the Beer and Wine Revenue Act on the grounds that the country needed the tax money. (Roosevelt thought they needed a drink.) One newspaper cartoon showed FDR as a waiter, towel over his arm, a tray loaded with foaming beer, running to a table. The caption read, "I Call That Service."

By the end of FDR's first year in office, all alcohol was legal again. On December 5, 1933, the 21st Amendment to the Constitution repealed the 18th Amendment. Prohibition was over. However, the decision of whether to be wet or dry was left to the individual states. Utah is still dry. Also in 1933, a California man invented a handy machine that solved a problem that had been a bane to mankind: it took the pits out of green olives, making them suitable for dropping into martini glasses.[4]

Although people could begin drinking again, the industries that produced alcohol had gone out of business or been closed for 13 years. In 1933, there were about 130 wineries left in California and around 150 total in the United States, down from more than 1,000 pre-Prohibition. Equipment was rusted, casks rotted. The 1934 vintage "may well have been the worst commercial American wines ever produced. Some, still fermenting when first shipped, literally blew up on store shelves."[5] The reputation of wine fell, further depressing the wine industry. It took decades to recover.

Bill W. and Dr. Bob: Alcoholics Anonymous and the Twelve Steps

Some people began to admit, after years of trying to deal with it themselves, that they were alcoholics. Two, Bill W. and Dr. Bob, both Vermont natives, had severe blackouts (24 hours at a time) and had been hospitalized multiple times; they were considered hopeless. Bill W. was on the verge of being committed to an institution when a friend told him about the Oxford Group, a worldwide religious organization founded by a Lutheran minister and dedicated to changing the world "one person at a time." One of the men Bill W. met at a meeting had gone to Europe in desperation to see the famous psychoanalyst Carl Jung, who told him that medicine and science could do nothing to help him; it would take a spiritual conversion. Bill W. had such a conversion, and then "there came a vision of a society of alcoholics, each identifying with and transmitting his experience to the next—chain style."[6] He proceeded to bring this philosophy to others, including Dr. Bob. The official date of the beginning of Alcoholics Anonymous is June 10, 1935, known as the day Dr. Bob took his last drink. In 1938, the Twelve Steps—the guidelines to recovery—were developed. AA has spawned Overeaters Anonymous, Narcotics Anonymous for drug addicts, and many other twelve-step programs. In Germany, Hitler dealt with alcoholism by sterilizing between 20,000 and 30,000 alcoholics.[7]

New Marketing Concepts to Sell Food

During the depression, American ingenuity went into overdrive to come up with new ways to sell food. Apple sellers appeared on street corners in cities. Little pieces of paper that told fortunes were baked into cookies in a Chinese restaurant in Los Angeles. Movie theaters started selling popcorn to help the corn farmers. Before that, going to a movie was like going to a play. The theater was an elegant "palace" with heavy velvet draperies and chair coverings, gold on the walls, elaborate paintings on the walls and ceiling. You did not eat. Now, theaters also had nights where they gave away dishes and other prizes. Oregon fruit growers Harry and David used the United States mail to save their pear orchards and their business. They became the largest mail order shippers in the United States. In cities, Horn and Hardart had a chain of automats. Putting coins in a slot opened the latch on a little door so customers could pick the food they wanted, visible behind glass in vertical cases.

The Joy of Cooking and Depression Cooks

After the stock market crash, many upper-middle-class women found themselves merely middle-class or worse. They suddenly had to live without household help, the maids and cooks on whom they had always relied. One woman who found herself in what was referred to then as "reduced circumstances" was a 53-year-old widow of old German stock in St. Louis, Missouri. When she began collecting recipes from women friends and restaurateurs, her family called what she was doing a "hobby" or worse, because they all knew "Irma can't cook." The result was *The Joy of Cooking,* which Irma Rombauer published herself in 1931 with half of all the money she had. Her daughter Marion Rombauer Becker, educated at Vassar and an artist, provided the illustrations for the 3,000 copies. As Anne Mendelson, the Rombauer/Becker biographer, points out, Irma "hit on . . . a new way of writing recipes." Instead of listing the ingredients, then giving the instructions, Irma swirled them together like a marble cake:

Sift----------------------------------1/2 cup sugar
Beat until soft--------------------1/4 cup butter[8]

The format was continued in following editions by her daughter and then her grandson Ethan Becker, a Cordon Bleu graduate.

Another woman who turned her kitchen into a gold mine during the depression was Margaret Rudkin. The Connecticut woman invented a special whole-grain bread for her son, who was suffering from allergies. Her bread developed a local reputation, so she placed it in stores. When bread was selling for a dime a loaf, Margaret insisted on charging a quarter and got it. That was the beginning of Pepperidge Farm.[9]

In Los Angeles, pies baked in her kitchen provided income for Marie Callender. In Texas, Cornelia Alabama Marshall realized that not everyone could afford her full-size pecan and fruit pies, so she loaded up her husband's truck with individual three-inch pies and sent him out to construction sites. The pies became known by a short form of her middle name, Bama Pies; she was "Gramma Bama."[10]

In 1935, a young man from Oregon with some college and a bit of experience as an actor needed to make money, so he began a catering business. Two years later he opened a small shop called Hors d'Oeuvre Inc., and the rest, as they say, is history. James Beard published his first book, *Hors d'Oeuvres and Canapés,* in 1940. Beard published many books, including *Cooking It Outdoors,* the first cookbook that went beyond scouting or survival food and treated outdoor cooking seriously. He was also the first person to have a television show on cooking. James Beard died in 1985; it was Julia Child's idea to preserve his brownstone home in New York's Greenwich Village as a foundation to promote fine food and drink, and as a memorial to the man known as the "father of American cooking."

Poisoned Food: Japan's Biological War Against China

Japan invaded China in 1931, then escalated their attacks in 1937. They intended to take China's massive natural resources, including food. The Japanese committed many atrocities, including the Rape of Nanking. In less than two months, the Japanese raped, dismembered, looted, tortured, and burned at least 100,000 people, most of them civilians. Japan denies this ever took place, even though they filmed it. In 2002, Japan opened a museum about World War II; it included nothing about Nanking.

The Japanese used food as a weapon against Chinese civilians, including children. Japanese scientists put anthrax bacteria in chocolates and plague bacteria in cookies. They dumped typhoid bacteria down wells, sprayed fields with contaminated grains of wheat and millet, and released rats carrying plague fleas into cities. Chinese food customs, like fish peddlers who went from village to village, accidentally helped to spread the diseases. Japanese doctors came to vaccinate people in the affected areas—but the "vaccines" were injections of cholera. They burned down villages and said they were cleansing them. They developed a concentrated version of toxin from the liver of the Japanese blowfish—*fugu*—to kill people, but a United States bombing raid destroyed the research facility. These tactics of terrorism, violence, and biological warfare were extremely effective: 6 million civilians died.[11]

1939

The last year of the decade ended with the best of events and the worst of events. The best: the New York World's Fair opened. Pavilion after pavilion displayed technological progress and the hope for a better life in the future. The French pavilion had a restaurant, called simply Le Pavilon, which was the latest in French food. After the fair closed the restaurant went directly into New York City, where it became a landmark for years and the training ground for many chefs, including the White House chef in the Kennedy administration.

The worst: in August 1939, Hitler and Stalin entered into a nonaggression pact: neither country would attack the other. The two countries, very wary of each other, were separated only by Poland. In effect, Stalin was giving Hitler the go-ahead to invade Poland. Britain and France, which had been counting on the threat of Russia to deter Hitler, were furious. They immediately informed Hitler that if he invaded Poland, Germany would be at war with them. They hoped this would prevent Germany from invading Poland.

WORLD WAR II

Germany invaded Poland on Friday, September 1, 1939, plunging the world into war again for the second time in a little more than two decades. England and France, true to their word, then declared war on

Germany. The match was uneven. Germany had been preparing for war for the better part of a decade while England and France had not. The heart of Germany's industrial production, the Ruhr Valley, was dominated by the Krupp family. They began in the 16th century as manufacturers of cutlery who went town to town peddling German knives.

Germany easily took Poland, then overran Denmark and Norway. In Denmark, when they ordered all Jews to wear a yellow star, everyone, including the king and queen, wore a yellow star. The Nazis continued west and attacked the Netherlands. As the Dutch army rushed to defend its borders, the Nazis attacked the interior of the country with a new kind of warfare: paratroopers, soldiers dropped from airplanes behind enemy lines. Overwhelmed, the Netherlands surrendered, then Luxembourg and Belgium. By May 1940, so did France. Hitler was making plans to invade England. And after that, the United States. For more than a year, England, the last country in Europe not under Nazi control, fought the entire Nazi empire alone in Europe and in Africa, where the Nazis were trying to capture the Suez Canal and get to the oil in the Middle East. The United States helped with the lend-lease program, in which it loaned— really gave—ships, ammunition, oil, and food to England.

The Nazi Siege of Leningrad: "Starve Them"

The Nazis looked at the Slavic people of Russia the same way they looked at the Jews, as *Untermenschen*—subhumans. On June 22, 1941, Hitler broke his nonaggression pact with Stalin. The German air force, the Luftwaffe, launched a *blitzkrieg*—a lightning strike—against the USSR and destroyed almost their entire air force before it could get into the air. Then Germany invaded on the ground. By September 8, 1941, the city of Leningrad was surrounded and under siege. The Nazis used incendiary bombs to deliberately set the warehouses on fire and burn the food supply. Two thousand five hundred tons of burning sugar turned into lava, flowed through the streets, then hardened. The government broke pieces off and sold the sugar in chunks.[12] The Nazi strategy: wait until winter and let the people of Leningrad starve. Then they would surely surrender.

December 7, 1941: Pearl Harbor

President Roosevelt told Japan to get out of China. When Japan didn't, the United States cut off Japan's oil supply. Japan bombed United States military bases in Pearl Harbor, Hawaii, on Sunday,

December 7, 1941, shortly before 8 o'clock in the morning. Pearl Harbor was only one prong in a multi-target attack. At the same time they bombed Pearl Harbor, the Japanese also bombed the Philippines, Guam, Wake Island, Hong Kong, and other places in the Pacific.

A kitchen worker was one of the heroes of Pearl Harbor and the first African-American hero of World War II. Mess Attendant First Class "Dorie" Miller, a Texas high school fullback and heavyweight boxing champion on the USS *West Virginia,* manned a .50-caliber machine gun on the deck of the ship and started firing even though he had not been trained to—the segregated armed forces taught only white sailors to use guns. Rumors spread that he shot down several Japanese planes, but Miller said he thought maybe he got one. He was awarded the Navy Cross for bravery. The African-American community wrote to President Roosevelt to have Miller admitted to the United States Naval Academy. It never happened. Miller was serving as a ship's cook third class when his ship, the *Liscome Bay,* was torpedoed by a Japanese submarine and sank on November 24, 1943. Miller was awarded the Purple Heart after his death, and a ship named after him, the USS *Miller,* was commissioned in June 1973.[13] In 2001, the actor Cuba Gooding Jr. played Miller in the movie *Pearl Harbor.*

Congress declared war on Japan on Monday, December 8, 1941. While they were debating whether to also declare war on Japan's allies, Germany and Italy, Germany and Italy declared war on the United States. Then the factories in the greatest industrial cities in the greatest industrial nation the world had ever seen—Detroit, Pittsburgh, New York, Chicago, Los Angeles—shut down. When they reopened, jeeps and trucks, not cars, drove off the assembly lines at General Motors, Chrysler, and Chevrolet in Detroit. Steel for battleships and bombers rolled out of the mills in Pittsburgh 24 hours a day, seven days a week.

When Pearl Harbor was bombed, Leningrad was deep in winter and its fourth month of siege. In January 1942, the bread ration dropped to four ounces per person per day. Two hundred thousand Russians starved to death. But they did not surrender.

Executive Order 9066

The sneak attack on Pearl Harbor enraged and terrified Americans, especially on the West Coast, where they were afraid the Japanese— some of them American citizens—would engage in sabotage to help Japan win the war. But the Japanese were in a bind: it was against the law in America at that time for anyone born in Japan to become a citizen, no matter how much they wanted to. President Roosevelt issued Executive Order 9066: arrest every person of Japanese ancestry, even children who were citizens because they were born in the United States. They were sent away from the Pacific coast to detention centers in remote inland areas. Before the detention centers were ready, the Japanese in Los Angeles were kept in the horse stalls at the Santa Anita racetrack near Pasadena. Japanese-Americans fought Executive Order 9066 all the way to the Supreme Court, which ruled against them in *Korematsu v. United States* in 1944.

One of the camps was Manzanar, in the Mojave Desert at the foot of the Sierra Nevada Mountains, which made escape nearly impossible. Some Japanese were sent to Indian reservations in Arizona, others to Wyoming. Japanese in Canada were sent to camps, too. Under American pressure, Peru's Japanese population—too close to the Panama Canal—was shipped to Texas. In the camps, these people, mostly farmers, continued to do what they had always done: grow fruits and vegetables, which they ate and sold to the soldiers at the camp. Those born in Japan were required to sign a loyalty oath; some refused because they were afraid if the United States lost the war they would have no country at all. Many young Japanese-American men got out of the detention centers by joining the armed forces. The Japanese 442nd Regimental Combat Team fought bravely in Europe and became the most highly decorated unit in the American military in World War II.

Spam and the War Cake

The United States was wealthy in food. It sent its men into battle with what only a few years before had been a luxury item: chocolate candy. Sugar was rationed for home use but was available for the commercial production of chocolate and soft drinks. Hershey and Mars got sugar; so did Coke and Pepsi. When Congress was on the verge of declaring the manufacture of candy illegal because it wasn't important to the war effort, Hershey convinced them that chocolate was crucial as a morale booster—it would remind the boys of home and what they were fighting for. So America's soldiers went to war and ate Hershey bars and M&Ms from Hershey's competitor, Mars.

Chances were good that the sugar came from sugar beets that were grown, cultivated, and harvested by Mexicans. With more than 16 million Americans in the armed forces, farms needed laborers. The United States began the *bracero* (laborer) program (from *brazo,* the Spanish word for "arm") to bring back the Mexicans they had just deported.

Under the *bracero* program, approximately 4 million Mexican agricultural workers came into the United States until the program was discontinued in 1964.

Soldiers on the front lines drank instant coffee made by 12 different companies in the United States, including Maxwell House and Nescafé.[14] It was fortunate that the men had coffee and candy, because they soon got tired of the main course in their army rations—Spam. During World War II, the United States government bought 90 percent of everything the Hormel Company put in a can. Some of Hormel's products included Hormel Chile Con Carne, Dinty Moore Beef Stew, and canned hams. But the product most identified with Hormel was Spam. GIs ate Spam fritters, Spam soup, Spam sandwiches, Spam salad, Spam stew, Spam and macaroni, Spam and dehydrated eggs, Spam and dehydrated potatoes, Spam meatballs, Spam chop suey, Spam and Spam and more Spam. Every bit of Spam was used, including the packaging. The valuable metal in Spam cans was recycled as pots and pans and stills to make alcohol. Spam grease lubricated guns, conditioned skin, and became candles. There was so much Spam that soldiers called Uncle Sam "Uncle Spam."[15]

Spam was also shipped overseas as part of the lend-lease program. In England, it was eaten by civilians in air raid shelters and cleverly disguised under French sauces in fine restaurants. They thought Spam was an acronym for "specially prepared American meat."[16] In Russia, Spam fed the army. After the war, the Red Cross fed Spam to grateful, starving European refugees, who thought it was a luxury.

To help the war effort, the American government asked consumers to voluntarily cut back on their consumption of vital foods like meat. It had worked in England. But Americans are not British. They didn't cut back until laws set quotas and forced them to. In response to rationing, Americans did the same thing they did when Prohibition went into effect: they took their babies out of carriages, grabbed their children's toy wagons, went to the stores, picked the shelves clean, and hoarded. Then the slogan was: "Use it up, wear it out, make it do or do without." Some of the things Americans on the home front did without (or with very little of) were rubber, gasoline, sugar, butter, meat, milk, and eggs. Without rubber, Americans didn't go on vacation. They did, however, go to the movies in record numbers, so popcorn consumption tripled. A chemist named Orville Redenbacher went into the popcorn business to feed the new movie theaters, including drive-ins, which had opened in 1933.

Nutrition became a matter of national defense. Men were "rejected for service with the armed forces because of faulty nutrition and thousands of man-hours are lost on the production lines for lack of proper food."[17] It was up to the housewives of America to change this and save the country—even though they might be working full-time in defense plants themselves. Newspaper and magazine cooking columns invented recipes based on shortages. Meat was extended with eggs, bread stuffing, rice, and cereal. Recipes for pseudo-ethnic foods were supposed to tempt the palate: Italian liver (tomato, green pepper, and mushroom sauce on spaghetti), tamale pie, Spanish rice, Swiss steak. For the truly desperate, there was "Gypsy's Joy," made of rice, water, bacon fat, condensed tomato soup, cooked ham, and "crumbled, nippy cheese."[18] Extensive use was made of macaroni: au gratin, loaf, ring, with spinach, in a casserole with fish and corn. Welsh "rabbit" made a comeback. Food writer M. F. K. (Mary Frances Kennedy) Fisher wrote a book called *How to Cook a Wolf,* about how to make nutritious meals with limited items. Americans continued to discover that Italian food was cheap, nutritious, and delicious.

Not just what was prepared for lunch but how it was packed was connected to national security: "Some defense plants insist on paper bags which can be inspected as they enter the plant."[19] Housewives were urged to collect and recycle cosmetics jars, peanut butter jars, salad dressing bottles, and cottage cheese and ice cream cartons to pack food along with the standard thermos bottle.

With sugar rationed, desserts posed a problem. In America's Down Under allies, Australia and New Zealand, women baked ANZAC

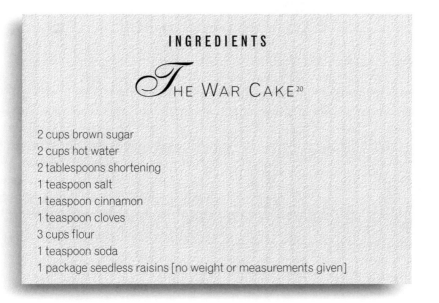

INGREDIENTS

The War Cake[20]

2 cups brown sugar
2 cups hot water
2 tablespoons shortening
1 teaspoon salt
1 teaspoon cinnamon
1 teaspoon cloves
3 cups flour
1 teaspoon soda
1 package seedless raisins [no weight or measurements given]

biscuits—an acronym for Australia and New Zealand Army Corps. They were made of oats and flour, sweetened shredded coconut, and honey.[21] In the United States, some cooks used Coke and Pepsi as sweeteners: bake a cake, poke it full of holes, pour the cola in. The "war cake" was made without butter, eggs, milk, or white sugar. It used brown sugar and water sweetened by soaking raisins in it, a technique used in the Middle East since ancient times. It tasted good and kept long enough to be shipped overseas to men and women in the armed forces.

Even though American civilians struggled to come up with creative ways to make cakes without key ingredients, and American soldiers complained about having to eat Spam, Americans were lucky. None of World War II was fought in the United States, and nobody starved to death because of food shortages in America.

Prison Camp Food

The 140,000 men held prisoner by the Japanese would have laughed at rationing in the United States. The men were all severely malnourished and suffered from beriberi, pellagra, and scurvy; thousands died. In their weakened state they also got malaria, dysentery, cholera, and typhus. Some swelled up grotesquely, and others went blind. Any small cut or mosquito bite could mean gangrene and death within days. The Japanese guards told the men their problem was that they needed to exercise more.[22] Scattered in camps throughout Asia, the prisoners—British, Dutch, Australian, American—worked at hard labor in salt mines or building a railroad in Burma (as in the movie *The Bridge on the River Kwai*). The United States Army ration for each enlisted man in peacetime was approximately four and a half pounds of food per day. In combat, it was much higher. The official Japanese ration for prisoners of war doing strenuous physical labor was one pound eleven ounces of food per day.[23] One bright spot in the months—for some, years—of imprisonment was when Red Cross packages arrived filled with food, cigarettes, and antibiotics. The men quickly traded items. Chocolate, tobacco, canned meat all changed hands. One food was almost never traded: cheese. The men had not had dairy in any form in so long, they craved it and held on to it. An exception: men who couldn't stop smoking starved to death because they traded their food for cigarettes.

In the United States, approximately 400,000 German prisoners of war were treated precisely according to the Geneva Convention of

1929, which stated that captured soldiers were to receive the exact same food that the capturing army fed its own troops. Troops were not subject to rationing; civilians were. So, during World War II, German prisoners of war in America ate better than American citizens.

The Hollywood Canteen

Hollywood actors and actresses volunteered their time and services to help the war effort. Male stars like Clark Gable, Jimmy Stewart, and Tyrone Power joined the armed forces. Actresses flew across the country selling bonds. In Hollywood, some of the biggest stars could be found at night at the Hollywood Canteen handing out coffee and doughnuts and chatting and dancing with men in the armed forces. Black and white movie studio musicians played live music. These humane gestures and simple food exchanges escalated into political acts when word got out that there were "mixed" couples—blacks and whites dancing together. There was talk of segregating the canteen. That ended when two-time Academy Award winner Bette Davis and John Garfield—major Warner Bros. stars and founders of the canteen—said if that happened, the actors wouldn't come. Without actors, there would be no canteen. So, unlike the armed forces in World War II, the Hollywood Canteen was integrated.[24]

The "Final Solution"

In early 1943, Hitler put into effect his "Final Solution," the plan to kill all the Jews in Europe. When Hitler was asked how he thought he could get away with killing millions of Jews, he said, "Who remembers the Armenians?"—a reference to the almost 2 million Armenians killed by the Turks in 1914–1915, and who had been largely forgotten by the world. Jews, Gypsies, homosexuals, political prisoners, and Christian ministers were rounded up and shipped in boxcars without food, heat, or sanitary facilities to concentration camps throughout Europe. Twelve million people, including six million Jews, starved to death, died of disease, or were sent to the gas chambers in camps like Auschwitz in Poland. People who were ordinarily civilized and kind became concerned only with their own survival. The motto in the camps was: "Eat your own bread, and if you can, that of your neighbor." A sign that humanity was returning at the end of the war was when people started to share food again.[25]

In his zeal to kill Jews, Hitler had not forgotten to keep killing Slavs. Leningrad was still under siege. No animals were left in the city. The people had eaten all the stray cats, dogs, and birds. And their own pets.

The Greatest Tank Battle in History; Mass Starvation

In July 1943, on the flat fields of Ukraine, near the town of Kursk, the greatest tank battle in history took place. For two weeks, the Germans and Russians fought each other with everything on wheels. The Russians finally emerged as the victors in what some historians consider the turning point of World War II, but it demolished the land that was the breadbasket not just of the Soviet Union but of Europe.

In Leningrad, still under siege, starving people ate anything that offered any semblance of nourishment—leather shoes, briefcases, lipstick. They stripped wallpaper off plaster walls and ate the wallpaper paste. Then they ate the wallpaper. Then they ate the walls.

As 1944 approached, millions of people were dying all over the world, many of starvation. In India, the British took rice to feed their troops fighting the Japanese in Burma; almost six million Indians starved to death or died from diseases brought on by malnutrition. In Japan, strict food rationing was in effect. They were also short on medical supplies, oil, and many other crucial items. In the Netherlands, Anne Frank, a 14-year-old Jewish girl in hiding with her family, wrote in her diary about the terrible monotony of their diet, which included slimy, very old preserved cabbage. Other people in the Netherlands ate tulip bulbs boiled to mush or sliced and fried like chips.

In Leningrad, still under siege, people resorted to cannibalism. Children didn't dare go outside.[26] The siege finally ended in January 1944, after 900 days. The death toll from starvation was approximately one million people, one-third of the city's total population; more were killed by the bombs.[27] During all that time, the only ones who expected the people of Leningrad to surrender, the only ones who ever uttered the word *surrender*, were the Nazis.

The Atom Bomb

In the United States, President Franklin D. Roosevelt died on April 12, 1945, and left his successor, President Harry S Truman, with a difficult decision. A plainspoken man from Missouri, Truman's motto was "If you can't stand the heat, stay out of the kitchen." The decision was whether or not to drop the new $2 billion weapon the United States had developed, the atomic bomb. Truman knew he was in the kitchen, and the heat was turned up full blast. He also knew that conventional warfare was not effective against the no-surrender samurai warrior mentality of Japan's rulers. After repeated clear warnings to the Japanese government that they would face a "rain of ruin" if they did not surrender, the United States dropped the first atom bomb on the city of Hiroshima, Japan, on August 6, 1945. The center of the city was completely destroyed. Approximately 73,000 people were killed outright; thousands died later from the aftereffects of radiation. When Japan still didn't surrender, the United States dropped another atom bomb on Nagasaki on August 9. Several days later, Japan surrendered, ending World War II. The airplanes that had dropped bombs began dropping crates of food. Some prisoners of war, so hungry, ate too much and died. Sometimes the parachutes on the 250-pound packages didn't open, and buildings and people were destroyed. One of the last American casualties of World War II was a marine killed by flying Spam.[28]

POST–WORLD WAR II AND THE COLD WAR

World War II caused a major shift in global politics and economics. The United States, England, and Russia used American oil in eastern and western Europe, Asia, Africa, and the Pacific and Atlantic oceans to fly airplanes, run tanks, trucks and jeeps, and sail ships. After World War II, the United States was still producing oil, but not enough to meet its needs. The world's attention shifted to the area that was richest in oil—the Middle East—especially the countries of Iran and Saudi Arabia. At the same time, the USSR and the United States, countries that had been uneasy allies in World War II, became bitter enemies, especially after the USSR exploded its own atom bomb in September 1949. In October 1949 Mao Zedong triumphed over Jiang Jieshi (formerly Chiang Kai-shek) in China's civil war and announced that the most populous country on earth—500 million people, onefourth of all the people on the planet—was now the communist People's Republic of China. Thousands of Chinese fled communist China and went to Taiwan, then called Formosa.

This was the Cold War between two different political and economic systems, capitalism and democracy versus communism. It consisted of a massive military buildup including nuclear weapons and espionage. Americans dug bomb shelters in their yards and stocked them with canned goods just in case the Cold War heated up.

The Russians took heavier casualties in World War II, both military and civilian, than any other country. About 20 million people died, killed either in the war or by starvation. (In comparison, a little more than a quarter of a million Americans died in the war—about 290,000.) In the Russian countryside, more than half the horses were gone; only 3 million pigs were left out of 23 million. Almost 5 million houses were destroyed, as well as hundreds of thousands of tractors and wagons and thousands of farm buildings.[29]

The United States poured millions of dollars into European countries, especially Italy, France, and Greece, to help them rebuild. The United States Army brought a new word into the Italian language: *ciao*. It is pronounced "chow" and means "hello" or "good-bye." It came into use after World War II, when starving Italians begged for food from American soldiers and knew only the one word of English they heard soldiers say when they went to eat—*chow*.

Food had become a political issue in Italy in the 1930s when the fascist dictator, Mussolini, declared pasta was passé because it was making Italians soft and sluggish. Mussolini's "New Roman Empire" needed new foods that would make people strong and hard. A huge debate arose all over Italy. The keep-the-pasta movement was supported with protests and petitions. Other people wanted the new cuisine, dishes with names like "Raw Meat Torn by Trumpet Blasts" and "The Ox in the Cockpit." Finally, a conference of chefs was held to decide the issue for the culinary community; the chefs decided to beat each other up instead.[30] At the end of the war, an Italian mob killed Mussolini and his mistress and hung them from a lamppost on a butcher's meat hook.

The period immediately following World War II saw a move for independence in colonial countries. In India, devastated by famine and disease, the Indian army followed Indian officers who wanted independence from Britain. A religious leader, Gandhi, used the same tactic to gain independence from England that Americans had used almost 200 years earlier: a boycott of British goods. One of these was salt, because England had a monopoly on salt production in India. From 1930 to 1932, Gandhi led hundreds of thousands of Indians to the sea on salt marches. Getting salt by evaporation from the sea broke the law—and the monopoly—and encouraged the Indian people to engage in other acts of civil disobedience until they were granted their independence in 1947.

For the 16 million American GIs returning home, many wanted to change jobs. Some had discovered during the war that they had a talent for cooking. By the end of the war, the Quartermaster Corps was

---

ℱOOD ℱABLE

❊ AMERICAN SOLDIERS AND WORLD WAR II FOOD ❊

The myth was that American soldiers, impressed by the food they were exposed to in European countries, especially Italy and France, came back to the United States eager to eat more of it. This would be inaccurate. During and after the war, there were tremendous food shortages in Europe. The food exchange went from Americans to Europeans, not the other way. The Italian food that GIs had been exposed to, many for the first time, was given to them by the army—canned Chef Boyardee spaghetti.

---

preparing more than 24 million meals every day.[31] In 1946, the cooking school that became the Culinary Institute of America was founded in New Haven, Connecticut.

Also in 1946, an American woman from Pasadena, California, a graduate of the Smith College class of 1934, went with her husband to Paris, where he was stationed at the American embassy. She went to the Cordon Bleu cooking school there and became fascinated with French cooking. She wanted to spread the word on how good French food was and show Americans how to make it. And that is exactly what Julia Child did when she returned to the United States.

The Cold War heated up and became a shooting war (called a United Nations "police action") in Korea from 1950 to 1953 (the subject of the movie and TV series *M*A*S*H*). This caused a huge buildup of the military in the United States that continues to the present.

Korean Cuisine[32]

Rice is the staple of Korean cuisine. Glutinous lowland rice, *tap-kok*, is eaten. An upland variety is used for flour and beer. Flour is also made from ground mung beans. The staple condiment and national dish, which comes in more than 200 hundred varieties, is kimchee. It is traditionally made every fall—cabbage season—in Korean homes. Cabbage (and sometimes radishes), chili, pepper, and garlic are packed into stone crocks and fermented. What Americans know as Korean barbecue is *pulgogi*—meat or seafood marinated in soy sauce, sesame oil, garlic, ginger, pepper, and green onions, then broiled. Wheat or buckwheat noodles or dumplings like wontons but larger are served in soup. Soup provides the liquid during a meal; beverages like rice water or barley water are consumed after. What Americans would consider dessert—rice cakes or fruit—is eaten between meals as a snack.

The Koreans, like the Japanese, are formal people. There are many rules controlling relations between people and regarding food. Koreans consider it rude to look people in the face while speaking to them or to compliment anyone, like the cook, directly. It is more polite just to say that the food is good. Elders are deeply respected. They are spoken to first, served food and drink first, and eat first. No one can begin eating until the oldest person does. Dining tables are low; diners sit on cushions on the floor. The service is *à la française,* with all courses presented at once. Chopsticks and spoons are the utensils. Fingers are never used. The meal is over when the oldest person is finished. When dining out, Koreans never split the bill or ask for separate checks. The entire bill is paid by the person who had the idea to go out.[33]

THE FAST-FOOD FIFTIES

"Better living through chemistry" was the slogan in the 1950s, along with "I like Ike," referring to five-star general Dwight D. Eisenhower, who led the Allies to victory in World War II. After World War II ended in 1945, men returned from overseas, women gave up their factory jobs, and Americans got married in record numbers. Then they moved to the suburbs in record numbers, into houses financed by new government programs for veterans—the GI Bill—and built on what had often been farmland. They bought cars, stoves, refrigerators (20 million in one five-year period), dishwashers, washing machines, dryers, TVs, backyard barbecues (really grills), and the new home freezers invented by Amana in record numbers. Then they had children in record numbers—50 million from 1945 to the end of the 1950s. This baby boom resulted in food marketing aimed specifically at children. In 1951, Tony the Tiger appeared to sell breakfast cereal. Fish made into fish sticks transformed fish into finger food, appealing to children. Adults continued eating the foods they had been served in the armed forces: instant coffee and Spam.

Fast food and frozen food combined in 1954, when Swanson introduced a frozen, completely precooked meal that only needed to be reheated. For 99 cents, the consumer got an aluminum tray divided into compartments with an entree, vegetables, and dessert. The public called these "TV dinners," because they were often eaten in front of the television. As more people stayed home to watch television, movie attendance dropped and so did popcorn consumption. Popcorn producers started marketing to the home audience. In 1955, the principle of the assembly line finally came to food when Ray Kroc bought the McDonald brothers' hamburger stand. Down the street from them in San Bernardino, California, was the restaurant that became Taco Bell.[34] Disneyland also opened in July 1955, and was so successful that they ran out of food on the first day.

Civil Rights: The *Brown* Decision; Cesar Chavez

Civil rights advocates had been using lawsuits to chip away at segregation in the United States. They were aided by black athletes whose talents were so spectacular they could not be ignored. Jesse Owens ran like the wind at the Nazi Olympics in Berlin in 1936 and won four gold medals. In 1938, the phenomenal fists of Joe Louis, the "Brown Bomber," beat Germany's Max Schmeling for the world heavyweight boxing championship. And in 1947, UCLA graduate Jackie Robinson integrated baseball when manager Branch Rickey put him on the Brooklyn Dodgers (they didn't move to Los Angeles until the mid-1950s). The Tuskegee Airmen, black pilots, also served with distinction in World War II.

In the South, discrimination continued after World War II. In restaurants, the front of the house was segregated, but blacks still did the cooking and serving. Blacks felt that they had served their country honorably and risked their lives, so they should be treated equally. In 1948, one veteran, wearing his uniform and war medals, refused to move to the back of the bus. White men pulled him off the bus, beat him, and blinded him. An angry President Truman picked up a pen, issued an executive order, and integrated the army.

In 1954, the NAACP and others in the civil rights movement brought a case before the Supreme Court. In a rare unanimous decision in *Brown v. the Board of Education of Topeka, Kansas,* the Supreme Court justices stated that segregation was wrong. Period. In another decision, they ordered that schools be integrated. The South resisted. The governor of Alabama said, "Segregation now! Segregation tomorrow! Segregation forever!" It was going to be a long fight.

Another group was fighting for survival, too. The plight of migrant workers was shown to Americans in *Harvest of Shame,* a TV documentary that aired, deliberately, the day after Thanksgiving in 1960. Narrated by respected newsman Edward R. Murrow of CBS, it showed the deplorable conditions under which migrants worked—for $900 per year. One thing that made their lives so difficult was the short-handled hoe. The 12- or 14-inch handle forced workers to literally bend in half for up to 12 hours a day out in the fields. At the end of the day it was nearly impossible to stand up. There was also no place for workers to go to the bathroom. A leader emerged. Cesar Chavez forged a political movement of migrants and appealed to the American public to boycott table grapes (not wine grapes) and lettuce until those producers provided more humane working conditions. Chavez had a slogan: *Sí, se puede*—"Yes, We Can." And they did.

The Cuban Revolution: Castro and Rum, 1959

On New Year's Eve, December 31, 1958, Cuban revolutionary Fidel Castro finally succeeded in overthrowing the government. Dictator Fulgencio Batista had been very friendly to American businesses, including organized crime and the casinos and other operations they ran. This is captured on film in *The Godfather, Part II,* when the representatives of organized crime and American corporations literally cut up a cake in the shape of Cuba and hand out pieces. Castro also nationalized the rum industry, which means that the country took it by force. The Bacardi family fled to Puerto Rico. When Castro came to power in 1959, he promised free elections. The Cuban people are still waiting. Many of them—the educated, upper classes—moved to America after the revolution and brought their cuisine with them. Like other Caribbean countries, the staples are black beans and rice, and plantains. Cubans also love pork marinated in vinegar and orange juice and stewed with onions; chicken roasted with garlic; and tropical fruit drinks, some with rum.

Hawaii Becomes a State; the Puu Puu Platter

Hawaii became a state in 1959. Alaska joined in 1960, making a total of 50 stars on the American flag. Mainland Americans suddenly "discovered" the tropical Hawaiian islands, 2,500 miles away. James Michener's best-selling novel *Hawaii* became a blockbuster movie in 1966. A 1970 sequel, *The Hawaiians,* in a moment of deep fiction, showed Academy Award winner Charlton Heston changing the economy of Hawaii forever by stealing the pineapple from South America in the 19th century and bringing it to Hawaii. In reality, pineapples came to the Pacific with Captain Cook in the 1770s. Hawaiians began canning them in 1892. (They were grown in Europe shortly after Columbus found them on Guadeloupe in 1493.) Elvis Presley visited *Blue Hawaii* in 1961 and returned to enjoy *Paradise Hawaiian Style* five years later. On television, the islands provided exotic scenery for three series: *Hawaiian Eye* (1959 to 1962), *Hawaii 5-0* from 1968 to 1979, then *Magnum, P.I.* beginning in 1981. In each series the main characters were *haoles* (pronounced "HOW-lees")—white people—with Asian locals taking a distant second place or absent.

Haole Mark Twain visited Hawaii—then called the Sandwich Islands—in the 1860s, when there were still people alive who remembered native life and customs before missionaries arrived in the 1820s and converted them to Christianity. Dogs were raised for food and prized; 300 were sacrificed when King Kamehameha died in 1819. The dying king had to be carried from the house he slept in to the house where he ate because eating and sleeping in the same building was taboo. His wives had to eat in a separate house.[35] It was also taboo for women to eat bananas, pineapples, or oranges; the missionaries changed that.[36] Twain tried a cherimoya—"deliciousness itself"; a tamarind— "sour"; and saw natives eating raw fish—"Let us change the subject!"[37] In the marketplace he saw poi, a staple Hawaiian starch that "looks like common flour paste" and was kept in four-gallon bowls made of gourds. The natives "bake it [taro root] underground, then mash it up well with a heavy lava pestle, mix water with it until it becomes a paste, set it aside and let it ferment, and then it is poi."[38] It was eaten by sticking a forefinger into the bowl.

In the 1920s, 100 years after the religious missionaries came to Hawaii, food missionaries—home economists from Columbia Teachers College in New York City—introduced standard American food to Hawaiian schools: ground beef in the form of hamburger, meat loaf, and Salisbury steak.[39] Hawaiians refer to themselves as "locals" to distinguish themselves from *haole* missionaries and tourists. "Local Food" is their fusion of native, Japanese, Chinese, Filipino, Pacific Islander, and American cuisines. Rice is a staple starch. A whole pig marinated and roasted underground is the centerpiece of the luau. Spam appears in its Japanese form as Spam sushi and Spam tempura, in its Chinese form as Spam wonton, and in its Filipino form as Spam *lumpia*. As food historian Rachel Laudan notes, "In Hawaii Spam continues to be something to be reckoned with."[40]

Hawaii is part of Polynesia, what are now called the Pacific Islands: the Marianas, the Solomons, Guam, Fiji, Samoa, New Caledonia, the New Hebrides, and others. In the 1950s and 1960s, something that claimed to be Polynesian food appeared in American restaurants. Sweet, fruity drinks were garnished with small, colorful paper umbrellas. The puu puu platter was an excuse to deep-fry food and smother it in canned pineapple chunks, maraschino cherries, and corn syrup. Real Polynesians eat food steamed or baked in banana leaves: taro, poi, yams, plantains, coconut, and fresh tropical fruit. They also eat fried forest rat and insects. The stewed flesh of fruit-eating bats (*civet de roussette*) is regarded as such a delicacy that some species are near extinction.[41]

In the 1950s, Americans began a love affair with things Italian and French. On one of America's most popular television shows, *I Love Lucy*, Lucy and her real-life and television husband Ricky went to Europe. Lucy got more "local color" than she bargained for when she climbed into a wine vat to stomp grapes with her bare feet and ended up in a wrestling match with a strong, angry Italian woman. *Roman Holiday* (1953) was about a runaway princess; even ancient Rome was featured in a series of movies about the Roman Empire, including Shakespeare's *Julius Caesar*. Italian movie stars Sophia Loren and Anna Magnani were so well liked by American audiences that they both won Academy Awards for Best Actress.

France was equally photogenic. *An American in Paris,* about an American GI who stays in Paris to paint after the war, won the Academy Award for Best Picture in 1951; in *Sabrina* (1954), the plain-Jane title character went to a cooking school with a view of the Eiffel Tower and came back looking like a *Vogue* model—and she could crack an egg one-handed. *To Catch a Thief,* directed by suspense master Alfred Hitchcock in 1955, showed the glories of the French Riviera. It also had dialogue that was very suggestive for the time: gorgeous Grace Kelly asks Cary Grant if he wants a breast or a leg—but all she's offering him is chicken. Brigitte Bardot, the French "sex kitten," popularized the new bikini bathing suit. Americans went on whirlwind tours through Europe, where the dollar was strong. They fell in love with the food.

In France, a new style of cooking was developing throughout the 1950s and 1960s. Its leading chefs were Ferdinand Point, Paul Bocuse, Michel Guérard, Jean and Pierre Troisgros, and Alain Chapel. This new style altered the *grande cuisine* of Escoffier in several ways. It broke the three-century-old tradition of relying on roux as a thickening agent and used lower-fat stock reductions instead. Presentation was Asian-influenced and asymmetrical, with the focus on color, texture, size, and shape. Food was "art on a plate." Escoffier's parsley garnish was gone. In 1973, two food critics, Gault and Millau, gave the new cooking a name—*nouvelle cuisine*.

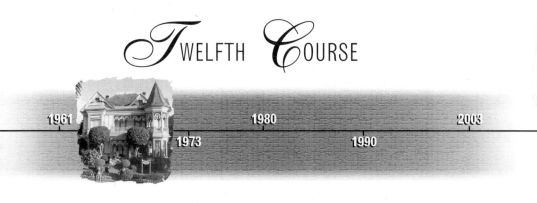

TWELFTH COURSE

Revolutions in Cuisines and Cultures: The 1960s Through the Next Millennium

THE SIXTIES: THE CIVIL RIGHTS REVOLUTIONS

The 1960s was a decade of political and social upheaval throughout the world. Students rioted in Paris, New York, and California. Millions of Americans protested the war in Vietnam, a former French colony. African countries revolted, shaking off their colonial masters. And African-Americans pointed out that one hundred years after President Lincoln freed the slaves in the Civil War, they still couldn't vote, serve on juries, attend schools with white people, or sit at public lunch counters. In 1963, hundreds of thousands of Americans of all races, ages, and genders marched at the Washington Monument and heard the Reverend Dr. Martin Luther King Jr. tell the world, "I have a dream"—that people will be judged by what's inside them, not by the color of their skin; millions more saw him on television. African-American men shook off hundreds of years of being insulted by being called "boy" and started addressing each other as "man." Because of the civil rights movement, advertising icons like Aunt Jemima and Uncle Ben got face-lifts to look more like professional people and less like happy slaves. Not only African-Americans struggled for rights; so did women, gays, Chicanos, Native Americans, and Asian-Americans.

Americans continued their love affair with speed in cars, airplanes, and food. At first, if you wanted food, you had to go to a restaurant.

Then you could call ahead and the food was ready when you got there. At some restaurants, you didn't even have to go inside—there was a drive-through window. In the 1960s, food got even faster—the restaurant came to you. Domino's Pizza was the first fast food delivered to your door. And Julia Child came to your television.

"Bon Appétit!"—Julia Child and Jackie Kennedy

In 1961, after years of writing and recipe testing, and 11 years after graduating from the Cordon Bleu, Julia Child, along with Simone Beck and Louisette Bertholle, wrote *Mastering the Art of French Cooking.* It revolutionized Americans' relationship to food, especially French food.

In 1963, Julia Child revolutionized the teaching of cooking when she appeared on Boston's public broadcasting station, WGBH, as *The French Chef.* Her purpose was to take the mystery out of French cooking, to make it accessible to anyone in America, and she did. The kitchen on Julia Child's television program looked like an average American kitchen because it was hers, designed by her husband, Paul. She cooked on an electric stove and used average kitchen knives and ingredients that could be found in any American supermarket. Quiche and other French foods became extremely popular.

In 1966, her picture was on the cover of *Time* magazine, which called her "Our Lady of the Ladle." The television programs *Julia Child and Company, Julia Child and More Company,* and *Dinner with Julia* followed. In 1981, she was one of the founders of the American Institute of Wine and Food (AIWF). In 1989, she wrote *The Way to Cook,* the first cookbook offered as a main selection by the Book of the Month Club. She was one of the founders of the James Beard Foundation and, with Jacques Pepin, of the new culinary history program at Boston University. Her name is on an award for Best Cookbook given by the International Association of Culinary Professionals (IACP), which she also helped to found. Her numerous books are on the shelf of every professional and amateur cook in America. Her kitchen is now at the Smithsonian's National Museum of American History. Her pots and pans are at Copia. Her generosity and commitment to food are everywhere.

Although Julia Child made it possible to cook French food without special equipment, Chuck Williams liked special equipment. Beginning as a hardware store owner in Sonoma, California, north of San Francisco, Williams went to France and brought equipment back to his store. It was immediately popular, so he opened another one, in Beverly Hills, then more. As a character on the television show *Sud-*

denly Susan remarked, "Once you've discovered fire, it's just a short hop to Williams-Sonoma."

French food reached Washington, D.C., too, in 1961, when John Fitzgerald Kennedy (JFK), the young, good-looking, Harvard-educated Irish Catholic senator from Massachusetts, and his wife, Jacqueline Bouvier Kennedy, became president and first lady. The White House became a social focal point of the United States. The Kennedys hired a chef who was trained in classical French cooking, René Verdon. Jackie, as she became known, was of French descent and had spent her junior year at Vassar in France. When the couple attended state dinners in France, she spoke to the guests in French; when they went to South America, she gave speeches in Spanish. Unfortunately, the first lady was not fluent in German, so when Kennedy went to Berlin and gave a speech to show solidarity with the people of Berlin, which had been split into two cities by a wall the communists built, he said, "*Ich bin ein Berliner.*" He thought he said, "I am from Berlin," which would have been "*Ich bin Berliner*"; what he really said was, "I am a Berliner"—which is a jelly doughnut.

Feast and Famine

In the 1960s, overabundance caught up with Americans—obesity became a problem. Weight Watchers held its first meeting in 1963. Other diet organizations followed: Overeaters Anonymous, patterned after the Alcoholics Anonymous program; the Australian program Jenny Craig; even a Christian Weigh Down Diet, which urged its members to get "slim for Him."[1] Millions of Americans were going to health clubs and drinking diet soda—Diet-Rite, Tab, Diet Pepsi, Fresca. In 1975, dieting even reached beer when Miller introduced Miller Lite. The slogans were "Thin is in" and "You can't be too rich or too thin"—except for the increase in eating disorders like anorexia nervosa and bulimia.

In the 1960s the United States saw food as an issue of national security. Underfed populations in other countries could revolt. Scientists had nearly wiped out malaria by spraying with DDT, invented a liquid vaccine that prevented polio, and cured infections with antibiotics like penicillin and sulfa. After these medical miracles, what was left? Miracle food—genetically engineered soybeans and dwarf rice that had a short growing time, a phenomenal yield, and would grow anywhere in Asia would stamp out famines like the one that killed approximately 20 million people in China between 1958 and 1961.[2] The United States, the largest grower of rice in the world, built the International Rice Research

Institute in the Philippines. In 1965, Ferdinand Marcos was elected president of the Philippines on the slogan "Progress is a grain of rice." The technical name of the rice was IR8, but it was called Than Nong, after the Vietnamese god of agriculture. The miracle rice did everything it was supposed to do except taste good.

THE SEVENTIES: THE FOOD REVOLUTION

California Cuisine—Alice Waters

If California were a country, it would be the fifth richest one in the world, after the United States, Japan, Germany, and England, and ahead of France, China, Italy, Canada, and Brazil. The tenth wealthiest economy in the world is the Los Angeles, California, area, ahead of Mexico and the remaining countries in the world. California, with an annual economy over one trillion dollars, has more people than any other state in the United States[3] and the most abundant food-producing area in the world—the vast Central Valley that runs north and south, half the length of the state, between the coastal mountain range and the Sierra Nevada mountains.[4]

In 1971, a landmark in the history of food took place in Berkeley, California—Alice Waters opened a restaurant called Chez Panisse. Panisse was a character who displays unconditional love in the French film trilogy *Marius* (1931), *Fanny* (1932), and *César* (1936). The movies take place in Provence, the home of the cuisine that inspired Alice Waters. Like other famous food people, Waters didn't start out intending to have a career in food. She was a kindergarten teacher who went to France and fell in love with the country and the food. When she found mesclun salad greens, she brought the seeds back and grew them herself. She was also inspired by British writer Elizabeth David's passion for Mediterranean cooking, her desire to bring the "flavour of those blessed lands of sun and sea and olive trees into . . . English kitchens."[5] In turn, Waters influenced another generation of chefs and food producers like Mark Miller, Lindsey Shere, Wolfgang Puck, and Francis Ford Coppola. Her cookbook, *Chez Panisse Fruit,* came out in 2002.

Another food landmark occurred in 1971, also on the West Coast. Three friends got together and opened a coffeehouse in Seattle, Washington. They named it after a character in Herman Melville's 19th-century novel about an obsessed sea captain's hunt for a great white whale, Moby Dick—Starbucks.

Healthy Food: Spa, *Minceur*, and Vegetarian Cuisine

In 1973, the Moosewood Restaurant, a collectively owned vegetarian restaurant, opened in Ithaca, New York. The food and the seasonings made vegetarian cooking exciting, spicy, and ethnic. Cookbooks like *The Moosewood Cookbook, The Enchanted Broccoli Forest,* and others followed. They gave vegetarianism a new taste.

Nouvelle cuisine, pared down even more and stripped of fat, resulted in super-lean cuisines like spa cuisine and *cuisine minceur* (French for "lean cuisine"). Many people thought that cutting out fats was the way to immortality. Nathan Pritikin, who ran the Pritikin Longevity Center near the beach in Santa Monica, California, touted the physical benefits of eating no fat and jogging. In 1983, *The Pritikin Promise: 28 Days to a Longer Life* became a *New York Times* best-seller. The Pritikin diet allowed absolutely no fat, sugar, or oil. Around the same time, a young medical doctor, Dr. Dean Ornish, had an idea that patients recovering from heart attacks and surgery would do better and with less medicine if they changed their diets drastically. He contacted a food writer, Martha Rose Shulman, who came up with "heart-healthy" recipes. The pilot program was a great success. The American Heart Association adopted the concept and soon restaurants were sporting menus with a ♥ next to the healthy, approved dishes. Shulman went on to write many other cookbooks, like *Mediterranean Light.* (For more heart-healthy recipes, see Martha-rose-shulman.com.) Spas like the Golden Door north of San Diego, California, founded in 1958 (the same year as the Barbie doll), provided very low-calorie cuisine based on organic fruits and vegetables from their own gardens prepared by classically trained chefs. In 2003, the Golden Door's weekly rate was $6,275. Farmers' markets and food festivals sprang up all over the United States in response to the demand for the freshest ingredients. In 1990, California passed the toughest organic food law in the United States.

At the other end of the food spectrum were desserts. In 1977, a woman opened a store in Palo Alto, California, in spite of having been told by everyone that she could never make a living selling nothing but cookies. Mrs. Fields proved them wrong. The following year, two friends learned how to make ice cream through a correspondence course from Pennsylvania State University and sold what they had learned in their lessons in a run-down converted gas station in Burlington, Vermont. Ben & Jerry's became an ice cream empire.

The Gingerbread Mansion Inn.
Courtesy Bob Von Norman

Urban Renewal and Gentrification: Boston Market and B&B's

Faneuil Hall Market, Boston, which spawned the Boston Market restaurant chain, was one of the first urban redevelopment projects. It took a downtown area that had been warehouses and public space and renovated it into small retail and food shops. The same trend continued in other cities. New Yorkers discovered old factories and warehouses with solid wood floors that could hold thousands of pounds; they turned the raw space, sometimes an entire floor, into artists' lofts. In more remote areas, old farmhouses and even lighthouses were turned into the newest getaway craze: the bed-and-breakfast, or B&B. Unlike an impersonal hotel, the B&B provided chatty owners who lived on the premises, comforting fireplaces in the bedrooms (and sometimes the bathrooms), goose-down quilts, liqueur nightcaps, and freshly baked breads, rolls, and muffins for breakfast. The California coast abounds in B&B's; one town that made a fortune turning California redwoods into lumber and then went into a decline revived by recycling its past and restoring its architecture. Eureka, California, has more places on the National Register of Historic Places than any other town in the United States. Eureka and the surrounding area north of San Francisco boast many B&B's, hotels, restaurants, and private homes that began as Victorian mansions with the elaborate trim and detail known as gingerbread. The photograph on the previous page, a bed-and-breakfast in Ferndale, California, is a real gingerbread house—the Gingerbread Mansion Inn.

THE EIGHTIES: THE RESTAURANT REVOLUTION

In the 1980s, Americans continued their healthy living and exercise craze. The baby boomers drank designer waters, joined health clubs, and exercised until their joints wore out. They looked for herbal and vitamin solutions to their problems. Eventually, glucosamine chondroitin arrived to help their joints. Saint John's Wort eased their depression. Echinacea cured their colds. They took gingko biloba to help them remember when to take everything else.

The Zagat Guide

In 1979, two New York City attorneys, both Yale Law School graduates (he went to Harvard, she went to Vassar), turned a hobby into a business. Their informal system of rating restaurants for friends evolved into best-selling guides for Tim and Nina Zagat and revolutionized the business of restaurant criticism. Unlike newspaper and magazine reviews, Zagat reviews don't depend on just one person. Over 100,000 people review restaurants in 45 cities by filling out a detailed questionnaire.

The Iranian Revolution Comes to Beverly Hills Restaurants

There was another important shift in world politics in the 1970s. In 1971, England withdrew from the Middle East, leaving a power vacuum. In 1978, an Islamic fundamentalist revolution led by a religious leader, the Ayotollah Khomeini, overthrew the shah of Iran and took the American embassy in the capital, Teheran, and all of its employees hostage. The shah and the royal family had to flee, as well as thousands of Iranians who were used to doing business with Western countries, especially the United States. The women didn't wear long dresses and veils; they went to college, had jobs, and drove cars.

These Iranians brought their Persian cuisine and culture with them to the United States, especially to southern California. Iranian restaurants, groceries, and bakeries sprang up in Beverly Hills and West Los Angeles, including one restaurant with a *tannur*, a freestanding clay oven like an Indian tandoor. Signs in the Farsi language lined Westwood Boulevard just south of the University of California. Menus offered items like *hummus, polos* (rice-based meat dishes), and *fesenjan* (meat stew in a pomegranate and walnut sauce). Fine pastry shops that sold baklava side by side with eclairs and *petits fours* showed the French influence on Middle Eastern food.

Iran stopped selling oil to the United States. Prices rose. Americans experienced something they had not experienced since World War II—shortages. They got up before dawn to drive to gas stations and wait in long lines for a limited number of gallons of expensive gas. The situation in the Middle East was stabilized briefly after the Gulf War in 1990, when the United States stepped in at the request of Kuwait to protect it and its oil fields (originally developed and owned by America's Gulf Oil and British Petroleum, then nationalized by Kuwait) from invasion by Iraqis under their leader, Saddam Hussein.

One long-term result of the oil crisis of the 1970s was that Japan, always short of energy, made a conscious decision to focus on electronics, including energy-efficient ones. Now this technology runs many appliances. Electronic sensors stop cooking food when it's done, switch lights off when people leave a room, and sense what's in the dishwasher.

The New Immigration and Ethnic Restaurants

In the 1980s, changes in immigration laws passed in 1965 began to show in an explosion of new immigrants—about 1 million a year in the last two decades of the 20th century. The immigration wave that had occurred in New York and other eastern cities at the end of the 19th century occurred on the West Coast at the end of the 20th, with one crucial difference. The eastern cities got immigrants from southern and eastern Europe; western immigrants were from Asia, the Middle East, and Central and South America. Just as New York had Little Italy,

German Yorkville, and the Jewish Lower East Side, southern California has Little Saigon (with more Vietnamese than anywhere outside of Vietnam), Little India, Koreatown, and a sprawling new Chinatown in Monterey Park.[6] (There was already a Little Tokyo downtown and a thriving Japanese community on the west side.) The census of 2000 showed that for the first time, whites were not a majority in California. The Hispanic migration was so massive—almost 50 percent of the population of New Mexico, for example—that many of the immigrants do not assimilate, but live in parallel cultures. This immigration caused an explosion of ethnic restaurants. On the same street with Jamba Juice and Jack in the Box are Islamic *halal* butchers, Mexican *panaderias* (bakeries), sushi bars, Brazilian sports bars for watching soccer, Hong Kong–style seafood restaurants, Franco-Caribbean restaurants, bagel stores, Argentine *empanadas,* Thai takeout, and Iranian restaurants. Southwestern can mean Tex-Mex or a region of India.

Southeast Asian Cuisines

Rice is the staple crop in Southeast Asia—the Philippines, Laos, Cambodia, Vietnam, Thailand, Burma, Indonesia. But during the Vietnam War, which ended in a cease-fire in 1973, Vietnam went from a rice-exporting country to a rice-importing one. President Nixon's bombing of Cambodia to flush out Vietnamese communists damaged the country. A terrible tyrant named Pol Pot came to power and killed approximately 2 million Cambodians.

Since what Americans knew about these cuisines was connected to war, they didn't like them. Soldiers complained about fermented fish sauce (called *nuoc mam* in Vietnam, *nam pla* in Thailand). They knew nothing of delicate spring rolls with wrappers made of rice flour instead of wheat flour, or of seafood seasoned with lemongrass and ginger, or of chili and mint combinations. Cilantro was a familiar herb, but Thai basil (also called holy basil) was not. Also foreign were oils flavored with chili, garlic, or scallions. Noodle soups, called *phô,* and peanut sauces, *sate,* fared no better. Now, however, many Americans have acquired the palate necessary to appreciate these sophisticated combinations of Asian fusion food. Thai hot and sour foods show the influence of Chinese Szechwan and Yunnan cuisine. They are intensely flavored with citrus leaves, coriander root, chilis, and lemongrass like the shrimp soup *tom yung kung.* Noodles like crisp-fried *mee krob* also show the Chinese influence. Desserts perfumed with jasmine oil were probably introduced by Arabs.

In America, these immigrant groups followed the same pattern as earlier groups. At first, cooking was done at home, then in restaurants that catered to the immigrants, then in crossover restaurants for the general public. The first Thai cookbook, *The Original Thai Cookbook* by Jennifer Brennan, wasn't published in the United States until 1981. By the end of the 1990s, mainstream American publishing was producing many cookbooks devoted to the foods of Southeast Asia. They are the new style of cookbook writing, which includes not just cuisine, but culture, history, and memoir. More and more, in the global world and the global economy, people want to know not just what they are eating, but why. Like the cuisine, the authors of many of these books are multicultural and have lived in Asia, Europe, and the United States. Some recent Vietnamese cookbooks include *The Vietnamese Cookbook, Pleasures of the Vietnamese Table, The Food of Vietnam, Foods of Vietnam, Lemongrass and Lime,* and *Hot, Sour, Salty, Sweet.* Thai cookbooks include *Cracking the Coconut: Classic Thai Home Cooking; The Food of Thailand; Thailand, The Beautiful Cookbook; True Thai; Simply Thai; Easy Thai;* and *Thai Cooking Made Easy. The Best of Vietnamese and Thai Cooking* covers both bases.

There were changes in more than just the food in restaurants. Hispanics went into kitchens in record numbers. By 2002, they were 25 percent of all commercial cooks, including in high-profile restaurants.[7] Women caused changes in the front of the house. When a professional woman took a male client to dinner at the elegant L'Orangerie restaurant in the late 1970s, her menu had food items but no prices on it. The male client's had food *and* prices. Only male patrons at the restaurant were given menus with prices, because it was assumed that they would pay the bill. Women were not allowed to know how much things cost to spare their poor brains the effort of dealing with numbers and money. A lawsuit later, all patrons at restaurants get the same menu. Although women had been able to get credit in their own names since 1973, it was still unusual for a woman—even a professional woman—to buy dinner for a man. In the 21st century, it is commonplace.

Northern Italian

In the 1980s, Americans "discovered" Italian food all over again. This time it was the (mostly) tomatoless northern Italian food from Tuscany, Emilia-Romagna, Genoa. Pesto Genovese ("from Genoa")—basil, pine nuts, olive oil, and Parmesan cheese—became popular and soon had innumerable imitators. Parsley, sage, and cilantro were mixed with pecans, almonds, walnuts, or pumpkin seeds. Pasta sauces were cream and Parmesan cheese: alfredo, not tomato. Americans discovered other starches like rice and corn—risotto and polenta. *Tiramisù* (literally, "pick me up") became a popular dessert. It was assembled, not cooked, made from food that would be on hand in an average Italian household: coffee, ladyfingers or leftover sponge cake, mascarpone cheese, cocoa. In 1975, nouvelle spread to Italian when pasta primavera—"springtime pasta," with vegetables—was invented at New York's Le Cirque restaurant. Spaghetti and meatballs in tomato sauce were *finito* in upper-class restaurants.

Fetal Alcohol Syndrome

In 1989, Michael Dorris, a Native American professor of anthropology at Dartmouth College in Hanover, New Hampshire, published a book called *The Broken Cord*. It was the agonizing story of his discovery of the disease from which his adopted son was suffering, fetal alcohol syndrome or FAS. Drinking during pregnancy could cause severe central nervous system damage to the fetus; and seizures and a shortened life after the child was born. Dorris exposed the history of United States–Native American relations that had led to such despair on the reservations that young men carry can openers in their pockets to puncture spray cans of Lysol, smear the gel on bread, eat it to get high—and suffer severe nervous system damage. Soon after, Congress passed a law stating that labels warning women of the dangers of consuming alcohol during pregnancy had to be placed on all bottles of alcoholic beverages.

THE NINETIES: THE RISE OF THE CELEBRITY CHEF

In 1991, the communist government of the USSR came to an end and the Cold War was over. But a war for control of the television food audience was heating up.

The Food Network and Food Empires: Puck, Stewart, Lagasse

Some of the shows on the Food Network: Sarah Moulton's *Cooking Live,* Gale Gand's *Sweet Dreams,* and *Two Hot Tamales,* hosted by Susan Feniger and Mary Sue Milliken. Bobby Flay traveled across America, unearthing clambakes in Massachusetts and burgoo in Kentucky. Mario Batali and his sidekick Rooney ate their way across Italy from antipasto to zeppole. A knock on the door could be Gordon Elliott, bringing along a chef to surprise Mr. and Mrs. Average American and family with an amazing dinner cooked from odds and ends they found in the refrigerator, freezer, and kitchen cabinets. Chefs explained food chemistry with the aid of pop-up experts and graphics. *Food 911's* Tyler Florence could cure a sick bouillabaisse or whatever else ailed your food.

One of the most popular shows on the Food Network was *Iron Chef*. Dubbed from Japanese, this one-hour show pitted chefs cooking in Japan—male chefs—against each other. Each show centered around a theme food that was literally unveiled for the contestants for the first time: giant clam, eggplant, pumpkin. It is cooking as spectacle, cooking as contest, cooking as gladiatorial combat. It is the "straight" version of a comedy routine that John Belushi invented on the television show *Saturday Night Live* called "Samurai Chef," in which he hacked sandwiches to ribbons with a samurai sword.

In the 1970s, a shy young Austrian named Wolfgang Puck was the chef at Ma Maison, a Hollywood restaurant with an unlisted telephone number. A few years later, with the encouragement of his wife, Barbara Lazaroff, he broke out on his own. Puck reinvented pizza and pasta. Spago opened on Sunset Boulevard in West Hollywood, California, in 1982 and became wildly popular, especially with celebrities. Parties were held there after the Academy Awards. Frozen Puck pizzas and soups were sold in mainstream supermarkets. In January 2001, Wolfgang Puck began his own television show on the Food Network.

Martha Stewart went from model to Barnard graduate to Wall Street stockbroker to Connecticut caterer to Martha Stewart OmniMedia. The Polish-American seemed to discover what alchemists in the Middle Ages couldn't: how to turn everything she touched into gold. However, at the time this book was being written, Ms. Stewart was facing possible charges of insider trading—that she used advance knowledge of the stock market to sell stock in a company before its value dropped. Because of this accusation, there was talk that Martha Stewart might be forced to resign. Many felt this would seriously damage the company, which depends on her image.[8]

Emeril Lagasse, a Portuguese-American from Massachusetts and a 1978 graduate of Johnson & Wales, developed a tremendous following throughout the United States, even though his first half-hour television show was not exceptional. The second time around he based the show on his outgoing personality, and audiences responded. He now has a one-hour daily television show, a line of sauces, cookware, and cookbooks. Lagasse, with his down-to-earth style, became so popular that the Food Network sometimes seems like "all Emeril, all the time."

Comfort Food

As the Baby Boomers aged, they lapsed from their low-fat diets and went back to the comfort foods of their 1950s childhoods: meat loaf with gravy and mashed potatoes, and Rice Krispies Treats. They also comforted themselves with $6 billion worth of cookies a year and food they had eaten sitting around fires at summer camp.[9] Two of the old favorites were s'mores and banana boats.

RECIPE

 'MORES[10]

First make a campfire. Then take a graham cracker and cover it with a Hershey bar. Then put some marshmallows on a stick and roast them over the campfire. Slide the hot, toasted marshmallows off the stick (making sure to get some on your fingers, so you have to lick them) and onto the Hershey bar on the graham cracker. Cover with more Hershey bar and top with another graham cracker. The hot marshmallow melts the chocolate and welds the entire sandwich together. It is a symphony of taste and texture: hot marshmallow, melted chocolate, crunchy cracker. Everybody wants "s'more."

RECIPE

ANANA BOATS

First make a campfire. Then take a banana and peel one side of it, being careful not to detach the peel from the banana. Then scoop out some of the inside of the banana and eat it. Stuff marshmallows and pieces of chocolate into the scooped-out section. Put the flap of peel back down, wrap the banana in foil, and put it in the coals of the campfire for a few minutes until the banana is warm and the marshmallows get gooey and the chocolate melts.

Soon, s'mores went upscale, served with a knife and fork in restaurants with tablecloths, napped in pools of raspberry coulis. Banana boats suffered the same fate.

Frankenfood and Zoonoses

Americans introduced irradiated food to extend the shelf life of food that would otherwise perish. Soon, "nuked" food like soups appeared in pop-top or pour-spout boxes even in health food stores. Americans also introduced the concept of genetically modified (GM) food. The purpose was to produce foods that resisted disease. France resisted the foods. Other European countries were not keen on GM food, either; they especially didn't want GM techniques applied to wines. In France and Italy, where wine is a traditional and sometimes family business going back generations and hundreds of years, wine and wine making methods are sacred. How much this might change remains to be seen.

Zoonoses—diseases that leap from animals to humans—reached frightening proportions in England when bovine spongiform encephalitis, also called BSE or "mad cow disease," crossed over to humans and attacked their brains as the fatal variant Creutzfeldt-Jakob disease. The cause was traced to feeding cows with ground-up parts of other animals like sheep. It caused widespread panic in Europe, and a return to eating vegetables and fish.

Sugar Blues: The Twinkie Defense and "Diabesity"

In the 1970s, sugar became a villain. It had gone from being a medicine and a cure-all in the Middle Ages to an upper-class condiment, a popular sweetener, and finally a drug. Sugar intoxication and a sugar "high" were followed by a crash in blood sugar levels that supposedly produced "sugar blues." It even became an excuse for crimes. In San Francisco in 1978, former policeman and city supervisor Dan White shot and killed Mayor George Moscone and openly gay city supervisor Harvey Milk in San Francisco City Hall. He claimed that it was not premeditated even though he brought extra bullets and avoided metal detectors by climbing in a window. His defense: "diminished mental capacity," a chemical imbalance in his brain from eating too much sugar-rich junk food just before the murders. This became known as the "Twinkie defense." The jury found White guilty of only the lesser charge of manslaughter. In 1985, shortly after he was paroled from prison, White shot and killed himself, but there is no record of what he ate immediately beforehand. In 1982, California voters eliminated the diminished-capacity defense.[11]

While sugar as a cause of criminal behavior remains open to debate, sugar as a cause of physical illness is well established. Diabetes is a disease in which the pancreas cannot process sugar properly, which can lead to organ damage. Ninety to 95 percent of those with diabetes have what is called type 2. This usually strikes after the age of 40, which is why it is also called adult-onset diabetes. However, from 1990 to 1998, diabetes increased by one-third in the United States. The vast majority of this increase—76 percent—was among people age 30 to 39. It is much more prevalent in the southeastern and midwestern states and in California. It also has preferences: Native Americans, Alaskan natives, and African-Americans have a much higher incidence of the disease. The two major causes are an increase in obesity and a decrease in exercise. Sixty percent of Americans do not exercise regularly, and 25 percent do not exercise at all.[12] A new word entered the English language: *diabesity.*

Some obese people view these medical facts as a personal attack. They have organized and claim it is possible to be fat *and* fit, despite all evidence to the contrary. One class of deliberately obese professional athletes provides an example. Sumo athletes eat foods that are healthy—vegetables, meat, and fish—but portions that are not, so they can gain weight. And they suffer from all the illnesses caused by obesity: diabetes, high blood pressure, heart and joint problems. Their life expectancy is ten years less than that of the average Japanese male. The Japan Sumo Association decided to set weight limits because the sport was going out of sumo—extremely heavy men (412 pounds average) couldn't execute complicated moves and it was becoming simply a matter of one big-bellied man trying to push another big-bellied man out of the ring.[13]

Fat Blockers and the French Paradox

Americans say they want to lose weight. They just don't want to have to change what they eat or feel deprived while they do it. They want to have their cake and eat it, too. One of the first attempts at fat blocking was a drug combination unregulated by the FDA. Fen-phen was removed from the market when its users began experiencing serious side effects, even death. Then came Olestra, a fat-like substance that was not absorbed in the intestines but had side effects such as

𝒞ULINARY 𝒫UZZLE

≫ THE FRENCH PARADOX ≪

Americans do not understand how the French can eat the way they do and stay healthy. The French diet is high in fat, but there is much less heart disease in France than in America. This is called the French Paradox.[14] Many theories have been advanced as to why. Smaller portions in France? Higher wine consumption keeps them healthier? Or maybe it's their attitude, their *joie de vivre*—joy in living. After all, the entire country stops work in August and goes on vacation. There are also close ties with family, and the French workday ends at a reasonable hour so everyone can go home for dinner, unlike the American workday, which is 24/7. Although the French have less heart disease than Americans now, nutritionists say this will change if the French diet shifts to more fast food.

diarrhea. There were other fat blocker substances, and low-fat or no-fat desserts that compensated for the reduction in fat with an increase in sugar. Lay's came out with potato chips that were baked instead of fried, and the company mounted one of the most expensive campaigns in advertising history, using supermodels and Miss Piggy the Muppet.

THE NEXT MILLENNIUM

"What we eat has changed more in the last forty years than in the previous forty thousand."

—*Eric Schlosser* in *Fast Food Nation*[15]

On December 31, 1999, much of the world went into a panic over the coming year 2000 (Y2K). Like people in the Middle Ages one thousand years earlier, some expected the world to end at the beginning of the new millennium; others stockpiled food, water, and ammunition because they feared a worldwide breakdown of the computer systems that control telephones, traffic lights, electricity, and national security systems. None of this came to pass.

However, drastic changes had occurred in American life by the year 2000. Just as by 1920 a majority of Americans lived in cities, by 2000 a majority of Americans lived in suburbs. In the beginning of the 19th century, the vast majority of Americans were farmers. In the beginning of the 20th century, most Americans worked in factories. In the beginning of the 21st century, the fastest-growing sector of the economy was service jobs, especially restaurants, which employed 3.5 million people, many at minimum wage. About 50 cents of every dollar Americans spent on food was spent in a restaurant, predominantly fast food, often drive-through—more than $110 billion.[16] The typical American diet of meat and potatoes became hamburgers and french fries, mostly frozen, freeze-dried, high in fat and salt.

At the same time, part of the population was very concerned about nutrition. On December 20, 2000, the United States Department of Agriculture (USDA) set national standards for organic foods and ordered that labels be applied to foods in 2002, after farms have been inspected. To rate the label "100 percent organic," foods must meet the following criteria: (1) no irradiated food, (2) no genetically altered food, (3) no synthetic insecticides, (4) no chemical fertilizers, (5) no chemical herbicides, (6) no sewage sludge, and (7) no growth hormones.[17]

The minimum daily nutritional requirements also changed from the four basic food groups to a food pyramid. It still relies more heavily on meat than the food pyramids of other countries. It is also different in what it lacks: other pyramids include exercise and water, as the illustrations on pages 310–311 from Oldways Preservation Trust (www.oldwayspt.org) show.

A Few Words About Windows on the World

Tuesday morning, September 11, 2001. At the southern tip of Manhattan stand the twin towers of the World Trade Center, the tallest buildings in New York since the south tower was completed in 1973. Every day, 50,000 people file into the buildings, which have their own zip code, to work and to visit. They come from New York, New Jersey, Connecticut, Pennsylvania, and more than 60 countries. And all of them have to eat.

At street level is the Big Kitchen, a food court with many small, fast restaurants: Ben & Jerry's ice cream, Mrs. Fields cookies, Pastabreak, the Italian delicatessen Sbarro, and others. In private dining rooms throughout the building, private chefs are preparing meals. On the 106th and 107th floors—the very top—of 1 World Trade Center, 79 staff members are in the kitchens of the Windows on the World restaurants preparing for the rush that will come later in the day and swell the kitchen staff to 450. Some are bringing breakfast to the 500 people attending a business seminar. George Delgado, the head bartender, is sometimes in at this hour, but he worked late the night before, until almost 2:00 A.M.—unusual for a Monday—so he will come in a few minutes later. Carmen Newman, the wine school coordinator in the school run by Kevin Zraly, would be there taking inventory and organizing, but a series of classes has just ended, so she and her husband are on their way to the airport for a vacation. Executive chef Michael Lomonaco, the gifted man who turned around "21" and raised the Windows restaurants to award-winning excellence, will take the 58-second elevator ride up 107 stories in a few minutes, after he gets his new eyeglasses.

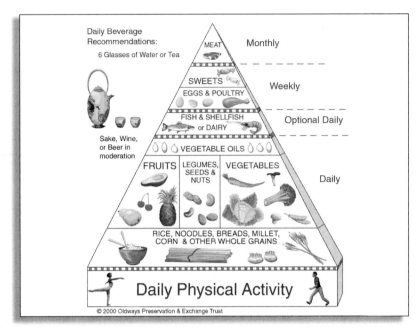

The Asian Diet Pyramid. © *2000 Oldways Preservation & Exchange Trust*

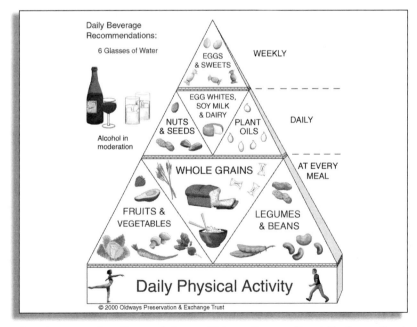

The Vegetarian Diet Pyramid. © *2000 Oldways Preservation & Exchange Trust*

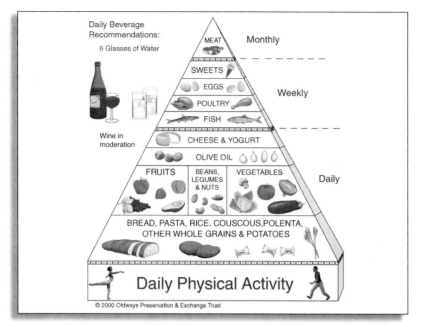

The Mediterranean Diet Pyramid. © *2000 Oldways Preservation & Exchange Trust*

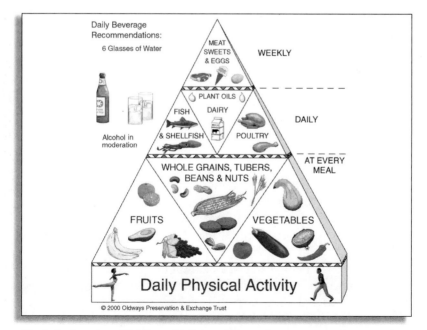

The Latin American Diet Pyramid. © *2000 Oldways Preservation & Exchange Trust*

But Michael Lomonaco will never get into the elevator, because the building will be on fire, filled with exploding jet fuel. Seventy-nine people who worked under him in the kitchens in the sky will not be seen again except in pictures on telephone poles, walls, and bulletin boards all over New York City: Jaime Concepción, from Santo Domingo; José Bienvenido; Ivanh Carpio, a Peruvian; Manuel Ostinbay, from Ecuador; Enrique Gomez; Ysidro Hidalgo, from the Dominican Republic; Antonio Javier-Alvarez, from Mexico. They share wall space with others in the melting pot: O'Doherty, Kawauchi, Benedetti, Snell, Gilligan, Koppelman, Cho, Andrucki, Jones, Mirpuri, Metz, La Fuente, Chin, Amanullah, Takahashi, Samantha.

The Zagat Guide says Windows on the World "put diners close to heaven." The view from the top of the world on the 107th floor was indeed spectacular. As you looked down into the harbor, the Statue of Liberty raised her torch up toward you. There is a special place in my heart for Windows on the World. I got one of my favorite recipes from there—chef Nick Malgieri's frozen amaretto soufflé. I am looking at that soufflé-spattered recipe now. It lists the restaurants that were in existence when Windows first opened: the Restaurant, the Cellar in the Sky, the City Lights Bar, the Hors D'Oeuvrerie, and the Statue of Liberty Lounge. Now, there is—there were—Windows on the World, Wild Blue, and the Greatest Bar on Earth, all award-winning and all gone. The lunch special on Tuesday, September 11, would have been crisp sweetbread salad; at dinner, roast suckling pig. Gone are the soft-hearted devil's food cupcakes and the private dining and catering rooms that served two to 2,000: the Ballroom, where I attended the wedding of two college classmates; the Hudson, Manhattan, and Pinnacle Suites; the Cellar in the Sky; the Liberty Suites. But some of the recipes live on.

George Delgado, the mixologist at Windows on the World (now at www.barmanac.com), invented many drinks, some inspired by the vistas from Windows. One mimics the colors of the Statue of Liberty, a gift from our French friends in 1886. The famous words "Give me your tired, your poor, your huddled masses yearning to breathe free" by Jewish-American poet Emma Lazarus are on the base of the statue. Delgado posted the recipe on the July 2001 Windows on the World Web site.

In the weeks after the attack, looking at the pictures of the firemen at ground zero, so many of them big, strong, Irish lads, it could have been 150 years ago, and them just off the coffin ships, fleeing the famine, stepping ashore in New York, working to build the city the way they were sifting through its rubble now—one shovelful at a time.

WINDOWS ON THE WORLD

DRINK OF THE MONTH—JULY 2001

GEORGE DELGADO'S
LADY LIBERTINI MARTINI

"The Statue of Liberty . . . may seem diminutive from up here (107 stories up), but what she stands for is far greater than the tallest buildings on earth. . . . As I gaze out over what is now called Liberty Island, I think of this statue's rich history as well as her symbolic significance, and decide that she needs a tributary cocktail of her own. Not just any cocktail would do. It would have to be the truly American classic, the king of cocktails, the Martini.

3 oz. Grey Goose Vodka
¼ oz. Monin Kiwi Syrup

In an ice-filled mixing glass, add the kiwi syrup and the Grey Goose Vodka (which I consider to be 'the other great gift from France'). Shake it thoroughly and give a quick check on the color. It should match the green, rusted copper color of the Statue of Liberty. If it's too pale, add up to ¼ oz. more of the kiwi syrup. But remember, the syrup is for color only; the end result should be a vodka martini. Now you can strain the cocktail into a chilled martini glass. For aesthetics you may try a red-colored garnish like a speared cherry or an orange twist to represent the 'torch of liberty.'

I wish you could join us here at Windows on the World to make this celebratory tribute, but if you can't, please try this at home and enjoy! Have a happy and safe 4th of July."

Source: © 2001 George Delgado/Promixology, Inc.

Fine Dining: Life as a Work of Art

I had a transforming dinner shortly after September 11, 2001. I arrived on the East Coast after more than ten hours of travel from Los Angeles—getting to the airport in the middle of the night, standing in lines of nervous, somber people for hours, going through checkpoint after checkpoint, changing planes, renting a car. I was tired, hungry, and cranky. The beautiful dining room and the kind people who treated me—a grubby walk-in off the street—like a queen put me in mind of ancient Greece: these people understood the needs of the weary traveler and the obligations of the host. They made me feel for the first time since the attack that there was beauty in life. The restaurant was the St. Andrews Café in Hyde Park, New York, the first restaurant rotation for students at the Culinary Institute of America. This is life lived as art.

The great American architect Frank Lloyd Wright believed in life lived as art, too. At Taliesen, the school he founded in Spring Green, Wisconsin, it is the job of one student to get up early every morning and create a work of art for the others. This work of art is composed of furniture, napkins, and cups and saucers. The tables in the dining room are a variety of shapes, like Tinkertoys: round, square, rectangular. The student arranges them in a new design, chooses napkins and placemats, picks wildflowers in season. This way, first thing every day, everyone is stimulated and challenged by new shapes, forms, colors, textures. And that's *before* the food. It is an old concept that is still new and meaningful.

Everything Old Is New Again

As the new millennium begins, history repeats itself with new twists. Now, meats like buffalo and ostrich, formerly consumed by Stone Age tribal people, are sold in American supermarkets. Pomegranate juice, used 5,000 years ago in the Middle East, is marketed in the United States as a health drink, an antioxidant more powerful than green tea or cranberry juice. Ancient butchering practices proved their worth again after an outbreak of hyperthyroidism—too much thyroid hormone—made many people seriously ill in the Midwest. It was traced back to a butcher shop that had switched from kosher to traditional butchering and had mixed toxic animal organs in with the ground beef, something that would have been impossible with kosher butchering. Roman excesses returned in the availability of truffles, chocolate, caviar, fine wines, and other foods that were affordable only by royalty when they first entered the culinary world. Verjus, the juice of unripe grapes and out of vogue since the Middle Ages, is produced commercially in Napa, California, as the wine-friendly alternative to vinegar in salad dressing. *Moros y cristianos,* the black beans and rice from Spain in the Middle Ages, is still a staple in Cuban restaurants, but it is called just *moros,* and in an age of increased health consciousness, sometimes the rice is brown. The Aztec food that the Spaniards couldn't bring themselves to eat—spirulina—is sold in health food stores.

In the summer of 2000, locust plagues infested the American West as they had more than one hundred years earlier.[18] This time, they were fought with poisons and pesticides instead of hopper dozers. Almost 100 years after the ice cream cone was invented, chef Thomas Keller of the French Laundry in Napa Valley reinvented it as a savory cone or cornet and scooped salmon tartare into it. Chefs Mark Miller, Stephan Pyles, and John Sedlar took tamales upscale with jerk shrimp, truffle butter, foie gras, roasted pheasant, duck confit, and venison chorizo. Chefs were celebrities again, as they were after the French Revolution. Soft-drink giants like Coke and Pepsi extended their markets by inventing "health" drinks with herbal additives that, like the patent medicines of 100 years earlier, promised to cure whatever ailed the consumer. The FDA sent them warning letters.[19] Heirloom tomatoes with names like Black Zebra, Box Car Willie, and Big Rainbow returned to supermarkets again, while the food of new ethnic groups joined the food of older ethnic groups in becoming "typically American." Just as Italian and German foods like pizza, hamburgers, and hot dogs had become "typically American," a Mexican food, salsa, replaced ketchup as the leading condiment in the United States.[20] Fine wining and dining on the railroad reappeared on the Napa Wine Train. In 2001, the chefs who began nouvelle cuisine—Paul Bocuse, Michel Guérard, Paul Haeberlin, Pierre Troisgros, and Roger Vergé—declared it *fini.*[21] California chef Roxanne Klein brought food full circle, from the cooked back to the raw, at her restaurant with no stoves in the kitchen and no food heated higher than 118°F. "Cookies," Dutch in origin and first described in print by Amelia Simmons in 1796, now mean computer files. The Internet also gave America's most popular canned luncheon meat a new meaning and turned it into a verb. Through everything, still surviving, but now meaning junk mail on the Internet, there is Spam.

On January 1, 2002, eleven countries in the European Union began using the same currency, the euro. The countries, in alphabetical order, are Austria, Belgium, Finland, France, Germany, Ireland, Italy, Luxembourg, the Netherlands, Portugal, and Spain. These countries (with the exception of Finland) had waged almost constant war against each other for 1,500 years, including nine world wars. They had been city-states, had monarchs, civil wars, revolutions, been split up, been reunified with different boundaries, and, finally, had been turned into democracies or limited monarchies. Now, for the first time since before the Roman Empire fell in A.D. 476, peace reigned among these countries. And menus in every single one had to be rewritten to reflect the new currency.

The Future of Food: Native Seeds, Sustainable Salmon, the Ark, and the Edible Schoolyard

The future of food lies in its past. While some plants are cultivated in increasing numbers, hundreds of species become extinct every year. Scientists call this an ecological disaster. Part of the tragedy is that we do not know what new foods or medicines might have been in these plants that are gone forever. In 1983, Native Seeds/Search (www.nativeseeds.org), a nonprofit organization based in Tucson, Arizona, was founded. It has reclaimed 2,000 varieties of plants cultivated by Native American peoples like the Apache, Yaqui, Paiute, Pima, Hopi, and Navajo. Fifty-five percent

RECIPE

$\mathcal{J}$OY MARTIN'S SALMON CARPACCIO

About 2 pounds of salmon, frozen (flash-frozen at sea is best or have the fish market do it because it removes any chance of parasites)
2 tablespoons salt
Freshly ground pepper
2 tablespoons fresh thyme
2 tablespoons fresh chopped tarragon
2 tablespoons fennel seeds (wild are best), chopped or milled in a grinder
2 tablespoons sugar (optional)
1 cup olive oil
Juice of 2 lemons
2 tablespoons capers

Thaw the salmon. Remove the skin and pin bones. (Most fish markets will do this.) Put the salmon in a nonreactive container. Combine the dry ingredients and sprinkle the salmon on both sides. Add the liquids. Cover the salmon tightly and refrigerate for at least two days and up to five. Turn twice a day. Remove from refrigerator one hour before serving. Hold the fish up to drain all the liquid, strain it, and save. Cut very thin slices of salmon slightly on the diagonal and place them on a serving platter. Whisk the reserved liquid until thick and spoon it over the salmon. Scatter the capers on top.

© The Fish Lady

of the seeds are for the native three sisters—maize, beans, squash. The remaining 45 percent are both Old and New World: black pinto, orange lima, and scarlet runner beans; purple string beans; pink lentils; yellow-fleshed watermelon; wild tomatoes and tomatillos for green salsa. Chili pepper connoisseurs appreciate the locally grown Jemez, Isleta, and Chimayo chilis. Organizations like the Nature Conservancy preserve seeds, too. In addition, governments throughout the world have established more than one hundred germ plasm banks to store seeds and cells. In the United States, the NSSL—the National Seed Storage Laboratory—began at Colorado State University in 1958. Today, more than 232,000 types of seeds are stored there, with plans to save more than one million.[22]

Not only sustainable agriculture, but sustainable livestock production and fishing are important to the future of food. Seafood, halibut, sole, and all five kinds of salmon from Alaska—pink, chum, coho (also known as silver), sockeye, and king (chinook)—are wild because fish farming has been illegal in Alaska since 1990. Salmon are unique. Born in freshwater, they swim out into the ocean, sometimes thousands of miles, live there for years, then return—only once—to the *exact spot* where they were born to lay and fertilize their eggs, sometimes thousands of feet above sea level. (This is beyond the comprehension of mere humans, even scientists.) The salmon are caught at spawning time, when they are heaviest and most loaded with nutrients. Wild Alaska salmon eat marine life like shrimp, herring, and squid, which makes them high in the antioxidant vitamin E and omega-3 oils. They also change color then, to their distinctive pink. (Farmed salmon, in pens, are dyed salmon color.) The state of Alaska monitors how many fish are running, water quality, and other factors to ensure no overfishing. Within one hour of being caught (some by hand on a line), wild Alaska salmon are flash-frozen in a -40°F blast freezer and glazed with a coat of water that freezes and forms an airtight seal to prevent oxidation. (See www.alaskaseafood.com or www.gourmetsalmon.com.) The recipe on the previous page is straight from Alaska, from fisherwoman Joy Martin.

In 1989, the Slow Food movement (www.slowfoodusa.org) was founded in Paris to combat the fast-food trend. Now based in Italy, it has 65,000 members in chapters, called convivia, in 45 countries.[23] Its symbol is the snail; its main project is the Ark. Like Noah's ark, its goal is to save the living things of the earth and to promote biodiversity and high-quality, sustainable food production. Recently, in conjunction with the American Livestock Breeds Conservancy, it reintroduced to the marketplace four excellent-tasting heritage turkeys that have been crowded out by the big-breasted Large White variety.[24] Near extinction are the

Narragansett (fewer than 100 alive), Jersey Buff and American Bronze (fewer than 500 breeding birds each), and Bourbon Red (664 breeding hens).

On Sunday, August 26, 2001 (coincidentally, the eighty-first anniversary of the day the Constitution was amended to give women the right to vote), Chez Panisse turned 30. The $500-per-person celebration was a benefit for the Chez Panisse Foundation. This supports, among other things, the Edible Schoolyard, a project with the Martin Luther King Jr. Middle School in Berkeley, California (www.edibleschoolyard.org). Alice Waters wanted children to learn about food from gardening to cooking to serving so they will eat better. Sustainable, earth-friendly agriculture also teaches children respect for nature and for themselves. Waters believes that "the most neglected schoolroom is the lunchroom."[25] This is especially true since school budget cuts at the end of the 20th century got rid of most of the home economics programs started by Ellen Richards and other professional women at the beginning of the 20th century. It also made cash-needy schools easy targets for corporations. Food giants like Taco Bell and Pizza Hut served students lunches; Coca-Cola machines sold them sodas. In 2002, the Los Angeles Unified School District began to reverse this trend when they voted to take the soda machines out of schools.

There are a growing number of projects that promote the healing power of nature and of food: the Garden Project at the San Francisco County Jail, run by Catherine Sneed; the Veterans Administration Hospital garden project in west Los Angeles; Les Dames d'Escoffier school projects throughout the United States; the Vassar farm; chef Ann Cooper's school on Long Island; in the Midwest, chefs Charlie Trotter and Rick and Deann Bayless. Julia Child, who turned 90 on August 15, 2002, funds children's educational programs with part of the proceeds from the sale of seeds for Julia Child Heirloom Tomatoes. There are many others, and they all have one goal: ensuring good, healthy food for this generation and for all those to come.

> Let us live and eat in peace and good-fellowship, for when God sends the dawn, he sends it for all.
>
> —*Sancho Panza, 1602*[26]

♥

APPENDIX A:
FRENCH PRONUNCIATION

1. THE CIRCUMFLEX ACCENT: ^

This just means that the letter *s* got dropped on the way from Latin to French; it has nothing to do with pronunciation. For example, *goût* (pronounced *goo*) means "taste," which in Latin is *gustus*. *Château*—castle—used to be *castellum*.

2. THE LETTER *S*

The final *s* is not pronounced unless there is an *e* after it, and then it sounds like *z*. For example, the knife cut *brunois* is pronounced *broon-WAH*. Add an *e*—*brunoise*—and it becomes *broon-WAHZ*. The same holds true for *françoise, niçoise,* and all the other words that end in *-ois*.

3. THE CEDILLE: Ç

This is used to make a *c* sound like *sw*. For example, *niçoise*, as in *salade niçoise*, is pronounced *nee-SWAHZ*.

4. THE FINAL *E*

The final *e* in words like *brunoise* is not pronounced. To indicate that the *e* is supposed to be pronounced, an accent mark is added. Then the *e* is pronounced *ay*. For example, *velouté* sauce: without an accent on the final *e*, it would be pronounced *veh-loot,* instead of *veh-loo-TAY.*

APPENDIX B:
ITALIAN PRONUNCIATION

There are few pronunciation rules in Italian. All the letters are pronounced, and the Italian alphabet has only twenty-four, two fewer than English. The letters *j* and *k* are missing; *g* and *c* fill in for them. Some simple things to remember about Italian pronunciation:

1. PLURAL

Any word that ends in *i* in Italian is already plural; do not add an *s*. For example, *ravioli* and *cannoli* are plural. *Raviolis* is incorrect. So is *cannolis*.

2. EMPHASIS

The emphasis is usually on the second-to-last syllable. For example, spa-GHE-tti.

3. SOMETIMES THE LETTER *C* EQUALS THE LETTER *K*

The letter *c* is pronounced hard, as in *cat*. There are two exceptions: *ce* and *ci* are pronounced *chay* and *chee*. Example: the mushroom, *porcini*, is pronounced *por-CHEE-nee*. To keep the hard *c* sound, put an *h* between the *c* and the *e* or the *i.* Examples: *zucchini,* pronounced *zoo–KEE–nee;* the Italian pasta dish *checca* is pronounced *KAY-kah.*

4. SOMETIMES THE LETTER *G* EQUALS THE LETTER *J*

The letter g is pronounced hard, as in *got.* There are two exceptions: *ge* and *gi* are pronounced like the letter *j.* Example: *gelato* is pronounced *jay–LAH–to.* To keep the hard g sound, put an *h* between the g and the *e* or the *i.* Example: spaghetti. Also, the first syllable of the San Francisco chocolate company Ghirardelli is pronounced like *gear,* not *jeer.*

APPENDIX C:
COOKBOOK AND FOOD BOOKS CHRONOLOGY

Date	Area/Language	Author	Book Title	Importance
	Greece/Greek	Archestratos	(Fragment)	
1st c. A.D.	Rome/Latin	Apicius	*Cookery and Dining in Imperial Rome*	First real cookbook; many sauces
10th c.	Tunisia/Arabic	*Abū Bakr al-Mālikī*	*Riyād al-nufūs*	"Fabulously valuable manuscript for culinary matters"; first mention of the Arab cheese dessert *kunāfa*[1]—Clifford Wright
1061	China/Chinese		*The Illustrated Basic Herbal*	Hundreds of foods described; set standards for botanical illustration in China
Early 13th c.	Muslim/Arabic		*Kitāb waf al-at'ima al-mutada*	94 out of 155 recipes use rosewater
13th c.	Arabic		*Kitāb al-tabīkh fī, al-Maghrib wa'l-Adalus*	Hispano-Muslim; early written reference to couscous
1215	Japan/Japanese		*Kissa yojoki*	First treatise on tea published in Japan
1226	Muslim/Arabic	Al-Baghdadi	*A Baghdad Cookery Book*	Wide variety of foods; sugar; beginning of pastry/confection
Circa 1300	Switzerland/French		*Sion viander*	Little Arab influence; little sugar, no honey

DATE	AREA/LANGUAGE	AUTHOR	BOOK TITLE	IMPORTANCE
14th c.	Naples/Latin	Anonymous	*Liber de Coquina*	First lasagna recipe
1306	France/French		*The Little Treatise*	Little Arab influence; few herbs or vegetables; no sugar or honey
Circa 1370	Switzerland/French	Taillevent	*Le Viandier*	Little Arab influence; little sugar; no honey.
1392/1393	France/French		*Ménagier de Paris*	Compilation of other recipes; daily household cooking
1440	Germany		Gutenberg invents printing press	Books can be more widely read
1457	Rome/Latin	Apicius	*Cookery and Dining in Imperial Rome*	Vatican gets manuscript; Rome rediscovers Apicius
1474	Rome/Latin	Platina	*De honesta voluptate*	First printed cookbook; contemporary Italian cooking; influenced French
1490	France/French	Taillevent	*Le Viandier*	First printed French cookbook
1498	Europe/Latin	Apicius	*Cookery and Dining in Imperial Rome*	Because of printing press, widely available
1505	France/French	Platina	*Platine en francoys*	*De honesta voluptate* translated into French
1510	Brussels/Dutch	Thomas vander Noot	*Eeen notabel boecxke van cokerije*	First cookbook printed in Dutch
1520	Barcelona/Spanish		*Libre del coch*	Catalan cuisine
1604	Brussels/French	Casteau	*Ouverture de cuisine*	Italian influence on international cuisine in original, non-medieval recipes; first *pâte à choux*
1607	France/French		*Le Thresor de santé*	Dietitics
1651	France/French	La Varenne	*Le Cuisinier françois*	Beginning of classical French cooking; first roux
1653	France/French	La Varenne	*Le Pastissier françois*	Probably written with/by an Italian pastry chef
1667	Netherlands/Dutch		*The Sensible Cook*	Dutch food in Old and New Netherlands
1691	France/French	Massialot	*Cuisinier roïal et bourgeois*	First recipes organized under alphabetical headings
1742	America/English	Eliza Smith	*The Compleat Housewife*	First cookbook published in the colonies; author is British
1746	France/French	Menon	*La Cuisinière bourgeoise*	First French cookbook directed to women

DATE	AREA/LANGUAGE	AUTHOR	BOOK TITLE	IMPORTANCE
1796	U.S./English	Amelia Simmons	*American Cookery*	First cookbook written by an American and published in U.S.; chemical leavening, cookies, pumpkin pie
1810	France/French	Nicolas Appert	*L'Art de conserver pendant plusieurs années toutes les substances animales et végétales*	First book on food preservation by canning
1824	U.S./English	Mary Randolph	*The Virginia Housewife*	Considered by some the most influential cookbook in 19th-century U.S.
1829	U.S./English	Lydia Maria Child	*The Frugal Housewife*	Reprinted at least 35 times
1841	U.S./English	Sarah Josepha Hale	*Early American Cookery*	
1841	U.S./English	Catherine Beecher	*Treatise on Domestic Economy*	Anatomy, democracy, health, and diet
1859–1861	Britain/English	Isabella Beeton	*Beeton's Book of Household Management*	Middle-class British Victorian cooking
1864	Australia/English	Edward Abbott	*The English and Australian Cookery Book*	First Australian cookbook
1881	U.S./English	Mrs. Abby Fisher	*What Mrs. Fisher Knows About Old Southern Cooking*	First African-American cookbook; author illiterate
1881	U.S./English	Ellen Richards	*The Chemistry of Cooking and Cleaning*	First woman Ph.D. from MIT; chemistry in cooking
1891	Italy/Italian	Pellegrino Artusi	*La scienza in cucina e l'arte di mangiar bene*	Cornerstone of the Italian culinary tradition
1896	U.S./English	Fannie Farmer	*The Boston Cooking School Cook Book*	Effects of industrialization on cooking
1901	U.S.	Lizzie Black Kander	*The Settlement Cookbook: The Way to a Man's Heart*	Jewish and Jewish-American recipes
1903	France/French	Escoffier	*Le Guide culinaire*	5,000 recipes from the master; first English translation published 1979

DATE	AREA/LANGUAGE	AUTHOR	BOOK TITLE	IMPORTANCE
1930s	Italy/Italian	Marinetti	*The Futurist Cookbook*	Fascist Italian cooking
1931	U.S./English	Irma Rombauer	*The Joy of Cooking*	3,000 copies self-published by widow become best-selling cookbook
1936	U.S./English	Apicius	*Cookery and Dining in Imperial Rome*	First English translation published in the United States, by Vehling
1938	France/French	Montagné	*Larousse gastronomique*	Encyclopedia
1941	U.S./English	Frank Schoonmaker	*American Wines*	
1960	Britain/English	Elizabeth David	*French Provincial Cooking*	Influenced generations of cooks
1961	U.S./English	Simone Beck, Julia Child, Louisette Bertholle	*Mastering the Art of French Cooking*	Made French cooking accessible to Americans; revolution in American cooking.
1968	U.S./English	Claudia Roden	*A Book of Middle Eastern Food*	Comprehensive with ancient recipes
1970	U.S./English	Harva Hachten	*Best of Regional African Cooking*	First continent-wide African cookbook
1973	U.S./English	Madhur Jaffrey	*An Invitation to Indian Cooking*	Regional, accessible, written for Americans; "perhaps the best Indian cookbook available in English"—Craig Claiborne
1973	U.S./English	Molly Katzen	*The Moosewood Cookbook*	Vegetarian, spiced up and ethnic
1979	English trans.	Escoffier	*The Culinary Guide*	First English translation
1981	U.S./English	Jennifer Brennan	*The Original Thai Cookbook*	First Thai cookbook published in the U.S.
1982	U.S./English	Alice Waters	*The Chez Panisse Menu Cookbook*	Seminal California French
1982	U.S./English	Nathan Pritikin	*The Pritikin Promise*	Extra-lean diet
1983	U.S./English	Dean Ornish, M.D., and Martha Rose Shulman	*Stress, Diet, & Your Heart*	First heart-healthy cookbook

Date	Area/Language	Author	Book Title	Importance
1984	U.S./English	Harold McGee	*On Food and Cooking: The Science and Lore of the Kitchen*	Chemistry
1989	U.S./English	Julee Rosso and Sheila Lukins	*The New Basics*	Reflected the changes that had been occurring in American cuisine
1996	Italy/French	Flandrin and Montanari, eds.	*Histoire de l'alimentation*	Invaluable
1999	U.S./English	(in English, Sonnenfeld)	English title: *Food: From Antiquity to the Present*	
1998	U.S./English	Ntozake Shange	*If I Can Cook//You Know God Can*	African-American food/history book with a poetic soul
1999	England	Alan Davidson, ed.	*The Oxford Companion to Food*	Encyclopedia
2000	U.S./English	Clifford Wright	*A Mediterranean Feast*	Massive combination of 500 recipes plus history
2000	U.S./English	Su-Mei Yu	*Cracking the Coconut*	Thai by a Thai
2001	U.S./English	Eric Schlosser	*Fast Food Nation*	Examines the way many Americans eat now
2002	U.S./English	Marion Nestle	*Food Politics*	First hard political/history

$\mathcal{N}$OTES

Chapter 1

1. Pyne, *World Fire*, 3.
2. *Los Angeles Times,* July 11, 2002, 1.
3. Brothwell & Brothwell, *Food in Antiquity,* 32.
4. Tannahill, *Food in History,* 32.
5. Klein with Edgar, *The Dawn of Human Culture,* 156.
6. Flandrin & Montanari, *Food,* 17; Farb & Armelagos, *Consuming Passions.*
7. Tannahill, *Food in History,* 15.
8. Achaya, *Indian Food,* 5.
9. Cass, *Dancing Through History,* ix.
10. Ibid., 3–8.
11. Ibid., 7.
12. Frazer, *The Golden Bough,* 21, 24. See also Janson & Janson, *A Basic History of Art,* 32–35.
13. Brothwell & Brothwell, *Food in Antiquity,* 19.
14. Achaya, *Indian Food,* 3.
15. Ibid., 202–203.
16. Ibid., 199.
17. Klein with Edgar, *Human Culture,* 17.
18. McGee, *Food and Cooking,* 234.
19. Ibid., 275.
20. Brothwell & Brothwell, *Food in Antiquity,* 194.
21. Woodier, *Apple Cookbook,* 1–2.
22. Courtwright, *Forces of Habit,* 9.
23. There was an early civilization around the Niger River in Africa, but there is little information.
24. Spodek, *World's History,* 48–49.
25. http://news.nationalgeographic.com/ news/2001/05/0518_crescent.html; accessed August 1, 2002.
26. http://news.nationalgeographic.com/ news/2002/07/0723_020724_cuneiform. html; accessed August 1, 2002.
27. Brothwell & Brothwell, *Food in Antiquity,* 165.
28. McGee, *Food and Cooking,* 370.
29. Davidson, *Oxford Companion,* 384.
30. Spodek, *World's History,* 48–49.
31. Brothwell & Brothwell, *Food in Antiquity,* 166.
32. Bresciani, "Food Culture in Ancient Egypt," in *Food,* 40.
33. Phillips, *Wine,* 24.

34. Brothwell & Brothwell, *Food in Antiquity*, 200.
35. Joannes, "The Social Function of Banquets in the Earliest Civilizations," in *Food*, 35.
36. Ibid., 19.
37. Tannahill, *Food in History*, 47.
38. Woodier, *Apple Cookbook*, 2.
39. Spodek, *World's History*, 71.
40. McGee, *Food and Cooking*, 170–171.
41. History Channel, *Egypt Beyond the Pyramids.*
42. Flandrin, "Introduction," in *Food*, 13; Brothwell & Brothwell, *Food in Antiquity*, 54.
43. History Channel, *Egypt Beyond the Pyramids.*
44. Tannahill, *Food in History*, 52–53.
45. Bresciani, "Food Culture in Ancient Egypt," in *Food*, 39.
46. Zborowski & Herzog, *Life Is with People*, 368.
47. Ibid., 368–369.
48. *Exodus*, 12; Zborowski & Herzog, *People*, 388–389.
49. The Holy Bible. *Exodus*, 5–11.
50. Anderson, *Food of China*, 45.
51. http://www.math.nus.edu.sg/aslaksen/calendar/chinese.shtml.
52. http://www.educ.uvic.ca/faculty/mroth/438/CHINA/15-day_celebration.htm; accessed March 3, 2002.
53. http://www.new-year.co.uk/chinese/history.htm; accessed March 2, 2003.
54. Miller, *Spice Trade*, 43.
55. Kurlansky, *Salt*, 31.
56. Achaya, *Indian Food*, 18–29.
57. Ibid., 11.
58. Ibid., 18.
59. Ibid., 110, 113, 108, 111.
60. Ibid., 38.
61. Ibid., 9.
62. Farb & Armelagos, *Consuming Passions*, 141–146.
63. Anderson, *Food of China*, 6.

Chapter 2

1. Beck, et al., *World History*, 111; Amos & Lang, *These Were the Greeks*, 5.
2. Toussaint-Samat, *History of Food*, 299–301.
3. Tannahill, *Food in History*, 61.
4. Amos & Lang, *Greeks*, 143.
5. Farb & Amelagos, *Consuming Passions*, 62.
6. Amouretti, "Urban and Rural Diets in Greece," in *Food*, 82.
7. Montanari, "Introduction: Food Systems and Models of Civilization," in *Food*, 69.
8. Davidson, *Oxford Companion*, 551–553.
9. In Greek, the final *e* is pronounced like the *ee* in *beet*. For example, the name of the Greek goddess of victory, Nike, is pronounced "nighkee."
10. Depending on which translation. Rose, in *Handbook of Greek Mythology*, says pennyroyal; Hamilton's *Mythology* says barley water and mint.
11. Courtwright, *Habit*, 10.
12. Schmitt-Pantel, "Greek Meals: A Civic Ritual," in *Food*, 94.
13. Asimov, *Words of Science*, 20; *Oxford English Dictionary*, 1119.
14. Vetta, "The Culture of the Symposium," in *Food*, 97.
15. Ibid., 100.
16. Tannahill, *Food in History*, 65.
17. Amouretti, "Diets in Greece," in *Food*, 82.
18. Brothwell & Brothwell, *Food in Antiquity*, 201.
19. Peyer, "The Origins of Public Hostelries in Europe," in *Food*, 288.
20. Grant, *Founders*, 68.
21. Amouretti, "Diets in Greece," in *Food*, 87, quoting Antiphanes in *Apud Athenaeum*, 370e.
22. Toussaint-Samat, *History of Food*, 622.
23. An identical statue is in Rome, Georgia. Dictator Benito Mussolini sent the copy in 1929 as a gift from one Rome to the other to honor the opening of a Georgia silk mill whose

parent company was in Italy. During World War II, the American statue had to be taken down and hidden after angry citizens threatened to blow it up.

24. Grant, *Founders,* 144, 145.
25. This is disputed; Tannahill says that the Romans preserved the land and grew grain on it (72–73).
26. Miller, *Spice Trade,* 23, 278, 279.
27. Woodier, *Apple Cookbook,* 2.
28. Tannahill, *Food in History,* 64.
29. Toussaint-Samat, *History of Food,* 296–297.
30. The male warrior society of Rome assumed that bee society was just like theirs: headed by a powerful male, like an emperor bee, who brought all the other bees out to wage war. The idea of a queen did not occur to them. Lacey & Danziger, 139.
31. Farrar, *Ancient Roman Gardens,* triclinium, 40–41; treehouse, 57.
32. Shelton, *As the Romans Did,* 75–78.
33. Shelton, *Romans,* 130–131.
34. Ibid., 83–84, quoting *Geoponica* 20.46.1–5.
35. Vehling, *Apicius,* 9–11.
36. Vehling, *Apicius,* xiv.
37. Corbier, "The Broad Bean and the Moray," in *Food,* 134.
38. Ibid., 137.
39. Vehling, *Apicius,* 161.
40. Ibid., 114–115 n.
41. Brothwell & Brothwell, *Food in Antiquity,* 48–49.
42. Ibid., 52.
43. Grant, *Founders,* 263.
44. www.gardenmedicinals.com.
45. History Channel, *The XY Factor: The History of Sex: Ancient Civilizations.*
46. http://www.gmu.edu/departments/fld/CLASSICS/apicius4.html; accessed May 7, 2003
47. Ibid., 112, 46–47, 111, 129, 102.
48. Shelton, *Romans,* 79.
49. Tannahill, *Food in History,* 74–76.
50. Shelton, *Romans,* 79 n. 6.
51. Corbier, "Bean and Moray," in *Food,* 136.

52. Shelton, *Romans,* 72–74.
53. Corbier, "Bean and Moray," in *Food,* 135.
54. Lacey & Danziger, *Year 1000,* 12–13, 53.
55. Visser, *Dinner,* 77.
56. Diamond, *Guns, Germs,* 205, 207.
57. Beck, et al., *World History,* 152.
58. Corbier, "Bean and Moray," in *Food,* 129–130.
59. Tannahill, *Food in History,* 92.
60. Miller, *Spice Trade,* 25.
61. Garnsey, *Food and Society in Classical Antiquity,* 68.

Chapter 3
1. Phillips, *Wine,* 75.
2. *Oxford English Dictionary,* 1557, 1663.
3. Ibid., 308; Rawcliffe, *Medicine & Society,* 33; Wheaton, *Savoring the Past,* 35; Farb & Armelagos, *Consuming Passions,* 119.
4. Grieco, "Food and Social Classes in Late Medieval and Renaissance Italy," in *Food,* 309–311.
5. Flandrin, "Seasoning, Cooking, and Dietetics in the Late Middle Ages," in *Food,* 318.
6. Flandrin, "Dietary Choices and Culinary Technique," 1500-1800, in *Food,* 407; Flandrin, "From Dietetics to Gastronomy: the Liberation of the Gourmet," in *Food,* 421.
7. Farb & Armelagos, *Consuming Passions,* 121.
8. Flandrin, "Seasoning, Cooking, and Dietetics in the Late Middle Ages," in *Food,* 316–317.
9. Flandrin, "Dietetics to Gastronomy," in *Food,* 422.
10. Flandrin, "Seasoning in Late Middle Ages," in *Food,* 314.
11. http://www-lib.usc.edu/~jnawaz/ISLAM/PILLARS/FastFiqh.html.
12. Achaya, *Indian Food,* 160.
13. Henisch, *Fast and Feast,* 106.
14. Wright, *Mediterranean Feast,* 118.
15. Roden, *A Book of Middle Eastern Food,* 234.
16. Ibid., 246–248.

17. Ibid., 250–251.
18. Ibid., 277.
19. Ibid., 305 (*imam bayaldi*), 302 (filling).
20. Wright, *Mediterranean Feast,* 325.
21. Ibid., 303.
22. Ibid., 499.
23. Davidson, *Oxford Companion,* 523.
24. Rosenberger, "Arab Cuisine and Its Contribution to European Culture," in *Food,* 208.
25. Pendergrast, *Uncommon Grounds,* 4.
26. Ibid., 5–6.
27. Montanari, "Introduction: Food Models and Cultural Identity," in *Food,* 189.
28. Ibid.
29. Borrero, *Food in Russian History and Culture,* 29, n. 34; 20, n. 21.
30. Phillips, *Wine,* 101.
31. Chianti gained more fame in the movie *Silence of the Lambs* with Hannibal "the Cannibal" Lecter's remark about one of his victims: "I ate her liver with some fava beans and a nice Chianti."
32. Phillips, *Wine,* 98–99.
33. Ibid., 96.
34. Ibid., 104–105.
35. Ibid., 107–111.
36. Dupont, "The Grammar of Roman Dining," in *Food,* 117–119.
37. Phillips, *Wine,* 85.
38. McGee, *Food and Cooking,* 236.
39. Riley-Smith, ed. *Crusades,* 49.
40. To see what happens when an apprentice thinks he knows more than he does, see Walt Disney's animated movie, *Fantasia.* In the "Sorcerer's Apprentice" segment, while the sorcerer is away, apprentice Mickey Mouse tries to get out of his cleanup duties by casting a spell on a broom to make it carry a bucket of water. Unfortunately, he knows only part of the spell, and the one broom turns into an army of brooms and a flood.
41. Desportes, "Food Trades," in *Food,* 281.
42. Ibid., 275.

43. Phillips, *Wine,* 111.
44. Levenson, *Habeas Codfish,* 13.
45. Elias, *Manners, Vol. I,* blow nose, 64; spit on table, 153; helmet on, 87; clean teeth with knife, 87; gnaw on bone, 64, 85; pick nose, 64, 88.
46. Lacey & Danziger, *Year 1000,* 137.
47. Cass, *Dancing,* 41.
48. Woodier, *Apple Cookbook,* 42.
49. For an excellent fictitious telling of the story of this colony, see Jane Smiley's novel, *The Greenlanders.*
50. Willan, *Great Cooks,* 9.
51. *Cooking Live,* November 5, 2001, Elizabeth Ryan, pomologist.
52. Achaya, *Indian Food,* 11.
53. Siberia is in remote eastern Russia. The communists used it as a prison where they sent exiles.
54. Quoted in Wheaton, *Savoring the Past,* 7.
55. Ibid., 6.
56. Ibid., 16.
57. Willan, *Great Cooks,* 9.
58. *Durum* means hard in Latin (like "durable").
59. Wright, *Mediterranean Feast,* 622.
60. www.silk-road.com/artl/marcopolo.shtml.
61. Foot binding, which crippled women and turned them into expensive objects, ended in China with the revolution in 1911. It continued for several years after that among Chinese in the United States.

Chapter 4

1. Anderson, *The Food of China,* 65.
2. Ibid., 58.
3. Kurlansky, *Salt,* 35.
4. Anderson, *An Introduction to Japanese Tea Ritual,* 14–15.
5. The Chinese might have been on to something. Scientists have recently discovered that green tea is a powerful antioxidant, a cancer-fighting agent.
6. Anderson, *The Food of China,* 63.
7. Chang, *Food in Chinese Culture,* 169.
8. Ibid., 144.

9. Ibid., 151, 147.
10. Anderson, *The Food of China,* 81.
11. Chang, 151.
12. Ibid., 149.
13. Chung, 282–284.
14. Davidson, *Oxford Companion,* 662–664.
15. Ruth Benedict, *The Chrysanthemum and the Sword.*
16. Anderson, *Tea Ritual,* 57–58.
17. Ibid., 150.
18. Ibid., 165.
19. Ibid., 166–172.
20. Mason & Caiger, *A History of Japan,* 120–121.
21. Le Goff, *The Medieval World,* 116.
22. http://www.crs4.it/~riccardo/ Letteratura/Decamerone/Ottava/ 8_03.htm.
23. Schama, *History of Britain,* PBS.
24. Flandrin, "Seasoning in the Late Middle Ages," in *Food,* 313.
25. Ibid., 319.
26. Grieco, "Classes," in *Food,* 307, 303.
27. Klapisch-Zuber, *Women, Family, and Ritual in Renaissance Italy,* 106–107.
28. Burke, *The Italian Renaissance,* 70.
29. Willan, *Great Cooks,* 23.
30. Davidson, *Oxford Companion,* 613.
31. Ibid., 144.
32. Barer-Stein, *You Eat What You Are,* 397.
33. Chamberlin, *The Bad Popes,* 167.
34. Flint, *The Imaginative Landscape of Christopher Columbus,* 4–5.
35. Kamen, *Inquisition and Society in Spain,* 11.
36. www.press.uchicago.edu/Misc/ Chicago/101363.html.
37. http://medinfo.wustl.edu/~McKinney/ cahokia/Introduction.html
38. Sokolov, *Why We Eat,* 86.
39. Coe, *America's First Cuisines,* 174–175.
40. Ibid., 182.
41. McGee, *Food and Cooking,* 170.
42. *Oxford English Dictionary,* 559.
43. Fussell, *The Story of Corn,* 17.
44. Beck, et al., *World History,* 213.
45. Sokolov, *Why We Eat,* 82.
46. Sokolov, *Why We Eat,* 83.
47. Fussell, *Corn,* 249–250.
48. Coe, *First Cuisines,* 98.
49. Ibid., 111.
50. Ibid., 110.
51. Coe & Coe, *True History of Chocolate,* 89–93.
52. Ibid., 97.
53. Ibid., 98.
54. Coe, *First Cuisines,* 97.
55. Ibid., 99–100.
56. Ibid., 100–101.
57. Nabhan, *Gathering the Desert,* 126.
58. Ibid.,123–124.
59. Ibid., 128.
60. Dor-Ner, *Columbus and the Age of Discovery,* 119.
61. The *Niña* was 90 feet long; compare with Zheng He's 400-foot-long ship.
62. Dor-Ner, *Columbus and the Age of Discovery,* 120.
63. Ibid., 133–134.
64. Ibid., 118.
65. Ibid., 125.
66. No one is sure exactly which island this is.
67. Ibid., 149.

Chapter 5
1. Crosby, *Columbian Exchange,* 53.
2. Ibid., 106.
3. Ibid., 79.
4. Silverberg, *Pueblo Revolt,* 63.
5. Coe, *First Cuisines,* 70–71.
6. Roueché, *Medical Detectives, Vol. II,* 19. In 1980, the World Health Organization declared smallpox eradicated, but after September 11, 2001, and the threat of bioterrorism, the United States is considering resuming smallpox vaccinations.
7. *New York Times,* August 14, 2002.
8. Bayless, *Mexican Kitchen,* 276, 286–287.
9. Coe & Coe, *Chocolate,* 216–218.
10. Diana Kennedy, *The Cuisines of Mexico,* 16–18.
11. Silverberg, *Pueblo Revolt,* 27.
12. Sokolov, *Why We Eat,* 88.
13. Phillips, *Wine,* 156–159.
14. Sokolov, *Why We Eat,* 84.
15. Crosby, *Columbian Exchange,* 84–87.
16. Ibid., 85.
17. Ortiz, *The Book of Latin American Cooking,* 153–157.

18. Molina, *Secretos de las Brasas*, 20, 22, 26.
19. Ortiz, *Latin American Cooking*, 38–39.
20. Crosby, *Columbian Exchange*, 83.
21. Beck, et al., *World History*, 497.
22. Davidson, *Oxford Companion*, 141.
23. Ortiz, *Latin American Cooking*, 333.
24. Ibid., 50.
25. Beck, et al., *World History*, 497.
26. Mintz, *Sweetness*, 45.
27. Phillips, *Wine*, 153.
28. Mintz, *Sweetness*, 45.
29. Ibid.
30. McPhee, *Oranges*, 71.
31. Mintz, *Sweetness*, 53.
32. Ibid.
33. Ibid., 44.
34. Ibid., 53.
35. Ibid., 45.
36. Ibid., 53.
37. Ibid.
38. Ibid., 54.
39. Ibid.
40. Davidson, *Oxford Companion*, 94, 103.
41. www.backusturner.com/demarera/history3.
42. Courtright, *Habit*, 150.
43. www.history.ufl.edu/west1/nar1.htm.
44. See Steven Spielberg's 1997 movie, *Amistad*.
45. McPhee, *Oranges*, 86, quoting Samuel Pepys.
46. Davidson, *Oxford Companion*, 627.
47. Ibid.
48. Dor-Ner, *Columbus*, 266.
49. Toussaint-Sarnat, *Food*, 711.
50. Ibid.
51. Davidson, *Oxford Companion*, 628.
52. Dor-Ner, *Columbus*, 266.
53. Ibid., 268.
54. Ibid., 266.
55. Beck et al., *World History*, 535.
56. Dor-Ner, *Columbus*, 267.
57. Toussaint-Samat, *Food*, 717.
58. Dor-Ner, *Columbus*, 269.
59. Viola and Margolis, *Seeds of Change*, 48.
60. Dor-Ner, *Columbus*, 267; Toussaint-Sarnat, 717.

61. Davidson, *Oxford Companion*, 627.
62. Ibid., 628.
63. Toussaint-Samat, *Food*, 723.
64. McGee, *Food and Cooking*, 133.
65. Davidson, *Oxford Companion*, 267.
66. Toussaint-Sarnat, *Food*, 725.
67. Dor-Ner, *Columbus*, 270.
68. Viola and Margolis, *Seeds of Change*, 255.
69. Dor-Ner, *Columbus and the Age of Discovery*, 171.
70. Miguel de Cervantes, *Don Quixote*, Chapter I; http://ibiblio.org/gutenberg/etext97/1donq10.txt, accessed February 24, 2003.
71. Ibid., Chapter II.
72. Davidson, *Oxford Companion*, 494.
73. Cervantes, *Don Quixote*, Chapter LIX, accessed February 24, 2003.
74. Ibid., Chapter II.
75. Ibid., Chapter LIX.
76. Ibid., Chapter LXII.
77. Ibid., Chapter XLIX.
78. Ibid., Chapter XX.

Chapter 6

1. Bailey & Kennedy, *American Spirit*, 29.
2. Cronon, *Changes in the Land*, 22.
3. Brillat-Savarin, *Physiology of Taste*, 78.
4. Cronon, *Changes in the Land*, 45, n. 17.
5. Simmons, *The First American Cookbook*, 28.
6. Kurlansky, *Cod*, 51.
7. Ibid., 81.
8. Nearing & Nearing, *The Maple Sugar Book*, 26.
9. Ibid., 23–24.
10. Ibid., 35–37.
11. Ibid., 29, 38.
12. Brown, *Early American Beverages*, 40.
13. Ibid., 39.
14. Ibid., 67.
15. Ibid., 19.
16. Ibid., 17.
17. Rose, *Sensible Cook*, 26.
18. Spodek, *World's History*, 408.
19. Anderson, *Food of China*, 7–8.
20. Spodek, *World's History*, 407.
21. Schama, *Embarrassment of Riches*, 169.

22. Ibid., 176.
23. Rose, *Sensible Cook,* 43.
24. Ibid., 26–127.
25. Ibid., 66.
26. Ibid., 67.
27. Ibid., 51.
28. Schama, *Embarrassment,* 177, quoting Burema, L. *De voeding in Nederland von de Middeleeuwen tot de twintigste Eeuw.* Assen, 1953.
29. Rose, *Sensible Cook,* 6–7.
30. Schama, *Embarrassment,* 186, 184.
31. Tempest, "Stovelore in Russian Folk-life," *Russian History and Culture,* 3.
32. Ibid., 4.
33. Ibid., 3–11.
34. http://samovars.net.; accessed May 3, 2003.
35. Wheaton, *Savoring the Past,* 43.
36. Ibid., 44.
37. Willan, *Great Cooks and Their Recipes,* 59.
38. Davidson, *Oxford Companion,* 232.
39. Pendergrast, *Uncommon Grounds,* 10.
40. Ibid., 15–16.
41. Ibid., 7–18.
42. Kagan, Ozment, & Turner, *Western Heritage,* 436.
43. Wheaton, *Savoring the Past,* 136.
44. McPhee, *Oranges,* 70.
45. Ibid., 69.
46. Ibid., 82–84.

Chapter 7
1. Davidson, *Oxford Companion,* 254.
2. Ibid., 150–151.
3. Hutchinson, *The New Pennsylvania Dutch Cookbook,* 93.
4. Hazelton, *The Swiss Cookbook,* 48.
5. Brown, *Early American Beverages,* 20.
6. The Americans weren't the only ones smuggling tea. By 1784, the British were paying taxes on only slightly more than one-third of the tea they consumed. The rest had entered the country illegally.
7. Bailey, Kennedy, & Cohen, *American Pageant,* 136.
8. History Channel, *Save Our History: Valley Forge National Historical Park.*
9. Phillips, *Wine,* 170.
10. Ambrose, *Undaunted Courage,* 41.
11. Simmons, *First American Cookbook,* 3–4.
12. Gutman, *Black Family,* 332–333.
13. Simmons, *American Cookery,* 2nd ed. www.opendoorboks.com; accessed September 30, 2002.
14. Election Cake, *The Boston Cooking School Cook Book.* www.bartleby.com/87/rl550.html; accessed December 22, 2001.
15. Wheaton, *Savoring the Past,* 99.
16. Pascal Ory, quoted in Spang, *Restaurant,* 206.
17. Kaplan, *Bakers of Paris,* 23–24.
18. Ibid., 464.
19. Ibid., 66–70.
20. Ibid., 215–218.
21. Ibid., 470.
22. Ibid., 475.
23. Ibid., 464–466.
24. Ibid., 101–102.
25. Ibid., 106.
26. Schama, *Citizens,* 314–315.
27. Waters, *The Chez Panisse Menu Cookbook,* 111.
28. Spang, Restaurant, 123-127.
29. Bailey, Kennedy, & Cohen, *American Pageant,* 219.
30. Hatch, *Democratization of American Christianity,* 96.
31. Land, *New Orleans Cuisine,* 36, 29.
32. Ibid., 23.
33. Ibid., 23.
34. Shephard, *Pickled, Potted, and Canned,* 226–227.
35. Spang, *Restaurant,* 139.
36. Ibid., 191.
37. *Oxford English Dictionary,* 1119.
38. Brillat-Savarin, *Physiology of Taste,* 51.
39. Ibid., 95.
40. Ibid., 311–313.
41. Escoffier, *The Complete Guide to the Art of Modern Cookery,* 528.
42. Roueché, *The Medical Detectives, Vol. II,* 302–305.
43. Willan, *Great Cooks,* 143.
44. Ibid., 144.

Chapter 8

1. Stewart, *Overland Trail*, 293.
2. Ibid., 182.
3. Ibid., 78.
4. Ibid., 79.
5. Holliday, *The World Rushed In*, 313.
6. West, *Growing Up with the Country*, 13.
7. Holliday, *World Rushed In*, 315, 331.
8. Dunaway, *No Need to Knead*, 32.
9. Pendergrast, *Uncommon Grounds*, 56–57.
10. http://www.levistrauss.com/about/history/timeline.asp, accessed October 6, 2002.
11. Holliday, *World Rushed In*, 97.
12. Shephard, *Pickled, Potted, and Canned*, 216.
13. Hurtado, *Indian Survival on the California Frontier*, 3.
14. Kennedy, Cohen, & Bailey, *American Pagent*, 353.
15. Gutman, *Black Family*, 336.
16. Fox-Genovese, *Within the Plantation Household*, 159.
17. Fisher, *What Mrs. Fisher Knows*, 90.
18. Ibid., 24.
19. Ibid., 37.
20. Fox-Genovese, *Plantation Household*, 118–119.
21. Ibid., 103.
22. White, *Ar'n't I a Woman?*, 100.
23. Bailey & Kennedy, *American Spirit*, 321–322.
24. Sklar, *Catherine Beecher*, 155.
25. Blockson, *Underground Railroad*, 26.
26. http://hnn.us/comments/1802.html; "Are the Media Right to Single Out William Tecumseh Sherman as the Most Reckless Civil War General of Them All?" by Dr. Michael Taylor.
27. Bailey & Kennedy, *American Spirit*, 471.
28. Pryor, *Clara Barton: Professional Angel*, 142.
29. http://www.amazon.com/exec/obidos/tg/detail/-/0807072419/ref=lib_rd_next_13/102-420; accessed December 3, 2002.
30. Rafter, *Partial Justice*, 143–144.
31. Twain, *Roughing It*, 46–47.
32. Ibid., 89.
33. Luchetti, *Home on the Range*, 56–57.
34. Twain, *Roughing It*, 292.
35. Ambrose, *Nothing Like It in the World*, 150.
36. Ibid., 162–163.
37. From a *New York Times* article, quoted in *Roughing It*, 48.
38. Martin, *The Land Looks After Us*, 91.
39. Faragher, "The Midwestern Farming Family, 1850," in *Women's America: Refocusing the Past*, Linda K. Kerber and Jane De Hart Mathews, eds., 117–122.
40. *New York Times*, June 18, 2001.
41. Atkins, *Harvest of Grief*, 30–33.
42. Luchetti, *Home on the Range*, 92.
43. McCallum, *The Wire that Fenced the West*, 132–133.
44. Josephson, *Union House, Union Bar*, 14.
45. Williams, *Savory Suppers*, 39–44, 80, 86–89.
46. Ibid., 95–96.
47. Brumberg, *Fasting Girls*, 175–176.
48. Andreason & Black, *Psychiatry*, 479.
49. Ibid., 480–486.
50. Rafter, *Partial Justice*, 165.
51. Benning, *Oh Fudge!*, 7.
52. Ibid., 12.
53. www.picture frames.co.uk/page/saint_valentine.htm; accessed February 14, 2003.
54. Hamilton, *Mythology*, 92–100.
55. Burns, Ric. *New York* video, Episode 3, "Sunshine and Shadow, 1865–1898."
56. Schlereth, "Home Utilities" in *American Home Life, 1880–1930*, 233.
57. Whorton, *Crusaders for Fitness*, 48.
58. Thoreau, *Walden and Other Writings*; Joseph Wood Krutch, ed., 112.
59. Thoreau, *Walden*, 150.
60. Whorton, *Crusaders*, 223.
61. Pendergrast, *For God, Country and Coca-Cola*, 16.
62. Ibid., 14–15.
63. Ibid., 422.

Chapter 9

1. Druett, *Rough Medicine*, 142.
2. Lincoln, *Food for Athletes*, 48.
3. Brennan, *The Original Thai Cookbook*, 23.
4. Druett, *Rough Medicine*, 142.

5. Rosenberg, *Cholera Years,* 47.
6. Phillips, *Wine,* 282–285.
7. Beeton, *The Book of Household Management,* title page.
8. Ibid., 259–260.
9. Ibid., 590–591.
10. Ibid., 242–243.
11. Swift, "A Modest Proposal," in *Swift: Gulliver's Travels and Other Writings,* 489.
12. http://www.stpatricksday.ie/cms/stpatricksday_history.html.
13. Gallagher, *Paddy's Lament,* 22–25.
14. Beck, et al., *World History,* 686.
15. Wright, *Mediterranean Feast,* 523–524.
16. Davidson, *Oxford Companion,* 220.
17. DeWitt, Wilan, & Stock, *Flavors of Africa,* 197.
18. Hachten, *Regional African Cooking,* 125–126.
19. Ibid., 114–118.
20. DeWitt, Wilan, & Stock, *Flavors of Africa,* 129.
21. Hachten, *Regional African Cooking,* 217.
22. Davidson, *Oxford Companion,* 790.
23. DeWitt, Wilan, & Stock, *Flavors of Africa,* 9.
24. Ibid., 20.
25. Ibid., 69.
26. Beeton, *Household Management,* 135–136 (#269).
27. Achaya, *Indian Food,* 176.
28. Ibid., 176–178.
29. Anderson, *Food of China,* 208–209.
30. Ibid., 210–217.
31. *Castles Neuschwanstein and Hohenschwangau,* Copyright by Verlag Kienberger
32. Shaw, *The World of Escoffier,* 24–27.
33. Beck, Bertholle, & Child, *Mastering the Art of French Cooking,* 147.
34. Willan, *La France Gastronomique,* 28–31.
35. Ministère de la Culture, *Les Français et la table,* 446–449.
36. Hazan, *The Classic Italian Cookbook,* 3.
37. Ibid., 6.
38. Davidson, *Oxford Companion,* 582.
39. Ibid., 800.
40. Ucello, *Pani e dolci di Sicilia,* 99.
41. Simeti, *Pomp and Sustenance,* 89.

42. Ibid., 284–293.
43. Mangione & Morreale, *La Storia,* xv.
44. Ibid., 60–80.

Chapter 10
1. Norton, et al., *A People and a Nation, Brief Edition (5th, Vol. B),* 358.
2. Mangione & Morreale, *La Storia,* 174.
3. Diner, *Hungering for America,* 201–202.
4. Ibid.
5. www.agh-attorneys.com/4_lochner_wnew_york.htm; accessed March 4, 2003.
6. http://caselaw.lp.findlaw.com/scripts/getcase.pl?court=us&vol=198&onvol=45; accessed March 4, 2003.
7. Hall, *Oxford Companion to the Supreme Court, Lochner,* 508–511, *Parrish,* 924.
8. www.biography.com/features/mother; accessed May 5, 2001.
9. www.rootsweb.com/~wvtaylor, accessed May 5, 2001.
10. Not in OED as of 1981.
11. www.federaljacks.com; accessed February 27, 2003.
12. www.raffelshotel.com; accessed February 27, 2003.
13. www.kapaluabayhotel.com; accessed February 27, 2003.
14. Strenio, *Testing Trap,* 79–80.
15. Shapiro, *Perfection Salad,* 40.
16. Kennedy, Randall. *Ni____r,* 8.
17. Escoffier, *Complete Guide,* ix.
18. Donovan, *Cooking Essentials for the New Professional Chef,* 19–20.
19. Ibid., 19.
20. Shaw, *World of Escoffier,* 52.
21. Poling-Kempes, *The Harvey Girls,* 238–241.
22. Ibid., 43.
23. Ibid., 87.
24. Ibid., 39.
25. Ibid., 87.
26. Ibid., 39.
27. Coleman, *The Liners,* 183.
28. Ibid., 66.
29. Archbold & McCauley, *Last Dinner,* 36.
30. Eaton & Haas, *Titanic Exhibition.*
31. *Slow Food,* April–June 2001, 47, 49.
32. Coleman, *Liners,* 71–81.

33. Ibid., 106.
34. MacClancy, *Consuming Culture,* 135.
35. Volokh, *The Art of Russian Cuisine,* 584–585.
36. Borrero, "Communal Dining and State Cafeterias in Moscow and Petrograd, 1917–1921," in *Food in Russian History and Culture,* 163.
37. Ibid., 169–170.
38. Ibid., 171–172.
39. Phillips, *Wine,* 303–304.
40. Wicker, *A Time to Die,* 89, 317.
41. Dickson, *Great American Ice Cream Book,* 79.
42. English, *Rin Tin Tin Story,* 125.
43. Leuchtenberg, *Perils of Prosperity,* 192.
44. Ibid., 186.

Chapter 11
1. Berolzheimer, *The United States Regional Cook Book,* 631.
2. Second inauguration, January 20, 1937.
3. Porter, "The Enchanted Forest," *The Quartermaster Review,* March–April 1934.www.qmmuseum.lee.army.mil/ccc_forest.htm; accessed August 29, 2002.
4. Davidson, *Oxford Companion,* 153.
5. Lukacs, *American Vintage,* 105.
6. Bill Wilson letter to Dr. Carl Jung (undated); http://members.tripod.com/aainsa/frames.html.
7. Philips, *Wine,* 302.
8. Mendelson, *Stand Facing the Stove,* 96–97.
9. www.kingarthurflour.com; accessed October 12, 2002.
10. emails, Bama Company to Civitello; November 19 and 21, 2002.
11. Harris, *Factories of Death,* 77, 78; fugu, 62.
12. http://motlc.wiesenthal.com/text/x19/xm1962.html; accessed March 2, 2003.
13. http://www.navysna.org/awards/Miller.htm; http://www.history.navy.mil/faqs/faq57–4.htm; http://www.dorismiller.com; http://www.dorismiller.com/history/dorismiller/ussmiller.shtml;

http://www.tsha.utexas.edu/handbook/online/articles/view/MM/fmi55.html.
14. Pendergrast, *Uncommon Grounds,* 224.
15. Wyman, *Spam,* 17–18; 23.
16. MacClancy, *Consuming Culture,* 47.
17. Thompson, *Canning,* 2.
18. Ibid., 20.
19. Ibid., 9.
20. Thompson, *Canning,* 38.
21. Malgieri, *Cookies Unlimited,* 47.
22. Daws, *Prisoners of the Japanese,* 120–121.
23. Ibid., 111.
24. Andrews & Gilbert, *Over Here, Over There,* 62–63.
25. MacClancy, *Consuming Culture,* 102.
26. Ibid., 47–48.
27. http://motlc.wiesenthal.com/text/x19/xm1962.html; accessed March 2, 2003.
28. MacClancy, *Consuming Culture,* 340.
29. Kennedy, *Great Powers,* 362.
30. MacClancy, *Consuming Culture,* 134.
31. www.qmfound.com/short.html; accessed August 29, 2002.
32. I am indebted to Korea historian Mary Connor for the information on Korean cuisine and culture.
33. Connor, *The Koreas,* 246–256.
34. Food Network, *More American Eats.*
35. Twain, *Roughing It,* 369.
36. Ibid., 359.
37. Ibid., 342, 355.
38. Ibid., 354.
39. Davidson, *Oxford Companion,* 373.
40. Ibid. 742.
41. http://www.lbl.gov/Publications/Currents/Archive/Apr-21–1995.html; accessed November 24, 2002.

Chapter 12
1. *New Yorker,* January 15, 2001; 48–56.
2. Beck, et al., *World History,* 864.
3. *New York Times,* June 15, 2001.
4. *New York Times,* June 18, 2001.
5. http://www.bbc.co.uk/arts/books/author/david/pg3.shtml; accessed November 23, 2002.

6. www.harcourtschool.com/articles/ video_updates/050/050_160_80.html; accessed August 23, 2003.
7. *Sacramento Bee,* October 17, 2002; B1, B7.
8. *New York Times,* October 23, 2002 (nytimes.com, accessed October 30, 2002).
9. www.mrsfields.com; accessed October 30, 2002.
10. From the author: that's how we made s'mores and banana boats when I was a Girl Scout.
11. http://www.law.cornell.edu/background/insane/capacity.html; accessed March 2, 2003.
12. http://www.cdc.gov/nccdphp/sgr/shalala.htm; accessed March 2, 2003.
13. www.sumoweb.com/sumo_guru/question71.html;
www.dimensionsmagazine.com/news/083958.htm; accessed August 13, 2002.
14. Donovan, *Cooking Essentials,* 7.
15. Schlosser, *Fast Food Nation,* 7.
16. Ibid., 3.
17. Los Angeles Times, December 21, 2000.
18. *New York Times,* June 18, 2001.
19. *New York Times,* June 7, 2001.
20. Food Network, *In Food Today.*
21. *Saveur,* "Nouvelle Schmouvelle," Sept./Oct. 2001, 15.
22. Mauseth, *Botany,* 729.
23. www.slowfood.com; accessed November 2, 2002.
24. "The Snail," December 2001, 4–5.
25. http://www.edibleschoolyard.org/feedingfuture; accessed March 2, 2003.
26. Cervantes, *Don Quixote,* Chapter XLIX, accessed February 24, 2003.

BIBLIOGRAPHY

BOOKS

Achaya, K. T. *Indian Food: A Historical Companion*. Delhi: Oxford University Press, 1994.

Ambrose, Stephen. *Nothing Like It in the World: The Men Who Built the Transcontinental Railroad, 1863–1869*. New York: Simon & Schuster, 2000.

———. *Undaunted Courage: Meriwether Lewis, Thomas Jefferson, and the Opening of the American West*. New York: Simon & Schuster/Touchstone, 1996.

Amos, H. D., and A. G. P. Lang. *These Were the Greeks*. Chester Springs, PA: Dufour Editions, Inc., 1982.

Amouretti, Marie-Claire. "Urban and Rural Diets in Greece," in *Food*, eds. Jean-Louis Flandrin & Massimo Montanari. English ed. Albert Sonnenfeld. New York: Columbia University Press, 1999.

Anderson, E. N. *The Food of China*. New Haven: Yale University Press, 1988.

Anderson, Jennifer L. *An Introduction to the Japanese Tea Ritual*. Albany: State University of New York Press, 1991.

Andreason, Nancy C., M.D., Ph.D., and Donald W. Black, M.D. *Introductory Textbook of Psychiatry, Second Ed.* Washington, DC: American Psychiatric Press, 1995.

Andrews, Maxene, and Bill Gilbert. *Over Here, Over There: the Andrews Sisters and the USO Stars in World War II*. New York: Zebra Books, 1993.

Apicius. *Cookery and Dining in Imperial Rome*. Trans. Joseph Dommers Vehling. NY: Dover Publications, Inc., 1977. Originally published: Walter M. Hill, 1936.

Archbold, Rick, and Dana McCauley. *Last Dinner on the Titanic: Menus and Recipes from the Great Liner.* New York: Hyperion/Madison Press, 1997.

Asimov, Isaac. *Words of Science and the History Behind Them*. New York: New American Library, 1959.

Atkins, Annette. *Harvest of Grief: Grasshopper Plagues and Public Assistance in Minnesota, 1873–78*. St. Paul: Minnesota Historical Society Press, 1984.

Bailey, Thomas A., and David M. Kennedy. *The American Spirit: United States History as Seen by Contemporaries*. 9th Ed., Volume I: to 1877. Boston: Houghton Mifflin Company, 1998.

Bailey, Thomas A., David M. Kennedy, and Lizabeth Cohen. *The American Pageant, Vols. I and II*. 11th Ed. Boston: Houghton Mifflin Company, 1998.

Barer-Stein, Thelma. *You Eat What You Are: People, Culture and Food Traditions*. Willowdale, Ontario, Canada and Buffalo, NY: Firefly Books, 1999.

Bayless, Rick, with Deann Groen Bayless and Jean Marie Brownson. *Rick Bayless's Mexican Kitchen*. New York: Scribner, 1996.

Beck, Roger B., *et al*. *World History: Patterns of Interaction*. Evanston, IL: McDougal Littell, 1999.

Beck, Simone, Louisette Bertholle, and Julia Child. *Mastering the Art of French Cooking*. New York: Alfred A. Knopf, 1961.

Beebe, Lucius. *Boston and the Boston Legend*. New York: D. Appleton-Century, 1935.

Beeton, Isabella. *Mrs. Beeton's Book of Household Management*. [Facsimile.] Lewes, East Sussex: Southover Press, 1998.

Benedict, Ruth. *The Chrysanthemum and the Sword: Patterns of Japanese Culture*. Boston: Houghton Mifflin, 1946.

Benning, Lee Edwards. *Oh, Fudge!* New York: Henry Holt and Company, 1990.

Berolzheimer, Ruth, ed. *The United States Regional Cook Book*. Chicago: Consolidated Publishers, Inc., 1939.

Blockson, Charles L. *The Underground Railroad: First-Person Narratives of Escapes to Freedom in the North*. New York: Prentice Hall, 1987.

Boorstin, Daniel J. *The Discoverers: A History of Man's Search to Know His World and Himself*. New York: Vintage Books, 1983.

Borrero, Mauricio. "Communal Dining and State Cafeterias in Moscow and Petrograd, 1917–1921," in *Food in Russian History and Culture*, eds. Musya Glants & Joyce Toomre. Bloomington, IN: Indiana University Press, 1997.

Bourdain, Anthony. *Kitchen Confidential: Adventures in the Culinary Underbelly*. New York: Bloomsbury, 2000.

Brennan, Jennifer. *The Original Thai Cookbook*. New York: Perigree/Putnam, 1981.

Brenner, Joël Glenn. *The Emperors of Chocolate: Inside the Secret World of Hershey and Mars*. New York: Broadway Books, 2000.

Brenner, Leslie. *American Appetite: The Coming of Age of a National Cuisine*. New York: HarperCollins, 1999.

Bresciani, Edda. "Food Culture in Ancient Egypt," in *Food*, eds. Jean-Louis Flandrin & Massimo Montanari. English edition ed. Albert Sonnenfeld. New York: Columbia University Press, 1999.

Brillat-Savarin, Jean Anthelme. *The Physiology of Taste or, Meditations on Transcendental Gastronomy*. Trans. M. F. K. Fisher. Washington, DC: Counterpoint, 1949.

Brothwell, Don, and Patricia Brothwell. *Food in Antiquity: A Survey of the Diet of Early Peoples*. Expanded edition. Baltimore: The Johns Hopkins University Press, 1998.

Brown, John Hull. *Early American Beverages*. Rutland, VT: Charles E. Tuttle Company, 1966.

Brumberg, Joan Jacobs. *Fasting Girls: the History of Anorexia Nervosa*. New York: Penguin Books U.S.A., 1988, 1989.

Burke, Peter. *The Italian Renaissance: Culture and Society in Italy*. Princeton: Princeton University Press, 1986.

Burns, Ric, dir. *New York: a Documentary Film*. New York: Steeplechase Films, 1999.

Calhoun, Creighton Lee, Jr. *Old Southern Apples*. Blacksburg, Virginia: The McDonald & Woodward Publishing Company, 1995.

Camporesi, Piero. *The Magic Harvest: Food, Folklore and Society*. Milan: Arnoldo Mondadori Editore S.p.A., 1989. Trans. Joan Krakover. Cambridge: Polity Press, 1993.

Carley, Eliane Amé-Leroy. *Classics from a French Kitchen*. New York: Crown Publishers, Inc., 1983.

Cass, Joan. *Dancing Through History*. Englewood Cliffs, NJ: Prentice Hall, 1993.

Castles Neuschwanstein and Hohenschwangau [pamphlet]. Verlag Kienberger, n.d.

Cervantes, Miguel de. *Don Quixote*. Trans. John Ormsby. *http://ibiblio.org/gutenberg/etext97/1donq10.txt;* accessed February 24, 2003.

Chamberlin, E. R. *The Bad Popes*. New York: Dorset Press, 1969.

Chang, K. C., ed. *Food in Chinese Culture: Anthropological and Historical Perspectives*. New Haven: Yale University Press, 1977.

Clark, Alan. *Barbarossa: The Russian-German Conflict, 1941–45*. New York: Quill, 1985. Originally published: New York: Morrow, 1965.

Coe, Sophie D. *America's First Cuisines*. Austin: University of Texas Press, 1994.

Coe, Sophie D., and Michael D. Coe. *The True History of Chocolate*. London: Thames & Hudson Ltd., 1996.

Coleman, Terry. *The Liners*. Middlesex: Penguin Books, 1976.

Connell, Evan S. *Son of the Morning Star: Custer and the Little Bighorn*. New York: Harper & Row, 1984.

Connor, Mary. *The Koreas*. Santa Barbara, California: ABC Clio, 2002.

Cooper, Ann. *"A Woman's Place Is in the Kitchen": The Evolution of Women Chefs*. New York: Van Nostrand Reinhold, 1998.

Corbier, Mireille. "The Broad Bean and the Moray," in *Food*, eds. Jean-Louis Flandrin & Massimo Montanari. English edition ed. Albert Sonnenfeld. New York: Columbia University Press, 1999.

Cott, Nancy F. *The Bonds of Womanhood: "Woman's Sphere" in New England, 1780–1835*. New Haven: Yale University Press, 1977.

Courtwright, David T. *Forces of Habit: Drugs and the Making of the Modern World*. Cambridge: Harvard University Press, 2001.

Cowan, Ruth Schwartz. *More Work For Mother: The Ironies of Household Technology from the Open Hearth to the Microwave*. New York: BasicBooks, 1983.

Cronon, William. *Changes in the Land: Indians, Colonists, and the Ecology of New England.* New York: Hill and Wang, a division of Farrar, Straus & Giroux, 1983.

———. *Nature's Metropolis: Chicago and the Great West.* New York: W. W. Norton & Company, 1991.

Crosby, Alfred W., Jr. *The Columbian Exchange: Biological and Cultural Consequences of 1492.* Westport, CT: Greenwood Press, 1972.

Darnton, Robert. *The Great Cat Massacre and Other Episodes in French Cultural History.* New York: Vintage Books, 1985.

Dash, Mike. *Tulipomania.* New York: Three Rivers Press, 1999.

Davidson, Alan. *The Oxford Companion to Food.* Oxford: Oxford University Press, 1999.

Daws, Gavin. *Prisoners of the Japanese: POWs of World War II in the Pacific.* New York: Quill/William Morrow, 1994.

De Kruif, Paul. *Microbe Hunters.* New York: Harcourt, Brace, 1926.

De Talavera Berger, Frances, and John Parke Custis. *Sumptuous Dining in Gaslight San Francisco, 1875–1915.* Garden City, New York: Doubleday and Company, Inc., 1985.

Desportes, Françoise. "Food Trades," in *Food*, eds. Jean-Louis Flandrin & Massimo Montanari. English edition ed. Albert Sonnenfeld. New York: Columbia University Press, 1999.

DeWitt, Dave, Mary Jane Wilan, and Melissa T. Stock. *Flavors of Africa Cookbook: Spicy African Cooking—From Indigenous Recipes to Those Influenced by Asian and European Settlers.* Rocklin, CA: Prima Publishing, 1998.

Diamond, Jared. *Guns, Germs, and Steel.* New York: W. W. Norton & Company, 1997.

Dickson, Paul. *The Great American Ice Cream Book.* New York: Galahad Books, 1972.

Diner, Hasia R. *Hungering for America: Italian, Irish and Jewish Foodways in the Age of Migration.* Cambridge, MA: Harvard University Press, 2001.

Donovan, Mary Deirdre, ed. *Cooking Essentials for the New Professional Chef.* New York: John Wiley & Sons, Inc., 1997.

Dor-Ner, Zvi, with William G. Scheller. *Columbus and the Age of Discovery.* New York: William Morrow and Company, Inc., 1991.

Dornenburg, Andrew, and Karen Page. *Becoming a Chef, with Recipes and Reflections from America's Leading Chefs.* New York: John Wiley & Sons, Inc., 1995.

Dorris, Michael. *The Broken Cord.* New York: HarperPerennial, 1990.

Druett, Joan. *Rough Medicine: Surgeons at Sea in the Age of Sail.* New York: Routledge, 2000.

DuBois, Ellen Carol. *Feminism and Suffrage: The Emergence of an Independent Women's Movement in America, 1848–1869.* Ithaca: Cornell University Press, 1978.

Dupont, Florence. "The Grammar of Roman Dining," in *Food*, eds. Jean-Louis Flandrin & Massimo Montanari. English edition ed. Albert Sonnenfeld. New York: Columbia University Press, 1999.

Eaton, John P., and Charles A. Haas. *Titanic: The Exhibition.* Florida International Museum. Memphis: Wonders, 1997.

Elias, Norbert. *The History of Manners.* Trans. Edmund Jephcott. New York: Pantheon Books, 1978.

English, James W. *The Rin Tin Tin Story.* New York: Dodd, Mead & Co., 1949.

Escoffier, A. *The Complete Guide to the Art of Modern Cookery.* Trans. H. L. Cracknell and R. J. Kaufman. New York: John Wiley & Sons, Inc., 1979.

Evans, Joan, ed. *The Flowering of the Middle Ages.* New York: Barnes & Noble Books, 1998.

Fagan, Brian. *The Little Ice Age: How Climate Made History, 1300–1850.* New York: Basic Books, 2000.

Faragher, John Mack. "The Midwestern Farming Family, 1850," in *Women's America: Refocusing the Past*, eds. Linda K. Kerber and Jane De Hart Mathews. New York: Oxford University Press, 1982.

Farb, Peter, and George Armelagos. *Consuming Passions: The Anthropology of Eating.* New York: Pocket Books, Washington Square Press, 1980.

Farrar, Linda. *Ancient Roman Gardens.* Phoenix Mill, UK: Sutton Publishing Limited, 1998.

Fisher, Abby. *What Mrs. Fisher Knows About Old Southern Cooking.* Facsimile, with historical notes by Karen Hess. Bedford, Massachusetts: Applewood Books, 1995. Originally published: San Francisco: Women's Co-operative Printing Office, 1881.

Flandrin, Jean-Louis, & Massimo Montanari, eds. *Food: A Culinary History from Antiquity to the Present.* English edition ed. Albert Sonnenfeld. New York: Columbia University Press, 1999.

Flint, Valerie I. J., *The Imaginative Landscape of Christopher Columbus.* Princeton, NJ: Princeton University Press, 1992.

Foner, Eric. *Reconstruction: America's Unfinished Revolution, 1863–1877.* New York: Harper & Row, 1988.

Fox-Genovese, Elizabeth. *Within the Plantation Household: Black and White Women of the Old South.* Chapel Hill: The University of North Carolina Press, 1988.

Foy, Jessica H., and Thomas J. Schlereth, eds. *American Home Life, 1880–1930: A Social History of Spaces and Services.* Knoxville: University of Tennessee Press, 1992.

Frazer, Sir James George. *The Illustrated Golden Bough: A Study in Magic and Religion.* Abridged by Robert K. G. Temple. Britain: The Softback Preview, 1996.

Fussell, Betty. *I Hear America Cooking.* New York: Elisabeth Sifton Books/Viking, 1986.

———. *The Story of Corn.* New York: North Point Press/Farrar, Straus and Giroux, 1992.

Gabaccia, Donna R. *We Are What We Eat: Ethnic Food and the Making of Americans.* Cambridge, MA: Harvard University Press, 1998.

Gallagher, Thomas. *Paddy's Lament.* New York: Harcourt Brace Jovanovich, 1982.

Garnsey, Peter. *Food and Society in Classical Antiquity.* Cambridge: The Cambridge University Press, 1999.

Gillespie, Angus K., and Jay Mechling. *American Wildlife in Symbol and Story.* Knoxville: The University of Tennessee Press, 1987.

Gin, Margaret, and Alfred E. Castle. *Regional Cooking of China.* San Francisco: 101 Productions, 1975.

Gisslen, Wayne. *Professional Cooking, 4th Edition.* New York: John Wiley & Sons, Inc., 1999.

Gitlitz, David M., & Linda Kay David-son. *A Drizzle of Honey: The Lives and Recipes of Spain's Secret Jews.* New York: St. Martin's Press, 1999.

Glants, Musya and Joyce Toomre, eds. *Food in Russian History and Culture.* Bloomington: Indiana University Press, 1997.

Grant, Michael. *The Founders of the Western World: A History of Greece and Rome.* New York: Charles Scribner's Sons, 1991.

Gray, James. *Business Without Boundary: The Story of General Mills.* Minneapolis: University of Minnesota Press, 1954.

Grieco, Allen J. "Food and Social Classes in Late Medieval and Renaissance Italy," in *Food*, eds. Jean-Louis Flandrin & Massimo Montanari. English edition ed. Albert Sonnenfeld. New York: Columbia University Press, 1999.

Gutman, Herbert G. *The Black Family in Slavery and Freedom, 1750–1925.* New York: Vintage Books, 1976.

Hachten, Harva. *Best of Regional African Cooking.* New York: Hippocrene Books, 1970.

Hale, Sarah Josepha. *Early American Cookery: The "Good Housekeeper,"* 1841. Mineola, New York: Dover Publications, Inc., 1996.

Hall, Kermit L., ed. *The Oxford Companion to the Supreme Court of the United States.* New York: Oxford University Press, 1992.

Hamilton, Edith. *Mythology: Timeless Tales of Gods and Heroes.* New York: Mentor Books, 1953.

Harris, Sheldon H. *Factories of Death: Japanese Biological Warfare, 1932–45, and the American Cover-up.* London: Routledge, 1994.

Hatch, Nathan O. *The Democratization of American Christianity.* New Haven: Yale University Press, 1989.

Hayden, Dolores. *The Grand Domestic Revolution: A History of Feminist Designs for American Homes, Neighborhoods, and Cities.* Cambridge, MA: The MIT Press, 1981.

Hazan, Marcella. *The Classic Italian Cook Book: The Art of Italian Cooking and the Art of Italian Eating.* New York: Alfred A. Knopf, 1980.

Hazelton, Nika Standen. *The Swiss Cookbook.* New York: Atheneum, 1967.

Hedrick, Joan D., ed. *The Oxford Harriet Beecher Stowe Reader.* New York: Oxford University Press, 1999.

Henisch, Bridget Ann. *Fast and Feast: Food in Medieval Society.* University Park: The Pennsylvania State University Press, 1976.

Hess, John L., and Karen Hess. *The Taste of America.* New York: Grossman Publishers/Viking Press, 1977.

Hirtzler, Victor. *The Hotel St. Francis Cook Book.* Chicago: The Hotel Monthly Press/John Willy, Inc., 1919.

Hofstadter, Richard, and Michael Wallace, eds. *American Violence, a Documentary History.* New York: Vintage Books, 1971.

Holliday, J. S. *The World Rushed In: The California Gold Rush Experience.* New York: Simon & Schuster/Touchstone, 1981.

The Holy Bible. Cleveland: World Publishing Company, 1962.

Hsiung, Deh-Ta. *Chinese Regional Cooking.* Seacaucus, NJ: Chartwell Books Inc., 1979.

Hutchinson, Ruth. *The New Pennsylvania Dutch Cook Book.* New York: Harper & Row, 1985.

Janson, H.W., and Anthony F. Janson. *A Basic History of Art*. Englewood Cliffs, NJ: Prentice Hall, Inc., 1992.

Joannes, Francis. "The Social Function of Banquets in the Earliest Civilizations," in *Food*, eds. Jean-Louis Flandrin & Massimo Montanari. English edition ed. Albert Sonnenfeld. New York: Columbia University Press, 1999.

Josephson, Matthew. *Union House, Union Bar: The History of the Hotel and Restaurant Employees and Bartenders International Union, AFL-CIO*. New York: Random House, 1956.

Josephy, Alvin M., Jr., ed. *America in 1492: The World of the Indian Peoples Before the Arrival of Columbus*. New York: Vintage Books/Random House, Inc., 1993.

Kagan, Donald, Steven Ozment, and Frank M. Turner. *The Western Heritage: Since 1300*. 7th Ed. Upper Saddle River, NJ: Prentice Hall, 2001.

Kamen, Henry. *Inquisition and Society in Spain in the Sixteenth and Seventeenth Centuries*. Bloomington: Indiana University Press, 1985.

Kaplan, Steven Laurence. *The Bakers of Paris and the Bread Question, 1700–1775*. Durham: Duke University Press, 1996.

Keegan, John A. *A History of Warfare*. New York: Vintage Books, 1994.

Kennedy, Diana. *The Cuisines of Mexico*. New York: Harper & Row, 1986, 1972.

———. *Mexican Regional Cooking*. New York: HarperPerennial, 1978, 1984, 1990.

Kennedy, Paul. *The Rise and Fall of the Great Powers: Economic Change and Military Conflict from 1500 to 2000*. New York: Random House, 1987.

Kennedy, Randall. *N_____r: the Strange Career of a Troublesome Word*. New York: Vintage Books/Random House, Inc., 2002.

Kerber, Linda K., and Jane De Hart Mathews, eds. *Women's America: Refocusing the Past*. New York: Oxford University Press, 1982.

Kimball, Marie. *Thomas Jefferson's Cook Book*. Charlottesville: University of Virginia Press, 1976.

Klapisch-Zuber, Christiane. *Women, Family, and Ritual in Renaissance Italy*. Trans. Lydia G. Cochrane. Chicago: The University of Chicago Press, 1985.

Klein, Herbert S. *African Slavery in Latin America and the Caribbean*. New York: Oxford University Press, 1986.

Klein, Richard G., with Blake Edgar. *The Dawn of Human Culture*. New York: John Wiley & Sons, Inc., 2002.

Kuh, Patric. *The Last Days of Haute Cuisine: America's Culinary Revolution*. New York: The Penguin Group/Viking, 2001.

Kurlansky, Mark. *Cod: A Biography of the Fish that Changed the World*. New York: Penguin Books, 1997.

———. *Salt, a World History*. New York: Walker and Company, 2002.

Lacey, Robert, & Danny Danziger. *The Year 1000: What Life Was Like at the Turn of the First Millennium*. Boston: Little, Brown and Company, 1999.

Land, Mary. *New Orleans Cuisine*. South Brunswick: A.S. Barnes & Co., 1969.

Lang, George. *Hungarian Cuisine*. New York: Bonanza Books, 1971.

Langseth-Christensen, Lillian, with the cooperation of the Marine Historical Association, Incorporated. *The Mystic Seaport Cookbook: 350 Years of New England Cooking.* New York: Galahad Books, 1970.

Le Goff, Jacques, ed. *The Medieval World.* London: Collins and Brown, 1990. Originally published: *L'Uomo Medievale,* 1987, Giuseppe Laterza and Figli S.p.A., Roma-Bari.

Leuchtenburg, William E. *The Perils of Prosperity, 1914–32.* Chicago: The University of Chicago Press, 1958.

Levenson, Barry M. *Habeas Codfish: Reflections on Food and the Law.* Madison: The University of Wisconsin Press, 2001.

Levenstein, Harvey. *Paradox of Plenty: A Social History of Eating in Modern America.* New York: Oxford University Press, 1993.

———. *Revolution at the Table: The Transformation of the American Diet.* New York: Oxford University Press, 1988.

Lin, Jan. *Reconstructing Chinatown: Ethnic Enclave, Global Change.* Minneapolis: University of Minneapolis Press, 1998.

Lincoln, Ann. *Food for Athletes.* Chicago: Contemporary Books, Inc., 1979.

Luchetti, Cathy. *Home on the Range: A Culinary History of the American West.* New York: Villard Books, 1993.

Lukacs, Paul. *American Vintage: The Rise of American Wine.* Boston: Houghton Mifflin Company, 2000.

MacClancy, Jeremy. *Consuming Culture.* London: Chapmans Publishers Ltd., 1992.

MacLauchlan, Andrew. *The Making of a Pastry Chef.* New York: John Wiley & Sons, Inc., 1999.

Malgieri, Nick. *Cookies Unlimited.* New York: HarperCollins, 2000.

Manchester, William. *A World Lit Only by Fire: The Medieval Mind and the Renaissance.* Boston: Little, Brown and Company, 1992.

Mangione, Jerre, & Ben Morreale. *La Storia: Five Centuries of the Italian American Experience.* New York: HarperCollins, 1992.

Martha Washington's Booke of Cookery and Booke of Sweetmeats: being a Family Manuscript, curiously copied by an unknown Hand sometime in the seventeenth century . . . Transcribed by Karen Hess with historical notes and copious annotations. New York: Columbia University Press, 1981.

Martin, Joel W. *The Land Looks After Us: A History of Native American Religion.* Oxford: Oxford University Press, 1999.

Mason, R. H. P., and J. G. Caiger. *A History of Japan.* Tokyo: Charles E. Tuttle and Company, Inc., 1972.

Mauseth, James D. *Botany: An Introduction to Plant Biology.* Sudbury, MA: Jones and Bartlett Publishers, 1998.

McCallum, Henry D., and Frances T. McCallum. *The Wire That Fenced the West.* Norman: University of Oklahoma Press, 1965.

McGee, Harold. *On Food and Cooking: The Science and Lore of the Kitchen.* New York: Fireside/Simon & Schuster, 1984.

McNeill, William H. *A History of the Human Community: Prehistory to the Present.* Upper Saddle River, NJ: Prentice Hall, 1997.

———. *Plagues and Peoples.* New York: Anchor Books/Doubleday, 1976.

McPhee, John. *Oranges.* New York: Farrar, Straus, and Giroux, 1966.

Mendelson, Anne. *Stand Facing the Stove.* New York: Henry Holt and Company, 1996.

Miers, Earl Schenck, and Richard A. Brown. *Gettysburg*. American History Through Literature Series. Armonk, New York: M. E. Sharpe, 1996.

Miller, J. Innes. *The Spice Trade of the Roman Empire, 29 B.C. to A.D. 641*. Oxford: The Clarendon Press, 1969.

Miller-Cory House Museum and the New Jersey Historical Society. *Pleasures of Colonial Cooking*. Orange, NJ: The New Jersey Historical Society, 1982.

Milton, Giles. *Nathaniel's Nutmeg or, the True and Incredible Adventures of the Spice Trader Who Changed the Course of History*. New York: Farrar, Straus and Giroux, 1999.

Ministère de la Culture, Musée national des arts et traditions populaires. *Les Français et la table*. Paris: Editions de la Réunion des musées nationaux, 1985.

Mintz, Sidney. *Sweetness and Power: The Place of Sugar in Modern History*. New York: Penguin Books, 1985.

———. *Tasting Food, Tasting Freedom: Excursions into Eating, Culture, and the Past*. Boston: Beacon Press, 1996.

Molina, Martiniano. *Secretos de las Brasas: Cochina al Aire Libre*. Buenos Aires: Editorial Sudamericana S.A, 2001.

Montanari, Massimo. "Introduction: Food Models and Cultural Identity," in *Food*, eds. Jean-Louis Flandrin & Massimo Montanari. English ed. Albert Sonnenfeld. New York: Columbia University Press, 1999.

Nabhan, Gary. *The Desert Smells Like Rain: A Naturalist in Papago Indian Country*. San Francisco: North Point Press, 1987.

———. *Gathering the Desert*. Tucson: The University of Arizona Press, 1985.

Nash, Gary B. *The Urban Crucible: The Northern Seaports and the Origins of the American Revolution*. Cambridge: Harvard University Press, 1979, 1986.

Nearing, Helen, and Scott Nearing. *The Maple Sugar Book*. New York City: Galahad Books, 1950, 1970.

Nestle, Marion. *Food Politics: How the Food Industry Influences Nutrition and Health*. Berkeley: University of California Press, 2002.

Norton, Mary Beth, David M. Katzman, Paul D. Escott, Howard P. Chudacoff, Thomas G. Paterson, William M. Tuttle Jr., and William J. Brophy. *A People and a Nation*. Boston: Houghton Mifflin Company, 1999.

Ortiz, Elisabeth Lambert. *The Book of Latin American Cooking*. New York: Alfred A. Knopf, 1979.

Orton, Vrest. *The American Cider Book: The Story of America's Natural Beverage*. New York: North Point Press/Farrar, Straus and Giroux, 1973.

Oxford English Dictionary. Compact edition. Oxford: Oxford University Press, 1971.

Pares, Bernard. *A History of Russia*. New York: Vintage Books/Random House, 1965.

Peck, Gunther. *Reinventing Free Labor: Padrones and Immigrant Workers in the North American West, 1880–1930*. Cambridge: Cambridge University Press, 2000.

Pendergrast, Mark. *For God, Country, and Coca-Cola: the Unauthorized History of the Great American Soft Drink and the Company that Makes It*. New York: Scribner's, 1993.

_____. *Uncommon Grounds: The History of Coffee and How It Transformed Our World*. New York: Basic Books, 1999.

Penner, Lucille Recht. *The Colonial Cookbook*. New York: Hastings House, 1976.

Perdue, Theda, ed. *Sifters: Native American Women's Lives*. Oxford: Oxford University Press, 2001.

Peyer, Hans Conrad. "The Origins of Public Hostelries in Europe," in *Food*, eds. Jean-Louis Flandrin & Massimo Montanari. English edition ed. Albert Sonnenfeld. New York: Columbia University Press, 1999.

Phillips, Rod. *A Short History of Wine*. New York: HarperCollins Publishers, Inc., 2000.

Poling-Kempes, Lesley. *The Harvey Girls: Women Who Opened the West*. New York: Paragon House, 1989.

Polo, Marco. *The Travels of Marco Polo (The Venetian)*. Rev. and ed. Manuel Komoroff. New York: Boni and Liveright, 1926.

Pryor, Elizabeth Brown. *Clara Barton: Professional Angel*. Philadelphia: University of Pennsylvania Press, 1987.

Pyne, Stephen J. *World Fire: The Culture of Fire on Earth*. New York: Henry Holt and Company, Inc., 1995.

Rafter, Nicole Hahn. *Partial Justice: Women, Prisons, and Social Control*. Second ed. New Brunswick, New Jersey: Transaction Publishers, 1992.

Rawcliffe, Carole. *Medicine & Society in Later Medieval England*. London: Sandpiper Books Ltd., 1999, 1995.

Redon, Odile, Françoise Sabban, and Silvano Serventi. *The Medieval Kitchen: Recipes from France and Italy*. Trans. Edward Schneider. Chicago: The University of Chicago Press, 1998.

Riley-Smith, Jonathan, ed. *The Oxford Illustrated History of the Crusades*. Oxford: Oxford University Press, 1995.

Roden, Claudia. *A Book of Middle Eastern Food*. New York: Vintage Books/Random House, 1968, 1972.

Rose, H. J. *A Handbook of Greek Mythology Including Its Extension to Rome*. New York: E. P. Dutton & Co., Inc., 1959.

Rose, Peter G., trans. and ed. *The Sensible Cook: Dutch Foodways in the Old and the New World*. Syracuse University Press, 1989.

Rosenberg, Charles E. *The Cholera Years: The United States in 1832, 1849, and 1866*. Chicago: University of Chicago Press, 1987.

Rosenberger, Bernard. "Arab Cuisine and Its Contribution to European Culture," in *Food*, eds. Jean-Louis Flandrin & Massimo Montanari. English edition ed. Albert Sonnenfeld. New York: Columbia University Press, 1999.

Roueché, Berton. *The Medical Detectives*. 2 vols. New York: Washington Square Press, 1982, 1986.

Ruhlman, Michael. *The Making of a Chef: Mastering Heat at the Culinary Institute of America*. New York: Owl/Henry Holt and Company, 1997.

Sánchez, George J. *Becoming Mexican American: Ethnicity, Culture and Identity in Chicano Los Angeles, 1900–1945*. New York: Oxford University Press, 1993.

Sass, Lorna. *To the King's Taste: Richard II's Book of Feasts and Recipes Adapted for Modern Cooking* [from *The Forme of Cury*]. New York: Metropolitan Museum of Art, 1975.

Schama, Simon. *Citizens: A Chronicle of the French Revolution*. New York: Alfred A. Knopf, 1989.

————. *The Embarrassment of Riches: An Interpretation of Dutch Culture in the Golden Age*. Berkeley: University of California Press, 1988.

Schlesinger, Stephen, and Stephen Kinzer. *Bitter Fruit: The Untold Story of the American Coup in Guatemala*. Garden City, NY: Anchor/Doubleday, 1983.

Schlosser, Eric. *Fast Food Nation*. New York: HarperCollins Publishers Inc., 2002.

Schmitt-Pantel, Pauline. "Greek Meals: A Civic Ritual," in *Food*, eds. Jean-Louis Flandrin & Massimo Montanari. English edition ed. Albert Sonnenfeld. New York: Columbia University Press, 1999.

Shange, Ntozake. *If I Can Cook/You Know God Can*. Boston: Beacon Press, 1998.

Shapiro, Laura. *Perfection Salad: Women and Cooking at the Turn of the Century*. New York: Farrar, Straus and Giroux, 1986.

Shaw, Timothy. *The World of Escoffier*. New York: Vendome, 1995.

Shelton, Jo-Anne. *As the Romans Did: a Sourcebook in Roman Social History*. New York: Oxford University Press, 1998.

Shephard, Sue. *Pickled, Potted, and Canned: How the Art of Food Preserving Changed the World*. New York: Simon & Schuster, 2000.

Shindler, Merrill. *American Dish: 100 Recipes from Ten Delicious Decades*. Santa Monica: Angel City Press, 1996.

Silverberg, Robert. *The Pueblo Revolt*. Lincoln: University of Nebraska Press, 1970

Sim, Alison. *Food and Feast in Tudor England*. New York: St. Martin's Press, 1997.

Simeti, Mary Taylor. *Pomp and Sustenance: Twenty-five Centuries of Sicilian Food*. New York: Alfred A. Knopf, 1989.

Simmons, Amelia. *The First American Cookbook: A Facsimile of* American Cookery, 1796. New York: Dover Publications, Inc., 1984.

Sklar, Kathryn Kish. *Catharine Beecher: A Study in American Domesticity*. New York: W. W. Norton & Company, 1976.

Smith, Andrew. *The Tomato in America: Early History, Culture, and Cookery*. Columbia: University of South Carolina Press, 1994.

Smith, Eliza. *The Compleat Housewife; or, Accomplish'd Gentlewoman's Companion: being a Collection of upwards of Five Hundred of the most approved Receipts in Cookery, Pastry, Confectionary, Preserving, Pickles, Cakes, Creams, Jellies, Made Wines, Cordials . . . fit either for private families, or such publick-spirited gentlewomen as would be beneficent to their poor Neighbors*. London: 1727. Facsimile of the 1753 fifteenth edition: London: Literary Services and Production Limited; T. J. Press Ltd., 1968.

Sokolov, Raymond. *Why We Eat What We Eat: How the Encounter Between the New World and the Old Changed the Way Everyone on the Planet Eats*. New York: Summit Books: 1991.

Spang, Rebecca L. *The Invention of the Restaurant: Paris and Modern Gastronomic Culture.* Cambridge: Harvard University Press, 2000.

Spodek, Howard. *The World's History.* Upper Saddle River, NJ: Prentice Hall Inc., 1998.

Stewart, George. *The California Trail.* New York: McGraw-Hill Book Company, 1962.

Stewart, Katie. *The Joy of Eating.* Owings Mills, MD: Stemmer House Publishers, Inc., 1977.

Stewart-Gordon, Faith, and Nika Hazelton. *The Russian Tea Room Cookbook.* New York: Perigee Books/Putnam Publishing Group, 1981.

Strenio, Andrew, Jr. *The Testing Trap.* New York: Rawson, Wade Publishers, 1981.

Swift, Jonathan. "A Modest Proposal," in *Swift: Gulliver's Travels and Other Writings.* Miriam Kosh Starkman, ed. New York: Bantam Books, 1962.

Symons, Michael. *One Continuous Picnic: A History of Eating in Australia.* Adelaide: Duck Press, 1982.

Tannahill, Reay. *Food in History.* New York: Three Rivers Press, 1988, 1973.

Tempest, Snejana. "Stovelore in Russian Folklife," in *Food in Russian History and Culture,* eds. Musy Glants & Joyce Toomre. Bloomington: Indiana University Press, 1997.

Thomas, Lately. *Delmonico's: A Century of Splendor.* Boston: Houghton Mifflin, 1967.

Thompson, Ruth. *Ruth Thompson's Wartime Canning and Cooking Book.* New York: Bedford, 1943.

Thoreau, Henry David. *Walden and Other Writings.* New York: Bantam Books, 1962.

Toland, John. *The Rising Sun: The Decline and Fall of the Japanese Empire, 1936–1945.* Toronto: Bantam Books, 1970.

Toussaint-Samat, Maguelonne. *A History of Food.* Trans. Anthea Bell. Oxford: Blackwell Publishers Ltd., 1992, 1994.

Turner, Frederick. *Beyond Geography: The Western Spirit Against the Wilderness.* New Brunswick, NJ: Rutgers University Press, 1986.

————. *Of Chiles, Cacti, and Fighting Cocks: Notes on the American West.* San Francisco: North Point Press, 1990.

Twain, Mark. *Roughing It.* New York: New American Library, 1962.

Uccello, Antonino. *Pani e dolci di Sicilia.* Palermo: Sellerio, 1976.

Vetta, Massimo. "The Culture of the Symposium," in *Food,* eds. Jean-Louis Flandrin & Massimo Montanari. English edition ed. Albert Sonnenfeld. New York: Columbia University Press, 1999.

Viola, Herman J., and Carolyn Margolis, eds. *Seeds of Change.* Washington, DC: Smithsonian Institution Press, 1991.

Visser, Margaret. *Much Depends on Dinner.* New York: Collier Books, 1988.

Volokh, Anne, with Mavis Manus. *The Art of Russian Cuisine.* New York: Macmillan Publishing Company, 1983.

Von Drachenfels, Suzanne. *The Art of the Table: A Complete Guide to Table Setting, Table Manners, and Tableware.* New York: Simon & Schuster, 2000.

Ward, Susie, Claire Clifton, and Jenny Stacey. *The Gourmet Atlas.* New York: Macmillan, 1997.

Washington, Booker T. *Up from Slavery.* New York: Penguin Books, 1986.

Waters, Alice, in collaboration with Linda P. Guenzel. *The Chez Panisse Menu Cookbook.* New York: Random House, 1982.

Watson, Ben. *Cider Hard and Sweet: History, Traditions, and Making Your Own.* Woodstock, VT: The Countryman Press, 1999.

Wejman, Jacqueline, with essays by Charles St. Peter. *Jams & Jellies.* San Francisco: 101 Productions, 1975.

Wels, Susan. *Titanic: Legacy of the World's Greatest Ocean Liner.* Tehabi Books and Time Life Books, 1997.

West, Karen. *The Best of Polish Cooking.* New York: Weathervane Books, 1983.

Wheaton, Barbara Ketcham. *Savoring the Past: The French Kitchen and Table from 1300 to 1789.* Philadelphia: University of Pennsylvania Press, 1983.

White, Deborah Gray. *Ar'n't I a Woman? Female Slaves in the Plantation South.* New York: W. W. Norton & Company, 1985.

Wicker, Tom. *A Time to Die.* New York: Quadrangle/The New York Times Book Co., 1975.

Willan, Anne. *Great Cooks and Their Recipes.* London: Pavilion Books Limited, 1995.

———. *La France Gastronomique.* New York: Arcade Publishing, 1991.

Willan, Anne, and l'École de Cuisine La Varenne. *The La Varenne Cooking Course.* New York: William Morrow and Company, Inc., 1982.

Williams, Eric. *From Columbus to Castro: The History of the Caribbean.* New York: Vintage Books/Random House, 1970.

Williams, Susan. *Savory Suppers and Fashionable Feasts: Dining in Victorian America.* Knoxville: The University of Tennessee Press, 1996.

Wilson, David Scofield, and Angus Kress Gillespie. *Rooted in America: Foodlore of Popular Fruits and Vegetables.* Knoxville: The University of Tennessee Press, 1999.

Witty, Helen, and Elizabeth Schneider Colchie. *Better Than Store-Bought: A Cookbook.* New York: Harper and Row, 1979.

Woodier, Olwen. *Apple Cookbook.* North Adams, MA: Storey Books, 2001, 1984.

Wright, Clifford A. *A Mediterranean Feast.* New York: William Morrow and Company, Inc., 1999.

Wyman, Carolyn. *Spam: A Biography.* San Diego: Harcourt Brace & Company, 1999.

Young, Alfred F. *The Shoemaker and the Tea Party: Memory and the American Revolution.* Boston: Beacon Press, 1999.

Zborowski, Mark, and Elizabeth Herzog. *Life Is With People: The Culture of the Shtetl.* New York: Schocken Books, 1952.

INDEX

Columbus, Christopher, 92, 94, 102–104
Cookie:
in biological warfare, 276
comfort food, 305
computer files, 315
first recipes, 159–160
fortune, 19, 274
Mother's Cookies Company, 239
Mrs. Fields, 297, 309
as thickener, 141
Cooking:
barbecue, 113
boiling, 3
campfire food, 305
charcoal, 77, 175–176
clambake, 133
"correctly," 89
discovery of fire, 2
"fixing" food, 89
medieval humors, 55–56
open fire, 73, 183
pit roasting, 3, 113, 133
pot au feu, 162
spit roasting, 3
Coprolites, 5–6
Corn (maize):
in Aztec cuisine, 98–100
beer, 98, 135
canned, 198
chicha, 98
Corn Flakes, 207
corn-bread stuffing, 130
Corn–Maize Confusion, 97
cornmeal, sacred, 111
first recipes, 159
fritters, 184
green corn tamales, 191
grits, 170
hasty pudding, 134
hoe cake, 184
hominy, 170
in Inca cuisine, 97–98
in Irish potato famine, 217
johnnycake, 133
maize, 221
polenta, 229, 303
popcorn, 274, 280, 288
succotash, 184
syrup, 292
in three sisters, 101, 109
whiskey, 136
"white lightning," 159
Corpses, 5–6
Cortés, Hernán, 108
Cowboy:
cuisine, American, 195
culture, Argentine, 113–114
culture, Spanish, 113–114
Don Quixote and Sancho Panza, 123–125

gaucho, 114
vaquero, 114
Coyote, Café, 101; how to cook, 180
Cranberries, 66, 107, 130
Crocker, Betty, 264–265
Crusades, 56, 64, 66–68, 87
Children's Crusade, 67
Cuba, 117, 182, 210, 290
Cuisine:
African, 219–222
African, in American South, 129
America, colonial, 133–137
American Southwest, 100–102
American, beginnings, 159–160
American, cowboy, 195
American, Pennsylvania "Dutch," 153–155
American, slave, 184
American, stagecoach, 190
ancient Chinese, 18–19
ancient Egyptian, 14–15
ancient Greek, 25–31
ancient Indian, 20–21
ancient Mesopotamian, 10–12
ancient Roman, 34–46
Argentinian, 113
Armenian, 252
Aztec, 98–100
British, 215–216
California, 296
Cantonese, 224–225
Catalonian, 90
Classique, 242
Creole, 169–170
Cuban, 290
definition, 82
Dutch, 139–142
Eritrean, 222
Ethiopian, 222
Franco-Caribbean, 301
Franco-German, 227–228
Haute French, 147, 162
Hawaiian, 290–292
Hellenistic, 33
Inca, 96–98
Iranian/Persian, 299–300
Italian-American, 233–235
Italian, fascist, 286
Italian, Northern, 228–229
Italian, Southern, 229–231
Japanese, 85
Jewish-American, 235–236
Jewish dietary laws, 15–17
Korean, 287–288
Malaysian, 222
medieval European, 55–57,

64–66, 73–76
Mexican, 108–110
minceur, 297
Mongol, 79–80
Moroccan, 220–221
movie star, 266
Muslim Empire, 60–62
Native American maple-based, 132–133
Northern Chinese, 82
nouvelle, 292
Persian/Iranian, 299–300
Peruvian, 112–113
Polish, 236
Renaissance European, 88–89
Roman, ancient, 39–46
Russian, 255–256
Sicilian, 231–232
Southeast Asian, 301, 302
Spanish, 121, 123
Szechwan, 82
Thai, 301–302
Valentine's Day, 203
Vegetarian, 206–207, 297
Vietnamese, 301
Culinary Institute of America, 287, 314

Depression, economic, 269–275
Domestication, 7–8, 18, 95–97
Don Quixote, 123–125, 229, 318
Dutch East India Company, 142–143, 222

Easter, 48–49, 256–258
Ecuador, 95, 178, 212, 312
Efficiency experts, 238
Eggplant, 60, 61, 101, 232, 252, 304
Egypt, ancient, 12–17, 214
Electricity, 204–206, 240
Elephants, 35, 222
England:
in Africa, 219
anorexia, 198
boiled food, 176, 215–216
Britannia, 37
British East India Company, 223
canning, 173
Careme in, 176
cathedrals, 68–69
in China, 224
China plates, 162
cholera, 213
Christmas, 188
in colonial India, 222–224
colonies in North America, 127